COLLEGE
TEACHING

COLLEGE TEACHING

Practical Insights From the Science
of Teaching and Learning

....

Donelson R. Forsyth

American Psychological Association
WASHINGTON, DC

Published by
American Psychological Association
750 First Street, NE
Washington, DC 20002-4242
www.apa.org

To order
APA Order Department
P.O. Box 92984
Washington, DC 20090-2984
Tel: (800) 374-2721; Direct: (202) 336-5510
Fax: (202) 336-5502; TDD/TTY: (202) 336-6123
Online: www.apa.org/pubs/books/
E-mail: order@apa.org

In the U.K., Europe, Africa, and the Middle East, copies may be ordered from
American Psychological Association
3 Henrietta Street
Covent Garden, London
WC2E 8LU England

Typeset in Meridien by Circle Graphics, Inc., Columbia, MD

Printer: Bang Printing, Brainerd, MN
Cover Designer: Beth Schlenoff Design, Bethesda, MD

The opinions and statements published are the responsibility of the authors, and such opinions and statements do not necessarily represent the policies of the American Psychological Association.

Library of Congress Cataloging-in-Publication Data

Forsyth, Donelson R., 1953-
  [Professor's guide to teaching]
  College teaching : practical insights from the science of teaching and learning / Donelson R. Forsyth. — Second edition.
     pages cm.
  Revised edition of: The professor's guide to teaching. c2003.
  Includes bibliographical references and index.
  ISBN 978-1-4338-2081-6 — ISBN 1-4338-2081-1 1. College teaching—Methodology.
2. College teaching—Psychological aspects. 3. Educational psychology. 4. Student-centered learning. 5. Effective teaching. I. Title.
  LB2331.F632 2016
  378.1'25—dc23
                                        2015014049

British Library Cataloguing-in-Publication Data
A CIP record is available from the British Library.

Printed in the United States of America
Second Edition

http://dx.doi.org/10.1037/14777-000

To those who were my teachers, including Mrs. Boyd,
Mrs. Butterfield, Monsieur Baltz, Mr. Davis, Mr. Drick,
Mr. McCrory, and Coach Hosack; Dr. Bob French, Dr. Glade Whitney,
Dr. Charlie Madsen, Dr. Lee Sechrest, Russ Clark, and Steve West;
and Hank Pennypacker, Bob Watson, Dick Swanson, Bob Ziller,
Marv Shaw, Barry Schlenker, Tom Simon, Joel Cohen, Larry Severy,
Bill Yost, Bill Ware, Bill Froming, Bill Sanders, and Mike Burgoon.

Contents

Preface

am not a born teacher. In graduate school I was all about the research, and so when I took my first academic post I was ready to measure, manipulate, and publish, but I was unprepared to teach. Like many other new college professors, I was relatively untrained in the pedagogical arts, for I had adopted the worldview that, whereas scholarly research was a joy, teaching was a duty.

My first few years teaching were a struggle. I'd leave too many classes feeling I had failed. Then there were the intrusive thoughts, such as "I wish I were going someplace else," that popped into my mind during the too-short walk to each class. And the evaluations: I came to dread the time of year when students would let me know what they thought about my teaching expertise. I would sit in my office with the door shut, sift through the reviews, pick out the bad ones, and lose confidence in myself. Some were simply negative:

- Forsyth is a jerk; he should be fired.
- He is the worst teacher I have ever had.

Others were critical, if insightful:

- I force myself to come to this class and tolerate the elementary way you approach this class most of the time.
- Your jokes are seldom funny or effective as teaching methods and that shows how egotistical and self-centered you probably are.

Some were poignant:

- At first he had the attitude he didn't really care about us, then we all started flunking and dropping his course. He became somewhat concerned, but it was too late for us.

And, in response to the question "What was the single most important learning experience for you in this course?" one student wrote, "I cannot think of one, other than not to take this instructor again."

I wanted to blame my students—to question their abilities, preparation, and raw intellect. But I could not overlook the irony of the situation: As a psychologist, I was supposedly an expert on understanding people—how they think, feel, and act. If I had any faith in my own discipline, then why could I not use its accrued insights and findings to find ways to teach more effectively?

Turning to psychology to seek insight resulted not only in a comforting level of intellectualization but also in a set of guidelines for improving my effectiveness as a teacher. The understanding I gained eventually helped me improve my teaching, and in time those 2s and 3s on the 5-point rating scale became 4s and 5s, and students' comments changed from hostile and negative to complimentary and appreciative. This $n = 1$ case study suggests that, just like any other scholarly skill, good teaching can be learned.

This book assumes that the science of teaching and learning offers a means of organizing the diverse and varied factors that determine how the students in our classes are responding, psychologically, to our teaching, and so it offers both a general orientation to teaching as well as specific how-to recommendations. These recommendations are, in most cases, consistent with general theories of human thought, emotion, and action but, more than that, they are based on empirical research. This is because even though theoretical analyses provide predictions about teaching and learning, these predictions do not always stand up to empirical test. As a consequence, evidence-based suggestions about teaching are preferred to those based on logic, speculation, hearsay, or authority.

College Teaching: Practical Insights From the Science of Teaching and Learning is similar in organization and emphasis to the first edition, published by the American Psychological Association in 2003 and titled *The Professor's Guide to Teaching: Psychological Principles and Practices*. The present book's chapters are sequenced by a just-in-time heuristic, beginning with planning a course and ending with documenting one's work by developing a teaching portfolio. Each chapter frames the major issues surrounding one aspect of instruction. In Chapter 4, which deals with lecturing, for example, I conceptualize the lecturing method as a form of communication and then use research dealing with persuasion processes to identify how this teaching method can be best used. Similarly, in Chapter 5, which focuses on classroom testing, I approach the issue from the standpoint of psychological assessment and so consider how testing requires the same care that psychologists use when developing questionnaires and inventories.

This edition differs from the first, however, in that it does not assume the reader has studied psychology or even cares about it. It also includes an updated analysis of such topics as online teaching, instructional design, learning teams, and recent debates about the overall effectiveness of higher education. Like the first edition, however, this book strives to satisfy the needs of readers who are beginning their careers as well as those who have been teaching for many years. These two groups' interests are in some ways incompatible, for novice teachers are often searching for a sound footing to guide their teaching, whereas veterans seek insights into perennial problems that still nag them each time they teach a course. In this book, I try to satisfy both of these demands by adding novel interpretations of existing, taken-for-granted practices but also stressing the tried-and-true techniques of effective instruction.

I deserve the blame for the portions of this book that a reader may find objectionable, such as simplistic bits of advice about teaching, distracting personal opinions, and the use of too many words to make relatively simple points. Also, although I deserve some of the credit for the good parts, so do many other people. The book would be much shorter were it not for the dedication of researchers who are not content to merely speculate about teaching and learning but instead conduct scientific research to better understand these processes. Natalie Kerr Lawrence and Sandra Goss Lucas reviewed an initial draft of the entire manuscript, and their comments were instrumental in helping me improve the document. I also extend my appreciation to the many colleagues who have shared their approaches to teaching with me. Crystal Hoyt, Al Goethals, Jeni Burnette, Jim McMillan, and Tom McGovern merit special mention.

The list of people who deserve thanks for their support of and contributions to this project is lengthy and includes the Jepson School of Leadership Studies scholarship committee; Jon Messer, Fred Hagemeister, and the other good folks in the Center for Teaching, Learning, and Technology; and the capable staff of the American Psychological Association, including Linda Malnasi McCarter and Susan Herman. As always, Claire, David, and Rachel all deserve prizes for tolerating the distracting ways of a father and husband struggling with work–life balance issues.

COLLEGE TEACHING

Introduction

n early fall, the temperatures of the Earth's northern hemi-
sphere drop, the Monarch butterflies of North America begin
their migration to Angangueo, Mexico, and millions of college
students stream back to campus to extend their understanding of the world. These students are not novices just beginning
their studies but seasoned learners who have spent years in the
classroom. They are led in their quest by professors who have
achieved an extraordinary degree of mastery over their chosen
field. These professors know what students most need to learn,
and they have planned a series of activities and experiences—
discussions, laboratory exercises, lectures, readings, tests, recitations, reviews, and so on—all designed to facilitate their
students' learning. How complicated can that be?

Very complicated, it turns out. Teaching is an intentional
intervention designed to result in a cognitive, affective, or
behavioral change in another person: a student. It requires
a rich understanding of the fundamentals of one's field, skill
in organizing and communicating complex information, and
the ability to accurately appraise students' progress. Good

http://dx.doi.org/10.1037/14777-001
College Teaching: Practical Insights From the Science of Teaching and Learning,
by D. R. Forsyth

teaching, however, requires even more: a detailed understanding of the type of change desired, insight into the psychological and interpersonal processes that influence the teaching–learning process, command of a range of methods to help students reach their educational goals, discernment in determining when teaching is or is not successful, and a willingness to modify the intervention to improve its effectiveness.

Learning, too, is complicated. Our capacity to process information makes humans the envy of all the other primates (were they capable of envy), but learning requires substantial mental effort, energy, and self-regulation. College learning is also an interpersonal process, for students' level of motivation and willingness to devote time to their studies ebbs and flows in a pulse determined as much by their social networks as by their professors' academic demands. College students are capable learners who can grasp complex topics in the arts, science, mathematics, and business, but their busy lives can cause them to pursue activities that most interest them—and those activities may not be academic ones. In most colleges and universities the professor is not the only one doing the teaching.

Fortunately, the complexities of teaching and learning do not render these processes impenetrable. Professors know that their students' final grades result from the intermingling of many causes: the student's educational experiences, personality and values, parental and peer influences, the priorities and resources of the institution, the professor's skill as a teacher. But this complex assortment of causes, correlates, and outcomes can be tamed through systematic study and thoughtful analysis.

Many are the methods that can be used to unravel the processes that sustain, promote, or impede college-level learning outcomes, but the approach I take in this book draws primarily on theoretical and empirical studies of the psychological bases of teaching and learning. Psychologists have been studying teaching and learning—and the ways to enhance those processes—for as long as the social sciences have been around. That work is ongoing, but even now it offers a means of organizing the diverse and varied factors that determine how students learn and, as a consequence, how professors should teach. This book reviews that theory and research, for it assumes that once you understand a process you can then go about improving that process.

The Science of Teaching and Learning

Researchers in psychology and related disciplines study maze-navigating rats, depressed adolescents, disenchanted factory workers, forgetful Alzheimer's patients, and the minds of musical geniuses. They also study students and their teachers. The study of teaching and learning has been a core concern for more than 100 years, dating back to such distinguished educators and researchers as William James (1899), John Dewey (1910), G. Stanley Hall (1911), and Edward L. Thorndike (1913). Their faith in psychology as a source of principles and practices was expressed, unreservedly, by Thorndike back in 1910 in the first issue of the *Journal of Educational Psychology* when he wrote the following:

> Psychology contributes to a better understanding of the aims of education by defining them, making them clearer; by limiting them, showing us what can be done and what cannot; and by suggesting new features that should be made parts of them. (p. 5)

A psychological analysis of teaching and learning, if written 50 years ago, would have stressed classic theories of learning, relying heavily on such concepts as stimulus, response, conditioning, reinforcement, punishment—theories still being inflicted on students sitting in their introductory psychology courses. Contemporary psychology's analysis of teaching and learning is faithful to the idea that learning is a relatively permanent cognitive, behavioral, or emotional change resulting from experience, but as researchers burrowed more deeply into Skinner's (1953) black box, they discovered all sorts of psychological processes—memory systems, schemas, unconscious cognitive processes, motivations, traits, and so on—that augment the processes studied by the behaviorists. The law of effect (which states that behaviors followed by rewards occur more frequently) still shapes how students learn, but we also know that the kinds of learning that occur in college classrooms depends as much on cognitive, motivational, personal, and interpersonal processes as it does on behavioral ones (Reynolds & Miller, 2013).

COGNITIVE PROCESSES

What mental processes sustain students' learning? A psychological explanation usually starts by examining how people process information (Schank, 2011). Learners, we hope, are busily taking in information through their senses. They see, for example, the professor's scrawls on the chalkboard or hear the comments made by another student during class discussions. If they encode this information, the system translates it into an internal, psychological representation that is held briefly in working memory. At the same moment, however, the information-processing system is also retrieving data from long-term memory stores, for the human memory system is quick to associate the new with the known. In consequence, new (short-term) memories are aligned with existing (long-term) memories in a dynamic, active process (consolidation). This process is so dynamic, in fact, that most researchers assume information is constructed rather than simply stored. As the cognitive scientist Ulric Neisser (1967) put it, we are like paleontologists working with fossil evidence, for "out of a few stored bone chips we remember a dinosaur" (p. 285).

In some cases this system encodes, constructs, and consolidates information almost effortlessly, but the kind of deliberative, intentional processing needed to learn complex subjects is challenging. If Noah is texting on his smartphone, he may not hear what the lecturer is saying. If Sophia is worrying about a personal problem, the cognitive load may be so great that she cannot process the topic the class is discussing. If Liam reads the textbook and memorizes key facts and terms, but does not link the information to his stock of memories, he will learn only at a surface level rather than a deep level. If Emma is so unfamiliar with the topic covered in class that she has no way to cognitively organize the information flooding into her working memory, she may be unable to retrieve that information even though she made a diligent effort to create durable memories of it. If Jacob, in contrast, has a well-formed set of organized information about a particular topic, he may not remember information that is inconsistent with his existing memorial inclinations. If Olivia is feeling happy on the day she learns about the constructivist model of memory, she may not be able to retrieve those memories if she is sad and lonely on the test day. 'Tis considerable strain twixt the teaching and the brain.

Studies of learning quite naturally tend to focus on how information is encoded; consolidated in memory; retrieved; and used for making rational, well-informed decisions. However, this superb information-processing system, engineered by the challenges of a threatening social and physical environment, is not just an objective fact finder and information processor but a motivated system that seeks meaning, self-assurance, control, and inclusion. The same system that wants to identify why it missed the question on the test about field reversal across a first-order boundary of an Ising ferromagnet would prefer to blame the teacher, the test, or the text rather than one's finely tuned information-processing system. The same system that can decide when to use the words *comprise*, *literally*, and *reticent* correctly is also calculating the strength of its social network based on Facebook cover photo likes. The same system that can follow the professor's complex arguments about the differences between Derrida's concept of *deconstruction* and Heidegger's notion of *destruktion* is also calculating the odds of hooking up with the attractive student two rows over. The cognitive system processes all information, including that which is not strictly curricular.

MOTIVATIONAL PROCESSES

Why are some students more involved in class, better prepared for discussions, quicker to ask questions, and striving harder than other students with equal or better ability? A psychological explanation usually invokes the somewhat mysterious dispositional quality of *motivation* to explain relatively stable differences in purposeful engagement in academic tasks and study. Certainly some students come to the classroom ready to expend considerable time and effort in their quest to learn the course material and achieve personal goals of success. For many students, though, the motivational pump is unprimed. They are dogged in their pursuit of the goals that they themselves chose, but those goals may not be aligned with ones set for them by their parents, professors, major, school, or society. Students often have jobs and other life experiences to contend with, and these extracurricular activities may be far more exciting or involving than the act of learning. Students are energized by the prospect of pursuing a valued goal—earning the top grade in the class, writing a paper of such quality that it garners the professor's glowing praise, or mastering a complex field of study—but not if their intuitive odds calculator warns them that the probability of success is vanishingly small. In other cases, students' motivation drops down to nil as their initial interest in learning is wiped away by hours of uninspired lectures or too many low quiz scores (Brophy, 2004).

Teaching and learning are also emotional experiences. Like motivations, emotions guide behaviors, prompting people to move in directions that they associate with positive feeling states—happiness, contentment, pride, satisfaction, and the like—and away from people, places, and activities that engender the negative emotions: annoyance, anger, sadness, distress, and so on. Also, although extracurricular activities may offer no end of opportunity to maximize positive emotions, the hard work of learning often generates more negative ones. When, for example, the tests are handed back and the grade scrawled on the front page is less than what was desired, students may experience surprise, guilt, shame, resentment, or anger. These emotions may serve an adaptive function by providing the motivational energy students need to improve their work, but they may also trigger psychological responses that interfere with learning, such as withdrawal, denial of responsibility, and even depression.

Professors, despite stereotypes that stress their predilection for pondering rather than emoting, are by no means immune to the social and psychological processes that instigate emotional experiences. Many experience considerable happiness, satisfaction, and well-being as they help college students reach their learning goals. The college class can, however, be emotionally distressing for professors just as it is for some students. When professors learn, for example, that their evaluations at the semester's end were negative rather than positive, they report feeling *worried, angry, distressed,* and *upset. Lost, alarmed, stressed, negative,* and *defensive* also made the list. Professors, like most people, do not like feeling they have failed (Forsyth, 2012).

PERSONAL PROCESSES

Who are these students who populate the rosters of our courses? What are they like, as individuals, and what characteristics do they tend to share with their fellow students? There are, of course, aspects of individual learners that influence how they respond to different types of teaching modes and methods. For example, students whose epistemological model of knowledge leans toward the simplistic rather than complex side do not learn well when they must integrate information from multiple sources (Pieschl, Stahl, & Bromme, 2008). Students whose self-esteem is so high that they can be considered narcissists are more likely to cheat in college than are students with lower levels of self-admiration (Brunell, Staats, Barden, & Hupp, 2011). Some students are confident in their ability to use online resources in their classes, but others lack Internet self-efficacy (Kuo, Walker, Schroder, & Belland, 2014). Some individuals prefer to learn by reading textual information, whereas others favor charts, graphics, and other visual depictions of information (Kozhevnikov, Evans, & Kosslyn, 2014). Understanding the various learning modalities requires an understanding not only of the commonalities among students but also what differentiates each one from the others.

People differ in ways other than personality, and these *individual differences* (as they are termed in the jargon of psychology) are equally influential determinants of feelings, thoughts, and actions. Colleges were once populated by a relatively slim sliver of the population, and so heterogeneity was low and individual differences between students did not matter so much. But in 2016, over half of all graduating high school students will attend college, so the undergraduate student body is nearly as diverse as the population it samples. Students differ in ethnic, cultural, and socioeconomic background, religious affiliation, sexual orientation, and age, and these differences are systematically related to their interests, their level of academic preparation, and their familiarity with the norms and procedures common to, but often taken for granted, on college campuses.

INTERPERSONAL PROCESSES

A psychological analysis of teaching and learning recognizes the cognitive, motivational, and personal processes that influence the acquisition of new ideas, insights, and skills, but it also considers the interpersonal processes that inevitably come into play when people work collaboratively to learn from one another. Teachers and learners are linked together in a social relationship that may remain formal and unsubstantial or grow into one that is warm and influential. Each communicates regularly and richly with one another, exchanging information about the many and varied concepts examined in the course as well as creating a social connection that will help them understand one another. In most cases, too, professors work with students collectively, and thus learning is influenced by the dynamics of the classroom groups. Students in classes compete for status, compare themselves to one another, form strong friendships, and help one another (sometimes even when they should not), so a class is more of a social network than an aggregation of independent learners. And even when students are learning through the solitary study of text, film, art, or music they are nonetheless responding to another person's thoughts, ideas, and artifacts. Technology has evolved to the point where students can learn from teaching programs that move them along in their lessons with great efficiency, but automated methods of instruction do not generate as much enthusiasm as more social forms of teaching and learning. Students and their professors are, after all, social animals.

EVIDENCE-BASED PRACTICES

A psychological perspective on college-level instruction and learning offers two basic suggestions to those who teach. First, be mindful of the undercurrent of cognitive, motivational, personal, and interpersonal processes flowing through even the most routine of educational experiences. Second, favor teaching practices that have been tested through some type of systematic empirical procedure, because even the most revered bit of wisdom about how to best teach can turn out to be misguided when subjected to scientific scrutiny. For example, even though many educators favor teaching students in ways that mesh with their own natural learning styles, scientific evidence offers little support for this recommendation (e.g., Hattie & Yates, 2014). Even though many college students believe their study techniques are effective ones, researchers who tested their favored techniques drew much more negative conclusions (Dunlosky, Rawson, Marsh, Nathan, & Willingham, 2013). Many professors are distrustful of the value of grading students' performance too frequently, but research has confirmed the *testing effect*: Answering questions is a sure-fire way to improve information retrieval (Brown, Roediger, & McDaniel, 2014). Even though students who are intrinsically motivated to learn course material enjoy their learning more, they are less likely to ace the course; it is the students who are motivated to outperform their classmates who generally get the best grades in college (Harackiewicz, Barron, & Elliot, 1998). Whereas some professors may insist that newfangled online teaching methods are a poor substitute for "real" teaching, meta-analytic reviews of online classes all point to one conclusion: Well-designed and well-delivered online classes are as educationally effective—and often more effective—than face-to-face traditional classroom experiences (Schmid et al., 2014). The question "What is the best way to teach a college class?" is an empirical one.

Because teaching and learning are complex processes, with multiple causes, influences, and concomitants, pointing to one factor as the crucial factor that must be considered will oversimplify more than inform. Consider, for example, this basic assumption: Students will learn more if they are rewarded for learning. This principle, based on B. F. Skinner's law of effect, has been supported in countless studies—it is called the *law of effect* for a reason. In certain circumstances, however, rewards backfire, in particular, when they undermine students' natural interest in the topic. But that does not mean that mush is all we are after. An engineer knows that the carrying capacity of a bridge is based on a 100 different factors, but still the bridge, when built, must carry cars and trucks from one side to the other. Learning has multiple influences, but the classes professors build must nonetheless carry the students from a place of confusion and uncertainty to a place of wisdom.

A Look Ahead

The study of teaching and learning is an ongoing process and a very human one as well. Mistakes are made, conclusions firmly held are found to be flawed, exciting findings cannot be replicated, and disputes and controversies emerge that split scientists into opposing camps. The study of human thought, action, and emotion provides only guidelines rather than definitive answers to questions about the causes of learning and how teaching should proceed.

Nonetheless, the research that has been conducted, and the insights that it has yielded, are considerable. Hattie's (2009) synthesis of 800 meta-analytic studies identified 52,637 studies conducted with millions of students in all types of classes and at all grade levels. That mass of research suggests that everything matters when it comes to teaching and learning: the characteristics of the student, the quality of the curriculum, the school itself, the skills of professors and teachers, and a panoply of social and cultural factors. Many of these influences are ones that professors can neither measure nor manipulate in any way, but others—the class's level of intellectual demand, the quantity and quality of feedback students receive, the instructional methods used during the semester, and the relationship that connects professor to student—are both influential and controllable. The chapters in this book, which I summarize here briefly, examine the many choices professors make about their teaching, beginning with their initial planning of the course and its basic content through to the final decisions about grades and assessing effectiveness.

ORIENTING: IDENTIFY YOUR PURPOSES AND PRIORITIES

Chapter 1 asks the question "What is college for?" The professor's original charge—to provide instruction for schoolteachers and religious leaders—has expanded beyond intellectual outcomes to instilling moral values, a work ethic, citizenship skills, and even Googling prowess. Is every one of these goals essential for achieving higher education's end result: the transformation of students into well-educated citizens? Professors are prone to rumination and so will want to identify, through judicious deliberation, the educational outcomes they are seeking in their teaching. After all, as that great expert on human behavior, baseball player and manager Yogi Berra (2002), once warned, "If you don't know where you're going, you might not get there" (p. 53).

PREPPING: ALIGN YOUR PURPOSES WITH PRACTICES

We need to know not only where we are going but also how to get there. Physicians preparing for surgery, high school students studying for the SAT, managers planning a new initiative, and college professors readying themselves for another semester of teaching benefit when they take time to plan, even if they do not necessarily end up following the plan. Rare is the professor who strolls into class on the first day of the term or signs into his or her online course learning system and just begins to teach; most spend many months planning their process. This planning must take into account not only the nature of the class to be taught and the kinds of students who take it but also the purposes of the class itself. All who teach must decide how they will teach by selecting the techniques they will use to help their students reach their learning goals. They must plan discussions, write lectures, select readings and texts, design assessments, and sequence the topics they hope to cover. Chapter 2 assumes that this extensive planning is essential for meeting one of the fundamental requirements for effective instruction: aligning purposes with practices.

GUIDING: USE STUDENT-CENTERED TEACHING STRATEGIES

A knowledgeable instructor, a textbook brimming with information, rich online resources, and carefully designed assessments will all be for naught if students are not engaged in their studies, that is, if they do not devote time and energy to their learning. The student-centered teaching–learning methods examined in Chapter 3 offer empirically supported means of enhancing students' engagement in their learning. Discussions, learning groups, experiential activities, and other student-centered teaching methods, when properly executed, personalize and enrich the teaching–learning experience given that they bridge the gap between the conceptual and practical, the hypothetical and the concrete, and the uninteresting and the engaging. They require students to respond cognitively, behaviorally, and even emotionally to the material, and so they increase both intellectual understanding and personal engagement.

LECTURING: COMMUNICATE IN AN ENGAGING MANNER

Student-centered teaching methods are often called *active learning methods* given that they require more observable involvement by students in the teaching–learning process. But even professor-centered teaching methods—including the lecture—can trigger active learning when they draw students into the learning experience. Lecturers who stand at a lectern before a 400-person class (or appear as a talking head on the Internet) for an hour, reading from their detailed notes, with little variation in voice tone, likely fail to even reach the basic goal of transmitting information from teacher to learner, because the students cannot keep their minds focused on the lecture's content. However, as Chapter 4 explains, some lecturers know how to engage a class, provoking their students, stirring their emotions, and getting them thinking about questions they never before considered. That kind of learning is engaged learning, and that is the kind skilled lecturers can provoke.

TESTING: ALIGN TEACHING WITH EVALUATION

Developing effective ways to assess student learning is an essential component of good teaching. Tests provide the means by which to assign fairly grades based on student achievement, rather than whim or mood. Even though college students have years of experience in learning settings, many of them are still unable to calibrate their own learning; they do not always know when they have learned material and when they have not. Students also are not sufficiently skilled in regulating their time and motivation, so they need external goals to punctuate and validate their work. Chapter 5 reviews the basic steps professors should follow to ensure the validity of their testing methods, including identifying instructional goals, choosing among various types of tests (e.g., multiple choice, essay), writing items that assess students' attainment of the specified course goals, and evaluating the adequacy of the test through item analysis. The chapter takes seriously Thorndike's (1918) principle of measurement: "Whatever exists at all exists in some quantity. To know it thoroughly involves knowing its quantity as well as its quality" (p. 16).

GRADING AND AIDING: GRADE THEM, BUT ALSO HELP THEM

Chapter 6 is based on one core principle: The learning cycle requires a constant flow of useful feedback. Few achievements can be evaluated without reference to some standard that defines which outcomes are correct, successful, or satisfactory. Grades provide that clarity while also providing students with an additional incentive and a concrete goal. A grading system that is truly fair should be coupled with a second system: one that provides students with the assistance they need to learn from their errors and improve their performance. Instructors who set high standards for students are rated more positively than easy graders, so long as they grade fairly and provide students with the resources they need to reach their preferred outcomes.

MANAGING: FOSTER CIVILITY AND INTEGRITY

Even though professors' top priority is promoting students' learning and achievement, they must also enforce basic principles of academic integrity, civility, and tolerance. Classroom management, the focus of Chapter 7, includes all those "actions taken by the teacher to establish order, engage students, or elicit their cooperation" (Emmer & Stough, 2001, p. 103). A class is a social milieu, complete with norms, roles, relationships, cliques, statuses, conflicts, competitions, and other assorted interpersonal processes. These social dynamics sometimes contribute to the energy for and engagement in both the teaching and learning, but they can also be more disruptive than promotive. Of these difficulties, violations of academic integrity are the most significant in terms of their effects on the teaching–learning process. The student who shows no remorse when he naps in class each day may be irritating, but the student who cheats crosses a line that should not be crossed.

UPGRADING: USE TECHNOLOGY APPROPRIATELY

Despite the predilection for discomfiting terminology, such as *tweets, moocs, blogs, wikis, mashups, hypertext, podcasts,* and the like, technology offers professors new ways to reach their long-established goals. Some technologies, such as in-class projection systems, smartphones, and mediascape learning laboratories, are changing the nature of the traditional classroom lectures, discussions, and physical laboratories. But computer-based information technologies—most notably, the Internet—is the big player in the world of teaching technology: Each year, more classes move from bricks-and-mortar classrooms into virtual, online ones. A Gates Foundation survey of nearly 4,000 U.S. teaching faculty concluded that nearly 25% teach courses completely online, and another 20% teach blended courses in which at least 30% of the material is taught online (FTI Consulting, 2015). Chapter 8 reviews these innovations and their influence on teaching, for the effectiveness of these methods—like all tools—is determined by their consistency with pedagogical purposes and the skill of the user.

EVALUATING: ASSESS YOUR SUCCESS

In teaching, as in all things, many paths lead to excellence. One professor may be a superb lecturer who teaches listeners so stealthily they do not even realize their neural networks are being rewoven. Another may be the quintessential discussion leader who can draw out and organize students' viewpoints in a rich texture of insights. Others may develop novel methods of instruction, write textbooks that inspire students, or mentor colleagues in the craft of teaching. The steps taken in the evaluation of teaching discussed in Chapter 9 must reflect this diversity. Because professors reach excellence through many different paths, one must cast the net widely if one is to catch all the information needed to evaluate teaching. Teaching can and should be evaluated but, as with so many things in life, the easy way of doing something—in professors' case, surveying students—is not necessarily the best way.

DOCUMENTING: DEVELOP A TEACHING PERSONA

Professors are, in a sense, historians who are writing and revising their own autobiography. Each experience, each event, and each new insight adds to that ever-expanding archive of information that defines who they are, as individuals, as academics, and as educators. That history likely includes research, scholarship, and intellectual achievements, but a portion is also defined by their teachings: what they have done, across their career, to promote their students' achievement of their learning goals. A professor's teaching responsibilities are staggering, but Chapter 10 warns that the work in and out of the classroom can be overlooked and forgotten if it is never documented. Many teaching professors therefore gather together the artifacts of their teaching in a portfolio or dossier that describes their involvement in, and success at, teaching. Portfolios describe the teaching professor's work, guide development, and encourage innovation but, more important, they make explicit professors' central role in higher education.

The Idea of It All

College professors are not just philosophers, theoreticians, researchers, artists, scientists, and engineers; they also are educators. We are charged with a crucial responsibility: the transformation of our students into college graduates who possess the skills and capabilities that imprimatur promises. We effect that transformation by designing classes that inspire, motivate, and inform our students; by selecting and implementing effective methods of instruction; and by skillfully assessing our students' success in reaching their educational objectives. However, because we are rarely trained in instructional design, our practices—as impressive as they are—are often informed only by our personal experiences as learners, the well-meaning advice of colleagues, and feedback from students.

This book draws on a different source of information about teaching—theory and research in psychology—to offer insights into 10 key aspects of college-level teaching: (a) identifying purposes, (b) course planning, (c) student engagement, (d) lecturing, (e) assessment, (f) grading, (g) classroom management, (h) using technology, (i) course evaluation, and (j) developing a portfolio. For those who are new to teaching, the book, which is organized so that topics are covered in the order they gain our attention during the course of the semester, provides a guide one can follow from the semester's start to its end. Experienced teachers, in contrast, may use the book to gain new insights into issues that remain unsettled, even when viewed through eyes that have seen many classes, many students, and many changes to higher education itself.

How you use *College Teaching* depends on you and your purposes, but no matter what your experience or interest, I hope this book kindles (or rekindles) your curiosity about how people learn new things and that it prompts you to wonder again about how the students in your classes are transformed by what you do.

Orienting

Considering Purposes and Priorities

1

O nly people who have never taught a college course think it would be an easy thing to do. When new acquaintances discover you teach in a college or university, their comments and questions often betray their misunderstanding of what is involved in such an undertaking. How quick they are to overlook the hours spent preparing before first greeting a class: the years invested in learning your discipline's paradigm and principles; the late nights reviewing recent additions to the scholarly corpus and deciding which ideas must be purged so that room can be made for new ones; the time taken to develop ways to present the material, motivate and inspire students, and test their learning. And don't forget the logistics: finalizing the syllabus, creating online content, arranging academic accommodations, tracking attendance and grades, and so on. The uninformed ask, "What do you do with all that free time?" as you rush down the hall to your next class.

What is to be done when the situation's demands outstrip the time available to meet them? Dory, the *Paracanthurus*

http://dx.doi.org/10.1037/14777-002
College Teaching: Practical Insights From the Science of Teaching and Learning,
by D. R. Forsyth

hepatus in the animated film *Finding Nemo*, championed one strategy quite consistently: Just keep swimming. As the tasks pile up, plow through them by adding a few more hours for work, skipping all but the essential faculty meetings and presentations, scaling back on your scholarship, staying away from all forms of entertainment, and minimizing family obligations. Keep your head above water until the semester's end.

In this time-urgent world people facing a challenging task—such as transforming a roomful of students into polished scholars—often move too quickly into action. Like Dory, we just start swimming. But the coping strategy Dory recommends receives less-than-rousing support from those who study productivity, performance, and well-being. Performance prefaced by an orienting phase—when goals are set, procedures established, and strategies considered—results in a more successful and less stressful experience (Barrick, Mount, & Li, 2013).

But of the myriad purposes colleges and universities set forth in their mission statements, and promises they make to students and parents, which ones will you—this term, with these students, in this class—pull out of the "will get to if I have time" bin and slot into the rarified group of educational outcomes that you and your students must achieve? This chapter assumes that question must be answered before all others. It is important to not only know where you are swimming to, but also why.

Orienting Purposes

When Ken Bain (2004) was appointed director of a teaching center at his university he began a systematic analysis of the qualities of and methods used by the best college professors. His search led him to 63 different professors who had all reached or surpassed a set of rigorous criteria for excellence. These professors differed by discipline and experience, but they all had certain qualities and practices in common: They created critical learning environments in their classes, where students actively challenge ideas and learn to marshal evidence, question assumptions, and develop logically coherent analyses of issues. They crafted their lectures, their discussions, and their other teaching activities in ways that captured students' attention and held it. They trusted their students and developed positive reciprocal relationships with them.

In addition, all of these professors approached each course anew, taking time to revisit their purpose. Even when teaching a class for the 20th time, they did not walk into the class on the first day and repeat what they had done the previous semester but instead took a thoughtful, ruminative approach to their teaching. These professors recognized the scope of their broad charge to transform students into scholars, but they scaled that charge down to a manageable size by asking themselves, "What should my students be able to do intellectually, physically, or emotionally as a result of their learning?" (Bain, 2004, p. 49).

So, what should students be able to do when they complete their college education? Bloom's oft-cited taxonomy of educational outcomes, formulated in the 1940s, provides one answer (Bloom, Englehart, Furst, Hill, & Krathwohl, 1956). Bloom and his colleagues identified three domains—affective, psychomotor, and cognitive—but the cognitive domain is the one that so frequently structures educators' lists of learning goals. The cognitive domain consists of these levels:

- *knowledge*—remembering factual information, such as names, dates, studies, concepts, theories, and researchers (e.g., "List the six levels described by Bloom's taxonomy, in order from least to most complex");
- *comprehension*—understanding the meaning of an idea, concept, theory, or procedure (e.g., "Generate five verbs that describe the learning outcomes associated with each of the six stages of Bloom's taxonomy");
- *application*—describing the specific, concrete implications of a concept or idea in a new context or situation (e.g., "Give an example of a test question that measures learning at the application level of Bloom's taxonomy");
- *analysis*—identifying the elements of a complex concept and the interrelationships among these elements (e.g., "Compare and contrast Bloom's taxonomy to the revised model developed by Anderson and his colleagues in 2001");
- *synthesis*: integrating concepts and information to yield new insights or structures (e.g., "Use recent findings in the field of learning science to update and refine Bloom's original taxonomy of educational objectives"); and
- *evaluation*: gauging the value, quality, usefulness, and worth a concept, theory, set of works, and so on (e.g., "Critique Bloom's taxonomy, basing your analysis on the key characteristics of a good theory").

Other investigators have modified Bloom's taxonomy over the years (e.g., Anderson et al., 2001; Fink, 2013). Each model stresses some unique goals, but most converge on a common core of academic outcomes that include discipline-specific knowledge, basic literacies (reading, writing, oral communication, mathematics, technology, and information acquisition), and cognitive competencies (critical thinking, reasoning, problem solving, etc.). A second cluster of outcomes pertains to more personal outcomes, including an appreciation of the arts and other academic values, work and career preparation, and personal growth.

KNOWLEDGE: WHAT SHOULD STUDENTS KNOW?

Professors, given their uniquely exacting and exhaustive study of their disciplines, are committed to sharing their understanding with their students. A professor teaching an introductory physics course for nonscientists, for example, must select from his or her vast knowledge of the field those theories and findings that can be covered in the limited time available. Surely students must leave the class with a strong understanding of mechanics, energy, electricity, and thermodynamics, but what about the history of physics, optics, heat, relativity, and quantum mechanics (Häussler & Hoffmann, 2000)? An English professor teaching a first-year literature course may decide to cover the *Bildungsroman* genre (the growth and transition from adolescence to adulthood) but must selectively sample from the deep well of works that examine rites of passage, shifting sex roles, and the end of childhood (Showalter, 2003). Psychologists teaching students who may never again take another course in the field must ask themselves, "What theories, studies, facts, and findings constitute the core of psychology?" (McGovern et al., 2010).

Emphasizing knowledge is a bit old-fashioned when information is so quickly and easily acquired from places such as Wikipedia. Besides, the knowledge base of any field is continually mutating as conceptions and understandings are updated and reconfigured. The truths professors teach their students today may not be so highly prized by them tomorrow. But professors are after not *surface learning*—the recall of discrete facts and bits of information—but *deep learning*: the integration of new information within the learner's existing network of cognitive associations and structures. When students understand a concept or idea, then they grasp its basic meaning and interpretation. Instead of just naming the key features of a concept examined in a reading or class, students who understand the concept can describe the basic nature of each of its components, the dynamic interconnections among the components, and the relationship between the concept and other concepts. If students can interpret charts and graphs, translate text material into symbolic forms such as equations or predictions, defend the methods used in a particular study, or poke holes in the logic of a conceptual interpretation, then they have achieved a deeper comprehension of the field's intellectual yield rather than a surface-level, and likely fleeting, memory of facts and information. If students are to interpret, illustrate, classify, summarize, infer, compare, contrast, and explain, they must first acquire a foundation in the field's content (R. E. Mayer, 2002, pp. 228–229).

Cognitive scientist Daniel T. Willingham (2009) went so far as to argue that advanced intellectual skills, including critical thinking and problem solving, "*require* extensive factual knowledge" (p. 26). If two equally intelligent students—both certifiably excellent readers—review the same page from a textbook in your field, the one who has already studied the ideas, concepts, and information in depth will understand more of what was read. Individuals who are trying to solve problems do not first engage in logical analysis; they instead search for a solution in the memories they have acquired through previous study and experience. In general, the more one knows about something, the more easily new ideas and information are acquired.

Educating for understanding, however, also often requires the deletion of inaccurate data. Some concepts require more instructional time, not because they are complex but because they are not consistent with students' preexisting understanding and assumptions. For example, economics students who ace their examinations nonetheless fail to let go of their well-learned belief that price is a property of an object, so they never fully understand that price is a function of economic systems (Dahlgren, 1984). Some college graduates, despite having taken courses in physics and interplanetary motion, nonetheless misunderstand the causes of Earth's seasons (Schneps & Sadler, 1987). They mistakenly assume that the earth moves closer to the sun during the summer than the winter, even though they learned in class (and, for most, their year studying abroad) that it is the tilt of the Earth on its axis that causes seasonal fluctuations in temperature (Mastascusa, Snyder, & Hoyt, 2011).

CORE LITERACIES: ARE STUDENTS LITERATE?

A college graduate is, or at least should be, a literate person. A literate person was originally someone who could read and write: The word originates in the Latin *literatus,* as do such words as *literature* and *literary.* But a host of other literacies have joined those traditionally embraced within academia, with the result that competencies in mathematics, information acquisition, and technology have made the list of essential qualities of a well-educated person.

Reading

College professors assume that students can understand the meaning of the readings they assign, but they ask more of their students than just comprehension. Students must be skilled in the close reading of their textbooks; they must be able to extract information from the author's words, even when that information is not explicitly stated; they must be able to make connections and draw inferences from the text and link the information back to other ideas and concepts examined in the course. They must learn to analyze the author's arguments and descriptions, distinguishing between strong and weak claims, unsubstantiated declarations of opinion as fact, and gaps in the logic and meaning.

Unfortunately, even though most high school graduates in the United States can read English, only 44% can read with the speed and accuracy required for success in college—at least, as defined by the ACT (2013) benchmarks. Because of these deficiencies, many first-year students are directed into "developmental" (remedial) reading courses; estimates range from a low of 11% to well over 50% (Grubb, 2013). Even at graduation, a substantial number of students are not adept readers. The National Survey of America's College Students (Baer, Cook, & Baldi, 2006) tested the reading skills of 1,827 students graduating from either a 2- or 4-year college and graded them at three levels:

1. *Basic*: capable of reading simple documents, such as pamphlets
2. *Intermediate*: skilled in reading moderately difficult prose, can grasp the writer's purpose, capable of summarizing an argument and identifying causal inferences
3. *Proficient*: able to read lengthy, abstract prose and draw complex inferences from the material, can compare and synthesize multiple documents

Among graduates of 4-year schools, 6% were basic readers, 56% were intermediate readers, and 38% were proficient readers. For 2-year schools, these percentages were 11, 65, and 23, respectively (Baer et al., 2006).

Reading skills are also specific, to some degree, to each academic discipline. Students assume that reading their biology textbook requires the same cognitive skills and orientation as the books and papers they read in their English or philosophy class, for they view text as information. But for professors, reading is an interpersonal exchange between writer and reader, and so they consider meaning, motive, credibility, and connections to their own understandings as they read (Pearson & Cervetti, 2013). A historian, for example, does not read text the same way a chemist or a mathematician does. Historians are sensitive to the author's perspective, searching for the kind of selectivity in citations and source documentation that signals a biased agenda. Scientists read to learn about the procedures used by researchers who tested a theory, with a critical eye for methodological rigor and theoretical precision (Shanahan & Shanahan, 2008). Until students achieve disciplinary literacy, their understanding of what they read will not match their professors'.

Writing and Communication

Truth, as William James (1899) noted, "is too great for any one mind" (pp. 4–5). It must be traded, shared, exchanged, transmitted—communicated to—others. Communication often involves writing or speech and can range from an informal exchange of ideas among members of a class to more structured, formal presentations and texts. A proficient communicator must be skilled in identifying a topic, analyzing an issue or problem, developing arguments that are logically sound and supported by valid evidence, selecting information to include and exclude, and organizing this information to generate unified text or speech. A skilled writer must be able to produce writing that is coherent, grammatically correct, and sufficiently detailed. A skilled speaker must do the same, but with a spoken message that is both suitable for the situation's purpose and the audience of listeners (Morreale, Backlund, & Sparks, 2014).

Unfortunately, and as with reading, many students entering college have not yet mastered the subtleties of effective communication. When the U.S. Department of Education tested high school seniors' writing abilities, they discovered that the majority (52%) could develop and support a thesis concept in a paper with an introduction and a conclusion, but their writing was not very creative, analytically rigorous, or free of grammatical errors (see http://www.nationsreportcard.gov/). Only 24% of the students were "proficient writers" who wrote strong essays with few grammatical, spelling, and punctuation errors. Of the students tested, 3% were considered advanced, because they presented "thoughtful and complex ideas," wrote with a "structure that has a clear and effective logical progression of ideas," and "used specific and precise word choice" (National Assessment Governing Board, 2010, p. 80). Perhaps as a consequence, "My students can't write" routinely tops the list of professor's pet peeves, and this attitude is often associated with a profound reluctance to assign students writing assignments.

Numeracy

Numeracy is competency in processing, using, interpreting, and communicating numerical information. As the National Council of Teachers of Mathematics suggested back in 1991, "Every student can and should learn to reason and solve problems, to make connections across a rich web of topics and experiences, and to communicate mathematical ideas" (p. 21). People who are numerically literate should be able to solve problems and make decisions using basic mathematics, algebra, geometry, and statistics. They should be able to recognize when the numerical results others present are reasonable, given the circumstances, and be able to identify factors that place limits on the usefulness of the available numerical information. Numeracy also assumes a degree of skill in using data to make inferences and draw conclusions, even if the information is presented in complex tabular or graphic form.

Many students are ready and able to work their way through algebra, pre-calculus, and even calculus, but some entering college students (44%, in fact) have not reached the college math readiness benchmark set by the ACT (2013). More disconcerting, even students who can solve mathematics problems may not have a strong conceptual grasp of mathematics principles and processes. They may use procedures that they learned through rote repetition in high school and SAT preparation courses, but when they encounter an unstructured problem that requires mathematical thinking they are at a loss to solve it. Richland, Stigler, and Holyoak (2012) illustrated this possibility in their study of community college students who could pass math classes and solve well-structured problems yet were unable to solve problems that required understanding fractions, number lines, or percentages. For example, when researchers asked students to place the numbers −0.7 and 13/8 at their approximate location on a number line from −2 to +2, only 21% did so successfully. When researchers administered tests of mathematics problems that required several steps and the use of numbers to solve problems to more than 150,000 adults in 24 countries, one third of the U.S. college graduates failed to reach proficiency (Organisation for Economic Co-operation and Development, 2013). The United States ranked 17th of 24.

Emerging Literacies

The three Rs—reading, writing, and arithmetic—retain their place at the top of the list of literacies, but the Renaissance person of the modern era needs a few more talents to deal with life's complexities. The pages of Yahoo! and Google News, *The Huffington Post*, CNN, and the like are filled with discussions, debates, controversies, and analyses of all kinds of topics; to understand their meaning, innuendo, and implications requires a good grasp of science, technology, and cultural processes.

- *Science literacy* is a given for students in the sciences and social sciences, but all college students will likely benefit from an understanding of the philosophy of science and proper standards for scientific procedures.
- *Cultural literacy* has changed considerably since Hirsch, Kett, and Trefil (1987) first adjudged that American citizens should share a common stock of knowledge about key names, dates, places, events,

and so on; now the phrase is often used describe a general knowledge of past and current cultural events, including pop culture.

▪ *Digital literacy*, or information literacy, is no longer just a skill set monopolized by computer programmers and gamers. Sophistication in using Internet-based technology to acquire information is now considered by some to be an essential skill for lifelong learning. After students have graduated they will be acquiring the information they need via the Internet.

COGNITIVE COMPETENCIES: CAN STUDENTS THINK EFFICIENTLY, EFFECTIVELY, AND CRITICALLY?

French psychologist Jean Piaget (1950), in his theory of cognitive development, argued that children's mental processes are qualitatively different from the processes that sustain most adults' thinking and reasoning. Piaget explained that the errors and interpretations that characterize children's interpretations of the world are not the result of their lack of knowledge. They are not simply unschooled or inexperienced; instead, they have not developed the basic cognitive and metacognitive mechanisms required to solve complex problems, make difficult decisions, or critically evaluate arguments and interpretations. Piaget believed that cognitive maturation occurs over time as children experience situations that are difficult to reconcile with their existing cognitive structures.

Most beginning college students have reached the final level of cognitive development Piaget described in his theory: formal operations. Young adults can think abstractly and draw inferences that proceed in a logical way from premises to conclusions. They are capable of generating explanations of events and experiences, and they can test the value of these explanations by seeking out additional information. They can mentally reverse cognitive operations, use propositional logic, identify the assumptions made in a complex argument, and challenge a conclusion by examining the validity of its premises. But there is still considerable work to do. In Piagetian terms, students must confront questions, problems, and situations that they cannot understand fully just by calling forth previously learned solutions. These challenges disturb their cognitive status quo and entice them into joining the intellectual fray. As they turn the problem over in their mind, they are honing their cognitive capacities, becoming so expert that they can think clearly even when performing novel and demanding cognitive tasks under duress or the constraint of time.

Many professors accept as their cardinal objective the challenge of teaching students to think more clearly, logically, critically, and profoundly. Many universities, too, expressly endorse their commitment to cognitive outcomes in their statement of mission and goals; their websites are littered with such phrases as "Our Core Curriculum fosters critical thinking skills as students enter the life of mind," "Your university learning will begin with a foundation in general education that will help you learn to think clearly," and "Our faculty are committed to nurturing our students' ability to think analytically." Such laudable goals, however, are difficult to document through assessment, and each viral video of a college student doing something extremely injudicious during spring break suggests that this goal is more elusive than attainable. This anecdotal evidence of a failure to attain noteworthy gains in cognitive abilities is buttressed by harder evidence supplied by Arum and Roksa (2011) in their book *Academically Adrift: Limited Learning on College Campuses*. When they examined longitudinal data pertaining to college students' capacity to think critically and to express themselves in their writing, they were disappointed that 1,035 of the 2,300 students they tested showed no significant learning gains after taking college classes for 2 years. They concluded that students "may be acquiring subject-specific knowledge or greater self-awareness on their journeys through college" but that "many students are not improving their skills in critical thinking, complex reasoning, and writing" (p. 36).

APPLICATIONS AND SKILLS: WHAT CAN STUDENTS DO?

The expression "That's just academic" suggests that much of college learning has little applied value, but nurturing the skillful application of knowledge to solve practical problems is a high priority for many professors. Computer science students must know not only the complexities of information systems but also how to program those systems to perform essential tasks. Sociology students, after learning the various explanations for crime, must be able to use those theories to identify workable solutions for reducing this social problem. Finance students must not only understand the reason why the price:earnings ratio is an important indicator of a company's potential, but they must be able to calculate and use that index to make recommendations to investors. Professors value knowledge for its own sake, but they also recognize that knowledge provides the means to improve human existence.

Application as Learning Transfer

Bloom's taxonomy of teaching outcomes ranks application above such cognitive skills as remembering and comprehension because of the significant cognitive demands of the application domain. Application requires that one use existing knowledge structures—the stored and subsequently retrieved previous learning—for problem solving, and so it relies on a series of interrelated cognitive processes. Experts easily apply their knowledge to unfamiliar tasks and novel situations because they have, over time, developed a set of concepts and principles that guide their analysis of the problem and their search for solutions. Novices are still building their conceptual structures, and so they struggle to connect the elements in specific cases to theoretically meaningful concepts (Reimann & Schult, 1996, p. 124). They must identify the key features of the new situation. They must retrieve previous examples from memory in sufficient detail to match the elements with those of the new case. They must then generalize from their existing store of knowledge to the new problem. It is no wonder, then, that even students who know a content area backward and forward stumble when asked to apply their knowledge to a novel situation.

Procedural Skills

Psychologists distinguish between declarative and procedural memory systems. *Declarative memory* corresponds to knowledge of factual information and comprehension of relations among that information. *Procedural memory*, in contrast, is memory for doing things, including actions, skills, and processing information. When students practice specific skills for a class—say, they format a document, edit a wiki, solve a math problem, transpose a matrix, write a paragraph, stain a slide, conduct a statistical test, use a geographic information system to map an area, or determine the constituents of an alloy—they are strengthening their procedural memories. Direct instruction is often of little use in creating enduring procedural memories, for telling a person how to read, write, compute, or calculate is no substitute for practice. Transfer of learning from one situation to another often requires repetition of the task until the final product is judged, through comparison with some standard, to be of sufficient quality (Salomon & Perkins, 1989).

PERSONAL OUTCOMES: WHO ARE THEY?

In 1854, Cardinal John Henry Newman, as the rector of Catholic University in Ireland (now University College Dublin), spent considerable time pondering the following question: What is the purpose of a university? He concluded that the university is not a place for religious study or scientific research, but a place where students learn the distinctive gratifications of a studied and reflective life:

> It is the education which gives us a clear and conscious view of
> our own opinions and judgments, a truth in developing them,
> an eloquence in expressing them, and a force in urging them. It

teaches us to see things as they are, to go right to the point, to
disentangle a skein of thought, to detect what is sophisticated,
and to discard what is irrelevant. It prepares us to fill any post
with credit and to master any subject with facility. It shows us
how to accommodate ourselves to others, how to throw ourselves
into their state of mind, how to bring before them our own, how
to influence them, how to come to an understanding with them,
and how to bear with them. (Newman, 1891, p. 178)

Newman's charge remains a guiding principle for contemporary
colleges and universities. At the *personal level*, classes often help people better understand themselves and their problems. Some courses
address the goal of self-improvement or growth goal explicitly, but rare
is the course that does not yield ideas that have personal implications.
At the *value level*, many courses openly examine important contemporary issues, including racism, sexism, ethics, social policy, and political
values. Such courses teach not only disciplinary facts and intellectual
skills but also interpersonal sensitivity, respect for diversity, appreciation of individual differences, and ethical decision making. And at the
social level, colleges are communities of learners, scholars, and teachers,
and their years spent in that community should prepare them for a
life spent working, living, and joining with others. As Newman (1891)
wrote,

The educated person is at home in any society, has common
ground with every class, knows when to speak and when to
be silent, is able to converse, is able to listen, can ask a question
pertinently, and gain a lesson seasonably when he or she has
nothing to impart. (p. 178)

Orienting Issues

Whenever pundits and policymakers are incensed by a particular social
failing they often seek a remedy by adding another goal to college professors' already-long list of responsibilities. If the younger generation
seems unable to manage even the most simple of life's demands, tell
colleges to ramp up their educational efforts with regard to self-reliance
and personal responsibility. If the country's politicians and business exec-
utives disappoint more than they reassure, remind colleges that they are
the training grounds for tomorrow's leaders. If the country is lagging
behind other nations in research and development, tell colleges to pay
more attention to science, technology, engineering, and mathematics
(the STEM disciplines) in their curricula (Delbanco, 2012). Professors, as

the designers of their courses, have a louder voice in setting the course goals, but other stakeholders, such as students, parents, employers, may have their own priorities.

WHAT ARE YOUR SCHOOL'S PRIORITIES?

The place where one teaches will define, at least in part, which outcomes are considered essential and which are thought to be just niceties. Officially, the best-known taxonomy of colleges and universities in the United States, the Carnegie Classifications (see http://carnegieclassifications. iu.edu/), is mute on the issue of purpose. It considers size, types of degrees awarded, focus on undergraduate education, and research emphasis, but not on the specific educational outcomes sought by each college and university. However, research universities (those with multiple graduate programs, advanced professional schools, R1s or RU/VHs [research universities characterized as "very high research activity" per the Carnegie Classifications]) nonetheless tend to stress goals that are consistent with disciplinary knowledge and training for advanced study, whereas colleges with a high concentration of arts and sciences programs for undergraduates stress growth in cognitive complexity and literacy. Two-year colleges, which offer associate's degrees, are more circumscribed in their focus. Their goals include personal development, work and career preparation, and the development of basic skills (Ruef & Nag, 2015).

Liberal arts colleges and universities, too, tend to stress somewhat different goals than land-grant, public institutions of higher learning. *Liberal*, derived from the Latin *liber* (free), implies the intellectual freedom that comes from an enhanced capacity to think clearly, argue intelligently, and make choices expeditiously. *Arts*, in its broader sense, suggests skillful intellectual execution rather than the fine arts per se (e.g., painting or performance). Liberal arts colleges, therefore, focus less on application and instead prize intellectual growth, depth in traditional academic disciplines (e.g., history, arts, languages, philosophy), engagement in the community, self-development, and the value of knowledge as an end in and of itself (R. Howard, Kline, & O'Quin, 2014).

WHAT ARE YOUR DISCIPLINE'S PRIORITIES?

Angelo and Cross's (1993) Teaching Goals Inventory lists 52 learning outcomes that a professor may reasonably target for any given class, goals such as the development of analytic skills and creative thinking as well as those pertaining to academic success skills, liberal arts and academic values, work and career preparation, and personal development. When Angelo and Cross asked a sample of more than 2,000 professors at 2- and 4-year colleges to rate these objectives on a scale that ranged from *essential* to *unimportant*, the respondents displayed a quality rarely seen among college faculty: They agreed with each other. The three top goals, all rated by more than 50% of both community college professors and 4-year college professors as essential, were (a) "learn terms and facts of this subject," (b) "develop ability to apply principles and generalizations already learned to new problems and situations," and (c) "develop capacity to think for oneself" (pp. 399–406).

The professoriate, in general, agrees that students should learn their discipline's subject matter, develop cognitive and creative capacities, and become more self-directed learners (FTI Consulting, 2015), but each field's unique paradigmatic assumptions puts its stamp on that discipline's educational practices and priorities. Studies of the professoriate suggest that professors in the arts consider the development of appreciation of art to be an important goal; science professors, not so much. Math professors put problem-solving skills higher on their priority list of outcomes than do professors in business schools. Engineering and some business faculty (accounting, finance) stress the importance of preparing students for employment after college and creating an educated workforce. Faculty in the arts (art, music), humanities (English, philosophy, history), and some of the social sciences (sociology, political science) stress personal development, including self-understanding and moral character. Professors in the sciences and social sciences thought teaching students to write well was an important goal, although they rarely said it was *their* instructional goal (Angelo & Cross, 1993; Lattuca & Stark, 2009; Smart, 1982).

WHAT ARE THE PUBLIC'S PRIORITIES?

A college education remains a highly prized outcome, for most people assume that college graduates are significantly different—in a good way—from people who did not earn college degrees. This enduring support for colleges is predicated on the assumption that universities will transform the masses of matriculants into mature, cognitively sophisticated, and economically successful adults. Surveys of the public at large have found that most people feel that colleges are supposed to help students attain employment and success in a career (e.g., P. D. Hart, 2004). Over 90% of the Americans surveyed in one poll felt that career preparation was an important or very important purpose of a college education (Selingo, 2003). Many (62%) believed that a college education should help students qualify for a better job. General cognitive competencies were valued, although they tended to be second-rather than first-tier priorities. Fully 63% of the adults in one survey considered an "improved ability to solve problems and think analytically" was an essential skill to be gained during college—but nearly as many said the same thing about learning "high-tech skills, such as using computers and the Internet" (P. D. Hart, 2004, pp. 5–6). Other outcomes, including a sense of maturity, independence, and improved social skills, were rated as essential ones by a majority of the respondents but were not so uniformly acclaimed.

Business leaders, when asked about the most important skills needed for a career in business, stress practical skills such as digital literacy, work ethic, and experience in a business setting. They added, however, that long-term success in a business career requires the sorts of competencies stressed by a more traditional conception of higher education: critical thinking skills, problem-solving ability, skill in communicating with others, and self-discipline (e.g., Gallup–Lumina Foundation, 2014).

WHAT ARE YOUR STUDENTS' PRIORITIES?

Professors hope to engage with their students in the analysis of intellectual mysteries. Parents assume college will transform their children into mature, independent adults. Employers want colleges to turn out hardworking employees with strong cognitive, decision-making, communication, and collaborative skills. But what about the students? What are they seeking?

Given the great diversity of students currently attending college, any generalizations about the typical college student's hopes and aspirations will likely be overgeneralizations. For every student who expresses excitement about the opportunity to study the latest advances in nuclear physics or the lesser known works of F. Scott Fitzgerald will be a student who is seeking a work-required credential or a pre-adulthood moratorium. These diverse interests, however, generally coalesce into three broad categories of desired outcomes: (a) acquisition of knowledge, (b) development of skills and abilities required for success in a career, and (c) social pursuits. A substantial number of students endorse self-development as a priority as well (Acee, Cho, Kim, & Weinstein, 2012; Tinto, 1997).

Mastery and Achievement Goals

Students vary in their level of academic motivation. Some, perhaps realizing that colleges and universities are a type of school, recognize that their primary purpose in attending them is to learn. These students, however, differ in their degree of endorsement of two types of learning goals: (a) mastery goals and (b) achievement/performance goals (see Senko, Hulleman, & Harackiewicz, 2011, for a review). Students who adopt *mastery goals* are interested in learning the material in the class and strive to master that material. On surveys they strongly endorse such statements as "I want to learn as much as possible from this class" and "I desire to completely master the material presented in this class." In contrast, students who are pursuing *achievement/performance goals* are interested in demonstrating their competence, especially relative to other students. They tend to agree with such statements as "It is important to me to do better than the other students" and "It is important to me to do well compared to others in this class" (Elliot & Church, 1997, p. 223). A third cluster of students, however, is not as interested in either mastering a subject or demonstrating their competence. Some of these students are motivated primarily by a desire to avoid failing, whereas others lack any academic motivation whatsoever. These students are not committed to their identity as a student and as a consequence they do not acknowledge the importance of learning goals (Pizzolato, 2006).

Career Goals

Students, like the public at large, expect that their coursework will give them the skills needed for success in a profession. The National Norms survey, conducted by the Higher Education Research Institute, for example, asked 192,912 full-time students to rate the importance of several reasons for attending college, including to be able to get a better job, to gain a general education, and to develop an appreciation of ideas. Many (72%) considered learning, in general, to be an important goal, but even more of them (88%) rated getting a job as the most important reason to go to college. This survey also documented a mismatch in expectations regarding the length of time students would need to reach their educational goals. Although only about 40% of college students graduate in 4 years or less, 84.3% of the students in the Higher Education Research Institute sample believed they would wrap up their undergraduate careers 4 years after they enrolled as first-year students (Eagan, Lozano, Hurtado, & Case, 2013; Pryor et al., 2012).

Social and Personal Goals

Each year, *U.S. News & World Report* (2013) publishes its rankings of American colleges and universities. In most years, Harvard, Yale, and Princeton top the list of nationally ranked colleges, whereas Williams, Amherst, and Swarthmore dominate the list of liberal arts schools. But since 1993 the *Princeton Review* (http://www.princetonreview.com/) has been publishing another list: the Best Party School in America. The review bases its rankings on a survey of thousands of students at colleges across the United States that asks about drug and alcohol use, the proportion of students who belong to fraternities and sororities, and the number of hours students report studying each day. Schools at the top of the list are deemed party schools, and those at the bottom are labeled "stone-cold sober" schools. The *Review*'s list suggests that college students at some schools may have other priorities besides intellectual enlightenment and the development of skills needed for career success.

The *Princeton Review* is not alone in suggesting that students value social activities, peer relations, and personal gratification more than their academic pursuits (e.g., Arum & Roksa, 2011). For example, each year the Center for Postsecondary Research and Planning surveys students with its National Survey of Student Engagement. The survey asks students to estimate how much time they spend preparing for class—which could include not only studying but also doing the readings and any homework assignments. The center's conclusion was as follows: Very few students follow the general formula of spending 2 hours or more studying for each hour spent in class. Nearly half of the students surveyed averaged only 1 hour studying outside of class for every in-class hour, and only 15% of the students carrying a courseload of 15 or more hours spent more than 26 hours per week studying. Ten percent reported studying less than 5 hours a week—total (National Survey of Student Engagement, 2013).

Arum and Roksa (2011) also concluded that students are pursuing nonacademic goals with more vigor than academic ones. As noted earlier in the discussion of cognitive competencies, these investigators were disappointed to find that many students evidenced little or no gain despite performing well in their college classes. They identified a number of factors that could be blunting college's effect on students but highlighted one in particular: students' involvement in social, recreational, and personal activities. Drawing on ethnographies and their own survey data, they concluded that students are so heavily involved in clubs, sports, fraternities, sororities, and other social events and organizations that they hardly have time to study and complete their required assignments and readings. The students in their study reported spending 51% of their time on social activities but only 7% of their time studying. These findings suggest one more entry for college professors' long list of responsibilities: teach students that the primary purposes of college are learning and intellectual development instead of socializing and revelry (Arum & Roksa, 2014).

Orienting Alignment

Professors are the experimenters delivering the manipulation in one of the most elaborate social programs ever devised: higher education. Their students are experienced ones, but they have reached what will be, for most of them, the final stage in their transformation into a learned person, and professors are the ones who are charged with effecting that final change. Such a responsibility raises two sets of questions. First, what are the primary purposes of higher education? What are the standards that students must reach to be judged worthy of the label *college graduate*? What must they know, what intellectual skills must they command, and what kind of people should they be? Second, of the many lessons that students must learn in college, which ones are you, as their professor, going to teach them? Will you help them express themselves more clearly in their writing and speech? Will you share with them your unique understanding of your field? Will you stimulate their ability to think analytically, objectively, and with sophistication (see Table 1.1)?

Answering these questions deserves to be at the top of the professor's must-do list for at least three reasons. First, purposes determine procedures, for effective teaching requires aligning all the various and sundry activities associated with teaching with the goals one is seeking to achieve. Second, teaching and learning will proceed more smoothly

---

TABLE 1.1

A Summary of the Educational Objectives of Higher Education

Learning goal	Characteristics
Knowledge	Do your students have a deep understanding of the fundamental concepts of your field? Can they recall, define, interpret, illustrate, classify, summarize, compare, contrast, explain, and extend core concepts and issues?
Literacies	Have your students become skilled in reading, writing, using numerical information, scientific reasoning, and acquiring information?
Cognitive capacities	Can your students think efficiently, effectively, and critically? Can they analyze, synthesize, differentiate, organize, critique, evaluate, plan, and create?
Application	Can your students apply course concepts to new problems or novel situations? Have they developed practical skills, including learning skills?
Personal development	Have your students grown as persons? Are they continuing to develop as individuals and as members of society, exhibiting maturity in self-regulation, value clarification, morality, interpersonal skills, and cultural sensitivity?

when professors' and students' purposes intersect. Students cannot embrace the professor's purposes if they do not know what those purposes are. Third, knowing one's purposes gives the work of teaching and learning meaning because it clarifies the relationship between the quotidian aspects of teaching and its more lofty purposes.

ALIGNING PURPOSES AND PRACTICES

If professors had a code of best practices, probably the first principle on that list would be *primum non nocere*: First, do no harm. But their second principle might well be this: Align the purposes you seek in your teaching with the methods you use when you teach. Most professors find themselves in the enviable position of being able to design their courses, but the method they choose should be based on one guiding standard question: Will this intervention facilitate students' attainment of our learning goals? All will be confused by the professor who explains, "I want my students to learn to write well" but then never assigns any writing, or one who wants students to better understand the core concepts of the field but then covers the pertinent content superficially. And what of the professors who want their students to learn to work in teams but then never put into place procedures that will teach the basic skills required of collaborative activity? Identifying purposes does more than provide a general orientation to the semester's work; it guides the selection of the specific teaching methods to be used that semester (Biggs & Tang, 2007).

This recommendation to align purposes and practices applies to all aspects of teaching but, perhaps most important, to assessment. Even students filled with a love of learning, who are intrinsically motivated to pursue deeply the mysteries of your discipline, will lose some of their desire to study carefully if the tests, quizzes, and examinations you administer are not linked to the purposes you said you would be pursuing. Mager (1962) explained,

> Tests or examinations are the mileposts along the road to learning and are supposed to tell the teacher and the student the degree to which both have been successful in their achievement of the course objectives. But unless goals are clearly and firmly fixed in the minds of both parties, tests are at best misleading; at worst, they are irrelevant, unfair, or useless. To be useful they must measure performance in terms of goals. (p. 4)

Unfortunately, because memory of facts is easier to assess than analytic thinking skills or the development of self-awareness, the most important learning goals are often those that are least likely to be measured. One of the goals of higher education is to help students to make more rational, objective decisions, so it may be gratifying when they showcase their rationality by exerting effort only on the assessable aspects of your course. But one wonders about the rationality of the professor who tests students on their knowledge of X while hoping they have instead learned Y.

ALIGNING PROFESSORS' AND STUDENTS' PURPOSES

Both teaching and learning will proceed more smoothly if faculty and students are not working at cross purposes. College teaching is ideally a collaborative process whereby faculty and students pursue shared goals. Certainly some students and some professors, in some courses and programs, at some colleges and universities, are seeking compatible goals and outcomes. In many cases, however, professors' and students' goals are not just orthogonal but incompatible, given that the more intently professors pursue their educational goals the more likely their students will fail to reach theirs. This disparity in goal preferences may be irremediable, but at least its negative side effects can be partly repaired through preregistration advising, clarifying the rationale for the course's purposes, and even adding goals that are more in line with students' interests.

Advising and Registration

Journalists delight in poking fun at classes with curious titles, playing to the public's uncertainty about what college professors are actually doing in the classrooms. What, for example, will students be studying in Harvard's "Folklore 164, Maledicta," described as a course in "international traditions of vituperation and cursing"? And what are the learning goals targeted by Boston University's "Surfing and American Culture"; the University of Richmond's seminar "Baseballs, Body Parts, and Rosa Parks"; or the University of South Carolina's "Lady Gaga and the Sociology of Fame"?

In many cases, students learn of the course's objectives when it is too late: on the first day of class, when their schedules have been set in stone, at least psychologically. They may, of course, have been guided in their selections by reviewing the description of your course in the university or college catalogue, but in many cases those descriptions were crafted by a committee, and so they are not as informative as one might hope. This uncertainty can, however, be at least partly addressed by diligent preregistration advising and by providing detailed information about courses on university and personal websites. Many professors' online profiles provide information about their publications, office hours, and hobbies, but fewer provide details about what students will learn from these professors in their courses (Döring, 2002). Improving the match between the course's purpose and students' interests will likely yield positive results. After all, students who deliberately choose to take a course because they know what the course covers and are interested in the topic rate their learning experience more positively at the semester's end (Cashin, 1995).

Setting Goals (Together)

Studies of academic performance and goal setting offer one clear suggestion: Clarify for students the purpose of the course you are teaching and they are taking. Goals sit atop a pile of factors that psychologists have identified in their studies of motivation and performance. People working at jobs ranging from hauling logs to generating creative ideas to proofreading were found to be unproductive if their goals were vague or absent but productive if they were laboring to attain clearly established goals (Austin & Vancouver, 1996). Students tend to be more interested in course materials, and their performance improves, when they can identify the goals they are seeking (Forsyth & McMillan, 1991). As I note in Chapter 2, this clarification can be achieved by discussing the goals of the class during the initial class session and including the goals of the course on the syllabus.

Accommodating Students' Interests

Modifying one's teaching goals after considering students' interests and proclivities is sound practice, but only so long as their interests are not inconsistent with the primary objectives of the class. Some students have long- and short-term goals that are unified, clearly articulated, and reasonable. Other students, however, are still exploring their options for the future, and hence they cannot reasonably judge your course's value. It is one thing to respect students' interests, and to take advantage of those interests to increase their engagement in the course. However, the professor, as the expert, is the best judge of what a course's goals should be. With a nod toward the bard (Bob Dylan, not Shakespeare), students may know what they want, but professors know what they need.

Aligning Purposes and Meaning

Orientation requires ascertaining one's position relative to the goals one is seeking, whether these goals are the short-term outcomes sought that day, week, or month, or the longer term goals for one's year, career, or even life. A guiding orientation makes the work more meaningful by ensuring "the cognizance of order, coherence, and purpose in one's existence, the pursuit and attainment of worthwhile goals, and an accompanying sense of fulfillment" (Reker & Wong, 1988, p. 221).

Professors, as the makers of meaning, will likely prefer to take a more planful approach to the situation and its demands. This visioning helps professors cultivate and maintain a thoughtful, coherent approach to their teaching. Like a corporation's mission statement, a set of strategies gives purpose to the small, day-to-day actions that, although insignificant in isolation, sum to create an overall approach to teaching. Such an inclusive perspective provides an antidote for the relentless drift toward meaninglessness that can overtake action. The original purpose of an act can change over time until its meaning is replaced by some new, and less coherent, understanding (Vallacher & Wegner, 1987). A professor reading over material that must be covered in tomorrow's lecture may forget she is prepping a class and instead think she is just reading. A professor who stops on the street to answer a student's question may think he is wasting time, when in fact he is teaching. If people enter a situation without a conceptualization of action in mind, their actions are easy targets for reinterpretation. Before they know it, they become test givers, attendance takers, experts, disciplinarians, or speakers, but not what they intended to be: professors.

Orienting Redux: Identify Your Purposes and Priorities

Many are the purposes of higher education, in general, and a specific college class, in particular. Professor A, after reviewing the list of educational goals summarized in Table 1.1, may decide to focus on content; when the term ends she hopes the students will be familiar with the basic assumptions of the field's theories, theorists, and major findings. Professor B may be more interested in teaching his students the analytical and methodological skills of the field. He hopes that successful students can "do" things when they finish the course. Professor C may insist that her students learn to think critically, and she may let students sharpen these skills by debating controversies. Professor D may want students to apply material in their own lives. He wants his students to recognize the extent to which their own lives are shaped by factors discussed in class. Professor E may share the goals of Professors A, B, C, and D but also want students to apply an academic field in a practical pursuit, such as a business enterprise.

At least for now, academic freedom ensures that each scholar can pursue his or her own interests and teach those interests in his or her own way. However, this chapter's primary recommendation—identify your purposes and priorities—enjoins us to mindfully consider the essential purposes we seek. It does little good to teach the wrong thing effectively.

Prepping
Planning to Teach a College Class

2

The dream always begins the same way. I stand in a teaching auditorium I have never seen before. Students pack the hundred-seat rows that stretch back into the room's dark, distant recesses. I lean forward, clear my voice in the microphone, and the students fall silent as I welcome them to this, the first day of class. But as the word *welcome* echoes around the room I realize that I have forgotten to prepare any erudite remarks. I decide to just review the syllabus, but the empty desk by my side tells me that I forgot to make one for this class. So I steel myself to the task of bluffing my way through 30 minutes of reviewing the course's goals and procedures until the awful truth becomes apparent: I have no idea what course I am supposed to be teaching.

The nightmare's lesson: Prepare. College professors' teaching-related thoughts often revolve around *prepping*: "I haven't finished prepping that class yet." "Is that course a new prep for you?" "I cannot go to that talk—I have to prep for a class." "How many preps do you have this semester?"

http://dx.doi.org/10.1037/14777-003
College Teaching: Practical Insights From the Science of Teaching and Learning,
by D. R. Forsyth

"I need to have a few minutes of quiet so I can prep." Apparently, professors are so busy preparing that they do not even have time to say the whole word.

In Chapter 1, I examined the first step in planning: identifying the overarching purposes of the class. But if the first step in preparing to teach is the identification of goals—the knowledge base to build, the intellectual skills to foster, the personal development to actuate—then the next step requires identifying the means to achieve those ends. A professor's planning must take into account not only the nature of the class to be taught and the kinds of students who take it but also the instructional methods themselves. Professors must plan discussions, write lectures, select readings and texts, design assessments, and sequence the topics they hope to cover. This planning comes to an end on the first day of class when these plans, and the syllabus that details them, are shared with students. All the goal clarification in the world will not boost performance if the paths to take to reach those goals are uncertain.

Clarifying the Conditions

When Joan Stark and her colleagues asked faculty how they prepare for their classes, few of them said, "I think deep thoughts about my general approach to teaching and learning" or "I ask myself, 'What qualities should I build into my classroom to promote learning?'" Instead, they said that they spent time reviewing the topics they would be covering and the materials they would need for the teaching activities they had planned. They also claimed that they considered the characteristics of the students who would be taking the class, as if to coordinate their planned teaching approaches with the students' abilities, goals, and needs. Pondering arcane questions about goals, long-term outcomes, and strategies is all well and good, but professors cannot do it for too long, for they must get ready to teach the class (Lattuca & Stark, 2009; Stark, Lowther, Ryan, & Genthon, 1988).

CONSIDER THE CLASS

Professors who teach the same courses repeatedly may not have to review the content, but professors with a "new prep" or who are teaching the course again after several years away from it need to refresh their memories of the course's topics. One obvious source to consult for information is the university course catalogue. These descriptions, in most cases, have been officially sanctioned by curriculum review committees, but they can also be out of date and thus inaccurate. Colleagues who have taught the course regularly are another good source of information about content, and they can clarify local mores about veering away from the catalogue's description. If the class is a common one—an introductory survey course or even an advanced class in a popular major—then the standard content of the class can be gleaned from textbooks.

Do You Have a Commanding Grasp of the Course's Contents?

Many professors remember their first term teaching with mixed emotions. They were thrilled to have completed their graduate training and to at last be a professor. But in many cases they did not feel as though they were ready to teach. First, many felt uncertain about teaching because they had not been trained in teaching per se (e.g., Benassi & Buskist, 2012). Second, even though they were well trained in their particular field, their expertise was often narrower in scope than the courses they would be teaching (Boice, 1992).

Fortunately, professors are scholars, and so they are experts when it comes to transforming themselves from novitiate into expert. Beginners and more seasoned pros who are asked to take on a new preparation can also take solace in the fact that researchers have not been able to confirm the expertise–effectiveness relationship; students taught by professors with a well-developed and detailed understanding of their content area do not necessarily learn more than students taught by professors who are still developing their own understanding of their discipline. Professors who are active scholars in their fields tend to be slightly superior teachers, but the correlation between teaching skill and research stature is relatively small (rs ranging from .06 to .12; Zaman, 2004). As Hattie (2009, p. 127) suggested, it may be that effective teaching requires a certain level of proficiency but that once that baseline is reached, further advances in depth and sophistication contribute little to teaching effectiveness.

What Is the Level of the Course?

Skilled professors strive to match their instructional and assessment strategies to the level of the course. Course level is often confounded with other influential variables, such as course size; general goals; and student maturity, interest, and skill. A 100-level course is often a large-enrollment one, in contrast to a senior capstone course or a graduate seminar in some highly refined topic. Lower level courses are also more content focused than process focused because in many cases they are prerequisites for advanced classes that assume students are familiar with basic concepts. Course level also determines, in large part, the types of students who will enroll in the course. At many universities, introductory courses include a relatively high proportion of students who may not yet have developed the learning skills they need for academic success. Care must therefore be exercised when setting the course's level of difficulty.

What Is the Size of the Course?

If one applies to class size Simmel's (1902) taxonomy of groups, a small class ranges from four to 20 members, a moderate class from 20 to 40 members, and a large class contains more than 40 members. Two other categories should be considered as well: (a) huge classes, with 100 or more students taught in lecture halls, and (b) dispersed classes that are taught online rather than face to face (offline).

Size changes many of the structural, pedagogical, and practical features of a class, including the following:

- *Style*. As groups increase in size, the need for a task-organizing leader increases. As a consequence, an informal style that works so well in a small class may fail when applied to a large class, just as a highly structured approach may be overly constraining in small classes.
- *Interdependence*. In smaller classes, all the members can develop individualized relationships with one another, and each student has more of an impact on each class session.
- *Instructional choices*. As classes get larger, the reliance on student-centered teaching methods becomes smaller. Smaller classes can be taught through discussion, student presentations, and small-group activities, but as classes grow larger, lecturing becomes more likely in offline classes, and the level of student–professor interaction drops in online classes. Even professors who consider helping students improve their writing to be their No. 1 priority will not be able to pursue that goal if they are teaching hundreds of students.
- *Engagement*. The intimacy of smaller classes and the anonymity of larger classes create unique demands for students. Because smaller classes involve more personal social experiences, confident students often enjoy the opportunity to work closely with others. Less confident students may find the evaluative pressures of the small group to be too great. Students in larger classes often describe these classes as impersonal and uninvolving, yet some find the anonymity comforting: If they read the text material casually and cursorily, their lack of engagement goes undetected.
- *Management*. Some of the most time-consuming aspects of teaching—office hours, record keeping, make-up examinations, help sessions, advising, answering e-mails, responding to specific students' questions—multiply in direct proportion to the number of students in a class. Technical problems, too, arise as classes swell

in size and professors become media specialists, photocopy wizards, and crowd control experts. Students must take more responsibility for their own learning in larger classes, and fewer exceptions can be made for them in terms of testing procedures, missed classes, and so on.

In general, larger classes require more time to plan and organize. Basic tasks, such as taking attendance or returning printed assignments, require complex logistics in large classes. One can give a few students a make-up test when they are sick on test day, but what about 20 sick students? Small classes can also create unique challenges. The small class size partially reduces the psychological distance between professor and student, and so students in small classes are more likely to visit during office hours. They are also often more interpersonally dynamic, resulting in positive effects if the group unites in its support of the professor and the class goals but negative effects if the group members are united in their disgruntlement (Forsyth, 2012). A professor who is not comfortable interacting with students informally may find that resolving logistics is less challenging than exchanging pleasantries with them.

CONSIDER THE SPACE

It never hurts to take a peek at your assigned classrooms before the term begins, because all classrooms are not created equal. If you assume a fast wireless Internet connection, a 3,200-Lumen projector, and video-conferencing capability but on Day 1 discover the room has only a chalkboard and an overhead projector with a burned-out bulb, you will need to reconsider your options. If your course plan includes a series of breakout group discussion activities but your room's chairs are bolted to a floor that has a steeper pitch than seating in a basketball arena, those plans must change. The same advice holds for online classes: If you teach an online or hybrid course you need not check the chairs and chalk, but you do need to test the capability of the technology you will be using to deliver your instruction.

CONSIDER THE STUDENTS

Each year, Beloit College releases a list of facts about the incoming first-year class. The list recognizes that these students, if they are entering college immediately after they complete high school, were born only 18 years before. The Beloit College (2014) Mindset List notes the following characteristics of these students:

- If they miss *The Daily Show*, they can always get their news on YouTube.
- Their lives have been measured in the fundamental particles of life: bits, bytes, and bauds.

- Bill Clinton is a senior statesman of whose presidency they have little knowledge.
- They have never seen a paper airplane ticket.
- Exposed bra straps have always been a fashion statement, not a wardrobe malfunction to be corrected quietly by well-meaning friends.
- History has always had its own channel.
- They have known only two presidents.
- With GPS, they have never needed directions to get someplace, just an address.
- They have always been able to plug into USB ports.

The Beloit list reminds professors to consider their students' background—their life experiences, their attitudes and interests, their level of preparation, their ethnicities, their cultural backgrounds, and their goals—when ruminating about the best ways to teach them. Students will not know what you are talking about when you mention "old" rock groups (they are not even called *rock groups* anymore), ancient history (e.g., the Bill Clinton–Monica Lewinsky scandal), or long-gone television programs (e.g., *The Wire*) in your examples. Nor can you cite interesting local incidents or community events, because in many cases students know nothing of the local lore of the town or city where their school is located.

Who Are the Millennials?

Any given college class may comprise students ranging in age from teen-agers to older adults, but each year more than 13 million high school graduates will continue their education by attending a college (see https://nces.ed.gov/programs/digest/d12/tables/dt12_003.asp?referrer=report). These students differ from one another in many significant ways—personality, outlook, life experiences, attitudes, and so on—but they share one common quality: They are all Millennials. A generational approach to individual differences assumes that people who are born and raised in a particular culture, during a particular era, will be similar to one another in certain ways and that these qualities may make them quite different from those born before or after them. Such analyses are best approached with skepticism: How exceptionless are the general-izations made about people based only on the year in which they were born? Many educators, however, believe that much can be gained by considering differences between learners from different generations (e.g., K. Stewart, 2009).

The Millennials began entering college in 1998 (±2 years). Researchers do not agree about this generation's attitudes, values, and orienta-tions, but many consider them a mix of admirable and not-so-admirable qualities. These students are comfortable with certain types of technology but usually not the kinds that are useful for learning. They can control their privacy settings on Facebook and navigate smoothly across shopping sites, but they are less adept at manipulating a spreadsheet, formatting a document, creating webpages, and so on. They are group oriented, but in most cases their groups are social ones rather than task-focused ones; they are not uniquely skilled in collaborating with others in the pursuit of shared goals. They can process information quickly. They are prone to multitask, but researchers have not confirmed their claim that they are good at it (Wei, Wang, & Klausner, 2012). Many Millennials have served their communities, but their motives were not always humanitarian ones; their schools either required them to do volunteer work or they got involved to pad their profiles for their college applications (Twenge, 2006).

Twenge and her colleagues, in their generational research, searched through data archives to find records that would precisely document changes over the past 30 years. Their work suggests that Millennials are, as some professors might have suspected, uniquely insecure and anxious but also self-confident, entitled, and narcissistic. They are so self-focused that she dubbed them "Generation Me" (Twenge, 2006; Twenge & Campbell, 2010).

Teaching a roomful of narcissists requires redefined expectations, a change in instructional tactics, and renewed resilience. K. Stewart and Kilmartin (2014), after comparing the Millennials' self-reported personality traits with those same traits reported by students prior to 1979, concluded that Millennials were significantly lower in their willingness to expend effort in the pursuit of academic goals, in both highly structured situations and in self-regulated settings. As a consequence, direct instructional interventions that increase their level of preparedness, such as required worksheets and frequent quizzing, help keep them on track. Millennials also respond positively to more active and more student-centered educational practices, such as discussion, group activities, and self-discovery teaching methods.

Traditional or Nontraditional?

Not all students are fresh out of high school; many college classes include a mix of traditional and older, "nontraditional" students who are returning to school after a hiatus. The National Center for Educational Statistics projects a rise of 13% in enrollments of students under age 25, but a slightly larger increase in enrollments of students age 25 and over, by the year 2020 (see http://nces.ed.gov/fastfacts/display.asp?id=372). Such students may need more review of concepts covered in earlier courses, particularly if significant shifts in emphasis or analysis have taken place recently in the field in which you are teaching. Because nontraditional students tend to be taking classes on a part-time basis, they sometimes have difficulty taking advantage of on-campus resources: If you give credit for attending lectures or events on campus, you may be unintentionally favoring traditional students, who usually live on or near campus, over those who have to commute, who most often are the older, nontraditional students (M. J. Allen, 2000).

Socially Diverse or Homogeneous?

In the 1950s, most college students were men in their early 20s; they lived on campus, attended classes full time, and their parents were college graduates. Over the past three decades, however, women, African Americans, Hispanics/Latinos, Asians, Pacific Islanders, people with disabilities, international students, openly gay and lesbian students, and students from families whose members never went beyond high school have entered college in record numbers (see http://nces.ed.gov/programs/digest/d13/tables/dt13_306.50.asp). As college classrooms become more diverse, professors must sometimes revisit their methods, policies, and course contents to be certain they are appropriate for, and fair to, the students in their classes (Stulberg & Weinberg, 2011). When classes are filled with students who hail from a variety of ethnic, cultural, personal, and social backgrounds, the professor must be ready to respond positively to variations in communication styles and skills, interactional and learning styles, achievement orientation, and experience with Western culture's norms and expectations. As I discuss in Chapter 6, classes with a diverse array of students provide both professors and the students with an opportunity to meet one of the key goals of higher education: experience working in diverse groups and communities.

Novice Learners or Savvy Seniors?

The matching of students with their classes is an assortative social process that reflects students' stages of their academic careers; their personal interests; and, in many cases, the requirements of their chosen program of study. If you are teaching introductory courses in English, biology, history, or other general education classes, know that the majority of the students in the class will be first-years (freshmen) whose readiness for college may be uncertain. They may also be coping with a number of personal issues related to such things as dormitory living, establishing friendships, and even homesickness, so their performance can be surprisingly variable as their concentration on the course material ebbs and flows.

Students new to college may also be grappling with the differences between high school and college classes. First-year students have been students for most of their lives, and some have even completed courses that shadow college-level courses (e.g., Advanced Placement courses). College professors, however, are not high school teachers, and this difference is rarely covered in orientation sessions. Professors expect their students to take responsibility for their own learning, which means acquiring the textbooks, supplies, and other resources they need for the course; studying diligently; tracking when assignments are due and tests are scheduled; monitoring their performance; and seeking help if help is needed. It takes time for first-year students to learn these self-regulatory learning skills.

College professors also tend to adopt different instructional strategies than do high school teachers. High school teachers spend more time with their students, they are cautious in their movement through the material, and they provide more details and opportunities for questions and practice. They test more frequently, but with lower stakes, gently guiding students from ignorance to understanding. Professors move at a more brisk pace and expect students to do more of learning through independent, self-guided study. They examine with care both key concepts and ones that are known to cause difficulties for novice learners, but they expect students to handle the basic content on their own.

Then, too, the grading of performance differs between high school and college. In high school, students often have numerous graded assessments: attendance, projects, quizzes, book reports, papers, worksheets, homework, participation, service learning contributions, conduct, and, of course, test grades. Professors may include some of these activities in their grade calculations, but the majority of points will be generated by grades on major papers and examinations. Because high school teachers reward seat time and effort as well as competence, students are puzzled when in college they are not given credit for just "working hard" (Zinn et al., 2011). Good grades on small quizzes, completed homework, and active engagement rarely counterbalance an inability to demonstrate mastery of course material on the midterm and final examinations.

Professors who wish to break first-years' fall into college learning may want to test more frequently, prepare and post a more elaborate calendar of course milestones (e.g., readings, papers, tests), and shift topics that require heavier mental lifting to later in the semester, when students are further along in their transition to this new form of teaching and learning. But not too much later in the semester: Students tend to reach their satiation point in terms of studying and learning by early November of the first semester and spring break of the second (Duffy & Jones, 1995).

Majors or Nonmajors?

The introductory course and advanced courses that are particularly relevant to other disciplines often are required "service courses" in which a substantial proportion of the students who enroll are majoring in another degree program. In service courses one is not teaching the devoted majors in the discipline but students whose interests lie elsewhere: earnest sociology and psychology majors, serious premeds, pragmatic business students, creative art students, expressive theater majors, and so on. But many advanced courses are populated primarily with majors, and so some basic goals—capturing students' interest, helping students understand the discipline's perspective, eradicating misperceptions about the field—are more easily achieved.

Instructional Design

Where do plans come from? G. A. Miller, Galanter, and Pribram (1960), in their classic *Plans and the Structure of Behavior*, pondered this question before coming to the following conclusion:

> The major source of new Plans is old Plans. We change them around a little bit each time we use them, but they are basically the same old Plans with minor variations. Sometimes we may borrow a new Plan from someone else. But we do not often create a completely new plan. (p. 177)

So, if you are like most professors, this year's syllabus looks very similar to last year's. New professors base their teaching on the way they themselves were taught. Professors use familiar assessment methods; give lectures from ancient, yellowed notes; and forget to try anything new. The old plan becomes the template for all future plans. G. A. Miller et al.'s (1960) warning about the power of old plans to shape new plans suggests that professors, before they rush to write the syllabus, sequence the topics, and craft compelling lectures, should take a little time to consider the general strategies that will guide their teaching (for a review, see Lattuca & Stark, 2009).

CONSIDER THE TEACHING

Professors, like most people, differ in their approach to making their plans. Some sketch out their plans in extraordinary detail, laying out each step along the way to the final goal. Others prefer the flexibility of a sketchy plan or just a set of heuristic orienting principles. Some, too, prefer to craft their own plans and refuse to listen to the advice of others. Others seek out information about others' plans and adopt them as their own if they deem them to be effective. But the complexity of the task facing a college professor increases the need for an explicit plan of action for each course taught. This plan need not be extensive, but it must at least consider the topics to cover, the teaching methods to use, the various projects and activities students will undertake, the readings to be assigned, and the learning assessments to be implemented.

How Will I Teach?

One hundred years ago, professors lectured, led discussions, graded papers, and grilled their students in recitation sessions. Nowadays these tried-and-true methods can be supplemented with, or altogether replaced by, a variety of more targeted teaching techniques. In Table 2.1, I offer a suggestive sampling of these alternative methods, but the list is by no means comprehensive.

Researchers have examined the effectiveness of most of the methods given in Table 2.1, but they have not identified any one method as the best one for all learning settings. Hattie (2009), for example, in his meta-analysis of meta-analyses, compared such methods as direct instruction, cooperative learning, problem-based learning, web-based instruction, audiovisual presentation, and computer-aided instruction. He concluded that all of these promoted student achievement.

However, any method of teaching will be more effective if it is aligned with the educational outcomes sought. If your goal is to help students improve their writing, lecturing on the key features of good writing or testing their knowledge of Strunk and White's (2014) *The Elements of Style* will be less effective than a well-planned and -executed series of developmental writing assignments combined with detailed feedback. To encourage critical thinking, do not assign a 20-page term paper; instead, construct a series of problem-based learning exercises. If you believe that students who are only beginning their studies of your field will maximally benefit if they learn several general principles they can use to organize their understanding of a number of interrelated facts, concepts, and perspectives, then the best approach to teaching is direct instruction, which includes methods such as lectures, screencasts, and readings. Effective teaching requires the interleaving of learning objectives and teaching methods.

How Many Topics, Projects, Activities, Events . . . ?

Even a masterful instructional program, with powerful learning strategies and activities linked to well-specified learning goals and assessments, will falter if these learning experiences are ill timed. But professors, like

TABLE 2.1

A Sampling of Teaching Methods and Practices

Method	Examples/descriptions
Assessments	Tests, quizzes, critiques, reviews, class participation grades
Audiovisual materials	Sound recordings, images, video, film
Case studies	Analysis of specific examples, critical incident review
Data analysis	Statistical analysis, diagrams, graphs, GPS mapping
Debates	Pro–con argument lists, moot courts
Demonstrations	Illustrations of physical, biological, chemical, psychological, social, or interpersonal processes
Developing displays	Exhibits, posters, art, maps
Developing learning resources	Web pages, wikis, dictionaries of terms, selecting readings and cases
Developing study materials	Flash cards, study sheets, simulations
Discussions	Whole-class, student-led discussion; small-group, online discussion
Dramatizations	Skits, plays, role plays
Group activities and projects	In class, online, experiential, problem focused, community based, living-learning centered, service learning
Internships, field placements	Practica, residencies, volunteer work, tutoring
Laboratory work	Science laboratory exercises in biology, chemistry, physics, and so on
Learning games	Drills, bees, tournaments, contests
Lectures	Short, extended, podcasts, guest instructors, public speakers, online (MOOCs, TED talks, etc.)
Oral performances	Speeches, reports, exams
Panel presentations	Presentations by students, experts, professors
Presentations by students	Reports, summaries, reactions, video recordings, podcasts, exhibits, skits
Problem-solving activities	Problem-based learning, inquiry-based learning
Projects	Class level, team level, individual
Questioning	Recitation, Socratic, brainstorming, call outs
Readings	Assigning and reviewing texts, fiction and nonfiction books, chapters, articles
Research	Library, online
Reviewing	In class, supervised, online
Science projects	Field, experimentation, interviews, surveys, simulations, replications
Self-assessments	Personality measures, self-descriptions
Service projects	Community placements, volunteer work, civic projects
Tutorials	Student–teacher, peer, Oxford-style, computer-based programs
Worksheets	Puzzles, workbooks, problem sets
Writing	Reaction papers, prompt responses, formal research papers, book reports, term papers, diaries, journals, magazine article, blog post, editorials

Note. *MOOC = massive open online course.*

most people, tend to overestimate how much they can accomplish in a single semester. As Kahneman and Tversky's (1973) studies of the planning fallacy suggest, most of us inaccurately estimate how much time we will need to complete future tasks.

Given the limited amount of time available during the term and students' commitments of time and energy to any one class, one must take care when calculating the number of topics, learning activities, and readings to cover or assign. Like work environments in which workers have too little to do and too much time in which to do it, classes with too few assignments and activities are often boring, unchallenging, and inefficient. Too many assignments, though, will leave the students, and the professor who must grade the activities, feeling harried and unhappy (Walsh, 2003).

Classes also go more smoothly—and students learn more easily—when academic demands are consonant with what Duffy and Jones (1995) called the "rhythms of the semester." Every term has unique events—religious holidays, big football games, and so on—and the ideal schedule works around these events. Few students will, for example, use their spring break to study for an exam that is scheduled for the day they return to campus, so scores will be better if the assessment is administered before, rather than after, the break. And do not save your favorite topic for the week just before the Thanksgiving holiday, for you will be disappointed when your pearls of wisdom are scattered to so few students.

What Technology and Media Will Be Used?

Years ago, high-tech professors prepped by ordering films from distribution centers, sorting their slides, and changing the bulb in the overhead projector. Today's professors source their materials from films, videos, DVDs, TED talks, Vimeo, and YouTube; update their PowerPoint and Prezi presentations; and check to see whether their smart classrooms have gotten any smarter. Many, too, will use a learning management system (LMS; one of many software applications that help you administer, document, and track a course's educational information) as either an adjunct to their in-class teaching methods or as total replacement for face-to-face classroom instruction. Some still hand out hard copies of the syllabus and administer quizzes in class, but others now rely on Blackboard, Moodle, or some other LMS to quiz, post readings, hold discussions and office hours, and organize group projects.

What Will You Do to Support Students' Learning?

Depending on the course's degree of difficulty, the adeptness of the learners, and the goals of the class itself, you may need to find some time in the course schedule to deal with a too-often taken-for-granted learning outcome: the skills of learning. It may seem presumptuous to offer advice about the proper means of studying to college students who have spent years honing their personal approach to knowledge acquisition, but even the most proficient student may have picked up some bad habits in a lifetime spent in less-than-pristine learning environments. As I note in Chapter 6, many of the most common methods students use—such as cramming, rereading, highlighting textbooks and written notes, and studying in groups—are relatively ineffective (Dunlosky, Rawson, Marsh, Nathan, & Willingham, 2013).

CONSIDER THE READINGS

Humans' capacity to read others' words gives literate people access to the knowledge of past generations while reducing their dependence on oral forms of communication and information exchange. McKeachie (1999) went so far as to suggest that students learn more from their textbooks than they do from their teachers, making the choice of texts and readings one of the most important components of adequate preparation.

Should You Use a Textbook?

Textbooks, despite their controversial cost, remain a mainstay of many college courses. If well researched, written, edited, and designed, they provide comprehensive coverage of key concepts and topics in any given field of study. Good ones also provide an extensive scaffolding for learning, such as headings, summaries, sidebars, learning checks, and glossaries. If the textbook is a teaching one, then professors focus more on application, analysis, and evaluation. Some textbooks also come with test banks, teaching suggestions, video banks, and so on, that offer the professor additional time savings.

These strengths are also weaknesses, however. As the constructivist approach to learning warns, too much structure can result in superficial rather than deep learning (Banyard & Grayson, 1999).When students read the textbook only, they study only the book author's description of the field, or what Rheingold (1994) called "restless thought distilled into static outlines" (p. 36). In consequence, some professors assign readings of original sources. Such readings require students to organize the material themselves and make decisions about the importance, meaning, and implications of the various topics covered; however, they are often the only way to teach students to read and process material in ways that are unique to your discipline. Journal articles and other shorter readings, however, have one primary limitation: They can be narrow in focus, so the yield for the student who labors through the work may be rather meager.

Which Textbook Should You Select?

When identifying a textbook for your class, you can turn to colleagues for input, both informally and more formally by reading reviews of textbooks published online and in professional journals. You can also ask students to evaluate which textbooks they prefer. In one study, when researchers asked students to read textbook passages that had been previously tested for clarity and "learnability," they found that students accurately discriminated between books that they could learn from and books that likely would baffle them (R. G. Benjamin, 2012).

McKeachie (1999) was correct, however, when he stated, "There is no substitute for detailed review of the competing texts for the course you are teaching" (p. 13). That review requires that you obtain copies of all the textbooks that you are considering, so the selection of a book usually occurs well before all other preparatory activities. Some characteristics to consider include the following:

- *Scope, accuracy, and currency.* Does the text present a unified but comprehensive review of all major topics and concepts in the field you are teaching? The material itself should be clearly presented, painstakingly accurate, and representative of current thinking in the field.
- *Level of difficulty.* Is this book a hard or easy read? Some textbook are more challenging than others. Students who know very little about the material they are studying learn the most from a basic text (R. G. Benjamin, 2012).
- *Conceptual orientation.* Will you be comfortable using this textbook? Even the textbooks for such redoubtable courses as introductory biology or psychology differ in theoretical emphasis, perspectives, key terms, currency, and theoretical orientation. Disagreements with the text are inevitable, but the fewer there are, the better, both in terms of learning and classroom relations. Adopting a textbook and then not using it or frequently criticizing it makes the Top 10 list of students' pet peeves (Ludewig, 1994).
- *Writing quality.* Is the book well written? A good textbook should not just present information but also teach it through a clear, engaging presentation. Students will learn more when the author replaces wordiness with crisp sentences that use the active voice; peppers the text with vivid examples that touch on familiar topics; helps the reader grasp the overall organization of the chapter by signaling its structure with headings, summaries, and transitions from section to section; varies sentence and paragraph structures appropriately; and creates coherent paragraphs that make one or two points clearly.

- *Organization*. Is the book well organized? If the book's materials are not ordered in the way you want them to be, you can always ask students to read them in the order you prefer. But assigning entire chapters at a time, and following the order of the chapters, is less confusing for students. Telling students to "read the next chapter" is far simpler than having them check the syllabus, e-mail, or the LMS to find out where to go next.
- *Pedagogy*. Does the textbook include elements that will help the reader understand and remember the material? Most modern textbooks use boldface type for key terms, a glossary, learning objectives, chapter preview, chapter summaries, review questions, embedded self-assessments, boxed material, graphs and charts, summary tables, annotated readings list, and suggested activities to help readers understand the content.
- *Format*. Is the book available in various formats, including electronic formats (eBooks)? Most students prefer hard copy books over eBooks, but as hand-held devices for reading text continue to improve and textbook prices climb, many will appreciate the option of downloading the text. Publishers of enhanced eBooks, by building useful tools into the reader software, may make it easier for students to remember the information contained in the text. Many programs already include notepads, bookmarks, search options, and pop-up dictionaries, and these tools are sometimes supplemented with embedded simulations, animations, charts, and other informative graphic material. If, too, you are teaching a course online, the textbook publisher's materials may be available directly through your LMS.

Which Original Sources Should You Select?

Some of the same principles that guide the selection of a textbook should also guide professors' selections of required or recommended articles, chapters, monographs, and books (nontextbook books), but the consequences of a poor choice are less severe. Students will tolerate a dull or opaque reading or two, but a dull textbook's prolonged damage will be harder to undo.

Problems can arise, however, in simply getting the outside readings to students. Copyright laws have made it more difficult for faculty to create packets of readings, and in some cases university libraries will not even place photocopies of articles on reserve for fear of running afoul of U.S. copyright laws. Some academic publishers will create a customized package of readings, provided your classes are sufficiently large to justify the cost of production. Some journals permit the use of their contents in educational settings, provided your university's library subscribes to the journal. Alternatively, if you are willing to use someone else's collection of readings, then you can adopt an edited volume. Nilson (2010, pp. 63–70) provided a clear analysis of issues related to fair use in teaching.

How Will You Prompt Students to Do the Readings?

Few instructors would be shocked to learn that students sometimes come to class unprepared. It would be nice if students' intrinsic motivation and love of learning motivated them to spend the necessary hours reviewing the text material prior to each class, but the data suggest otherwise. The students in one survey explained that they "know it is important to read, know the professor expects them to read, and know it will impact their grade, yet most students still do not read" (Berry, Cook, Hill, & Stevens, 2010, p. 31).

Hatteberg and Steffy (2013) took this question directly to the students by asking them to rate various "Oh, won't you please do your readings?" interventions and their effectiveness. They sampled students from a range of sciences, social sciences and business majors, concentrating on first- and second-year students. Student also were asked to rate only reading stimulants that they had themselves experienced in a college class. Their recommendations, ranked from most to least effective, were as follows (p. 350):

1. graded quizzes on the reading administered when the reading was due;
2. graded responses to a structured guide or question set on the reading turned in when the reading was due;
3. short writing assignments, such as reaction papers, reading memos, or response cards;
4. required journaling;
5. call outs (called on in class to answer questions);
6. pop quizzes on the readings; and
7. optional reading guides or questions.

Students reported quizzing as the most frequently used method, but they also considered quizzes to be coercive. As Ewell and Rodgers (2014) explained, "Quizzes come across as a heavy-handed, high-schoolish attempt to get recalcitrant students to do the work. Although effective for grade-conscious students, quizzes do nothing to foster the mores of higher education" (p. 207). They therefore recommended *course preparation assignments* (CPAs): structured writing assignments that help students process the content of the readings in depth. They discovered that students in an introductory political science were more likely to prepare diligently on class days when a CPA was assigned and in classes that used CPAs consistently.

CONSIDER THE ASSESSMENTS

Well-prepared professors usually know what kinds of tests and scored assignments students will complete during the 12 to 16 weeks of the term, although the possibilities are nearly limitless; *tests* may include examinations, quizzes, take-home tests, and pop quizzes, and *scored assignments* may include reaction papers, book reviews, article summaries, term papers, research reports, journals, and group projects. Assessment planning requires a series of difficult choices about the number, timing, and type of tests and assignments that generate opportunities but exact costs as well.

Are Your Tests Aligned With Your Goals?

The semester's procession of educational events—its lectures, discussions, activities, and assignments—is punctuated by tests. As I note in Chapter 5, tests serve as explicit milestones that break up the months of continuous study and so provide a clear deadline that forces students who would otherwise procrastinate to review what they have learned. Tests also yield feedback for students about their progress toward their learning goals, with grades functioning as powerful motivators for all kinds of useful behaviors, such as studying, attending class, taking notes, and reading the textbook. Tests' contribution to student learning is far greater, however, when two conditions are met: (a) the tests assess students' attainment of the course's learning goals and (b) the process provides students (and the professor) with feedback they can use to improve their performance (Roediger, Agarwal, McDaniel, & McDermott, 2011). The professor who ranks creativity in thought, skill in designing scientific studies, confidence in judging the meaning of an author's textbook, or ability to solve practical problems should not give students multiple-choice tests that focus on memory for discrete facts and information. Furthermore, the positive impact of testing on learning is far greater when the graded assessment includes feedback rather than just a score (Hattie & Yates, 2014). Providing a large group of students with feedback about each one's strengths and weakness, as indicated by a test, can be a difficult undertaking, but such a review is sometimes needed to help certain students learn from their mistakes.

How Many Tests Should You Administer?

Researchers have repeatedly confirmed the *testing effect*: "Even a single test in a class can produce a large improvement in final exam scores, and gains in learning continue to increase as the number of tests increases" (P. C. Brown, Roediger, & McDaniel, 2014, p. 41). Both self-administered and teacher-initiated quizzing yields improved recall relative to simply reading material, but frequent tests on smaller amounts of material are more desirable than infrequent tests on massive amounts of material—especially for learners who are less advanced. Frequent tests not only improve students' ability to retrieve information from memory, but they also give them feedback about their studying, desensitize them to the testing process, provide them with samples of the types of questions on the major course exams, and increase their level of preparation for class. Some systems of instruction, such as Keller's (1968) programmed learning with integrated feedback, even require constant testing.

The general warning against "too much of a good thing" also applies to tests, however. Frequent testing keeps students on task, but too frequent testing distracts them from the ultimate goal of learning. Instructors who stress tests, evaluations, and grades over all else produce students who are striving to earn a particular grade rather than to learn the course material (cf. Harackiewicz, Barron, & Elliot, 1998). Professors should also describe carefully the nature and purposes of assessments. Tests described as "achievement tests" become extrinsic motivators, whereas tests described as "feedback mechanisms" function as intrinsic motivators (Forsyth & McMillan, 1991). Frequent tests may also create high levels of competition among students. Although introducing competition among students is a popular way to prompt them to expend greater effort, competition may focus students' attention on outperforming others and thus reinforces the tendency to assume the goal is a high grade rather than mastery of the material. Tests administered offline also take up class time, with the result that the more one administers tests, the less one lectures, leads discussions, presents demonstrations, and so on.

Cumulative Tests

Learning is more durable when cumulative testing methods are used. Students who were tested weekly outscored students who were tested biweekly, but students achieved the very best scores when all the tests were cumulative: when each test contained not only items dealing with the current material but also items that evaluated students' understanding of material from previous units (e.g., Lawrence, 2013). Because students must revisit previously learned material as they prepare for a cumulative test, these assessments take advantage of the *spacing effect*: Learning is more durable when material is learned in multiple sessions, separated by days or even weeks, rather than when learned in a single session (*massed practice*). The delay between the initial learning and subsequent review facilitates the consolidation of long-term memories and so creates stronger connections between the learners' existing knowledge structures and the new information (Carpenter, Cepeda, Rohrer, Kang,

& Pashler, 2012). Studies of spacing effects suggest that, for optimal learning, instructors should not cover a course topic, test students, and then move to the next topic; instead, they should return repeatedly to core concepts during the semester, reintroduce additional information pertaining to them, and, by using cumulative exams, prompt students to space their studying.

Cumulative testing methods require, however, that more time be spent reviewing the results of tests with students. When students will be confronting the material again in the near future, they expect and deserve clear feedback about the items they answered incorrectly. Because this review can be both time consuming and contentious when conducted in an open-class discussion, many instructors prepare standardized feedback information that can be distributed to all students. This feedback identifies common problems and alerts students to which learning objectives will likely be tested on future examinations. Such feedback procedures also reduce the need to return the actual examination items to students. Control of items is less of an issue for professors who use short-answer and essay tests, but instructors who reuse selection-type items each year may find that their items begin to lose validity if they return the tests to students to use in preparation for cumulative finals. If old tests become part of the test files maintained by campus groups (e.g., fraternities), or they are posted on online document-sharing sites (e.g., CourseHero, studyblue.com, koofers.com), their value as indicators of student learning declines.

Sharing the Plan

Professors' plans for their classes are what G. A. Miller et al. (1960) called *shared public plans*. Unlike private plans, which can remain vague and protean, public plans must be "prescribed in great detail because an attempt has been made to obtain optimal, not just satisfactory, performance" from each person who is part of the plan (G. A. Miller et al., 1960, p. 100). Professors can achieve this communication and specification of their shared plan in two ways: (a) writing a syllabus; and (b) carefully presenting that syllabus, and the overall plan, to the class at its first online or offline meeting.

CONSIDER THE SYLLABUS

A syllabus was originally a very concise list of the topics that would be covered by a lecturer during a protracted course of study. In time, though, the syllabus has evolved to include all sorts of basic information about the course. Different schools and departments have varying standards about a course syllabus and its contents, but a syllabus is usually considered a contract that defines professors' and students' responsibilities. A syllabus forces professors to share their private plan: It "compels you to publicly reveal your previously well-concealed assumptions. In other words, it makes explicit that which was implicit" (Appleby, 1999, p. 20). Table 2.2 describes some of the categories of information included on a syllabus and summarizes the preceding analysis of course planning.

Professors may not include all of the categories listed in Table 2.2 on their syllabus, and students may not pay much attention to all of them, either. As Becker and Calhoon (1999) discovered when they surveyed students about syllabi, students pay the most attention to the dates of the exams and when assignments are due. They take less notice of general course information, dates regarding when they can withdraw from the class without penalty, and the titles and authors of the readings. Becker and Calhoon also noted that first-year students were more interested in prerequisites than were continuing students, and they were more concerned about sources of academic support and the location of course materials. Nontraditional students attended to the syllabus's description of course goals and the readings, but they were not as concerned about holidays and penalties for late work and honors infractions. All students do expect, however, that professors will honor the syllabus as they would a contract. Hence it is important to include, somewhere on the syllabus, a statement that explains that aspects of the course may be changed if unforeseen circumstances arise and that these changes will be announced before they are initiated.

CONSIDER THE POLICIES

A classroom, like any group, develops its own set of *norms*: consensual standards that describe what behaviors members should and should not perform. A classroom's norms, however, are often deliberately manipulated by professors who hope that they can create normative structures that are consistent with, or even supportive of, scholarship and learning. They do so by developing policies and letting students know the consequences of violating their policies on the syllabus. As a professor, use the syllabus to reduce uncertainty (Tomlinson, 2002).

Is Attendance Required?

College students are adult learners, so many instructors feel that students should be given the right to miss classes without being penalized. Students who attend class regularly get better grades, but attendance

TABLE 2.2

Types of Information Supplied to Students in a Typical Course Syllabus

Subject	Questions answered
Instructor	What is your name, and what should students call you? Where is your office, and do you hold office hours? What is your educational, research, and teaching background?
Course description and goals	What are the overall goals of this course? How does this course contribute to general educational goals? What are the specific goals? What should students know when the course is over? How will this course change them?
Course topics	What topics will be covered in this course? Why these topics? Why this order? What are the prerequisites?
Teaching and learning methods	What methods (online learning, lecture, discussion, seminar, tutorial) will be used to teach this material? Will the course make any unusual demands on students (e.g., heavy writing requirements, use of technology, special projects)? Does the course make use of a learning management system and, if so, how can it be accessed? Why are these methods being used?
Textbook and readings	What textbook will be used? Will other reading assignments be made? Why were these textbooks chosen? Are these primary or secondary sources?
Activities and assignments	What types of learning activities and assignments will be made? Will papers will be required? What is their purpose, and how will they influence grades?
Grades	How will student progress be measured? Is the grading criterion-reference based or norm based? How much is each activity and test worth? Can tests be dropped? Is the final examination cumulative?
Policies	What is the attendance and test make-up policy? Do you have any other special policies or expectations about the class? Will any extra credit opportunities be offered?
Sources of support	Will you hold review sessions prior to examinations? Are the lecture notes or the outline available? Will students be given the opportunity to form study groups? Does this institution have academic support programs students can use if they encounter academic problems?
Calendar	What is the timeline for covering the various topics? When are the assignments due, and when should readings be completed? When are the tests? When will vacations occur?
Academic integrity policy	What type of academic integrity policy is in force at the university? How is this policy applied in this class?
Special issues	What special considerations apply to this class? Should students be warned about material and activities they might find objectionable? Should students with special needs contact the professor? What are the rights of students who need academic accommodations? Can students use computers and other devices in class?

may not be a causal factor in this relationship. As Golding (2011) noted, highly motivated students attend class and are likely to excel academically anyway, and so attendance's impact on achievement itself is difficult to discern. Regular attendance, however, is crucial for student success in certain kinds of classes: discussion-based classes, online classes, classes in which each unit builds on an understanding of the material presented in the previous unit, and so on.

A strict no-skip policy can create both organizational (roll must be taken, excuses for missed classes processed) and instructional (classes filled with unprepared, uninterested students) complexities. Carbone (1998, pp. 80–82) and other veterans of large classes have offered a number of suggestions for regulating attendance:

- collect homework as students enter the classroom and accept no papers once class begins,
- give low-stakes tests during class to create a record of attendance,
- monitor students' online activities in the LMS and intervene quickly if they are not keeping up with course requirements,
- reward students who leave class early after getting permission by acknowledging their use of appropriate procedures, and
- make the class so engaging that students will be intrinsically motivated to attend.

Can Students Take Make-Up Tests?

Because of circumstances both within and beyond their control, students sometimes miss tests. Although some professors tell students that no make-up tests will be given, these same professors must then bend their policies for students who have excuses from their physicians, who are required to take part in institution-sponsored activities (i.e., sports), or who are experiencing life events that psychologists recognize as extremely distressing (e.g., death of a loved one). Rather than simply installing a rigid policy that punishes students who miss examinations, many professors establish student-centered make-up test policies that include (a) advance notification of the absence or delay, (b) a time limit for taking a make-up test, (c) procedures for taking the make-up test, and (d) the type of test to be given (e.g., multiple choice, essay, true–false). They also share their rationale for their policy with their students so that the system is viewed as a fair, nonarbitrary one (Whitley, Perkins, Balogh, Keith-Spiegel, & Wittig, 2000).

Some professors avoid the problems associated with make-up tests by letting students drop their lowest test grade when computing their final score in the class or by counting another test (or the final) twice. Such procedures, however, likely reduce the overall level of student learning. Grabe (1994), for example, compared the performance of students who could drop tests with that of students who could not. He found that scores on individual tests were lower, overall, when students' grades were based on a subset of their tests, although the impact on final examination scores was not significant. These findings nonetheless suggest that students may not prepare as diligently when they know that they can drop a test score. The findings also underscore the importance of having a cumulative final examination when using such methods. A "nondroppable" cumulative final prevents students who are satisfied with their grade based on the earlier tests from skipping class entirely during the final segment of the term because they will drop that test anyway.

What Will Happen if Students Violate the Honor Code?

All colleges and universities have some form of an academic integrity policy that describes the kinds of activities that are considered inappropriate, immoral, or punishable (e.g., plagiarism, cheating, destruction of materials). In preparing for class, familiarize yourself with your university's code and let students know that you will enforce it. Also, be careful to add any restrictions or specifications that are not addressed in the local honor code but that you feel are important to maintain in your class. For example, if your college's honor code is mute on such issues as posting course material to sharing sites or multiple submissions (e.g., submitting the same paper to multiple professors), define your position on these issues clearly on the syllabus.

What Technology Should Students Use?

Although most students are well versed in the types of technology often used for instruction, it may still be prudent to explain to students that they are expected to read their e-mail, check the LMS for readings, take part in required online discussions, and so on. Your students may, for example, be avid readers of text messages but not e-mailed ones, and so they may not readily respond to e-mailed content. Students may be adept at navigating the Internet but inexperienced in using the Web 2.0 tools featured in your LMS.

Providing guidance in the use of technology is particularly important for blended or fully online classes. For starters, students will need to check to be certain that their technology is sufficient to meet the demands of the course and download any apps they need to do the work you assign. They also will need to learn to find their way around the various content areas and tools that make up your course's online system. Simply saving the syllabus as a pdf document and posting it to the site may not be sufficient, especially if students are not able to locate the pdf to open it (Ko & Rossen, 2010).

What Technology Should Students not Use?

You may also need to specify what sorts of technology students should *not* be using, in particular, in offline classes. College students tend to be wired, that is, continually connected to Internet resources through various types of electronic devices. Some students use these devices in the service of learning: to display the readings under discussion, take notes, and access related online materials. Other students, however, will use their devices to multitask—check their e-mail, post a yak, monitor stock prices, and so on, in the midst of the class's discussion of challenging intellectual ideas.

Unfortunately, studies of learning and distraction do not support students' strongly held beliefs about their multitasking skills. Correlational research indicates that students who bring their laptops to class use them to perform nonrelated tasks, and the more they do so, the poorer their performance in class (Fried, 2008). Experimental research offers a similar conclusion. In one study, researchers randomly assigned students listening to a lecture to one of two groups. Some were allowed to use their laptops during the lecture, but others were told to keep their laptops closed. As expected, the students who were permitted to use their laptops multitasked (including social networking, e-mailing, and web browsing), and they exhibited "decrements on traditional measures of memory for lecture content" (Hembrooke & Gay, 2003, p. 46).

Cell phones also are problematic. Nearly all the students in one recent survey reported they used their phones during classes, and many (10%) even reported texting while they were taking a major course examination (Tindell & Bohlander 2012). However, and as with laptops, students who are weaker in their capacity to self-regulate are more likely to text in class, and their messaging interferes with their capacity to maintain attention to course material for a long period of time (Wei et al., 2012).

Many professors view the use of laptops and cell phones as the student's decision, so long as their behavior does not negatively influence other students in the class. If a student wishes to disengage from the class for a period of time via his or her cell phone, that is that student's right. Other professors, in contrast, ban laptops and phones and indicate so on their syllabus, or restrict their use to class-relevant activities.

What Special Considerations Apply to This Class?

Students should be warned about any unique, distinctive, or potentially irritating aspects of the class. If, for example, students will be completing some of their work in small groups, attending presentations on campus, taking part in research studies, or visiting off-campus locations, tell them of these requirements before the add–drop period ends. Warn them, too, if your course deals with sensitive topics that they might find personally upsetting; some examples include political issues, social injustices, religious arguments, and personal inadequacies (H. L. Miller & Flores, 2012). You may also need to connect these contentious topics to the requirement for civility in the class. Although discourteous actions may not qualify as actionable under your school's honor code, some behaviors are considered to be so rude, distracting, or disturbing to others that they create tension in the classroom, and you may wish to ban them.

When Should Students With Disabilities Contact You?

Section 504 of the Rehabilitation Act of 1973 and the Americans With Disabilities Act of 1990 require colleges and universities to provide academic adjustments or accommodations for students with documented disabilities. Disabilities are not limited to sensory and motor limitations (e.g., sight impairment, mobility restrictions) but also can include problems in psychological adjustment and information processing. Students seeking academic adjustments or accommodations should be invited to identify themselves as soon as possible so that adjustments or accommodations can be arranged, but you cannot set a deadline for notification.

Colleges and universities vary significantly in the level of support they provide to students with disabilities and to professors who are trying to create a positive learning environment for them. Most ask students with a disability to register with the campus office that confirms the student's disability and determines the types of services and accommodations the student requires. Those accommodations may include extended time for examinations, permission to record lectures, use of a laptop or a scribe for taking notes, release from group learning activities, and reduction in distractions when completing tests. Students' requests for these accommodations should be honored without hesitation.

CONSIDER THE FIRST SESSION

Asch's (1946) classic studies revealed a *primacy effect* when perceivers form impressions of others: Initial judgments influence subsequent judgments even when subsequent information contradicts these initial inferences. Asch's findings remind professors to take full advantage of the ambiguity, excitement, and potential of the first meeting with a class. That day comes but once, and it is an opportunity to be seized, a chance to do far more than simply take roll and disseminate information about the textbook and forthcoming tests. Hilton (1999), who has taught classes with as many as 1,200 students, wrote: "I firmly believe that I win my class or lose them in the first 15 minutes, and 50 years of person perception research supports that belief" (p. 118). The first day of a class is the ideal time to give a clear introduction to your course that includes information about yourself, your goals, and the nature of evaluation; set the norms and tone for the classroom; motivate students by arousing their interest, involving them in the learning process, and displaying your enthusiasm for the course material; and correct any misperceptions or inaccurate social norms that pertain to the class.

What Is Your Teaching Style?

Instructors vary in their approaches and methods, and courses vary in difficulty and demandingness. In both face-to-face and online classes students are busy searching for information that helps them understand who you are and what you expect of them. You can help them gain clarity by adopting the behavioral style that you will take for the entire term. If you hope to start class on time, start the first day on time. If you will keep the class to the very end of the hour, do the same on the first day. If you expect the students to discuss issues actively in the class's online forum, require that they introduce themselves to the other students before the first week of class ends. You should also begin to build a relationship with your students by disclosing personal information about yourself, gathering some information about them, and responding to their questions.

What Will This Class Require?

Students often enter courses with a set of expectations about the course and its content, and in many cases these expectations are inconsistent with reality. They may assume that the introductory course will concentrate, almost entirely, on facts and information and so be surprised when a 20-page term paper is required. They may think that the courses will demand little of their time, in particular if the course meets a general education requirement or covers a popular subject. They may assume that their instructor is a compassionate individual who is willing to listen to their personal problems and give them advice. The first class session is an excellent time to prepare them for the realities of the class: the topics to be covered, the procedures to be used, and the amount of time they can expect to spend each week in and outside of class.

Care should be taken, however, when discussing the course's level of challenge. Positive expectations, even if somewhat unrealistic, facilitate performance. Students who assume that their skills and abilities can be improved and developed (*incremental theorists*) are more likely to persevere in the face of failure than are students who intuitively assume their dispositional qualities are fixed and stable (*entity theorists*). Students who "think they can," in comparison with students who "think they can't," work harder on class assignments, take a more active role in their learning by asking questions, learn more material, and come to think of themselves as high achievers (Dweck, 2012). However, students also need information about the types of behaviors in which they will need to engage to achieve desired outcomes and the amount of time they must spend on the class. Base rate information, such as a chart of the distribution of grades from prior sections of the course, should be sufficient to help students calibrate the class's demands (Forsyth & McMillan, 1991).

Why Should Students Take the Class?

Students are not always excited about plunging into a new area of study, so a little motivational packaging on the first day never hurts. Although many professors simply review the syllabus, explain how grades will be determined, or install their policies about absences and make-up tests, others take the opportunity to highlight the stimulating intellectual tasks to be accomplished, pique students' curiosity, challenge traditional views, and hint at inconsistencies to be resolved. Instead of spending the entire session dealing with procedures and logistics, they instead consider such basic questions as "Why take this course?" "What will people learn by the end of the course?" and "How does this course relate to fundamentally important personal and academic goals?"

Teaching will also likely progress more smoothly when you help students reach the learning goals they (i.e., the students) have set for themselves. As Schank (2011) put it: "Effective teaching means helping students do what it is they wanted to do and not what it is that you wanted them to do" (p. 31). To increase students' buy-in to the course and its goals, ask students to identify five critical goals they hope to accomplish in the class. Pool their goals through a class-wide discussion, and contrast their goals with the ones on the syllabus. This goal-setting exercise provides a way to break the ice on the first day of class and sets a norm of engagement and analysis.

Prepping Redux: Align Your Purposes With Your Practices

Many professors, facing the new semester, tend to recycle and reuse more than invent and innovate. They adopt the same textbook, show the same PowerPoint slides, ask the same discussion questions, and test the way they always do. However, instead of relying on the values provided by their default program, they should review those strategies and consider replacing them with alternative, innovative, and possibly more effective ones.

What alternative strategies should they consider? Although no one has succeeded in forging a definitive guide to teaching, Chickering and Gamson's (1987) "Seven Principles for Good Practice in Undergraduate Education" is a reasonable place to begin the search for alternatives. Chickering and Gamson, working with a select group of experts in higher education, developed a set of principles that they believe define "effective practice" in college teaching. Their final product, the "Seven Principles," does not focus on content, for it assumes that good professors know which theories to teach, which skills to nurture, and which findings to push into students' memories. Instead, the "Seven Principles" focuses on the *way* in which the content, skills, and knowledge of the course are taught to students. Chickering and Gamson's list (paraphrased from pp. 3–7) comprises the following recommendations:

1. Encourage contact between students and faculty: Cultivate frequent contact in and out of classes.
2. Encourage cooperation among students: Make use of collaborative, noncompetitive learning in small groups and student-to-student networks.
3. Encourage active learning: Use teaching methods that are engaging and involving, such as discussion and group learning.
4. Give prompt feedback: Assess baseline knowledge, frequently test progress in learning, and develop global assessments of educational outcomes.
5. Emphasize time on task: Set appropriate time demands and help students learn to manage their time.
6. Communicate high expectations: Set reasonable but high standards for achievement.
7. Respect diverse talents and ways of learning: Provide a variety of learning experiences and assessment options.

Research supports the value of these evidence-based recommendations: Students learn more in classes where professors heed their recommendations (Gamson, 1991). You should also consider adding one more best practice to their list. Effective professors, recognizing the limits of time, step back from the course, the semester, and the students, and consider their ultimate aims. Given the many possible goals to seek in teaching, identify your key goals and design your courses to maximize the probability that you will achieve those goals. Put in place teaching practices, including assessments of learning that are consistent with the goals you have set for yourself and your students. So, one more guiding principle can be added to Chickering and Gamson's (1987) list: As you plan your course, be certain to align your teaching and assessment methods with the course's purposes and priorities.

Guiding
Student-Centered
Approaches to Teaching

3

P rofessors, by tradition, are the givers of grades, but recently blue ribbon panels, government commissions, and concerned citizens have been issuing their own report cards, asking, "Just how much learning is actually happening in the ivory towers of academia?" Their answer: Not enough. For example, the 1998 *Reinventing Undergraduate Education: A Blueprint for America's Research Universities* report (hereafter the *Boyer report*) concluded that "research universities have too often failed, and continue to fail, their undergraduate populations" (Boyer Commission on Educating Undergraduates in the Research University, 1998, p. 5). In 2002, the Association of American Colleges and Universities called for "a dramatic reorganization of undergraduate education to ensure that all college aspirants receive not just access to college, but an education of lasting value" (p. vii, "Greater Expectations" national panel report). Former president of Harvard University Derek Bok titled his 2006 book *Our Underachieving Colleges: A Candid Look at How Much Students Learn and Why They Should Be Learning More*. The 2006 report commissioned by U.S. Education Secretary

http://dx.doi.org/10.1037/14777-004
College Teaching: Practical Insights From the Science of Teaching and Learning,
by D. R. Forsyth

Margaret Spellings, *A Test of Leadership: Charting the Future of U.S. Higher Education*, concluded that there are "disturbing signs that many students who do earn degrees have not actually mastered the reading, writing, and thinking skills we expect of college graduates. Over the past decade, literacy among college graduates has actually declined" (U.S. Department of Education, 2006, p. vii). Arum and Roksa (2011), in *Academically Adrift: Limited Learning on College Campuses*, agreed, finding little evidence of intellectual gains when they tested students' critical-thinking skills.

Educators have recommended steps to take to address these challenges. Many have suggested that the problem lies elsewhere, such as in the quality of primary and secondary public education. Some advocate for smaller classes; others favor increased reliance on technology, but nearly all agree that steps should be taken to make sure students are fully engaged in the learning process. The Spellings report, after examining ways to improve teaching, recommended professors switch to "active learning strategies to engage students in course material" (U.S. Department of Education, 2006, p. 21). Innes (2003), extending a constructivist approach to higher education, concluded that "useful knowledge is acquired through active knowledge construction during goal-directed inquiry, rather than through transmission" (p. 16). Astin (1993), drawing on longitudinal data on 24,847 students at 309 different institutions, concluded that students who are actively involved in their classes learn more. Of their seven principles for good practice in undergraduate education, Chickering and Gamson's (1987) Principle 3 is Encourage Active Learning: "Learning is not a spectator sport. Students . . . must talk about what they are learning, write about it, relate it to past experiences and apply it to their daily lives. They must make what they learn part of themselves" (p. 5).

Professor-centered approaches, such as lecturing, showing videos, working problems at the board, or reviewing the readings, can engage students, but many professors adopt student-centered methods to increase engagement in learning. They orchestrate discussions so that students learn to express themselves orally and listen to what their classmates are saying. They assemble students into small groups and assign these groups tasks that can be completed only through active collaboration. They ask students to undertake writing assignments that require students to develop and organize their understanding of the course material. They even work with their students as they conduct research in their own field of study (see Table 3.1). When student-centered teaching methods are used appropriately, they personalize and enrich the teaching–learning experience, for they bridge the gap between the conceptual and practical, the hypothetical and the concrete, and the uninteresting and the intriguing. They require students to respond cognitively, behaviorally,

TABLE 3.1

Types of Student-Centered Teaching Methods

Teaching method	Characteristics
Discussion, recitation, Socratic dialogue	A two-way dialogue between the instructor and the intact class; students interact through the professor, but they also sometimes interact with one another directly.
Learning groups	The class breaks out into smaller groups to discuss topics, complete projects, solve problems, and so on.
Experiential activities	Structured and semistructured learning exercises such as case studies, problems, or simulations that students can complete either individually or in groups.
Presentations, panels, and seminars	Formal and informal presentations; in many cases, specific topics are assigned to individuals or groups, who are responsible for teaching the material to the rest of the class.
Projects, independent study, research	Various types of projects, such as library and scientific research, guided readings, and empirical research, that are carried out under the direction and supervision of the professor.
Field placements, internships, practica, service learning	Students use their knowledge of and skills as they perform services in community, educational, therapeutic, medical, business, military, or industrial settings.
Writing (composition)	Assignments such as term papers, freewriting, journaling, and response papers that require students to express themselves through their writing.

and emotionally to the material, and so they increase both intellectual understanding and personal engagement (Barkley, Cross, & Major, 2005; Weimer, 2013).

Discussions

Sykes (1988), in his tellingly titled book *ProfScam*, included discussions on his list of "Five Ways to Teach Badly." When unprepared, he suggested, professors should "turn their classes into rap sessions, a tactic that has the advantage of being both entertaining and educationally progressive" (p. 61). But a good discussion is not a rap session; it is instead an organized class session during which the professor and the students "consider a topic, issue or problem and exchange information, experiences, ideas, opinions, reactions, and conclusions with one another" (Ewens, 1985, p. 8). Although discussions are student-centered teaching methods, they nonetheless require more preparation and investment than many professor-centered methods.

DISCUSSION'S MANY FORMS

Discussion-type methods involve talk—communication of ideas and information between students and the professor—although sometimes that "talk" takes place online instead of in face-to-face gatherings. As with many conversational forms of communication, participants take turns expressing themselves in a free-flowing, socially sustained way. Discussion, however, is more about inquiry and exploration than socializing. It is an "effort by a group of two or more to share views and engage in mutual and reciprocal critique" (Brookfield & Preskill, 1999, p. 6). But if you were to put a dozen teachers in a room who all say they teach through discussion, chances are not one of them teaches like anybody else. Discussion methods are a fuzzy set.

Instructor-Facilitated Discussions

In a discussion, the students do more of the talking than the teacher— at least in theory. The professor leads the discussion, asking questions to move the group from one point to the next, summarizing key points, and interceding to redirect the flow of ideas and information, but students' voices should be heard more frequently than the professor's. This exchange is the foundation of *erotetic teaching* ("teaching with questions"), but variations in the kinds of questions that are asked produce distinct differences in process and outcome. For example, with *recitations*, the professor ask a fact-oriented question, a student answers, the professor provides confirmation or correction, and then asks the next question. With *oral reviews*, the professor asks a general question pertaining to the course material, the class members offer answers and ideas related to the question, and then the professor moves on to the next question. With *call outs*, the professor calls on a specific student in the class by name, and that student is expected to provide a response.

Recitations are often only slightly more student centered than lectures because the professor directs the content of the discussion and speaks more than students. But the recitation becomes a legitimate discussion when the professor asks questions that require analysis and interpretation and if more than one student takes part in the answering exchange. Recitation sessions with a large number of questions and a pattern of teacher–student–teacher–student exchange are effective means of assessing learning, but they do not elevate engagement (Gage, 2009).

Socratic Dialogue

Who would want to argue with Professor of Law Charles W. Kingsfield in *The Paper Chase* when he explained,

> We use the Socratic Method here. I call on you, ask you a question, and you answer it. . . . Through this method of questioning,

answering, questioning, answering, we seek to develop in you
the ability to analyze that vast complex of facts that constitute the
relationships of members within a given society. . . . You teach
yourselves the law, but I train your mind. You come in here
with a skull full of mush, and you leave thinking like a lawyer.
(quoted in Dillon, 1979, p. 529)

The *Socratic method* of teaching is a variant of recitation discussion—
or perhaps recitation is a variant of the Socratic method. Either view is
a legitimate one, because the question "What is the Socratic method?"
is considered "the most contentious of all the questions scholars have
tried to answer about Socrates" (Brickhouse & Smith, 2009, p. 182). This
ambiguity is due in part to Socrates himself, for he used questioning
in various ways in his teachings. When Socrates taught Meno's slave how
to solve a mathematics problem, he used a series of deliberate questions
that could be answered definitively to guide him to a solution, but when
he discussed the nature of virtue with Meno through questioning, he
prompted Meno to examine more closely his assumptions. This style
of questioning, the *elenchus*, systematically revealed inconsistencies in
Meno's conceptualization, and undermined Meno's certainty, but then
guided Meno to a more rational, defendable alternative. With Meno's
slave, Socrates was patronizing, but with Meno he leaned toward a more
challenging style of questioning. Despite claiming to be an ignorant
questioner seeking understanding he seemed to know exactly where
the question–answer exchange is headed, which is one of students' key
complaints about this method of teaching (Schneider, 2013).

Small-Group Discussions

Discussions can be not only student centered but also student led. As
classes increase in size, fewer and fewer students will be able to take
part in the process. Small group discussions (or break-out groups) solve
this problem by breaking the class up into subgroups. These groups may
report back at the end of the session and the professor may selectively
facilitate their discussion, but the group's deliberations are managed by
the students themselves.

THE PURPOSE OF DISCUSSION

Sykes (1988) may have thought that students in discussions waste time
chatting informally, but a good class discussion can be used to accomplish
a variety of instructional objectives, including exchanging information
about concepts, issues, texts, controversies; analyzing, differentiating,
synthesizing, and evaluating course-related topics; expressing one's
position on issues and understanding of concepts in the field; stimulating interdependence among students and faculty; and exploring and

clarifying attitudes and values. Discussions that serve one function, such as value clarification or self-expression, require different types of materials and preparation than ones that involve pooling of shared information or critical thinking. If, for example, the discussion takes place on the day students were told to complete their reading of an assigned chapter, you may wish to use a recitation discussion method to review their understanding. If, however, you wish to help students connect the reading to their personal experiences, then a different set of questions and procedures is required. Preparation is sometimes not required when students are discussing personal experiences, but they may nonetheless need to spend some time organizing their thoughts before the discussion. Some professors encourage preparation by asking students to write short papers before class or giving them 5 minutes at the beginning of class to write a brief statement pertaining to the topic (Bean, 2011). As with all methods of teaching, discussions should be designed to contribute to specific, identifiable learning outcomes.

LEADING A DISCUSSION

Discussion leaders are just that—leaders—and so they must guide the class members' analysis of the day's topics. Most professors are fully capable of conducting such sessions, so long as they are careful to include the two sorts of leadership behaviors described in Table 3.2: (a) task leadership and (b) relationship leadership (Forsyth, 2014).

Task Leadership

When leaders are task focused, they set group goals and standards, initiate structure, define responsibilities, facilitate communication, give evaluative feedback, and plan and coordinate activities. To move the session along smoothly, a task-focused professor should monitor the amount of time spent on each topic and encourage resolution when appropriate. Group discussions can bog down if members are not reminded of time constraints, and professors can win many friends and admirers by keeping the session interesting, lively, and fast paced. The professor can also work to improve communication among members by providing clear transitions from topic to topic (especially when a change in topic also involves a change in function), summarizing and synthesizing the points made in discussion, providing feedback to discussants, and drawing out reticent members through questioning. An adept task leader keeps an eye on the content of the discussion (points raised, ideas offered, questions resolved) and an eye on process (who is talking most, how involved students are, where the discussion is headed).

TABLE 3.2

Discussion Leadership Skills

Type of skill	Examples
Task behaviors	
Directing	"I would like to discuss Jan's point further." "Let's move on to the next question."
Gatekeeping	"Ed, you've been quiet; do you have anything to add? "Let's hear from someone else for a change."
Group and individual mirroring	"The group seems to be focusing on . . ." "I hear you saying that . . ."
Informing and contributing	"I think that your conclusion is consistent with a study conducted by . . ." "Those standards were substantially revised in 1929 by . . ."
Observing process	"Why do we drift off into tangents whenever the question of ethics comes up?"
Opening	"Here is the question that I would like us to consider today."
Paraphrasing	"Let me see if I can say Jim's idea in a different way . . ."
Questioning	"Let me follow that point up with another question. Are you suggesting that . . ."
Restating and clarifying	"Let me see if I understand your point: you are saying . . ."
Summarizing	"Let me sum up."
Time keeping	"We need to finish up in the next 10 minutes or so." "We have plenty of time, so let's not cut our discussion short."
Relationship behaviors	
Approving	"That's a great point . . ." "Jill made a good point there . . ."
Confronting	"Do you realize that when you make statements like that others might be offended?"
Energizing	"We still have 20 minutes left, and we are making great progress. Let's continue to nail these points down."
Expressing feelings	"I'm not happy about the way this discussion in going." "How are you people doing right now?"
Negotiating	"Can we come to a consensus on this issue?"

Relationship Leadership

Classes in which an intriguing theory, reading, finding, or issue is being discussed are focused on the task at hand: weighing evidence, generating new ideas, critiquing positions, and so on. But as the discussion progresses, professors must meet not only students' intellectual needs but also their personal and interpersonal needs. A professor who can create a class climate that supports the open exchange of ideas, rather than defensive posturing, argumentation, and silence, will be rewarded by more engaged and vociferous students. Students who perceive the classroom to be discussion friendly engage more actively in discussion and report learning more from their discussions (Witt, Wheeless, & Allen, 2004). Studies of leadership effectiveness suggest that groups perform best when their leaders mix together both task and relationship leadership skills, in proportions that mesh with the class's level of readiness to engage in discussion. According to *situational leadership theory*, groups often require substantial amounts of task leadership when they first begin their work because the students lack confidence in their discussion capabilities, or they are unwilling to contribute to the discussion. In time, as they become more willing and able, students will benefit from increased relationship leadership, whereas their need for task leadership will decline (Hersey, Blanchard, & Johnson, 2013).

IMPROVING DISCUSSIONS: SOME EVIDENCE-BASED SUGGESTIONS

Regardless of where the discussants are located—in a circle in a physical classroom or before a computer typing their comments into the class's online forum or discussion area—the discussion's success will be influenced by such group-level features as normative constraints, cohesiveness, organization, clarity of goals, and members' motivation. It is not an accident that some classes are better suited to learning through discussion than others; some classes' structures and processes facilitate this learning outcome.

Establish Discussion-Friendly Norms

Group interactions, in their early stages, are characterized by self-protective disinterest more than active involvement. When a group first meets, it is lodged for a time in what Tuckman (1965) called the *forming stage*, which manifests itself in a low level of self-disclosure, inhibited and awkward exchanges, and the discussion of relatively insignificant details. A few students may even test the boundaries of the situation to determine what sorts of behaviors will be accepted, condoned, and commended by the teacher. This phase should be not suffered through, but exploited, given that it provides an opportunity to shape the group's structure.

Norms will develop in any classroom discussion, so both professors and students would be wise to nurture those that serve learning purposes, such as the following:

- Prepare carefully for the day's discussion by reading and reviewing any assignments.
- Write notes to yourself listing any terms or concepts that you wish to discuss during the class session.

- If you do not understand a concept or idea, ask about it—others are likely confused, too.
- Do not keep ideas and contributions to yourself, but share them with the class.
- Use examples and personal experience to make your point.
- Pay attention to what others say: Everyone in a discussion is a teacher.
- Add comments, suggestions, statements, and questions at the right point in the discussion; timing can be critical.
- Explore rather than avoid sources of disagreement and tension.
- Join the discussion, for this method of teaching works only if people fully participate.

The enjoinment to nurture the class's normative structures is particularly critical when holding discussions online. Most students are familiar with discussions, but they may have never held one in a forum or threaded discussion page. Dunlap's (2011) suggestions for online discussions include "demonstrate knowledge of the topic," "offer assistance," and "contribute to group's sense of well-being and harmony" (pp. 93–94). She also recommended using icebreakers combined with substantial positive feedback until students engage fully.

Ensure Engagement

The primary limitation of discussion is that too few of the students take part in the exchange. Students should, therefore, be reminded that their principal duty, in discussions, is to contribute. They should do all they can to make the discussion a positive, productive experience by preparing, communicating carefully, and cooperating with each other. Specific duties can also be defined by rotating roles among the class members through the term. Some professors, before each discussion, select students to act as the timekeeper, recorder, and even devil's advocate. When the discussion focuses on content, individual students can also be selected to make presentations.

In some cases, students take their responsibilities more seriously if they are graded on the quality of their contributions. Some professors use a system of peer ratings, self-evaluations, reward tokens, and running tallies of contributions. Grading discussions can be problematic, though, because such evaluations are often "too subjective to be defended if challenged" (Davis, 2009, p. 110). Grading discussion may also inhibit the discussion process if students become too grade conscious to risk making comments that others may evaluate negatively. Some students will also attempt to game the system by preparing a single point that they plan to drop in during the discussion—even if the point is irrelevant and obviously forced. If too many students are just trying to wedge in one hastily prepared comment after another, the discussion will not be a particularly productive one.

Ask the Right Questions

The kind of questions the professor puts to the class determines the nature of the discussion process itself. When professors ask yes/no questions, or ones that require a student simply to recall facts, the resulting discussions are halting rather than free flowing, students' answers are short rather than detailed, and the professor talks more than the students. Discussions are also influenced by how the professor responds after a student answers. Some research suggests that when the instructor follows a student's answer with yet another question, the discussion lurches along from question to question. Nonquestions, such as "Okay," "That makes sense," and "I see your point" keep the discussion flowing by providing space for other students to join in the exchange (Dillon, 1994). Not all discussions, however, gather sufficient momentum to sustain themselves, so in such instances professors may wish to make use of questions to push the analysis along. Brookfield and Preskill (1999) identified a number of question types that professors can use to stimulate further discussion, including asking for evidence or clarification, extensions, hypotheticals, cause-and-effect questions, and calls for synthesis.

Discussions are also more engaging when students raise as well as answer questions. When Dillon (1988) observed professors teaching through discussion he was surprised that so few students asked any questions. Students apparently assume professors know not only all the answers but the questions as well. This assumption can be challenged by asking students to (a) submit their own questions for the discussion session and (b) ask questions during the discussion itself. Developing a question can be just as intellectually engaging as thinking of an answer to one. In general, the two roles should be intertwined: Teachers and students should be both question askers and answerers.

Plan the Transitions

Groups need help starting and stopping their discussions. Because group discussions build gradually over time through a process of social contagion, the first few minutes are often slow going as ideas and energy rise. Many discussion leaders help the group get started by using an opener that serves as a springboard for the discussion: an icebreaker activity, an intriguing case, a video clip, a puzzling question, an involving anecdote, or a straw poll (a show of hands) on a controversial question.

Discussions also have a natural ending point, although in many cases the group can continue to generate ideas, opinions, points, and insights after the first slowdown. Once the group's analysis has reached its conclusion, the professor should help students reach a degree of closure on the issues being considered. If the discussion was structured by a series of questions, each one can be displayed and the class's comments recapped. The professor may also ask students to spend 5 minutes at the end of class writing a brief analysis of the discussion, and this paper can be used as a record of participation that day. Some instructors generate their own summaries of discussion, which they circulate to students, or ask different sets of students to write summaries for the class.

Start Slowly

Never, as Kramer and Korn (1999) warned, surprise students with a day of discussion. When, after a month of lecturing, the professor unexpectedly says, "What do you think about that idea?" students are often slow to respond in a productive way. Similarly, Bligh (2000) recommended gradually working up to a full class discussion by first attempting subcomponents of discussion: "Start with simple tasks in small groups for short periods of time, and then gradually increase their respective complexity, size, and duration" (p. 4).

A WORD OF CAUTION ABOUT THE BACKLASH

R. D. Mann and his colleagues (1970), in their classic analysis of professors who use discussion methods, reported that students enjoyed the discussion approach initially but that, before too long, they began to rebel. This backlash stemmed, in part, from the deliberate ambiguity of a discussion approach: The material is not neatly packaged for learners, and so they must themselves create meaning in the flow of ideas and opinions. The conflict was also fanned by the type of tests the professors gave their students. When students were given content-based tests that covered only readings and not issues examined in their discussions, they began pressuring their professors to drop the discussion method and revert to lecture-based procedures. Other research suggests that students respond negatively to discussion-based classes because they do not realize how much they are learning from discussions. When Lake (2001) compared a lecture course with a discussion-type science course (physiology), he found that grades and learning levels were better in the latter, but students in the lecture section believed they learned more.

This backlash, even if unpleasant, is nonetheless predictable. Conflicts are so ubiquitous in groups that Tuckman (1965), in his classic theory of group development, included a *storming stage* in his model: a period when tensions erupt in the group, distracting the members from their concentration on the task at hand. This theory suggests that a class, like any group, moves through identifiable phases over time as relations among members strengthen and the class's norms become more entrenched. The initial, *forming stage* is marked by reserve, caution, and tentativeness; the storming stage is marked by conflict. The group enters the *norming stage* when roles, norms, and relations strengthen, creating regularity in interaction patterns. Once these social structures develop, the group transitions to the *performing stage* as students engage enthusiastically in their learning tasks. Classes, given their entrenched power structures, often bypass the storming stage altogether or experience it only after an assessment or when a major assignment is due. Ironically, a period of conflict is more likely in when professors use student-centered teaching methods because these approaches amplify students' voices—for better and for worse. Students in lecture halls may also be angry, disappointed, and dispirited, but the conflict never has the chance to surface (Forsyth & Diederich, 2014).

Learning Groups

An active, energetic discussion conducted by a skilled professor is unmatched in its educational impact, but when classes are large some of the benefits of full-class discussion are lost. Discussions in large classes can become unwieldy, for when too many students become too expressive, the skills of a ringmaster rather than a discussion leader are needed. One of the key benefits of discussion is the opportunity it gives students to express themselves and so become actively involved in the exploration of topics. A class-wide discussion, however, limits the number of students who can offer comments during the discussion. In all but the smallest of groups, communication rates are usually unevenly distributed among members. Some individuals initiate far more comments than others, and they are also the targets of more comments. Even in groups with as few as 10 members, the discussion is best considered a series of monologues rather than an interactive dialogue. In five-person groups, interaction is more evenly distributed across members, and interactants are most influenced by the people they talk to the most. In 10-person groups, communication becomes centralized. Certain dominant figures speak more frequently than others, and some never speak at all (Fay, Garrod, & Carletta, 2000). If, as Mathie et al. (1993, p. 185) argued, "active learning requires that all students have the opportunity for the complete experience," then full-class discussion sessions do not often qualify.

One solution is to break classes into even smaller groups for discussions and group-based activities. Learning groups are unabashedly student centered, given that the students themselves are responsible for guiding their groups in the exploration of topics, analysis of problems, and creation of products and outcomes. Learning, to be effective, requires a high rate of sustained social interaction among members, but they lighten the load put on each student. They also provide students them with an opportunity to develop useful interpersonal skills.

DESIGNING LEARNING GROUPS

Learning groups are not the college equivalent of grade-school recess. Some group-based activities may stress experiential learning and personal growth, but others are designed to achieve a specific set of clearly defined learning goals. Learning groups provide professors with an engaging means of achieving the essential goals of higher education, including the growth of students' understanding of the field, the development of cognitive capacity, the various literacies (e.g., writing, reading, numeracy, information acquisition), application, and personal growth and development. Group learning does not sacrifice rigor for engagement and entertainment.

Learning Tasks

What will students actually do when they are part of a group? Will they review the course readings? Answer multiple-choice items pertaining to the text? Debate fundamental issues? Dissect case studies and recommend courses of action? Apply concepts from the class to current social problems? Compare two authors' views of some topic or principle? Rank order solutions to a technical problem? Curate a collection for exhibition? Role-play a group facing a challenging situation? Simulate a psychological or social phenomenon? Practice and perform a play? Jointly write a paper or develop a PowerPoint presentation?

Students can complete a wide variety of educational activities in learning groups, but McGrath's (1984) taxonomy of group tasks offers a way of clarifying the kinds of learning outcomes they facilitate. McGrath identified four basic categories of group-level activity: (a) generating, (b) choosing, (c) negotiating, or (d) performing. In some groups, students concoct the strategies they will use to accomplish some outcome (*planning tasks*) or create altogether new ideas and solutions to a problem (*creativity tasks*). In others, they choose among options, making decisions about issues that have correct solutions (*intellective tasks*) or problems that can be answered in many ways (*decision-making* and *discussion tasks*). When the groups must negotiate, they resolve differences of opinion among the members regarding their goals or their decisions (*cognitive-conflict tasks*) or resolve competitive disputes among members (*mixed-motive tasks*). The most behaviorally oriented learning groups do things; for example, *executing groups* compete against other groups (contests) and perform in some way (presentations, plays, etc.).

Formation and Duration

Learning groups can be formed in a variety of ways, and they can range in duration from just a few minutes to a whole semester or more. In many cases, professors create groups very quickly, even haphazardly, and the groups disband once the session is over. Breakout discussion groups, for example, are often formed by simply asking students to count off by fours, for example, and having students with the same number form a group. With pickup groups, in contrast, the professor asks students to form the groups themselves, usually by turning in the direction of others who are seated nearby. These groups are what the sociologist Erving Goffman (1971) playfully called *withs*: small temporary groups that "maintain some kind of ecological proximity, ensuring the closeness that ordinarily permits easy conversation and the exclusion of nonmembers who otherwise might intercept talk" (p. 19). When the group members finish their assigned task, the group will dissolve and members will not regroup in the future.

Other groups, though, may meet regularly during the term, both in- and outside of class. Such groups can work on more complex projects, but because they exist long enough for meaningful relationships to develop among members they are likely to be more interpersonally involving for students. As they develop over the semester, the internal dynamics of these groups will intensify, with both good and bad effects. Some groups will become cohesive and, if that cohesion is coupled with a focus on their academic tasks, then these groups will be highly productive in terms of learning outcomes. However, long-term learning groups are often marked by conflict. Some of the negative effects of long-term groups can be reduced by taking care when forming the groups, providing the groups with training in teamwork skills, including peer evaluations of group mates in the grading system, and even offering to consult with groups as needed to head off relational disaster or help them repair afterwards. Some general principles to keep in mind when forming groups include the following:

- *Create small, diverse groups.* When groups are working on challenging tasks, care must be taken when composing the groups. If groups are formed at random, then by chance some groups may be composed of the most talented, hardworking students in the class, producing imbalances in group potentialities and undoing the benefits of peer-to-peer teaching (Sweet & Michaelson, 2012). As diversity increases, communication becomes more problematic, and cohesion less assured, but diverse groups can draw on more intellectual and experiential resources than less diverse ones. Do not, however, let the groups grow too large. Larger groups stimulate more dynamic interactions, but they also facilitate more *social loafing*: the reduction of individual effort that occurs when people work on shared tasks in large groups.
- *Clarify the assignment.* Inserting a line in the course syllabus that states, "Students will work in learning teams on a semester-long

project" provides students with too little information about the assignment's purposes and processes. A nicely detailed assignment guide, in contrast, will help students better understand the dual purposes of the assignment (to examine a course topic in depth and to develop collaborative skills), the type of projects groups will be completing (e.g., a group paper, presentation, research project, interviews), deadlines, and so on.

- *Segment the assignment.* Many professors, when they ask their students to complete a term paper, often break the task down into subtasks with specific deadlines; for example, they require students identify a topic, develop a thesis statement, annotate at least five resources, and so on. This method, applied to long-term group projects, argues for identifying graduated subgoals that must be completed at specific points in the process. Frequent, specific tasks will help the groups move forward at a more auspicious rate, but they also provide the groups an opportunity to practice working together. Sports teams do not play a single championship game at the end of the season; instead, they practice regularly to improve their coordination and effectiveness. Similarly, project groups should perform smaller, more specific problems early in the semester as they develop into an effectively functioning team.

- *Give the groups a group task.* The best kinds of group projects are ones that are so challenging that students must combine their individual talents and energy to achieve the identified goal. If students are assigned divisible problems, they usually spend their first meeting splitting up the problem and assigning each part to a specific member. Nondivisible problems, such as community-learning projects, program evaluations, research studies, and so on, are harder to solve in a piecemeal fashion, so students must work together to complete them. The greater the interdependence required by the group project, the more likely the project will stimulate higher level learning processes, including peer-to-peer instruction, strategy formulation, improved coordination of action, conflict management, and enhanced willingness to exert effort in the pursuit of learning goals.

- *Teach group skills.* Working in groups may help students develop teamwork skills, but in many cases they will need guidance as these skills develop. If tasks are not repeated frequently enough for the groups to learn by trial and error, a more directive training approach will yield more rapid and positive outcomes (Salas & Rosen, 2013). If you feel that you are not sufficiently well versed in team theory to teach it, then consider adopting a guidebook on teamwork skills for your group-focused courses (e.g., Bell & Smith, 2011; Kahn, 2009).

- *Include multilevel and peer evaluations.* One of the primary complaints about student learning groups stems from the uneven contribution of members. Some members work diligently on the group's tasks, but others exert little effort. This social loafing can be reduced in two ways. First, motivate students to prepare for their group-level experiences by quizzing them as individuals before the group begins its work. Second, ask the students to evaluate each other, and factor those peer evaluations into students' grades (Havard, Ellis, & Kingry, 2013).
- *Consult regularly.* Learning groups are, in most cases, self-managing, given that members are responsible for monitoring and managing their learning process and executing required tasks. Even a smoothly functioning group, however, will benefit from some well-timed coaching about proper procedures, deadlines, standards of performance, and dealing with conflict. Coaching is particularly critical in online classes. Online learning teams can become as cohesive as collocated ones, but members must often work harder to coordinate their contributions and sustain a high level of interaction.

FORMS AND VARIATIONS

The land of learning groups is densely populated: The basic small group discussion approach whereby students talk for a time in small clusters during class has mutated into a variety of techniques, including breakouts, buzz groups, problem-based learning groups, peer-to-peer learning groups, and learning teams.

Breakout Discussion Groups

Breakout discussion groups are easy to implement: Develop a set of questions or issues for the students to discuss, break the class up into small groups, give the groups time to examine the questions, and then reassemble the class in a plenary session. Breakouts, like full-class discussion, can be used to share information, stimulate critical thinking, and double-check comprehension. They are particularly useful, however, as an interpersonal arena where students can express their understanding of course concepts and terms in their own words, work closely with other students, and clarify their personal values through social comparison. Because the professor is not present in the group, the discussion topics must be chosen with care, and students must be ready to explore them without close faculty supervision. In many cases, discussion topics that work well with a skilled, informed moderator do not yield a productive discussion when used in leaderless groups. In general, small group discussions are most effective when the group's task is a structured one, when students are practiced in collaborative work, when the goal of the discussion is clear to them, and they are well prepared. Bligh's (2000) advice—start simple and gradually increase complexity—is particularly important to heed with such groups.

When breakouts are used in online classes, each group's conclusions can be posted to a shared forum or wiki. But sharing is more difficult in classes that meet offline. A typical method, which is to have one person from each group make a brief report, works so long as the number of groups is not so great that the reports become repetitive. Bligh (2000) preferred to monitor the groups and extract key points that can be reviewed in a full-class session or have each group write out their answers. Another effective method involves asking groups to summarize their discussion in a table or graphic form that can be presented to the entire class.

Buzz Groups

Buzz groups, named for the distinctive bee-like clamor they generate, are highly structured, problem-focused, and short-lived break-out groups. Bligh (2000) advocated using these groups periodically to break up extended lectures, even in large classes with theater-style seating. He created such small groups early in the term by asking students to spend a few minutes writing out their thoughts on a discussion issue. He deliberately gave the students more than enough time to complete the individual portion of the task, and in many cases they spontaneously began to form groups with people sitting nearby. He then asked the groups to continue their discussions but limited the groups to three members to control the noise level. Bligh found that students develop a clearer understanding of definitions, concepts, and issues when they have been given the opportunity to discuss such ideas with other class members. This method, when based on two-person groups, is sometimes termed *think–pair–share*.

Problem Analysis and Decision-Making Groups

A number of professors structure small groups' interaction and learning by presenting students with a case, problem, or decision to analyze and resolve. Case study and problem-based learning (PBL) groups in business classes, for example, give students information about a fictitious company, and students must decide its mission, organization, marketing, and management. Guided design discussion groups in engineering classes spend a semester immersed in detailed information about a mechanical, chemical, electrical engineering problem and its possible solutions. Students in a computer science capstone class must analyze a request for proposals from a business and then develop the software solutions that meets the business's needs. Students in medical settings are provided with information about specific illness and disorders and must make a diagnosis and recommend treatments. These techniques are all based on developing an intriguing problem that students, by working as a team, can solve by applying course principles, gathering relevant information, and weighing alternatives (Amador, Miles, & Peters, 2006; Dunlap, 2005).

The success of a PBL group ultimately depends on the features of the problem itself. The most educationally influential problems have the following characteristics:

- *Engaging*. The case, problem, or issue should be an intriguing one; practical, realistic problems are particularly motivating.
- *Multifaceted*. A good problem is one that has no obvious, simple solution. It should be ill defined and require that students research facts, gather information, generate solutions, choose alternatives, and reach a consensus.
- *Multistaged*. Problems should be relatively complex and include a series of interlocked stages. The first stage should be related to recently learned material but should be open ended or controversial. Once the group arrives at an initial decision, its members must then acquire additional information and make a series of subsequent decisions.
- *Nondivisible*. The task should a unitary, nondivisible one that calls for collaboration and interdependent action rather than the pooling of individual efforts. When students are assigned divisible problems (e.g., interview projects, research papers, chapter reviews), they often cut the task up into components and assign each one to an individual member. Nondivisible problems, as noted earlier, are harder to solve in a piecemeal fashion, so students must work together to complete them.
- *Significant*. The problem should raise issues that are central to the learning objectives of the course.
- *Resources* The best problems can be solved only by consulting with archival and text material rather than simply through the exercise of logic and reasoning. The problem should force students to identify and locate the information they need to resolve the problem.

McBurney (2000), for example, used PBL to teach students about research methods in the social sciences. He noted that his students often responded negatively to discussions: "I have seen students put down their pens, ostentatiously fall asleep, or walk out" when he stops lecturing and entertains discussion (p. 135). Because the problems he uses are closely linked to the course material—and require an application of that material to work them out—student interest remains high. McBurney hands out the problems, which vary in length from a paragraph to several pages, 1 or more weeks in advance of their analysis. Students generally work in pairs, and he requires a written paper that includes a summary of the problem, a suggested solution and justification for that decision, and an analysis of the alternatives that were rejected.

Peer Instructional Groups

Some learning groups promote student-to-student instructional activities. Writing groups, for example, involve systematic cross-critiques by students who provide feedback about writing style, grammar, and meaning. Supplemental instruction groups are voluntary meetings held outside of class, taught by students (often for pay), which use discussion methods to review course content. They are similar, in many respects, to methods that use advanced students as mentors or tutors for students in introductory classes. These mentors, who are supervised by the course instructor, lead discussions, provide general advising, stimulate debates, and encourage students to extend their own learning. These mentors provide each student with a tangible, personal link to the university by answering academic and nonacademic questions (Kochenour et al., 1997).

The *jigsaw method*, developed by Aronson, Blaney, Stephan, Sikes, and Snapp (1978), is one of the best-known examples of peer instruction. Before the group sessions, a unit of study is broken down into various subareas, and each member of a group is assigned one of these subareas; students must then become experts on their subjects and teach what they learn to other members of the group. In developing an understanding of their assigned topic, the students would leave their learning groups and meet with their counterparts in the topic groups to review the material and decide how to teach the material to others. Once they had learned their material, these students then rejoin their original groups and teach their fellow members what they had learned. Thus, the jigsaw class uses group learning and student-to-student teaching techniques. Carroll (2001), when using this method with college learners, required that the groups sign a contract and scheduled each step in the project so that no student would fail to do his or her share (see Perkins & Saris, 2001).

Learning Teams

Not all learning groups are *learning teams*. Learning groups are often too short in duration to develop teamwork processes and the group structures that maintain those processes. Long-term learning teams, in contrast, have more of the qualities of a true team: "a unified, structured group that pursues collective learning goals through coordinated, interdependent action" (Forsyth, 2014, p. 400). The following features characterize learning teams:

- *Interaction*. Teams require members to interact with each other frequently over a long period of time as they learn to combine their resources in a coordinated process. The team generally completes not just a single project or learning activity but instead a series of evaluated tasks. These repeated tasks provide members the opportunity to detect and correct the sources of members' errors.
- *Interdependence*. Learning teams pursue group-level goals. Individuals may receive grades for individual work, but they also receive grades for the group's outcome. Members cannot succeed if their group does not succeed.
- *Structure*. Teams are structured groups, so the performance norms, members' roles, and patterns of communication and influence in the group become reified over time.
- *Cohesion*. Learning teams are, in many cases, cohesive, but their cohesiveness is based on shared commitment to their learning goals and frequency of interaction, rather than friendships. The primary goal of a learning team is learning rather than team building.

The key logistical issue with learning teams, like other long-term groups, is scheduling meetings. College students' calendars tend to be densely packed with activities, events, and commitments, so even a small group (four or five students) may have trouble identifying a time when all can meet. Flipped classes offers one means of dealing with this problem. As I discuss in Chapter 8, a flipped class is one in which class time is rarely used for content-focused review but for activities, quizzing, working problems, and group work.

Virtual Learning Teams

Not all teams meet in face-to-face settings. In online classes, professors can still assign group projects, but the students use technology to collaborate: videoconferencing, e-mail, text messaging, shared file storage systems, and even virtual-world conferencing. Online teams often have more flexibility in terms of scheduling meetings, although they must often work asynchronously when class members live in different time zones (Maynard, Mathieu, Rapp, & Gilson, 2012). Communication, however, is critical to the success of these virtual learning teams. Learning outcomes are impressive in groups where members communicate with one another regularly, with the content focused both on clarifying ambiguities about the group's task as well as on the exchange of personal information. Groups whose members lack individual initiative and communicate with one another only sporadically usually have difficulty completing their assigned tasks and, as a consequence, achieving significant learning (Jarvenpaa, Shaw, & Staples, 2004).

Elevating Engagement

Class discussions and learning groups are the workhorses of the student-centered classroom, but they are by no means the only methods that shift the teaching focus from the professor to the students. Activities, student presentations, seminars, labs, projects, and the many other methods I examine in this section are similar in that they draw students into the learning experience.

EXPERIENTIAL LEARNING ACTIVITIES

Such teaching activities as bees, competitive games, debates, demonstrations, experiments, field trips, puzzles, role-plays, role-immersion games, and simulations offer professors an effective means of reaching traditional learning goals, and they provide a break from the humdrum routine that can overtake a class that relies too much on one form of teaching. These methods are similar in that they shift instruction from the usual route—organized, linear, convergent thinking—to a more experiential one that stimulates nonlinear, inductively rich, divergent thinking. In experiential activities, for example, students engage directly in a process or phenomenon that is related to a course topic. Simulations model situations that highlight course-related issues and ask students to respond as if they were in those situations. Demonstrations re-create interesting phenomena in the classroom, and replications involve reproducing the methods and results of studies with students (Wurdinger & Carlson, 2010).

Design Issues for Activities

The use of experiential learning activities in class (and outside of class, for that matter) raises a number of issues. Activities consume time, equipment, money, and personal energy. They may yield little in the way of content-based understanding, and if students equate learning with taking notes then a day spent completing an activity may leaving them thinking they learned little. Also, activities do not always turn out as planned and can sometimes lead to unintended side effects, such as personal stress and conflict. As a consequence, students who feel uncomfortable taking part in activities should be offered alternative options (Mathie et al., 1993).

Active learning methods also falter in their purpose if the students never really grasp the pedagogical purposes of the activities. Students often enjoy the experiential activities, but then they fail to make the connection between the experience and the course concept. As Kolb (1984) explained, through direct experiences people gain a firsthand understanding of the phenomenon they are examining, but only by reflecting on the meaning of the experience can they transform this concrete data into abstract knowledge. To help them make this connection, the professor may need to add descriptive, analysis, and application phases to complete the learning cycle. These phases include the following:

- *Experiential phase*. Students perform an active learning exercise individually or in small groups.
- *Descriptive phase*. Students describe their personal feelings, thoughts, and reactions through open-ended discussion or structured questioning, information-exchange procedures, or a written assignment.
- *Analysis phase*. The professor helps students conceptualize their experiences by guiding their analysis of underlying concepts that give meaning to the event.
- *Application phase*. Students identify ways in which they can apply their newfound knowledge in their own work, family, and other interpersonal settings.

Guiding Students' Inquiry

Empirical studies of experiential learning have confirmed the value of this method for elevating student engagement and thereby triggering learning gains (e.g., Kilgo, Sheets, & Pascarella, 2014; Prince, 2004). This affirmation, however, does not extend to activities that provide a high level of experience but a low level of structured analysis. When R. E. Mayer (2004) reviewed studies of how students best learned specific cognitive strategies, including problem-solving rules, conservation strategies, and computer programming concepts, he arrived at the following conclusions:

> Students need enough freedom to become cognitively active in the process of sense making, [but they also] need enough guidance so that their cognitive activity results in the construction of useful knowledge. . . . Activity may help promote meaningful learning, but instead of behavioral activity per se (e.g., hands-on activity, discussion, and free exploration), the kind of activity that really promotes meaningful learning is cognitive activity (e.g., selecting, organizing, and integrating knowledge). Instead of depending solely on learning by doing or learning by discussion, the most genuine approach to constructivist learning is learning by thinking. (pp. 16, 17)

PRESENTATIONS AND PANELS

In some classes, the students do more of the things traditionally associated with teaching—such as structuring content, providing information, and leading discussion—than the professor. The instructor organizes the class and supervises sessions, but students control much of the content and process. In such classes students make formal and informal presentations, including didactic overviews of specific topics, summaries of research studies, discussions of their own personal research, and reviews of the textbook material. Students may also be organized into panels ranging from two to 10 members, with each participant in the panel responsible for a portion of the class content (Benz & Miller, 1996).

SEMINARS

In a seminar course, professors may lecture or lead discussions on occasion, but their influence and input are no greater than those of each student. Seminar sessions often begin with a student presentation of a paper, followed by general discussion coordinated by the professor. In other cases, however, a number of subtopics or key readings are reviewed, with particular students coordinating each subtopic's or reading's analysis. In the most student-centered form, a specific student or group of students takes on the instructional activities typically carried out by the professor, including reviewing the topic, identifying key points to be covered, selecting general readings and those assigned to specific students, and developing any teaching methods that might be used for that week.

In general, seminars are often used with advanced students, such as graduate students, who already have a strong background in the topics or issues that will be covered in the course. Seminars promote the skills needed in a scholar, with a particular emphasis on the communication skills needed when discussing complex issues with colleagues. The professor remains available to students as necessary by moderating the discussion, clarifying issues, and interceding to correct errors in interpretation, but the students are the primary teachers in seminars. As a consequence, the success of this approach depends on the motivation, skills, and experience level of the student organizers. If they are unskilled in making presentations, inarticulate when discussing complex issues, insufficiently prepared, uninterested in the course itself, or do not understand their responsibilities, then little learning may occur. The results may be as bleak as those described by a seminar veteran interviewed by Sykes (1988): "I've taken six seminar courses, and in every one of them it's been almost impossible to learn a god damn thing" (p. 76).

PROJECTS, INDEPENDENT STUDY, RESEARCH

Some student-centered learning methods ask students to take an active role in the creation of knowledge. By carrying out projects, independent studies, theses, dissertations, and other types of research students not only learn the field's theories, concepts, and findings but also must take part in creating this content. They actually do the work of the discipline, rather than just studying it. The value of student research was affirmed in the Boyer report, for this group's first recommendation was "Make Research-Based Learning the Standard" (p. 15). Research offers strong support for this recommendation (National Science Foundation, 2000; Stage & Kinzie, 2009).

In some cases, such as honors theses, master's theses, and dissertations, the student is the primary intellectual owner of the project: If a publishable product resulted, he or she would be first or sole author. In most cases, however, a student works closely with professors on their projects rather than initiating a completely distinct, independent study. Professors are always working on a long-term project of some kind—a study, a literature review, grant-sponsored research, a book—and invariably students can play significant roles in these undertakings.

Students require considerable supervision throughout the course of their projects. When the general public and the media complain about the easy teaching schedules of college faculty who spend 6 to 12 hours in a traditional classroom setting each week, they overlook the large chunk of time professors spend helping students identify, plan, conduct, and write up their projects. Effective supervision requires frequent communication between the professor and student, including face-to-face meetings, e-mails, the exchange of papers and guidelines, and the development of feedback and reports. Students appreciate the support they are given by faculty who are available, and empathic, and who take a positive approach when mentoring and supervising student researchers, but faculty often find that the demands of multiple students carrying out diverse projects can drain them of the time they need for their own work (Zanna & Darley, 1987). Some faculty tame these multiple demands by approaching research supervision as they would any class: They develop a syllabus, multiple assignments with deadlines, scheduled group meetings, and so on (Horner, Stetter, & McCann, 1998).

FIELD PLACEMENTS, INTERNSHIPS, PRACTICA, SERVICE LEARNING

A number of student-centered activities—field work, internships, work-study projects, practicum placements, service learning, and so on—integrate academic study with work experiences in nonacademic settings.

These programs integrate the values of a traditional college course with the experiences gained in vocational settings such as businesses, mental health agencies, community organizations, or schools. With varying degrees of faculty assistance, students choose a placement service site where they can take on the responsibilities of a clerk or an intern. They carry out duties for their on-site supervisor while attempting to apply their course-related knowledge to the tasks and problems they confront.

Graduate-level training in many fields—the health professions, clinical and counseling psychology, engineering, marketing, education, entrepreneurship—relies heavily on the internship model for helping students develop their professional skills. When students are placed in business, industrial, educational, and health settings they have the opportunity to apply knowledge and skills gained in their courses to work with clients and to learn firsthand about the issues and concerns professionals confront in the workplace. Students in such programs sometimes attend regularly scheduled weekly seminars or practica meetings to review and share their experiences, gain advice and support from other trainees, review assigned readings on professional issues, and complete skills training exercises.

Service learning is another widely adopted model used to integrate academic preparation with practical experience. Students in courses with a service learning component, like those in traditional internships, work for as many as 10 to 20 hours a week in a community setting. Service learning courses require that the service component provide a public good for the community and that the community be fully involved in the students' educational experience. The service component must also be closely integrated into a content-based course. Unlike a traditional internship, in which a student works for several hours a week at a school, hospital, or business and then writes a short report of the experience, students in service learning courses must actively integrate their hands-on learning experiences with the content of their discipline. This integration can occur through student-centered methods, such as discussion, or in more traditional lecture classes, but this reflection process is usually structured by a supervising faculty member (see Bowdon, Billig, & Holland, 2008).

Writing

Light (2003), to identify the best teaching method to use to elevate student engagement, sought out and interviewed 365 undergraduates and asked them this question about each course they were taking:

"What is your level of personal engagement in this course?" He also asked them how much writing they were doing in the class. The results, he said, "are stunning. The relationship between the amount of writing for a course and students' level engagement . . . is stronger than the relationship between students' engagement and any other course characteristic" (pp. 28–29). The more students wrote, the more engaged they were in their learning.

The often-heard defense against writing assignments—"I'm not an English professor, so why should I assign writing activities?"—is a weak one. Many students certainly do need help with their writing, for despite years of schooling they still have problems with grammar, punctuation, sentence structure, and vocabulary. But writing assignments are not just exercises in grammar and grading; they also are exercises in learning.

Professors, given that they must "publish or perish," should well understand the close link between composition and knowledge. Yet many view writing as only a means of assessing a students' understanding of course material, and they overlook the profound impact that the writing process has on understanding itself (Boice, 1982). Writer and professor of English composition Donald M. Murray (1985) explained the writing–learning association well:

> Meaning is not thought up and then written down. The act of writing is an act of thought. This is the principal reason writing should be taught in the academy, yet, ironically, it is this concept that is most often misunderstood by academicians. They give writing assignments based on the assumption that writing begins after thinking is concluded, and they respond to those assignments as if the etiquette of language were more important than the thinking represented by the language. (p. 3)

Granted, students who just *write* a formulaic paper will experience few of the benefits of the experience, but students who *author* a paper become an "authority" on the subject. They must create, comprehend, analyze, synthesize, and evaluate as they fill the blank page or screen with text. They must identify their topic and the goals they hope to achieve. They must then plan out the paper, breaking down this complex process into manageable pieces that can be tackled in sequence. He or she must then generate the text: the words, phrases, sentences, and paragraphs that will communicate the content to a reader while conforming to the rules and etiquette of language. A good writer must also review and rewrite the text, making certain that the words convey the meaning clearly and, ideally, creatively.

Writing, then, is a profoundly active learning experience, for when people write they identify and define problems, evaluate evidence, analyze assumptions, recognize emotional reasoning and oversimplification, consider alternative interpretations, and reduce their uncertainty (Gopen, 2004). Indeed, in many cases writers do not understand a concept clearly until they must organize their thoughts on the topic and communicate those thoughts through composition. As a result, authors are often surprised by the ideas they themselves write, for understanding emerges during the struggle to make points clear to others (D. M. Murray, 1985).

TYPES OF WRITING ASSIGNMENTS

Professors who wish to add just one element of student-centered instruction to an otherwise professor-centered approach should start by asking students to write. These writing assignments may include the traditional favorites—term papers and essay tests—but Walvoord (1982, 2014) has wisely recommended giving shorter but more varied and frequent, writing assignments, such as the following:

- *Freewriting*. Experts on teaching composition agree that students need to write on a regular basis without having to worry about how their text will be judged. They therefore recommend that students spend time each day writing a paragraph or two about something. They should write quickly, without editing or rereading, and not worry about style or technique (see Hinkle & Hinkle, 1990).
- *In-class writing*. To help students find the time to do some writing, some professors stop class for 5 minutes from time to time for unannounced periods of freewriting.
- *Journals*. Journals are dated, autobiographical notes that offer personal reflections on daily or weekly experiences. Journaling prompts students to puzzle over personal experiences; apply course material to everyday events; and ask deep, probing questions that are difficult or impossible to answer. Unfortunately, if students are simply told to keep a journal, their entries tend to be descriptive and superficial (O'Connell & Dyment, 2011). Cowan (2014) recommended helping "learners to develop a clear understanding of what their reflective writings should feature, beyond and distinct from narrative reporting" (p. 54).
- *Abstracts*. Because published abstracts rarely contain sufficient information for their use in papers (also, they are protected by copyright law), students can themselves abstract articles and chapters. They should be urged to never copy the abstract in the original paper or plagiarize in any way, although they can quote clever or essential portions of the article so long as they include page numbers and the quote is not too lengthy. Writing abstracts and text material also improves students' performance (Radmacher & Latosi-Sawin, 1995).

- *Literature reviews.* When students write detailed reviews of the published literature, they learn a number of scholarly skills. Harris (2006) offered suggestions for helping students write literature reviews by (a) contrasting a critique or reaction paper and scholarly review, (b) reviewing the rubric to be used in grading the finished paper, and (c) reviewing the use of sources. Froese, Gantz, and Henry (1998) taught students to use meta-analytic strategies to help them narrow and integrate the material in their papers.
- *Research articles.* In the sciences and social sciences students, working individually or in teams, can in some cases collect the data they will need to generate a report of an empirical investigation. In such cases students can develop their project into a scientific report complete with abstract, introduction, methods, results, discussion, and references sections.
- *Reviews.* Students can write book and article reviews modeled after those published in the *New York Times Review of Books*. They should be reminded to not abstract the book but instead to critically review the purpose, ideas, and conclusions. The best reviews are those that aspire to literary as well as scholarly excellence.
- *Alternative genres.* Students can use alternative genres—poetry, fiction, letters—to write about ideas, information, and their understanding of course material. Dunn (2000), for example, asked students to write letters to peers in other sections of his classes to help them learn to express course concepts in their own words.
- *Open assignments.* Students can be given unstructured, free assignments to write about anything that interests them, so long as they connect the essay or paper to the contents of the course. They will often need guidance in selecting and narrowing down a topic, but their papers are generally more interesting because they presumably pick topics that they want to know about rather than topics their professor wants to read about.

COACHING AND GRADING

When students write, they are learning to use the "traditions of language to discipline their thinking and to make that thinking clear to others" (D. M. Murray, 1985, p. 52). Unfortunately, many students will need coaching on the process of writing and feedback about the quality of the writing they generate. As Walvoord (1982) suggested, the professor should

> make writing assignments meaningful, establish a wholesome and stimulating writing environment for their students, coach pupils in the writing process, respond accurately and specifically

to student papers, communicate clearly with students about their writing successes and failures, and help student improve writing *as they learn* and *in order to learn*. (p. 3)

Graham and Perin (2007), in their meta-analytic review of strategies that researchers have confirmed as effective in helping novice writers improve, recommended taking time to teach students about the writing process itself before immediately assigning an essay or a paper. Even college students require guidance in developing a sophisticated strategy in their writing; many are not sufficiently familiar with academic, as contrasted to personal, writing. They may know well how to express themselves in critiques and personal reaction papers, but they may not be as experienced in summarizing precisely the things they read or developing a logically coherent essay that supports a particular position or thesis. Graham and Perin recommended using collaborative, class-centered approaches, such as peer review of drafts and student mentoring, combined with direct instruction on writing strategy and purposes. Students also need to be told, directly, that writing is discipline specific: A student who crafts masterful papers in philosophy or political science may not write in ways that satisfy professors in business or biology. Other suggestions include the following:

- *Clarify the assignment.* Nodine (1999) noted that students need to learn about writing assignments as much as they need to learn about writing per se. Telling the students to "write a 5- to 10-page paper on one of the topics covered in this unit" is likely to frustrate students and disappoint professors. Instead, the assignment should explain the paper's purpose, the audience for the paper, the genre, voice, typical length, style, degree of documentation expected, and deadline.
- *Challenge myths and misunderstandings about writing.* Boice (1994) noted that many students misunderstand the process of writing. They feel that writing is a private, secretive process that requires huge blocks of time. Others feel that writers must be first moved by the Muse, and so they procrastinate too long before beginning. Most also fail to recognize the amount of planning, research, and drafting that are needed to generate a final paper. These misconceptions should be discussed and replaced with more accurate information about writing.
- *When giving feedback, focus on content first, then mechanics.* Writing experts recommend establishing a hierarchy of comments and putting content above mechanics. By circling misspellings and crossing out extra commas, professors may send the signal "I have read this paper," but may also convey to students that form is more important than substance (e.g., Bean, 2011; D. B. Willingham, 1990).

■ *Offer specific comments.* Writing experts recommend offering suggestions that are specific, but not too much so. Vague complaints, such as "Think more about what you're saying here," "Rephrase," "Vague," and the favorite "Awk," do not point students to the specific problems with their text. More specific comments, such as "This sentence is too long and wordy," "Help the reader connect the ideas you are discussing in this paragraph to the ones you discussed in the previous one," and "I'm confused by the way you are using the word *reward*" provide students with more direction for the next draft. (Table 3.3 contains other suggested wordings for feedback based on an article by Handelsman & Krest, 1996.) Avoid rewriting sentences for the student; students should not be able to revise their papers by typing in the professors' comments directly into the previous draft.

TABLE 3.3

Ten Most Common Problems in Students' Writing and Examples of Feedback

Frequent problem	Example of comment
The significance of the topic, issue, or paper is exaggerated.	"My first impression was that this paper was about stereotypes rather than a study of student attitudes. How about starting closer to your topic?" (p. 23)
Key details are omitted or ideas are not linked to the paper's overall themes.	"Readers who have not read Smith's article may not understand the basis of this argument." (p. 23)
Too much detail about specific studies or examples is included.	"Omit these details that readers don't need." (p. 23)
Large portions of the paper consist of summaries of studies with no interpretative framework provided.	"How do these two paragraphs tie into each other, and into the rest of the paper?" (p. 23)
Original sources are quoted extensively.	"Paraphrase these quotations, and explain their significance." (p. 23)
Only one ideological or theoretical position of many is examined.	"What are the distinctions between behavioral and psychodynamic approaches?" (p. 23)
Conceptual distinctions are examined, but their implications are not discussed.	"I need less definition of the principles and more about how they apply." (p. 23)
The paper draws conclusions that overreach the paper's contents.	"I don't understand how you came to your conclusions. Your reasoning is the most interesting, creative, and important part of your paper! Please share your thinking with me." (p. 31)
No conclusions are offered.	"After all your good analysis, I'd love to hear your personal conclusion; what is your judgment on the ethics of deceptive research?" (p. 31)
The writing is stilted or mechanically inadequate.	"Watch out for passive voice throughout the paper." (p. 31)

Note. Data from Handelsman and Krest (1996).

- *Comment kindly.* Comments that are too harsh will likely not be heeded, so they do not help students revise their work. The best comments are balanced ones that are written as if the professor were giving comments to a peer. Instead of bluntly criticizing the paper, skillful reviewers first comment on the paper's strengths before identifying weaknesses. Negative comments, too, should be conversational in tone and can often be phrased as questions rather than declaratives (D. B. Willingham, 1990).
- *Bolster students' motivation to write.* Writing, as Bruning and Horn (2000) explained, is a difficult task that requires "extended periods of concentration and engagement in which writers must marshal all of their cognitive, motivational, and linguistic resources" (p. 28). Their suggestions for augmenting students' motivation to write, summarized in Table 3.4, include nurturing their writing self-efficacy, assigning interesting topics, giving feedback carefully, and modeling positive attitudes about writing.

FINDING THE TIME TO TEACH WRITING

Adding writing requirements need not generate stacks of to-be-graded papers so tall that one's own writing, research, and mental health suffer. In many cases the papers need only be checked off as completed, rather than assigned a grade. Some professors emphasize revision and do not comment on the papers until they are revised. Some may give students an in-class writing assignment and then hold short feedback sessions in the back of the room with individual students. They may also walk around the classroom reviewing students' journals or brief papers (e.g., summaries, lab reports) informally, or meet with students in small groups. Technology, as I note in Chapter 8, also offers a way to ease the burden of commenting on students' writing. Comments can now be easily be embedded directly in the draft using the tracking and revision software or recorded using a laptop webcam and uploaded to student's grade center in the course's learning management system.

Time can also be saved by shifting the locus of evaluation elsewhere: to a set of guidelines, to peers, or to the students themselves. Some professors, before students begin their work, develop and review with students a set of numbered guidelines and frequent mistakes. This structuring information reduces the number of mistakes students make and speeds up the feedback process; if students violate an element of the guidelines, their error can be noted by referring to its number. Many teachers make use of peers. Students can comment on each other's early drafts, provided they receive some guidance in how to present their comments and suggestions. Writing groups are based on the same principle and work effectively as long as students are not competing for a limited

TABLE 3.4

Factors in Developing Motivation to Write

Cluster	Related motivation-enhancing conditions
Nurturing functional beliefs about writing	■ Creating a classroom community supporting writing and other literacy activities ■ Displaying the ways that teachers use writing personally ■ Finding writing tasks that assure students of success ■ Providing opportunities for students to build expertise in areas they will write about ■ Using brief daily writing activities to encourage regular writing ■ Encouraging writing in a wide variety of genres
Fostering student engagement through authentic writing goals and contexts	■ Having students find examples of different kinds of writing (e.g., self-expressive, persuasive, entertaining) ■ Encouraging students to write about topics of personal interest ■ Having students write for a variety of audiences ■ Establishing improved communication as the purpose for revision ■ Integrating writing into instruction in other disciplines (e.g., science, math, social studies)
Providing a supportive context for writing	■ Breaking complex writing tasks into parts ■ Encouraging goal setting and monitoring of progress ■ Assisting students in setting writing goals that are neither too challenging nor too simple ■ Teaching writing strategies and helping students learn to monitor their use ■ Giving feedback on progress toward writing goals ■ Using peers as writing partners in literacy communities
Creating a positive emotional environment	■ Modeling positive attitudes toward writing ■ Creating a safe environment for writing ■ Giving students choices about what they will write ■ Providing feedback allowing students to retain control over their writing ■ Utilizing natural outcomes (e.g., communication success) as feedback sources ■ Training students to engage in positive self-talk about writing ■ Helping students reframe anxiety [and] stress as natural arousal

Note. From "Developing Motivation to Write," by R. Bruning and C. Horn, 2000, *Educational Psychologist, 35,* p. 28. Copyright 2000 by Taylor & Francis. Adapted with permission.

number of high grades. Some professors also ask students to critique their own papers and to turn in with the paper a brief synopsis of their view of the work's strengths and weaknesses (D. B. Willingham, 1990).

Because writing must be practiced and developed over an extended period and in a variety of contexts, professors who take the teaching of writing seriously may also find that they must work with other professors—even ones in other departments and schools—to develop a collaborative, cross-class, system-level approach to writing. As the writing-across-the-curriculum movement suggests, skillful writing is best developed by a progression of more and more advanced assignments that unfold as students progress across the 4 (or more) years of their undergraduate careers (Soysa, Dunn, Dottolo, Burns-Glover, & Gurung, 2013).

Guiding Redux: Use Student-Centered Teaching Strategies

Many professors avoid using student-centered teaching methods and are wary of their limitations and problems. One concern involves how discussions can be controlled so that the key ideas that must be covered in the course emerge, as if spontaneously, during the natural give-and-take dialogue between professor and student. When students work in small groups, how can their relative contributions be balanced so that all group members do their fair share of the work? How can one find the time to grade all the writing that students should be doing? On what criteria will grades be based? What if the demonstration fails and students are left bewildered and the professor embarrassed?

Student-centered teaching, though, has much to recommend it. In theory, the method seems well suited for helping students achieve fundamentally important educational goals, including

- a more comprehensive understanding of the field, its concepts, its issues, and orientations;
- higher order cognitive skills, including critical thinking, analysis, synthesis, and evaluation;
- self-directed involvement in the learning process;
- fluency in the expression of significant issues and ideas;
- interdependence among students and increased faculty–student contact;
- allocation of responsibility to students for their educational direction and outcomes; and
- opportunities to clarify and reconsider personal opinions, attitudes, values, and ethics.

Do student-center methods stand up when subjected to empirical test, in particular, when contrasted with more professor-centered methods? The empirical evidence, although less than definitive in either design or results, suggests that such methods, when properly designed and implemented, are equal to traditional teaching methods in terms of their efficiency in delivering course content and are perhaps even superlative in terms of their impact on critical thinking skills. Bligh (2000), for example, after reviewing 123 empirical comparisons of discussion methods and other types of teaching, concluded that discussion is as effective as lectures and supervised readings.

Given these strengths, it is difficult to argue with Chickering and Gamson's (1987) conclusion:

> Learning is enhanced when it is more like a team effort than a solo race. Good learning, like good work, is collaborative and social, not competitive and isolated. Working with others increases involvement in learning. Sharing one's own ideas and responding to others' reactions sharpens thinking and deepens understanding. (p. 4)

Lecturing
Developing and Delivering Effective Presentations

4

T he lecturer paced about the front of the room, shifting his gaze from one student to another as he explained that today's lesson would reveal one of psychology's great truths: that behaviors followed by reinforcers increase in frequency of occurrence. We students listened properly and took a few notes as he systematically ticked off B. F. Skinner's basic assumptions about behavior, but before our minds could wander he launched into one of his stories. This one was set in his high school, which was ruled by an evil, autocratic principal. One day, a package arrived at the school, and the staff paid the exorbitant shipping charges. Imagine their surprise, he explained, when they opened the box: It contained only a 50-lb rock. Furious, the principal called an assembly of the entire school, wheeled in the rock, and demanded that the student who had managed the prank confess. No one moved. But, over the next few days, the post office delivered box after box to the school, all containing nothing but rocks. The principal had rewarded the wrong behavior: Instead of punishing the students who sent the rock, he unintentionally rewarded

http://dx.doi.org/10.1037/14777-005
College Teaching: Practical Insights From the Science of Teaching and Learning,
by D. R. Forsyth

them and provided other potential miscreants with a model to imitate. The lecturer's story made all these contingencies clear to us, and we left class that day capable of explaining the law of effect and applying it in a real life example.

Professors are often experts at certain techniques of instruction. Some of us are masters at leading discussions and Socratic questioning. Others excel in a one-on-one mentoring setting, or helping students perfect their writing. Nearly all of us, however, must be able to lecture (Cashin, 2010). Before books were either written or read, lecturing was the way teachers passed their special knowledge along to students and, despite the promise of many alternatives, lecturing remains a staple of college instruction. One expects college professors to *profess*: to state aloud their beliefs and understanding of topics on which they are academic authorities. Indeed, in many colleges our positions are lectureships; when we make presentations in colleagues' classes we are guest lecturers, and when our good teaching is recognized we are given awards with such names as "Outstanding Lecturer" or "Lecturer of the Year" rather than "Outstanding Professor." In a 1989 survey of faculty, 55.6% reported using extensive lecturing in their teaching. By 2014, that number had dropped—but only by 5 percentage points: Just over half (50.6%) of faculty in 2013–2014 reported using lecturing as their primary teaching method (Eagan et al., 2014).

Nonetheless, academics often debate the worth of the lecture as teaching tool. Critics complain that the lecturer actually teaches very little. With unverifiable statistics like "People remember only 10% of what they hear in a lecture" and "Seventeen percent of all information transmitted orally is forgotten in an average of 4.5 days," the "anti-lecturites" assault the usefulness of this old-fashioned method of teaching. Chickering and Gamson (1987), for example, argued that students do not learn much "just sitting in classes listening to teachers, memorizing pre-packaged assignments, and spitting out answers" (p. 5). Barkley (2009) proclaimed that "in the traditional model, teachers stand at the front of the room and teach by 'telling' students what they have learned with the expectation that they will transfer this knowledge into students' heads efficiently and accurately" (p. 25). And Arch (1998) concluded that "lecture hall education is . . . a terrible way for students to learn" (p. 1869).

"Pro-lecturites" counter that lectures provide professors with the means of not just disseminating information but also transforming that information into a coherent, memorable package. Scholars, when they reveal their unique interpretations based on years of research and analysis, are a rich source of information and interpretation. Pro-lecturites note, too, that the statistics offered about lecturing and learning rates rarely are based on data. For example, K. Wilson and Korn (2007) reviewed the scientific evidence supporting the claim that students' attention declines dramatically after about 10 minutes of a lecture. They examined studies of note-taking quality, physiological measures, observer ratings of students, and self-reports of students themselves and concluded that some students are inattentive, and some are attentive, but they found no evidence of the widely believed drop in attention after 10 minutes.

Both sides in this debate have merit, for the question, "Is lecturing an effective way to teach?" cannot be answered with a simple yes or no. Lecturing is a complex communication process, involving a series of reciprocal exchanges of semantic and nonverbal messages between the lecturer and the listeners, and the outcome of that exchange is shaped by the interaction of a host of personal and situational factors. Lecturers who read their dull talks in a monotone to bored students sneaking a peek at their cell phones are not communicating or teaching. But, as Penner (1984) put it, why abandon "the lecture method, just because there are many poor lecturers, who, in actuality, are not really lecturers at all but are unskilled blunderers in a perfectly legitimate educational activity?" (p. 79).

Instead of asking, "*Is* lecturing an effective way to teach?" in this chapter I ask, "*When* is lecturing an effective way to teach?" This question is similar, in many ways, to the one that guided the work of Hovland, Janis, and Kelley (1953) and their colleagues in the Yale Communication Group in their studies of persuasion and propaganda. They were puzzled by the dramatically differing impacts of communications on audiences. Some messages would prompt long-lasting change in the people who heard the message but, more frequently, the message was quickly forgotten and resulted in no change in attitudes or behaviors.

To explain these differences, the Yale group hypothesized that the impact of a communication depends on three factors: (a) the *source of the message*, (b) the *nature of the message*, and (c) *the person who listens to the message* (Hovland et al., 1953). First, the source of the message makes a difference. The Yale researchers discovered, for example, that listeners were sensitive to cues that helped them estimate the source's credibility and that listeners were more accepting of a message from a communicator who was similar to them in some minor, even trivial, way. Second, the message matters. A persuasive appeal that captures the listener's attention and is understandable and memorable will have a higher chance of leaving a lasting impact on the audience. Third, no two people react in the same way to a communication; some will respond positively, but others may remain indifferent. Applied to teaching, the model suggests that the impact of the lecture on learning depends on the professor, the professor's lecture, and the students; in short, who says what to whom.

The Lecturer

All communicators are not created equal. As the philosopher Frederick Mayer (1960) put it many years ago, "Every university has certain professors whose lectures are so stimulating, so challenging, and so exceptional that a student feels that his education is not complete unless he takes their classes" (p. 41). However, he added, "Unhappily, too many who lecture are not gifted that way" (p. 42). The educational benefits of a lecture depend, in part, on who delivers it.

LECTURE STYLE

The role of lecturer defines the behaviors that professors should and should not perform as they teach their classes. The role has certain standard features, regardless of who is lecturing: The professor, usually positioned in a cleared space facing a seating area, communicates verbally and nonverbally to students. But the way each teaching professor enacts that role varies. Like actors who bring unique interpretations to even the most stock characters, all professors create a lecturing persona that they carry with them from class to class.

The variety of professorial lecturing styles is undoubtedly vast, but G. A. Brown, Bakhtar, and Youngman (1984) identified certain common types when they asked 258 lecturers such questions as, "Do you write out your entire lecture when preparing?" "Do you use humorous asides in your lectures?" and "Do you like to lecture?" They categorized some common types of lecturers:

- *Ramblers* (amorphous lecturers) did not structure their lectures in terms of objectives, organization, or summaries. They did not have clear objectives when they began their lecture, and so they did not have any materials prepared to support the delivery of their ideas. They did not review prior lectures, provide an outline of the day's lecture, or summarize the content that they presented. G. A. Brown et al. used the word *amorphous* to describe this lecture style because it seems shapeless and unformed.
- *Orators* (oral lecturers) delivered solidly structured lectures. They often began the lecture by reviewing the prior lecture's major points and then described the objectives of the current lecture. In some cases orators provided students with a list of the major headings in advance of the lecture, but they relied almost exclusively on the spoken word to make their point. They did not write out their lectures in full before class, but they were nonetheless confident in their lecturing prowess.

- *Lecturers* (exemplary lecturers), like orators, confidently presented well-structured material without reading from or relying on detailed notes. However, lecturers augmented their oral presentation by using visual aids, stressing the relationship between ideas, and summarizing the major points at the class's end. They also reported using a wide range of pedagogical devices, such as humorous asides, repetition and restatement, involving the audience, questioning, and quoting from textbooks. The lecturers reported that they liked lecturing and were strongly interested in their material.
- *Self-doubters* did not reach the organizational and educational benchmarks set by the orators and lecturers, but they did present material adequately and efficiently. Self-doubters, however, confessed to considerable uncertainty about the contents of their lectures. They felt in many cases that they had structured the material inadequately and did not feel that they had achieved their teaching goals when the class was over.
- *Newscasters* (information providers) delivered well-organized lectures and, like the lecturers, used a variety of tools to communicate content to their classes. Newscasters, though, tended to write out their lectures in great or even complete detail. They tended to read their lectures, and so they rarely asked students questions, used humor, or digressed from the material. They generally delivered more content than any of the other types.

G. A. Brown and colleagues (1984), after reviewing differences in lecturing style by discipline and level of expertise, cautiously concluded that these teaching styles reflect dispositional tendencies rather than an unfolding developmental progression from one style (e.g., ramblers) to another (e.g., orators and lecturers) as the lecturer gained experience. They did discover that full professors were more likely to be classified as lecturers than were less senior professors but, for the most part, when they classified professors according to their level of experience (1–3, 4–7, 8–10, and 10+ years) they found few differences in terms of teaching style. Novice professors were as likely as seasoned veterans to be an excellent lecturer, a self-doubter, or a rambler.

STYLE AND LEARNING OUTCOMES

Professors' markedly different methods for lecturing are not just an intellectual curiosity, for certain styles are associated with more positive learning outcomes. Students learn more when their professors use more pedagogically sound methods, for example, when they pose questions to the class, summarize and reiterate key points, and effectively use technologically based teaching tools. Learning is also enhanced when lecturers display a passionate, enthusiastic interest in their field; they are not just knowledgeable but so engaged in the pursuit of understanding that they inspire others to join them. This enthusiasm is often paired with strong and personal connection to their students. Even when teaching in large classrooms or to students who are interacting with them remotely through Internet-based connections, outstanding lecturers build and sustain a personal relationship with their students (e.g., Buttigieg, 2010; Kessler, Dharmapuri, & Marcolini, 2011; Lau, Fallar, & Friedman, 2015).

These findings are consistent with Lowman's (1995) detailed analysis of master teachers. Lowman examined students' perceptions of teachers, observed expert teachers at colleges and universities, and systematically analyzed the content of letters written by students when they nominated their professors for teaching awards before concluding that these diverse sources all underscored two critical themes: (a) intellectual excitement and (b) interpersonal rapport. Masterful lecturers do not plod slowly through massive amounts of material and ignore students' questions before leaving the classroom through a back door behind the dais; instead, they spend the lecture hour fervently articulating their understanding of the subject's key issues and concepts while demonstrating that they care about their students' satisfactions and successes.

Intellectual Excitement

Lowman (1995), when comparing a professor who creates intellectual excitement with one who does not, pinpointed two key differences: (a) clarity of presentation and (b) degree of emotional stimulation. Exciting lecturers are clear lecturers: They convey their understanding of the material to others by defining, illustrating, clarifying, comparing, and contrasting. Students describe such lecturers with adjectives like *knowledgeable, organized,* and *prepared.* Master lecturers also seem to be excited about what they are doing: Students used the word *enthusiastic* frequently to describe such lecturers, followed by *inspiring, humorous, interesting,* and *exciting.* Less effective lecturers, in contrast, strayed too frequently from the path of clarity, leaving students confused and uncertain about what point was being made. Such professors also seem uninterested in the material themselves, and so their students also show signs of boredom and withdrawal. Lowman summed up these professors' style in two words: *vague* and *dull* (Lowman, 1995, p. 25).

Interpersonal Rapport

Lowman's (1995) findings in regard to rapport clash with the ideal of the impersonal and unapproachable "Herr Professor" of yesteryear. The lecture hall reduces the level of interaction among students, but it amplifies the bond between the professor and the class, and lecturers can use this bond to elevate learners' level of engagement. Such lecturers are warm and open in their dealings with students, show a high level of sensitivity to students' concerns and issues, and provide students with encouragement and praise for their accomplishments. Their students describe them with such adjectives as *concerned, caring, available, friendly, helpful,* and *encouraging.* Effective lecturers avoid doing things that will engender ill will. They rarely say negative things about their students' capabilities and interests, lose their tempers or display other signs of defensiveness, or act in dismissive ways when students ask questions. They stimulate positive emotions rather than negative ones.

STYLE + SUBSTANCE = EFFECTIVE LECTURING

The lecture method of teaching is often criticized for violating two of Chickering and Gamson's (1987) principles of good practice: (a) frequent contact between students and faculty and (b) use of active learning techniques. However, effective lecturers—those who are intellectually and relationally engaging—are in compliance with Chickering and Gamson's mandate. Lowman (1995) concluded, though, that intellectual excitement is a more important ingredient than rapport. A professor who has little rapport with students but is very exciting intellectually will likely be successful in the classroom, but a professor who is all rapport and no content is likely to be effective in only a limited range of situations. In particular, Lowman stated that professors who are high in intellectual excitement and at least moderately capable of establishing rapport will be the most successful in the large lecture setting, whereas professors who are very good at establishing rapport but only moderately strong on intellectual excitement will shine in smaller, nonlecture classes. Lowman's model of effective teaching suggests that professors who want to improve their effectiveness should strive to be clear, enthusiastic, knowledgeable, and interpersonally engaging.

Be Clear

Clarity requires not only an organized, well-constructed message but also an articulate, communicative messenger. Tongue-tied, note-reading ramblers and self-doubters are likely to leave a worse impression than silver-tongued orators and lecturers who weave together their ideas in a coherent texture of terms, examples, and implications. Clear speakers preview and summarize their presentations, stay on topic, use examples, explain in detail new or difficult concepts, and speak at an appropriate pace (Simonds, 1997). They also avoid, as much as possible, imprecise phrases and expressions that might confuse students (e.g., "So to speak," "Anyway," "Not too infrequently") and word mazes: discourse that does not make sense, including poor word choices, lack of detail, redundancies, and tangled explanations (Smith & Cotten, 1980).

Clarity in public speaking takes practice. Just as electricians become more skilled with each house they wire, and chess players become wilier with each game played, each time the professor delivers the lecture it becomes clearer. Practice also lessens the anxiety most people feel when they must speak before an audience. Standing before others in the lecture hall can be an unnerving experience, and those prelecture butterflies often interfere with clarity. Lecturers' nervousness leaks out in the form of stammers; long pauses; annoying filler sounds, such as "ah"; a loss of tempo; and repetitions. Nervous speakers' voices often quiver, and their mouths become so dry they have difficulty speaking clearly. Practice, however, will help replace nervousness with calm, as the once-novel experience of lecturing before an attentive audience becomes a mundane one (McCroskey, 2012).

Penner (1984) warned against trying to boost clarity by developing extraordinarily detailed notes and then following those notes too closely. Penner suspected that lecturers who read their notes may do so because they are worried that their weak grasp of the material will be obvious if they digress but, ironically, their reliance on notes betrays the very weakness they hope to conceal: "The lecturer gives the unmistakable impression to his students that he really does not know himself exactly what he is talking about" (Penner, 1984, p. 78).

Be Knowledgeable

Unlike persuaders, professors do not usually need to worry that their audience does not believe what they are saying, given that "Typically the classroom audience has initial expectations that the communicator's conclusions will be the 'correct answers'" (Hovland et al., 1953, p. 290). However, when the students in the class feel that the issues being discussed are matters of opinion—or, worse, they doubt the instructor's depth of preparation—then they are less likely to attend to and accept the information the lecturer is dispensing. Hendrix (1998) described the special credibility problems faced by faculty who are members of racial/ethnic minority groups or who are teaching about racism, ethnicity, or sexism but are not themselves members of the group they are examining. An Anglo American teaching about racism, for example, may be regarded as liberal but somewhat uninformed, in particular by African American students. As one wrote, "They can only get so close . . . I'd want a minority perspective" (Hendrix, 1998, p. 46).

Social psychological analyses of source credibility suggest that students likely notice three types of cues when estimating their professor's expertise (Corrigan, Dell, Lewis, & Schmidt, 1980). First are *evidential cues*, which include primarily nonverbal stimuli such as physical appearance, style of dress, office location, and age. As most young professors have always suspected, students likely associate age with wisdom and are thus more likely to conclude that an older professor is more of an expert than a newly minted PhD. Female professors, too, may find that some of their students do not grant them the same level of respect that they give to men, for the students unfairly assume a connection between sex and expertise (J. H. Wilson, Beyer, & Monteiro, 2014). The second type of cue comprises *reputational cues* that pertain to the professor's level of experience and expertise; examples include degrees, titles, and other professional credentials. Last, *behavioral cues* include the nonverbal and verbal actions that students associate with effective and ineffective interventions. A relaxed but poised physical posture, an attentive expression, a direct gaze, and loud voice all lay a claim to status.

Be Enthusiastic

In the late 1970s, Williams and Ware (1976; Ware & Williams, 1977) conducted a series of telling studies of the "Dr. Fox effect." They arranged for an actor named Fox to deliver a pair of lectures using one of two presentational styles. In the *expressive condition*, Dr. Fox spoke with much enthusiasm, charisma, warmth, and humor. In the *control condition*, he presented the scripted lecture adequately, but he did not put any emotion into its delivery. The lectures themselves were also manipulated to create three levels of useful content: (a) high, (b) moderate, and (c) low. After the students had listened to the lecture, Williams and Ware asked them to rate the speaker's skills, and they took a test on the content covered in the lectures. Students considered the expressive lecturer to be more interesting, and they earned higher scores on the test. But Dr. Fox's enthusiasm interfered with the students' ability to distinguish between an informative lecture and one empty of information. When Dr. Fox was enthusiastic, students felt the low-content lectures were just as good as the high-content lectures (Ware & Williams, 1977; Williams & Ware, 1976).

Subsequent studies of the Dr. Fox effect have suggested that students, over the course of a series of lectures, come to distinguish between a professor who is all style and no substance and one who knows the lecture material more thoroughly (Williams & Ware, 1977). However, research still indicates that students learn more from professors who can capture their attention by delivering material in an interesting way (H. W. Marsh & Ware, 1982), including using one or more of the following techniques:

- *Stimulating emotions.* Lowman (1995) noted that the outstanding lecturers in his studies "use their voices, gestures, and movements to elicit and maintain attention and to stimulate students' emotions. Like other performers, college teachers must above all else convey a strong sense of presence, of highly focused energy" (p. 23). A good lecture is not just informational but also inspirational. As Axtell (1998) so eloquently explained,

> Many students will soon forget the details and even general themes of their college courses, but few will forget the passion with which their professors approached the subject day after day or the inspiration they gave them to think the subject important and worth pursuing, at least for a semester. (p. 60)

- *Improving vocals.* A lecture is a spoken presentation to the class, and so its impact depends in part on the quality of the voice in which it is delivered. A variety of factors influence the quality of one's speaking voice—pitch, speech rate, loudness, vocal clarity, tone, and so on—but if any of these qualities is held constant, the result is monotony. When H. G. Murray and Lawrence (1980) taught professors how to vary their vocals, pauses, and nonverbal behaviors, their teaching ratings rose in comparison to faculty in a control group. Students also respond more positively to online lectures, such as streamed videos, podcasts, and screencasts, when the lecturer's voice is clear, appropriately paced, and varied in tone (Kay, 2014).
- *Improving nonverbals.* Skilled lecturers are usually in motion, and these body movements send implicit messages about their emotion, interest, and excitement. By adopting an open posture—knees and feet spaced apart, arms extended out, hands open, and body leaning forward toward the audience—one appears friendly, warm, and outgoing. Closed, symmetrical postures make the speaker seem unfriendly, cold, and nervous (Patterson, 2011). Certain hand gestures also communicate enthusiasm, and their use may also improve verbal performance by enhancing the retrieval and processing of verbal information (Krauss, Morrel-Samuels, & Colasante, 1991).
- *Declaring interest in the material.* Because enthusiasm, like perceived expertise and clarity, depends more on the subjective judgment of the perceiver than on the objective behavioral data the target provides, lecturers would do well to control their students' perceptual conclusions by monitoring self-disclosures. When one apologizes for having to "cover this boring material," one is letting students know that their attention will soon be wandering (Kessler et al., 2011).
- *Preparing for class.* Professors who are enthusiastic about their work usually prepare to teach it. Students take inadequate preparation as a sign of the professor's disinterest in the course.

These prescriptive recommendations can be summed up in a single proscription: Do not be boring. Boredom is, unfortunately, a relatively frequently heard complaint from students in classes, with 59% reporting considerable boredom and nearly one third complaining of nearly constant boredom (S. Mann & Robinson, 2009). Boredom, as a psychological process, occurs when individuals have difficulty focusing their attention on the content of the lecture. This difficulty can usually be traced to disinterest in the content itself, as when students drift off when a professor moves through a series of text-only PowerPoint slides or holds forth in an unbroken torrent of speech without ever asking the students what they think. Boredom occurs when a lecturer's "long-winded, rambling, and tedious exposition of an otherwise interesting subject" weakens even the best-intentioned students' control over their focus of attention (Leary, Rogers, Canfield, & Coe, 1986, p. 969).

Leary and his colleagues (1986) identified the key components of boredom by asking students to describe the things boring people do. Bores, they discovered, would make bad lecturers because they are passive, tedious, and easily sidetracked but, oddly, they are ingratiating. They show little enthusiasm, seem unnecessarily serious, are caught up in their own trivial concerns and they themselves seem to be bored. Leary et al. discovered that once a person is labeled a bore, his or her social value plummets; as boringness increases, one's apparent intelligence, competence, popularity, security, friendliness, and reliability decrease. Boring individuals "are at a distinct disadvantage in social life and may experience dysfunctional consequences" (p. 975).

Build Rapport

Lecturers are free to use techniques and tools that vary in terms of interpersonal involvement. Some lecturers rely primarily on more impersonal methods and maintain a teacher–student relationship that is similar to that of author–reader or newscaster–audience. They can, for example, remain apart from the class, lecturing in a detached, information-dissemination style and keep all their in-class discussions focused on the course material. But such an approach fails to take advantage of the unique interpersonal dynamics of the face-to-face lecture situation. When Samuel Johnson proclaimed "Now when we all read, and books are so numerous, lectures are unnecessary" (cited in Zakrajsek, 1999, p. 81), he was overlooking the human connection between lecturer and listener.

Just as there are many ways to engage students in the course material, so too are there many ways to strengthen the bonds between lecturer and class. Most, though, are consistent with Dale Carnegie's (1937) recommendations on how to win friends and influence people. Carnegie always maintained that the best way to create positive relationships with others is to become sincerely interested in them. Instead of ignoring the social needs of their students, interpersonally skilled lecturers use a variety of relatively simple methods to establish rapport, including the following:

▪ *Learn and use students' names.* Carbone (1998) suggested having students state their name each time they ask a question in class to help professors remember their names, but she also described more elaborate methods. Some professors record their students announcing their names in the first week of class, others download rosters with photographs from university databases, and some take photographs of each student so that they can learn their names. Ko and Rossen (2010), in their guide to online teaching, recommend using names as much as possible in email and discussion forums.

▪ *Decrease social distance.* Gleason (1986) suggested that lecturers think of their large halls as they would small, intimate classrooms and act accordingly. Come early to class, linger after class answering questions, and move about the room when lecturing if possible. Carbone (1998) described professors who eat regularly at the student dining hall and those who hold office hours at the student center. Twitter, Facebook, blogs, and other forms of social media also provide professors with the means to strengthen their connection with their students.

▪ *Decrease physical distance.* Rietz and Manning (1994) urged lecturers to get as close as they can to their students, even if it means leaving the rostrum and lecturing from the seating area. They flatly stated, "Never use a stationary or goosenecked microphone attached to a lectern. An immobile mike traps you in place: you cannot move or even turn and still be heard. Furthermore, the lectern becomes a barrier between you and the audience" (p. 247).

▪ *Lecture with less formality.* Another way of reducing the psychological gap between lecturer and lecturee is to use a less formal style of presentation. As Zimbardo (1997) noted, lecturers who move "vigorously about the teaching stage, hands flying, arms waving, gesturing broadly in best Italian fashion, talking fast, sometimes furiously, sometimes not completing sentences except with a finger flourish marking end points" (pp. 10–11) flatten the status hierarchy of the classroom. They move themselves closer to their students, all the while increasing their students' interest in what is being said.

▪ *Smile (and make eye contact).* Carnegie (1937) felt that people who smile are not only communicating happiness but also signaling their acceptance of other people. Eye contact also is a critical indicator of involvement. People generally assume that downcast eyes signal embarrassment, shame, and disinterest; lecturers who make eye contact with the class imply involvement, intimacy, attraction, and respect (Buskist & Saville, 2001). People also consider eye contact as evidence of certain personality traits. Exline and Messick (1967) found that people who gazed at others only 15% of the time were judged to be cold, pessimistic, cautious, defensive, immature, evasive, submissive, and indifferent, whereas those who maintained eye contact 80% of the time were seen as friendly, self-confident, natural, mature, and sincere.

- *Self-disclose, appropriately.* Hilton (1999) recommended using personal examples and anecdotes during the lecture when appropriate to the topic under discussion. Such materials, Hilton felt, "avoid the chasm of impersonal indifference" and remind students that their professor is a human being who experiences the field at a personal level. Hilton, of course, urged professors to monitor their level of self-disclosure, for there is "a fine line between personalizing your lectures and wallowing in narcissism" (p. 118).

- *Listen to students.* Only in the most formal of presentations do listeners hold their questions until the end of the presentations. In most cases, professors urge students to ask questions during the lecture, and they take the time to answer these questions respectfully. Many lecturers, too, punctuate their talk with carefully developed questions that require a response from students. Another way to gather feedback from students is to take a quick opinion poll about some issue relevant to the lecture topic through a show of hands, by using individual-response technology (IRT) units ("clickers," which I discuss in more detail later in this chapter), or by asking students to complete online surveys and questionnaires.

- *Take an interest in students.* Reciprocity is one of the most powerful determinants of attraction; people tend to like those who like them. Professors who show concern for their students, seem to like their students, and act as though they want their students to succeed are rated more positively by their students, and these more positive ratings are also highly correlated with students' self-reported motivational levels and grade expectations (J. H. Wilson & Taylor, 2001). Professors teaching online courses who diligently increase their social presence by responding promptly and personally to their students are perceived more positively by their students (Campbell, 2014).

Do Not Be Negative

Much of the good work done to build a relationship with students can be undone by an ill-chosen word or regrettable lapse of affect management (Buskist & Saville, 2001). When Ludewig (1994) asked students to name their pet peeves about professors, the following items made the list: assigning too much work, lecturing too quickly, making students feel inferior when they ask questions, delivering lectures in a boring way, getting behind schedule and then cramming in material just before the exam, and requiring a textbook and then never using it. MacArthur and Villagran (2015) generated an equally detailed list of professorial misbehaviors for teachers of online courses, including indecipherable course-related messages, messages replete with misspellings or bad grammar, sarcasm, favoritism toward certain students, and verbal abuse.

When these irritations mount, the professor–student relationship—which is so essential for a lecturer's success—is put at risk. Consider these examples (from R. D. Mann et al., 1970):

- One professor began his first class of the semester with a smile and an open, down-to-earth self-description, but when he described his goals for the class all he said was, "I want everyone to learn to spell the word *psychology*" (p. 226).
- During a lecture on learning theory, the professor asked the class questions every few minutes as he moved from point to point, but the students consistently gave incorrect answers. His lecture began to slow, and his enthusiasm dipped and reached a low point when no one responded to his question about a study of problem solving involving chimps. Finally he said, "Come on, people. The monkeys were able to solve it" (p. 55).
- After a student offered an opinion during a pause in the lecture, the professor seemed critical of the comment. The student, responding defensively, reminded the professor that he had said that all opinions were welcome. The professor replied, "What is the purpose of my giving you information if you don't use it? If I wanted your opinions, I would say, OK class, now we're going to do nothing for the next six weeks but sit around and listen to your opinions" (p. 60).

The professors in these examples could have managed these irritating circumstances more constructively than they did.

The Lecture

Even lecturers with all the right stuff—expertise, enthusiasm, and sincere interest in their students—will fail as teachers if they organize and present their lectures ineffectively. Anyone who has ever suffered through a disorganized lecture, listened to a colloquium that made no sense, or watched an online lecture that harped on trivial issues that were only vaguely relevant to the central topic can understand the importance of developing a powerful message. What makes a message powerful? According to the Yale group's analysis of the *what* component of their "Who says what to whom?" model of communication, an effective lecture must first *capture the students' attention,* for despite the claims for subliminal learning and the wisdom of the unconscious mind, communications that are ignored generate little in the way of learning. Second, the lecture must be *understandable;* the students must comprehend what the lecturer is saying. Third, the lecturer should *strive to make the message so compelling that listeners will accept it.* Fourth, *the points in the lecture must be memorable* so that they will be remembered long after the lecture ends. Lectures should, they suggested, be attention getting, understandable, convincing, and memorable (Hovland et al., 1953).

STRUCTURING THE LECTURE

College professors are not simply educators; they also are scholars with a well-defined command of a particular subject matter. As a consequence, their lectures should offer students their unique interpretation of their field's concepts and discoveries instead of a verbalized restatement of someone else's ideas and insights. The first lecture a professor gives on a particular topic may not completely satisfy the demand for originality, but with repetition and revision a pedestrian lecture can grow into a profound oration.

The content of the lecture should be established during those long hours of preparation with source materials. Once one reaches a comfortable level of understanding, however, the lecture itself must be built and decisions made about what topics are so important or complicated that they must be covered, the desired level of complexity and depth of the presentation, the amount of information that can be adequately presented given the time available, and—perhaps most important—the overall organization of the lecture.

Organizing the Topic

Learning is both a piecemeal and holistic process. Students learn not only by organizing discrete pieces of information into overarching conceptualizations (*bottom-up processing*) but also by integrating recently acquired information with their preexisting cognitive schemas, concepts, and associations (*top-down processing*). In general, learning proceeds more rapidly when it moves from whole to part rather than from part to whole. However, learning may be deeper—more lasting and more easily retrievable—when the students use parts to build a whole.

Most theories of memory and cognition suggest that people, as active processors of information, select and organize information in interconnected knowledge structures based on natural and perceived similarities, discontinuities, and clusters. A structured lecture that mimics this naturally occurring cognitive process by presenting information in a hierarchically tiered framework should, in theory, increase encoding and storage efficiency and retrieval success (Ambrose, Bridges, DiPietro, Lovett, & Norman, 2010). Bligh (1998) described two types of lecture organization: (a) hierarchical and (b) flat. In hierarchical lectures, the material is organized into a series of nested clusters, with more relatively specific concepts, examples, and applications organized into superordinate categories that connect the subordinate elements conceptually. Such lectures can typically be summarized in an outline form or as a graphic. Some material, though, is best presented in a flat, linear pattern rather than a tiered one. Bligh termed this type of organization *chaining* and recommended it when material is ordered in a temporal or cause–effect–cause–effect sequence.

Providing Advance Organizers

Given that the lecture has an organizational structure, should this organization be shared with students, either in advance of, or during, the lecture? And how detailed should these *advance organizers* be (Ausubel, 1963)? On the one hand, the effortful organization of the material may be a desirable difficulty: If students must actively detect the lecture's organization and then use it to build their own schematic cognitive structures, then their memories of the organization and the material it organizes will likely be more durable and detailed (P. C. Brown, Roediger, & McDaniel, 2014).

On the other hand, studies of students taking notes suggest that their cognitive load is already so heavy when they are listening to a lecture that they cannot divert sufficient cognitive resources to creating a suitable structure for the incoming information. If students cannot listen to the lecturer's points and simultaneously create an organizational cognitive structure, then well-structured advance organizers will improve their learning (Belland, Kim, & Hannafin, 2013).

Regardless of the level of detail in a lecture outline provided to listeners, lecturers should nonetheless use organizational signals in their presentations to let listeners know where they are in the sequence of topics. They can do this by using the verbal cues summarized in Table 4.1 to help listeners recognize key points, restatements, definitions, examples, comparisons, lists, asides, summaries, and so on. They can also signal movement through the elements of the lecture nonverbally, by counting on their fingers, referring to their notes when they want to summarize, and by raising their eyes to the classroom when opening the floor to questions (English, 1985).

TABLE 4.1

Cues Used by Lecturers to Reveal the Organizational Elements of Their Lectures

Organizational indicator	Example
Introductions, overviews, and orientations to the topic	"Today we will be discussing Freud's psychodynamic theory by focusing on four basic elements of that perspective: his assumptions, his beliefs about personality's structure, his notions about how people protect themselves from anxiety, and the implications of this perspective for treatment."
Shifters from lecture to question/answer and discussion	"Are there any questions about these three assumptions? . . . Let's discuss this for a moment. Specifically, what do you think of Freud's idea that women, because of their weaker superegos, are less moral than men?"
Enumerators	"Freud identified five stages of psychosexual development, if one counts the latency stage as a true stage. First. . . . Second . . ."
Definition indicators	"What did Freud mean by the word *repression?* Freud defined repression as motivated forgetting; the motivated caching of unpleasant or anxiety producing information in the unconscious rather than conscious mind."
Example and elaboration identifiers	"What are some examples of repression? One of Freud's patients, Little Hans, was very fearful of his father, but he was not aware of these feelings . . ."
Repetition designators	"This point is so critical that I need to say it again. Freud's belief that conflicts in the unconscious mind could be so anxiety-provoking that . . ."
Comparison and contrast identifiers	"So what is the difference, then, between Freud's conceptualization of dream imagery and Jung's interpretation of dreams? Freud, in calling dreams the 'royal road to the unconscious' . . ."
Elaboration markers	"Let's look more closely at one of Freud's most controversial ideas: his belief that boys' development depends on their ability to resolve the Oedipal conflict."
Sidetrack or aside identifiers	"Even though it's only peripherally related to the point I was trying to make, it's nonetheless interesting to consider the Freudian undercurrents in most modern advertising. Take, for example, . . . Anyway, to get back to our analysis of Freud's ideas about defense mechanisms . . ."
Transitioners	"We have seen that Freud believed that anxiety is, in many cases, caused by deep-seated conflicts that the ego cannot keep in check, even through the use of defense mechanisms. Given this assumption, what would be the best way to treat people who are suffering from such problems?"
Highlighters	"Sometimes people overlook the importance of this point, but it is a crucial one to grasp fully if one is to understand Freud's perspective. . . . What is the point in studying such an old theory that many people feel is sexist and historically limited? Well, Freud's thoughts pertaining to the unconscious mind are one of the cornerstones of modern psychology."
Summary and topic completion markers	"So, Freud's remarkable view of the human being is based on three key assumptions. As we have seen, Freud believed that psychological energy, our motivation, results from basic biological motives. Also, we are, in large part, unaware of these motivations because they are locked in the unconscious mind. Last, anxiety arises from the dynamic interplay of these psychic energies."

Connecting the Lecture to the Text

Penner (1984), a passionate advocate of the lecture method, was almost vitriolic in his condemnation of a lecturer who reads the textbook to the class:

> Any unqualified person can stand before a class and merely *flip pages* in the textbook! The combination of reading the text or stale notes, and poorly at that, in a monotonous manner, devoid of a sense of humor—that is really depicting a dullard. (p. 78)

If students can take notes in class just by following along and highlighting passages from their textbook, then the lecture adds little of value to the learning process.

Gray (1997) offered a strong argument for carefully integrating the textbook with the contents of a lecture. He noted that many instructors seem to be laboring under two false assumptions. First, they assume that they cannot test students' understanding of material covered in lectures if that material is not also examined in the textbook. Second, they assume that if material is covered in the textbook, but not discussed in a lecture, then students cannot be tested on that material either. Both assumptions, however, are false—or at least they can be defined as false by a clearly written syllabus:

> Students can read a textbook with understanding if it is well-written; they can also listen in class and take notes if the lecture is clear; and they do both of these if they know that the test includes ideas and evidence from both sources. My own formula, stated on the course syllabus, is that 70% of the points on each test are based on the textbook and 30% are based on lectures. (Gray, 1997, p. 55)

In many cases, too, the author of the textbook may have organized the material so carefully that modifying it into a different organization may render it less effective (Sternberg, 1997c).

CAPTURING ATTENTION

When William James (1892) discussed the nature of attention more than a century ago, he distinguished between passive and active attentional processes. *Passive attention* (stimulus-driven, bottom-up attention) is dictated by the stimulus itself: Students pay attention because the material itself is so arresting that it captures and holds attention. *Active attention* (goal-directed, top-down attention), in contrast, depends on those aspects of the perceivers (e.g., expectations, goals, conceptual structures) that determine what is noticed and what is overlooked (Egeth & Yantis, 1997). The following suggestions are based on James's two methods for capturing attention: (a) create attention-grabbing stimuli and (b) instigate cognitive mechanisms in the listeners that will increase their attention to what is being said.

Telling Stories and Anecdotes

Some lecturers teach critical concepts by embedding them in stories and anecdotes. Some stories may be personal ones, but others are retold tales of the experiences of others. Stories probably do much more than just increase interest on the students' part and help endear the lecturer to them. Interesting stories, instead of presenting information in a pallid, dull format, create an emotional reaction in the listener. Stories are more exciting, in many cases, than bulleted lists and charts. However, stories also work to create a deeper level of processing. Storytelling is an old and effective means of relaying information from one person to the next, and shared stories often form the basis for episodic and collective memories. These narratives, even though they were experienced by others, nonetheless have many of the memorial features of detailed episodic memories rather than semantic, paradigmatic memories (Bruner, 1996).

Asking Questions

A question will bring students back to the point at hand faster than any joke, aside, or anecdote. When lecturers question, they shift the class's focus attention from themselves to the students. Even a simple question, like "What do you think about that idea?" can be enough to make students perk up, or at least avert their eyes momentarily in the universally understood nonverbal message, "I don't have much to say. Don't ask me." But questions are also useful for stimulating a thoughtful analysis of information. Any lecture is, in essence, an organized series of answers to questions.

Questioning students, in particular in large classes, requires advance planning and the use of appropriate mechanics. Although a question that pops up on the spur of the moment might be an excellent one to use in class, lecturers should also develop possible questions to ask as they are writing the lecture itself. Some of these questions can be answered by the entire class, by vote, but even fact-based questions can provide a means of regaining students' waning attention. Lecturers should also use good mechanics when asking questions. The following list contains some suggestions:

- Signal the question clearly, perhaps by repeating it or presenting it on the board or projector.
- Give students time to think about the question; tolerate a period of silence in the room.
- If the room is a large one, repeat each student's answer to make sure all students hear the reply and to indicate the importance of listening to the answer.
- Use care when asking specific students to answer the question; students sometimes feel intimidated by faculty who cold-call students.

- Distribute the questions that will be considered during class to students in advance of the session.
- Praise students when they ask and answer questions.
- Correct students when their answers are inaccurate, but use tact to diffuse the students' embarrassment.
- Use rhetorical questions sparingly, if at all. Research suggests that such questions tend to distract students rather than stimulate them (D. J. Howard, 1990).

Quoting Original Sources

Professors who teach literature know how to use quotations in their teaching. When discussing some author's work they examine the author's words themselves, reading them aloud and asking the students to open their books and read along. This effective method can be used by professors across all disciplines. Studying the words scientists, researchers, historians, artists, and philosophers used in original sources lets another voice be heard in the classroom. Quotations can be particularly arresting when they are recorded in advance by a colleague with an expressive voice who reads the material with enthusiasm.

Using Humor

Evidence indicates that exposure to humor not only promotes health but also promotes learning. Most humor falls into one of four overlapping categories: (a) funny personal anecdotes, (b) descriptions of events and topics related to course material humorously related, (c) jokes concerning topics examined in the course, and (d) cartoons. Any of these forms may break up the monotony of the lecture and build rapport, but humor may also facilitate comprehension and strengthen students' cognitive responses. If students don't understand a particular joke, they likely also did not comprehend the ideas presented in lecture (Hackathorn, Garczynski, Blankmeyer, Tennial, & Solomon, 2012).

Not all students, however, appreciate a well-told joke or a humorous aside. When Babad, Darley, and Kaplowitz (1999) correlated students' rating of their instructors at Princeton University and the descriptions of these instructors in the student-generated university "Student Course Guide," they discovered that the instructors' humor was a significant predictor of students' ratings of course and lecture quality in general survey courses. In more advanced courses, however, humor became less important and was replaced by greater emphasis on the quality of course content and the absence of criticism. By the time students reached their senior-level courses, their evaluations were correlated with only judged quality of readings, course interest level, and instructor's knowledge and expertise.

Offering Asides and Personal Views

An *aside* occurs when the lecturer strays from the day's outline and presents information—personal views, a self-disclosure, a forewarning of a future topic—that is only tangentially related to the topic at hand. Like humor, asides provide the listener with a short recess and so reduce the cognitive burden of an information-rich lecture. Asides should be used sparingly, or the flow of the lecture may be sidetracked, and students may have difficulty concentrating on the main content when the lecturer returns to on-task material. Movement in and out of an aside should also be explicitly acknowledged to help students return to a note-taking mode, although the phrase "This won't be on the test, but it's interesting to consider" should probably be avoided because it invites students to woolgather.

Using Multimedia Material

When the angry adolescent says "Don't lecture to me," or the disgruntled employees mutter to one another "Here comes another lecture" just before the boss sits them down for a performance review, they are equating lectures with the delivery of words. But most lecturers combine their words with tables, charts, graphs, images, art, video, and audio materials. Images, graphs, sounds, and other media capture attention precisely because they are not words but instead salient stimuli that stand out as figures in the ground of the auditory verbal information. Although these materials may seem like gratuitous distractions, they are actually attention gatherers.

By combining voice with images, lecturers also can take advantage of the human information-processing system's capacity to simultaneously process auditory and visual stimuli. Although both systems are limited, in that excessive amounts of either verbal or visual information will overwhelm learners, these two systems function jointly to create richer, more detailed cognitive representations of information (R. E. Mayer, 1997; R. E. Mayer & Anderson, 1991; R. E. Mayer & Gallini, 1990).

Sequencing

When writing a lecture, professors must sometimes choose when to present the most challenging material. Should they begin with conceptually difficult information as soon as possible during the lecture (*primacy*), or should the initial minutes of lecture be used to set the stage for the intellectually challenging concepts revealed in the lecture's final minutes (*recency*)? This question has no obvious answer, for even though Hovland et al. (1953) spent considerable time trying to understand when primacy versus recency effects occur in persuasion contexts, they eventually concluded that "whether primacy or recency effects (or neither) occur depends upon the conditions of the communication situation" (p. 287). When listeners are unfamiliar with key issues in the communication and they grasp their significance only late in the presentation, then recency becomes more likely. Recency also trumps primacy when the lecture builds to a climax, or when listeners' energy rebounds after a midlecture sag as they anticipate the end of the session. The occurrence of primacy or recency effects ultimately depends on attentional variables: If attention is high, then the material will be better remembered regardless of where it appears during the lecture.

Demonstrations and Activities

Even the best lecturers can hold students' attention for only so long, so many punctuate their presentations with student-centered activities such as those discussed in Chapter 3: problem sets, demonstrations, short reaction papers, brainstorming sessions, buzz groups, think–pair–share sessions, and so on. These activities consume class time that could otherwise be spent lecturing, but research confirms the time is well spent. In one investigation of students in a content-focused class, scores were 8.6% higher when the professor interspersed activities with lectures, and this gain increased to 22.9% on the final examination (C. J. Miller, McNear, & Metz, 2013).

ENHANCING MEMORABILITY

Listening to a lecture on a new topic and taking notes that summarize key points is no easy feat. Given what researchers know about memory and the limited cognitive resources available for processing information, it is little wonder that students often do not remember when professors mention an upcoming test.

Repetition

Advertisers believe that any good ad is worth repeating—and repeating and repeating. As Cacioppo and Petty (1979) discovered in their studies of attitude change, when information is repeated several times listeners think more about the message and generate more promessage thoughts each time they hear the message. But they also discovered that too much repetition generated more anti-message and irrelevant thoughts, indicating that excessive repetition will interfere with learning (Bromage & Mayer, 1986).

Pace

Even though the expression "fast talker" is a pejorative one, calling up the image of a slick salesperson who talks a lot without saying anything of substance, listeners think that rapid-fire delivery is a sign of intelligence and expertise. A rapid delivery, however, interferes with students' ability to process the information at a deep level and causes encoding and retrieval problems because new information interferes with older information. As Bligh (1998) concluded, "Interference is probably the chief cause of forgetting in lectures, particularly when the lecture is too fast" (p. 39).

Pauses and Silences

Most lecturers, like radio DJs, scrupulously minimize "dead air": prolonged periods when no sound is issuing from the students or the lecturer. However, when professors pause every 10 to 15 minutes when lecturing, students' scores on subsequent examinations improve—sometimes by as much as a letter grade (Ruhl, Hughes, & Schloss, 1987). Such silences are adult learners' version of recess. They enhance learning by giving students the opportunity to review their notes for completeness, relax and let their minds wander, or identify questions about the material just covered. These periods should not be used by students for conversation or cell phone calls, so the instructor should explain the purpose of the periods of silence and explicitly signal their beginning and end.

Giving Examples

Skilled teachers recognize the value of a good example. Learners, and novice learners in particular, rely heavily on examples to build their understanding of concepts. Experts can often make sense of new information by relating it back to their existing stock of knowledge, but novices need concrete, specific illustrations of the concept. Novices are still building out their conceptual structures, so they use examples to connect the elements in specific cases to theoretically meaningful concepts. Examples also help them identify what elements, ideas, and concepts must be considered closely and which ones are superficial features that can be safely ignored. Examples, then, are a bottom-up cognitive strategy that facilitates the transfer of knowledge from one situation to another: "a very specific solution plan that contains no generalized conditions and actions, but only specific ones" (Reimann & Schult, 1996, p. 124).

A good example enhances encoding, elaboration, and depth of information processing, but what makes an example good? First, good examples are clear rather than fuzzy—they fit the concept under review neatly, with no distracting ambiguities. Second, a good example is memorable; a vivid, intriguing example will be remembered long after a pallid, mundane one. Third, a good example creates associations between students' existing knowledge and the new construct by relating the abstract concept to a topic that personally interests the students.

These aspects of strong examples signal the ways examples can mislead learners. Examples should be clear cut, but in many cases the example is so complex, or so forced, that students must strain to make the connection between the specific instance and the general construct. When lecturing on a particularly complex concept, be careful to assemble workable examples well in advance. Ad lib examples suggested by circumstances or students may fit the concept well, or only roughly. A vivid example can also be so distracting that students do not tie it back to the concept, and some examples are so involving for students that they lose their objectivity. Personally relevant examples can also estrange students in the class who are not interested in the example's focus. Sports examples, as Galliano (1999) noted, can irritate the nonathletic, just as scurrilous examples can offend those with heightened sensibilities. Because of these potential complications, once you find an example that works, save it and use it again.

Summaries

One of the most frequently recommended methods of lecturing involves three steps: (a) *preview* the information ("This is what I am going to say"), (b) *present* the material ("This is it"), and (c) *summarize* the material ("This is what I said"). This approach helps listeners follow the course of the lecture and provides them an opportunity to double-check their own interpretation of the material against the lecturer's recapitulation. As Lowman (1995) noted, however, excessive summarizing can dull the lecture's message. Indeed, when students know that the final few minutes of class will be spent in a review and recapitulation of material that they think they understood clearly the first time, they often use that time to zip and unzip their book bags and backpacks, collect their coats and belongings, and bid adieu to the students seated around them. Davis (2009), therefore, recommended a strong ending that will punctuate, rather than reiterate, the lecture's key themes:

> An impressive ending will echo in students' minds and prompt them to prepare for the next meeting. End with a thought-provoking question or problem; a quotation that sets an essential theme; a summation of the major issue; or a preview of coming attractions. . . . Don't worry if you finish a few minutes early; explain that you have reached a natural stopping point. But don't make it a habit. (p. 155)

USING POWERPOINT

Many lecturers rely on technology to increase the impact of their presentations. Microsoft's PowerPoint and Apple's Keynote, as well as Prezi, automate the development of visuals by offering templates that regulate the colors of the background and fonts, the format of the text material, and the location of any graphic materials. The software lets the user insert all types of material in a slide, including pictures, animations, and video and audio clips, and the material can be edited easily so that revisions are simple. Presentation software includes professionally designed templates that help the user provide an aesthetically pleasing consistency in appearance. The following are some suggestions for using presentation software:

- Configure the size, color (in particular, contrasts), and font of the type to match the requirements of the classroom or lecture hall; many of the figures and slides provided by textbook publishers or downloads from journal articles are too small to be used in large classrooms.
- Do not put too much information on a single screen; add images and graphics to counterbalance the text.
- Use the software's animation tools so that elements in the lists can be displayed one at a time. Students' attention is recaptured each time a new element is displayed.
- Upload your presentations to the Web so students can access them. Some studies suggest that it is a good idea to upload the slides prior to the lecture (e.g., Chen & Lin, 2008).

Presentation programs are becoming so common that a professor who lectures "naked"—who does not make use of information technology in his or her presentation—is now the exception rather than the norm (Bowen, 2012). However, building a presentation takes time, especially for novices. Because the equipment that runs the software is complex enough that small problems, such as an overlooked setting or a jack inserted into the wrong outlet on the projector, can bring the presentation to a standstill. Such presentations can also drive the lecture relentlessly, and students tend to write down the contents of each slide, then let their minds wander until the next slide is revealed. Some lecturers, too, do not spend enough time creating good visuals. Tufte (2003) called most PowerPoint displays "chartjunk" and concluded that most are so dull that they poke a "finger into the eye of thought."

CLICKERS: INDIVIDUAL RESPONSE TECHNOLOGY

The college class lecture hall, by tradition, limits communication between the professor and the student. Students can ask questions, but for the most part information flows primarily in one direction: from professor to student. IRT units, more commonly known as "clickers," make classrooms more student centered by improving the flow of information from the students back to the professor. With an IRT unit students do not need to raise their hands; they simply indicate their response using a computer keyboard, personal response pad, or a wireless clicker. Their responses can then be processed by the controlling computer program, recorded, and tallied for display to the instructor and the class. Clickers thus provide a means of escaping the routine of lectures and videos because students must respond continuously to the instructor's questions and take part in IRT-mediated activities. In most cases, the summary display presented to the entire class indicates only whether a response pad has answered: It does not indicate the specific answer a student gives. IRT units therefore protect students' confidentiality, reducing the possibility of embarrassment if one submits an incorrect answer. The specific answers can be scored by the program and saved to a data set, so the system provides the means for the instructor to take attendance, monitor student progress, and quiz students. Those who use classroom response systems have consistently described the technology as a catalyst for a significant shift in the classroom climate, pedagogy, and resultant learning. The results of studies conducted in a variety of classes suggest that clickers are very favorably evaluated by students, that they improved the quality of class discussions, and that they improve learning rates (e.g., Forsyth, 2006; R. E. Mayer et al., 2009).

The Listeners

An articulate, expert, and engaging lecturer prepares a well-organized lecture filled with vivid examples, memorable stories, and important points. Yet, some of the students, when tested on their understanding of the concepts covered, show little evidence of having learned the lecture's lessons. Why? Because learning does not depend only on "Who says" and "What is said," but also on "Who is (or is not) listening" (Hovland et al., 1953).

Hovland et al. (1953) offered a general orientation for organizing the many individual differences that influence message processing. They recognized that listeners vary in many ways, but they tied these differences back to the basic information-processing steps they identified in nearly all their empirical efforts. If differences among individuals influence their levels of attention, comprehension of the message, and acceptance of the message, then they will likely respond very differently to the same instructional experience.

LECTURES AND LEARNING STYLES

Studies of individual differences in how people acquire and process information have suggested that the lecture format, with its emphasis on sequential organization, verbal content, and minimal social interaction, is an ideal means of learning for only some students. Other students' preferred learning style may require more active processes, such as performing exercises or conducting experiments. Others may learn best through reading and independent study. Others may excel in small groups, whereas others may prefer visually stimulating experiences. Claxton and Murrell (1987) categorized these individual variations in learning styles into four groups: (a) personality, (b) information processing, (c) social–interactional, and (d) instructional preference. Personality models relate differences in learning style back to basic traits of the individual, such as field dependence–independence. Information-processing approaches suggest that students vary in the way they encode, store, and retrieve new information. Social–interactional models are based on variations in students' motivational goals, such as their interest in learning for learning's sake versus learning to outperform others. Instructional preference models take into account students' attitudes toward different teaching methods, such as small group discussions, formal lectures, readings, and so on.

Some educators feel that these individual differences are so powerful that students will not be able to learn in a setting that does not match their personal proclivities or characteristics. The data, however, do not offer consistent support for this view. Hattie (2009), in a meta-analytic review, found no consistent evidence that students' learning is enhanced when the material is taught in a way that meshes with their learning style. Pashler, McDaniel, Rohrer, and Bjork (2008) concluded that there is ample evidence to indicate that people have strong preferences about how they learn; however, they found "no adequate evidence base to justify incorporating learning styles assessments into general educational practice" (p. 105). Lilienfeld, Lynn, Ruscio, and Beyerstein (2009) considered learning styles to be "an urban legend of educational psychology" (p. 96).

Other researchers believe that particular types of learning style might be more prevalent in different cultural, ethnic, and gender groups; others feel that learning styles are likely confounded with stereotypes and may contribute to inappropriate and unfair treatment of group members. Moreover, even students who prefer to learn by doing, or assimilate knowledge more rapidly by carrying out projects in groups, should learn to augment their scholarly skills so they can learn in lecture classes as well as other settings. The ability to listen critically to a presentation and cull the most essential elements from the hour-long message is an important skill; even students with a visual or interpersonal learning style preference need to be able to understand the points made by the anchorperson on the evening news. Kozhevnikov, Evans, and Kosslyn (2014) judiciously recommended incorporating a range of methods when teaching, so that students become familiar with a number of modes for learning.

READINESS TO LEARN

College students are motivated to learn things that interest and challenge them, nd these interests are determined, in part, by their level of cognitive anu motional development (Widick, Parker, & Knefelkamp, 1978). Chickering's (1969, 1981) work, for example, assumed that traditional college students have particular developmental tasks or concerns pertaining to developing competence, managing emotions, developing autonomy, establishing identity, freeing interpersonal relationships, and developing purpose and integrity. Students' concern about autonomy, for example, expresses itself in their striving for independence from their parents, comparing themselves with peers to learn how to act in various situations, and relying more on their own thoughts and values than on those of others. Some of these motivations sustain their efforts to excel in the classroom, but others draw their attention away from scholastic concerns (Widick et al., 1978).

Perry's (1970) work with college students suggested that students are most likely to be engaged when they are challenged by thinking that is different from their current viewpoints. He contrasted students who were *dualistic thinkers*—those who feel that all questions can be answered clearly and definitively as either right or wrong—with more *relativistic thinkers*, who realize that, on most issues, different perspectives can be taken. Perry found that lecturers who introduce conflicting ideas, admit their uncertainty about questions, and encourage students to debate issues among themselves challenge dualists and help them move to a more relativistic stage of development (Schommer, 1998). But when professors also take a stance on an issue and base their commitment to that stance on their interpretation of relevant research findings, they stimulate relativists to move from ambivalence toward personal commitment (King, 1978).

LECTURES AND STUDENTSHIP

The range of students' scholarly skills can be striking. Some students attend class regularly, do the assigned readings before the day's lecture, take good notes, and study at least 3 hours for each hour spent in the class. Others, in contrast, lack what Pressley, Van Etten, Yokoi, Freebern, and Van Meter (1998) call *studentship*: the skills, knowledge, and attitudes needed to master their many academic demands. In large lecture classes, the general lack of studentship can escape detection. Students can skip classes, and their absence will go unnoticed. If they fall behind in their reading, this too likely will escape detection. If they are sick, hung over, or sleepy, they can "gut out" the lecture hour note free. But if students do not attend, if they do not connect to the professor, and if they do not take good notes, then they will likely learn little from even the best instructor.

Attending Class

No lecture will be effective if it is never heard (Knight & McKelvie, 1986); however, lecture classes, because they tend to be large and professor centered, provide students with the anonymity they need to skip class without fear of detection. In a small class, students who miss class regularly will be noticed, and their actions can be questioned and corrected, but when classes are large, and if attendance is not taken, students may soon find that other demands on their time will prevent them from getting to class. Unfortunately, as Lindgren (1969) reported, attendance and performance are highly correlated. When he reviewed the attendance records of high- and low-scoring students, he discovered that 84% of the high scorers attended nearly every class session, whereas only 47% of the low scorers attended faithfully. His findings argue in favor of required attendance in class, but such policies can result in classes filled with students who are so inattentive that they might as well be elsewhere rather than distracting the students who want to pay attention to the lecture. Sleigh and Ritzer (2001), recognizing this problem, suggested structuring the class "so that those who attend experience obvious benefits, such as better grades, personal growth, and 'informative entertainment'" (para. 10); specifically, a professor should

- include items on tests and exams that cover information and activities from the class sessions rather than the text;
- spend class time covering aspects of the material that are not considered in readings or online;
- provide only the outlines of classroom materials (e.g., lecture notes) at remote locations rather than verbatim transcripts;
- involve the students in the presentation by presenting ideas in interesting ways, making use of examples they can relate to, and involving them in the discussion;
- give students grades for classroom participation and make use of in-class quizzes and activities; and
- create an atmosphere of mutual respect and individual accountability in the classroom.

Listening and Note-Taking Skills

Every professor has had a student who did not take notes but performed marvelously in class. I once had a student who never took a single note, but got 100s on three exams and a 98% on the final. She stared at me throughout each class, never jotting down a single comment. It was eerie. Most learners, though, benefit in a number of ways from taking notes (Bligh, 1998). Memories are so fallible and fragile that most people must strengthen them by jotting down summaries of what they learn in each class. Note taking is even more important in large classes because these complex environments interfere with the sometimes-automatic production of lasting memory traces. Notes make salient the lecture's outline, organize information presented in the lecture, force students to identify key points, provide a written record for later review and study, and increase attention to the lecture's content (McKeachie, 1980). In Chapter 6, I offer some ideas for instructors who want to give their students pointers on how to take useful notes while listening to their lectures.

Lecture Hall Ecology

Even if students show up for class in a physical sense, they sometimes remain disconnected psychologically from the lecturer and the lecture's content. Indeed, many students deliberately select their seats in the lecture hall to avoid having to pay attention to the lecturer. According to Haber (1980), students who sit close to the front identify more with the lecturer and are likely trying to increase their focus on the course material. Those who sit in the rear areas of the class identify more with their peers than the professor, whereas those on the far sides of the class are connected to neither their peers nor the professor. In general, however, students in the center and front areas earn higher grades and participate more than students who sit at the rear of the room (Knowles, 1982; Sommer, 1969). Some evidence indicates that these differences are found because the more intelligent, talkative, or more interested students choose central territories (Levine, McDonald, O'Neal, & Garwood, 1982). Other studies underscore the impact of spatial factors, such as proximity to the instructor (Oluoch-Suleh, 2014). When Griffith (1921) assigned students to their seats alphabetically, students in the front rows scored 3% to 8% lower than students in the central areas, and students in the rear rows scored 10% lower than students in the central area.

Lecturing Redux: Communicate Engagingly

Professors who teach by lecturing are not a novelty at most universities. For decades, students have been filing into lecture halls, where they listen communally to professors' information-laden lectures on both basic and advanced topics. For just as long a time, professors have wondered whether the practical advantages offered by lectures offset their potential disadvantages. The lecture is an efficient means of transmitting course material and concepts to large numbers of students, but some consider these classes to be impersonal, uninvolving, and too teacher centered.

Is the lecture's checkered reputation as an old-fashioned and ineffective form of teaching deserved? A bad lecture, delivered by an unengaged professor, to students who are more distracted that inspired, likely teaches only one lesson: that lectures lead to little learning. However, a well-prepared lecture delivered by an enthusiastic professor who communicates engagingly to intellectually stimulated students is a superb means of constructing a shared understanding of a topic. Some important skills, such as expressing ideas in one's own words or collaborating with others, are best achieved through means other than a lecture. But how are students to learn to understand complex spoken information? How can they learn to listen critically to a presentation, and cull the most essential elements from the hour-long message? By listening to a lecture and developing the ability to extract its meaning. As R. E. Mayer (2004) concluded, "The most genuine approach to constructivist learning is learning by thinking" (p. 17) and an engaging lecture does just that: It makes students think.

Testing

Strategies and Skills for Evaluating Learning

5

The professor walks to the front of the room and makes the following announcement:

> Please switch off your phones and clear your desks. Part 1 of the test is multiple choice: 25 questions covering all the topics in this unit. Part 2 requires you to answer five questions with short answers of one or two paragraphs. Please write in complete sentences, and legibly; I cannot grade it if I cannot read it. If you have any questions as you work on the test, raise your hand. Before you begin, be certain to review and sign the honor code indicating that you neither gave nor received assistance in completing this assessment. Be mindful of the time as you work.

Side conversations die down, phones are secreted away, and the students shuffle through their things as the professor passes out copies of the questions they are to answer. Before long, all are working diligently, doing their part to perform in what is a grand academic tradition. It is test day.

http://dx.doi.org/10.1037/14777-006

College Teaching: Practical Insights From the Science of Teaching and Learning, by D. R. Forsyth

137

Assessment of the extent to which students have attained their educational goals is an essential component of the college learning experience. Students, when taking machine-scored tests, still scurry to find a No. 2 pencil. Some professors still prefer those quaint collections of pages stapled at the seam called *blue books*, although they are not books and in many cases are not blue. And students still spend the night before the exams engaged in what psychologists call *massed practice* but everyone else calls *cramming*. We might someday see colleges and universities without large lecture halls, fraternities and sororities, tenure, and academic freedom, but tests and their various forms—exams, quizzes, essays, term papers, response papers, projects, performances, presentations, portfolios—may be everlasting.

Their pervasiveness and longevity are due, in part, to their functionality (R. P. Phelps, 2009). Professors, as agents of educational systems that are based on credentialing only those students who achieve certain standards, use tests for the *summative assessment* of their students' learning. When the term ends and the dean's office asks who deserves credit for having mastered the course, tests provide answers that are ostensibly based on fair, objective standards. Tests are complicit in the growing trend to document with more certainty the outcome of higher education.

The stronger justification for testing, however, is its *formative* value. R. P. Phelps (2012), in a meta-analytic review, identified 177 studies conducted over the past century that had examined the relationship between achievement and testing. His conclusion: Testing promotes learning. Here are some of the reasons why:

- Tests increase motivation. They provide students with a concrete, clearly definable goal.
- A high grade on a test is a reinforcing event, just as a failing grade is a punishment, and so the delivery of grades by professors often increases the frequency of studious behaviors and decreases the occurrence of behaviors that undermine performance.
- Tests keep students on task by breaking up the relatively long semester into more compact segments. Goals that are too distant often fail to generate the same level of achievement-focused energy that more proximate goals produce.
- Students are more attentive to information presented in class when they know they will be tested on the information (R. P. Phelps, 2009).
- Testing stimulates learning directly. Studies of the *testing effect* have found that each time an individual must retrieve information from memory, his or her ability to retain that information is strengthened (Roediger & Butler, 2011, p. 20).

The positive effects of testing are even stronger when combined with clarifying feedback that pinpoints strengths and weaknesses

(R. P. Phelps, 2012). Such feedback helps students calibrate their competencies and thus closes what is often a too-wide gap between perceptions of learning and actual learning. Testing also provides professors with feedback about their own performance; testing makes learning visible (Hattie, 2009).

All these benefits of formative and summative assessment, however, apply to good tests, not poorly designed and haphazardly administered ones. Professors whose tests are filled with vague questions that are unrelated to the course learning goals or focus on trivial facts and minutiae are testing, but their students likely gain few educational benefits from such poorly constructed instruments. In this chapter, I discuss ways to create tests that maximize their positive impact and minimize their disadvantages.

Planning a Test

Some of the tasks of a professor are described with quaint euphemisms. They "give lectures to their students," as though professors were intellectually rich philanthropists. They "train their graduate students," as if advanced scholars learn best through regimented, structured teaching. They "hold office hours," as if they were jurists or monarchs holding court. And their tests? They "make them up," as if they were writing a piece of fiction, penning poetry, or cooking up a good excuse for some indiscretion. Certainly test construction has its creative aspects, but for the most part the task calls for careful planning, deliberation over choices, and the analysis of available data. Tests are not *made up*, like stories, poetry, or excuses; instead, they are *constructed*, like houses or intricate machines.

IDENTIFYING THE INSTRUCTIONAL OBJECTIVES

A professor's course has a set of purposes, and tests are designed to assess those purposes. Whether they are called *mastery learning targets* (Brookhart & Nitko, 2015), *behavioral objectives* (Mager, 1962), or *developmental objectives* (Gronlund, 1998), these explicitly identified objectives ensure the tests will be aligned with the course's goals and the professor's teachings. Objectives that focus on trivia, outcomes that are too advanced for most of the students in the class, and ideas that the discipline has long since abandoned should be replaced with ones that are consistent with the identified goals and purposes of the present class.

When students ask "What is on the test?" they are asking about its content: the topics, concepts, and skills that will be examined. Mager

(1962) championed the use of behaviorally oriented learning objectives that clearly communicate the professor's answer to this question. Descriptions of test content such as "Know all boldfaced terms in the text" or "Be clear on the accomplishments of the founders of the field" should be replaced with learning objectives that specify what students will *do* to demonstrate their learning. It is not enough to say, for example, that they will "appreciate the differences between schools of thought" or can "learn to experience the emotional significance of classic music." Such general verb phrases as *know, understand, appreciate, grasp the significance of, believe,* and *examine* should be replaced with words that are tied to the specific type of learning outcome sought. The following are some examples of knowledge objectives and some of the specific skills they encompass (Bloom, Englehart, Furst, Hill, & Krathwohl, 1956):

- *knowledge*—define, enumerate, identify, itemize, list, name, outline, quote, recall, recite, recognize, record, reiterate, repeat, replicate, restate, state;
- *comprehension*—convey, discuss, delineate, describe, explain, express, identify, locate, recognize, rephrase, report, reword, show, tell;
- *application*—act out, calculate, compute, carry out, demonstrate, employ, illustrate, implement, interpret, perform, role play, use;
- *analysis*—analyze, break down, chart, compare and contrast, diagram, differentiate, distinguish, dissect, inspect, relate, test;
- *synthesis*—combine, collect, compare and contrast, create, design, develop, formulate, integrate, plan, prepare, propose, reconcile, reunite; and
- *evaluation*—appraise, critique, gauge, evaluate, estimate, judge, rate, review.

PREPARING THE TEST SPECIFICATIONS

If specifying the learning objectives is Step 1 in developing a test, then Step 2 is making sure the test includes items that are related to those objectives. So, instead of selecting test items haphazardly, diligent test designers use a *table of specifications* (TOS) to keep track of the topics they sample and the level of learning outcomes the test requires. Consider, as an example, a midterm exam in a course on college teaching. Students have studied four core topics up to this point: (a) the purpose of higher education, (b) course planning, (c) student-centered teaching, and (d) lecturing. The test should therefore include items pertaining to all four of these topics, in proportion to their importance and the depth of analysis. However, the professor also wants to measure a range of learning outcomes. A few content-oriented questions, such as "Who developed the well-regarded Taxonomy of Learning Outcomes?" may be fine, but the test should also assess more conceptual, higher learning outcomes and applications. The TOS, then, should identify 12 categories of questions generated by the 4 (topics) × 3 (kinds of learning outcomes: content, conceptual, and application) chart.

TYPES OF ITEMS: SELECTED OR CONSTRUCTED

Student achievement can be measured in a variety of ways, but by far the most frequently used methods are *selected response* (SR) tests and *constructed response* (CR) tests. SR tests ask students to select the answer they feel is correct from a list of several possible answers; CR tests ask students to generate their own answers. Multiple-choice, matching, and true–false items are all SR tests, whereas completion, short-answer, and essays are CR tests (Haladyna & Rodriguez, 2014). Each offers unique advantages and disadvantages in terms of assessment.

Skills Assessed

True–false and matching items are best suited for testing recall and recognition of terms and facts. It is possible to craft multiple-choice questions that measure complex thought processes, such as analysis, organizing, critiquing, and planning, but these items tend to drift toward knowledge of content instead of asking the student to synthesize his or her understanding of broader concepts (Martinez, 1999). Instructional objectives that focus on creativity, evaluation, and expressive skills are usually assessed with CR items such as unrestricted essays.

Comprehensiveness

Multi-item SR tests are generally more comprehensive; they better sample the domain under study. The number of CR items that can be asked and answered during the time available for testing can be increased by asking shorter, more highly structured questions such as short-answer questions or fill-in-the-blank items.

Objectivity of Scoring

SR tests yield the same grade regardless of who scores them, provided the scorer uses the key appropriately. CR items that ask for specific types of information, such as lists or names of theorists, also can be scored objectively, but essay questions can be influenced by scorer characteristics (e.g., background, mood, and personal preferences).

Fidelity

Scores on SR tests accurately indicate the number of items a student answered correctly, but this score can overestimate achievement because students earn credit for correct responses that are based on guesses. Scores on CR tests are not influenced by guessing, but they can be inflated by other factors, such as adroit bluffing, impressive penmanship, or a pleasing writing style.

Writing and Reading

Only CR items provide students with the opportunity to express their understanding in their own words, but such tests may consistently underestimate the achievement of students who know the material well but do not possess advanced verbal skills. Both types of items are influenced by reading skill, but SR items put more reading demands on students in terms of amount and precision.

Feedback

Both types of tests provide students with useful information about their performance. SR items in particular can pinpoint specific areas of weaknesses; students who misunderstand certain topics but grasp others can be identified by analyzing the profile of their scores. CR items yield less information about specific strengths and weaknesses, but they do provide an opportunity for the instructor to make comments about general proficiencies and areas that need strengthening. Such items are also particularly useful for identifying errors in step-by-step problem-solving questions, as when students must show the steps they follow when solving a mathematics problem.

Pedagogical Implications

Martinez (1999) reviewed a number of studies that suggest students study differently for CR tests than they do for SR tests. When students anticipate multiple-choice tests they focus on details, but when they prepare for CR tests they focus on general concepts and connections between ideas. CR tests, because they involve writing, may also require more elaborate processing of course information during the test itself and therefore trigger increased comprehension as a side effect of the testing process.

Cheating

If students want to cheat, the test format alone will not prevent them from doing so. Short-answer CR questions can be copied from one test taker by the next, just as the answers to SR tests can be easily copied from a distance. Students have less success copying long-answer essay questions from one another, but these tests are nonetheless vulnerable to cribbing and leakage: If a professor uses the same questions in multiple sections of a particular class, students in one section can easily remember the few questions on the CR test and pass them on to students in the next section. Both SR and CR tests, when administered online, can become, in a sense, "open-book" exams; the professor can require that students complete these tests without using resources, but a mandate does not always result in compliance. As a consequence, as I discuss further in Chapter 8, online classes often use SR items for low-stakes testing and CR items (paired with other forms of assessment) for summative evaluations.

Practical Concerns

SR tests are scalable; they are so easily scored they can be used in any size class. CR items must generally be graded by knowledgeable or trained scorers, although the use of scoring rubrics can decrease the time needed. Still, most professors find the task of grading the essay tests of 100 students a daunting one. CR items can be constructed more quickly than SR items, especially those harder-to-write SR items that tap higher order learning outcomes. SR items, however, can be reused in some cases or drawn from test banks of items, if available. Tests that use SR items, if administered online, can give students immediate feedback about their performance.

RELIABILITY AND VALIDITY

The ever-entertaining website *Rate My Professors* (http://www. ratemyprofessors.com) allows students to make comments about their professors in a public forum. The students are permitted to remain anonymous, but the professors are identified by name. This website says much about students and their perceptions of tests. Very frequently, when students are unhappy with a testing experience, they use one adjective to describe the offending question or test: *unfair*. User ES144 wrote, "You will regret ever having stepped into his lecture, as his material is nonsensical and his tests are unfair." E1630 commented, "Class was alright [*sic*], but tests were unfair," and BMES1 opined, "Unfair tests, unfair homework grading, very unhelpful. Needs to be fired." Professors who give those allegedly unfair tests will find that their "easiness" scores will plummet on the site, along with their overall quality ratings. They may even lose their "hotness" chili pepper icon, a somewhat dubious distinction that can be selected by the site users.

However, individuals who wish to distinguish between good tests and bad tests eschew the value-laden word *fair* and instead stress two other attributes: (a) *reliability* and (b) *validity*. Tests should be dependable, stable indicators of learning, and this reliability should be indicated by the consistency of the students' scores across time and across the test's components. If students have successfully achieved the course's learning objectives, then a reliable test should yield nearly the same results each time the students take it, so long as the period between tests is not so great that students can no longer recall the material. Also, if a number of questions are asked about a particular learning outcome, then students' answers across the questions should be relatively consistent. A student who understood the concept well enough to answer Item 2 should not miss Item 16 if it revisits this same educational outcome.

Asking several questions about each learning outcome will improve a test's reliability, given that students who correctly answer one question dealing with a topic tend to respond correctly to the other questions pertaining to that topic as well. As a consequence, SR tests are usually more reliable than CR tests. Inconsistencies between different graders reading the same essay (low *interrater reliability*) and variations in a single grader's reaction to essays caused by fatigue, halo effects, order effects, and so on (*intrarater reliability*) can also lower a CR test's reliability.

Validity describes the extent to which the test measures what it is supposed to measure. Although Cronbach and Meehl's (1955) conceptualization of validity has been changed over the years, their basic assumption—that scores on a measure must be linked to a theoretically meaningful construct—is still accepted by most psychometricians (Messick, 1995; Shepard, 1993). A test has *content validity* if the items on the test adequately sample the material covered during the unit, *criterion validity* if the test yields grades that are correlated with other indicators of student achievement (*concurrent validity*) and are useful in predicting achievement-related outcomes (*predictive validity*), *construct validity* if the test measures what it was designed to measure (students' actual learning), and *face validity* if the test seems valid to those who are taking or interpreting it.

SR tests generally include many more items than CR tests, so their content validity is usually higher than CR tests—but only if the items adequately represent the domains identified in the TOS. If the TOS stresses higher order outcomes, but the test includes only fact-oriented selection-type items, then the test's construct validity is low. Conversely, if the learning objectives stress the acquisition of factual information, then a CR test may not be valid. If the learning objective states, "Students should be able to state and defend their personal positions," then an essay test likely will provide the most direct measure of this objective, whereas a multiple-choice test will only serve as a proxy for the desired outcome.

Both types of items can also be plagued by two types of problems identified by Messick (1995): (a) *construct-irrelevant difficulty* and (b) *construct-irrelevant easiness*. When a multiple-choice test, for example, demands a higher level of reading skill than the text requires, students who are slow or poor readers are penalized because both knowledge of the material as well as advanced reading skill are required. Similarly, students who have little experience in expressing themselves through their writing, and students for whom English is a second language, are at a disadvantage when taking CR tests. Construct-irrelevant easiness factors include any characteristics that make the items easy to answer by students who have not learned the material. Multiple-choice tests, for example, are easier for students who are test wise (skilled in the tricks of such testing procedures), just as essay tests are easier for the glib and the garrulous. These factors contribute to invalidity because they result in students receiving higher scores than they deserve.

Most students have idiosyncratic personal theories about the validity of both SR and CR tests. Many, for example, believe that one type is a more valid indicator of their achievement than another. They may also question the validity of items that are broad, humorous, and unusual in some way, in particular when the relationship between an item and the course's purposes is not clear to them. Perceptions of validity are also substantially influenced by individual performance outcomes: Students who do well on a test are often convinced that the test was more valid than students who perform poorly. However, even when many students are disappointed by their grades, the postperformance review session will be more constructive when the relationship between the test's contents and the course objectives is patently obvious (Forsyth, 1986).

SELECTING THE MEASURE

The great debate in testing circles pits the multiple-choice test against the essay test. The "multiple-choicers" staunchly defend their method as most efficient and accurate, and they emphasize the importance of reliability and validity to support their claims. The "essayists" ridicule the trivia of multiple-choice tests, which, to them, amount to little more than "multiple-guess" tests. They claim that the essay is the supreme measure of college-level learning (Traub, 1993). Both types of measures, however, are valid, provided they are properly constructed and congruent with the course's learning objectives. CR items are appropriate when measuring specific skills (e.g., quality of written communication, facility in graphing data) or complex cognitive processes such as knowledge integration and creativity. SR items, in contrast, are most useful for assessing understanding of a topic (Haladyna, 1994, 1997). SR tests are also appropriate for assessing higher order cognitive processes, such as critical thinking and reasoning, provided they are well constructed. Rodriguez (2003) found that when skilled testers create SR and CR tests to measure the same content, the scores on the two types are highly correlated—even approaching unity, once corrections for the lower reliability of essay tests had been made. Also, empirical studies do not support claims that choice-type items, relative to explanation-type items, are easier (e.g., Ercikan et al., 1998), require fundamentally different cognitive processes (e.g., R. Bennett, Rock, & Wang, 1991), or result in different grade outcomes for students (Hickson, Reed, & Sander, 2012).

Multiple-Choice Tests

In nearly all respects, the role of question-asker is more enjoyable than the role of question-answerer. Those who ask the questions can pick and choose which topics, issues, and concepts they will explore with the answerer, who has little time to reflect on his or her response and even less power to control the kinds of questions being asked. Researchers who studied the emotions of people who ask questions and those who answer them discovered that answerers usually felt more "relief than pride," but after asking questions themselves people felt more confident of their own knowledge of the topic (Ross, Amabile, & Steinmetz, 1977, p. 493).

The question-asker role does have one major drawback, however: Questioners must develop the questions, and multiple-choice type items can be particularly challenging to draft. These types of items usually have two parts: (a) a stem and (b) a set of choices or alternatives. The stem is usually a question or an incomplete statement; one of the alternatives is considered the correct answer, and the others function as foils. A quiz may contain as few as five items, but full-fledged tests generally contain 30 to 50. Crummy multiple-choice items are easy to write. Take a definition from the textbook, state it as the stem of the item leaving out the term itself, and then list the term and several other terms and the question is written. Writing *effective* multiple-choice items, in contrast, takes time, effort, and the judicious application of item-writing rules. Haladyna and Downing (1989a, 1989b) identified these rules by reviewing the recommendations of 45 experts and by searching the published literature for studies that confirmed or disconfirmed the rules. They discovered that the majority of the rules had never been empirically tested and that the experts did not always agree in their recommendations. Still, the rules discussed in the sections that follow offer useful guides for professors as they develop their items (see also Haladyna & Rodriguez, 2014).

MEASURE THE FULL RANGE OF LEARNING OUTCOMES

A valid test will measure student's achievement of all of the course's learning goals. If the TOS includes knowledge outcomes, critical thinking, and application, then the exam should include a mix of recall and recognition questions, conceptually challenging items, and questions that require the application of learned knowledge. Items that assess higher order learning outcomes, such as analysis and synthesis, are difficult to write and require careful posttest analysis to check their validity, but including them on exams rewards students who have learned the course material thoroughly and thoughtfully. If you tell your students you want them to think, but then test them on rote memory or trivial items, they will stop thinking.

USE MULTIPLE BUT CREDIBLE ALTERNATIVES

The ideal multiple-choice test offers test-takers a choice between one correct answer and several plausible, attractive, but undeniably incorrect options. When students answer the question, those who have not achieved the designated learning objective will not be able to differentiate the correct answer from the incorrect ones, so their choices should be distributed relatively evenly across the foils. An unprepared student will, some small percentage of the time, choose the correct answer by chance, but on a multi-item test the influence of guessing will be negligible. Each of the offered distractors should be chosen by some of the students who miss the question. An obviously incorrect distractor—one that is humorous, strange, or improbable—weakens the validity of the question. Distractors should be wrong. When students review the test, their suspicion that the question unfairly included several correct alternatives should be easily disconfirmed by the hard evidence of their notes and the readings.

Effective alternatives in a multiple-choice item parallel the structure, tone, and length of the correct answer. If the correct answer includes 10 words, the distractors should include about that many. Good foils are also as specific as the correct answer, although in some cases a more technically phrased distractor will capture the interest of poorly prepared students. Statements that are factually correct but irrelevant to the issue posed by the item's stem also make effective foils.

Traditional wisdom on the number of distractors stresses the need to have at least three decoys so that students who must guess have only a 25% chance of getting the question correct. This logic, however, underestimates the odds of an individual repeatedly guessing correctly on item after item. Generating highly plausible distractors is also very difficult. Rodriguez (2005), in a meta-analytic review of the strengths and weaknesses of multiple distractors, concluded that two plausible distractors were sufficient in most cases, particularly when the additional distractors are not plausible.

DO NOT USE TRICK QUESTIONS DELIBERATELY

A valid but difficult question is not a "trick" question. Valid questions include distractors that students who have an inadequate understanding of the material will find appealing, so they "trick" only the students who have not reached your learning standards. True trick questions, in contrast, are items that mislead students who actually know the material, with the result that students who have accomplished the level of understanding specified in the instructional objective are seduced into selecting one of the distractors. Trick questions sometimes use unnecessarily complex wording, double negatives, and deliberate misspellings. They sometimes, too, use the cues on which test-wise students often rely when taking tests, such as "If you must guess, pick the longest answer," to mislead students needlessly.

KEEP THE STEM, RESPONSES, AND STRUCTURE SIMPLE

The KISS principle (Keep it Simple, Stupid) applies to multiple-choice items. The item should focus on a single concept, and the options should be similar to one another in terms of structure and content. The question should not unfairly favor superior readers or native speakers of English, so wordiness, flowery language, elaborate setups, and verbosity in general should be minimized. Haladyna (1994) argued that the "vocabulary should be simple enough for the weakest readers in the tested group" (p. 66). The simplicity principle also suggests that intricate, intertwined options, such as "both a and b" or "both a and e"—which are typical of advanced tests in some fields—should be avoided.

MATCH ITEM AND INSTRUCTIONAL COMPLEXITY

Test questions should not use language, terminology, or writing styles that differ too greatly from the language and difficulty level that have been established during class lectures, discussions, and readings. If, for example, you have introduced a concept informally in class, using everyday language, students who understand the concept many not recognize it when it appears in a more formal form on the exam. Similarly, professors who set the level of difficulty of their lecture so that even their less well-prepared students can understand the material or who use a lower level textbook should not then use test items written in technically specific language or ones that require a much more thorough understanding of the material than the treatment in class suggested.

FAVOR QUESTION OVER COMPLETION FORMATS

Haladyna and Downing (1989b) and Statman (1988) both recommended using question-type stems rather than completion-type stems. Students have been asked questions about the material throughout the class, so they spend less time deciphering the item's purpose and more time identifying the answer. With a question-type item, the bulk of the verbal material is concentrated in the stem, so the student knows what concept is being assessed without reading through the options. Completion items, Statman suggested, require more concentration because students iteratively review the fit between the stem and each option, so performance may diminish when they are distracted or anxious. Also, if a completion-type item is used, the blank should appear at the stem's end (or beginning) to reduce the amount of time the reader spends testing the fit between the stem and each option.

USE NEGATIONS, "ALL OF THE ABOVE," AND "NONE OF THE ABOVE" ITEMS SPARINGLY

Some material lends itself to the use of negatively worded questions. Theoretical models that include a number of components are ripe for such items, because students' memory of the entire set can be easily assessed by asking, "Which one of the following is NOT one of . . . ?" Most assessment writers, however, are leery of such items: They worry that students may overlook the question's negative frame and pick an option that matches the model, theory, or concept. They therefore suggest that such items be placed together in a special section of the test with a notice that the items are asking students to identify exceptions rather than confirmations. The word *not* should also be accentuated, in boldface type, for example, or all capital letters.

Testing experts are also suspicious of the usefulness of "none of the above" and "all of the above" as options. The "none of the above" option, when it is the correct answer, is selected by students who know that all the other options are incorrect *and* by students who are totally baffled by all of the issues and concepts noted in the distractors. "All of the above" options can also introduce error into the measurement process if students answer the question by picking an option before reading the "all of the above" option that occurs as choice "d" or "e." There are four methods one can use to prevent this possibility: (a) the test instructions should emphasize the importance of reading the entire question and all of the alternatives, (b) these items can all be collected into a specific section, (c) the phrase "all of the above" can be emphasized, or (d) the "all of the above" alternative can be shifted to the first choice by phrasing it as "all of the following are true."

MINIMIZE DISTRACTIONS

A funny distractor added to more serious options, or a question with a touch of humor, can relieve the tension associated with exams, but humor can lead to some not-so-funny outcomes. For example, if a small group of students who have moved through a multiple-choice test so rapidly that you wonder if they are even reading the questions reaches the humorous questions, their guffaws will disturb students who are progressing through the test at a slower pace. Some students, too, take umbrage at humorous items, for they are deadly serious about their performance and expect the professor to be just as businesslike (Renner & Renner, 1999). A cautious tester avoids funny questions, as well as other types of distracting materials, such as outlandish or famous names for people or places in examples (Rosenfeld & Anderson, 1985).

Distractions during the test process, including ones that are generated by the test itself, should be kept to a minimum. When the test mislabels the options (including, e.g., two option "b"s), misspells key terms, uses an incorrect word that escaped the detection of the spell-checker, or includes matches between the stems and the options that are grammatically clumsy, students must refocus their attention on the content of the question, and some cannot tolerate the increased cognitive load.

BREAK ANY RULE YOU WANT

Haladyna (1997) offered one final rule for test-writers to consider and possibly heed: "This rule . . . states that since most of these rules do not have the common ground of expert agreement and research, *break any rule you want*" (p. 92). This rule is a reminder that some perfectly good test questions do not adhere to the general rules of thumb for question writing. These rules, then, are in actuality general guidelines instead of inviolate principles, and in some cases a question-writer must break free of them in order to create the most effective question for measuring student learning.

A NOTE ON TEST BANKS

Many professors, instead of writing their own questions, rely on the publishers of textbooks to provide a test bank filled with items they can swap into their own tests. Some publishers will even generate a test for a professor, who then needs to duplicate only enough copies for his or her classes. Such test banks can be helpful, because they take away much of the pain of preparing items and can save enormous amounts of time. However, they have some shortcomings that must be considered:

- *Too factual and trivial.* Because fact-focused multiple-choice questions are easier to write than conceptually challenging items, they tend to make up the bulk of the items in the bank. Also, because of the large number of items needed, in many cases the authors of the banks generate questions about relatively trivial material in the chapter.
- *Low content validity.* The exclusive use of a test bank will violate most professors' TOS. Test banks typically do not evenly sample the contents of the text, because definitions and facts are over-sampled and complex relational material is undersampled. The banks do not, of course, include items pertaining to material that was covered only in class, so students who attend class regularly will notice that discrepancy between course content and test content.
- *Not pretested.* In most cases, the items have not been pretested. Test bank authors must sometimes generate the items during the relatively short space of time between the preparation of the manu-script in final form and its publication, so they rarely have the time, or the students they need, to check the items, so the items remain untried until you test them on your students.
- *Low difficulty and discriminability.* Test bank items tend to be too easy. When Scialfa, Legare, Wenger, and Dingley (2001) exam-ined the psychometric performance of more than 4,000 items from test banks written for an introductory course in psychology they discovered that approximately 70% of the students passed each item. Neither did the items discriminate well. When Scialfa et al. subtracted the proportion of high-scoring students who got the question correct from the proportion of low-scoring students who got the question correct, the average for this index was only .36. They concluded that 20% of the items were too flawed to use on a test. Some items can, however, be salvaged by revising them.
- *Poor construction.* Some test banks include finely crafted items composed by authors with years of experience in teaching and testing, but others are compiled by inexperienced authors who violate many of the rules of good item preparation. The first test bank I ever wrote was rife with flaws because I developed it when I was a first-year graduate student who taken my share of tests but never written one.
- *Low content validity.* Some test banks permit testers to sample items randomly from the bank. Such tests are more likely to be low in content validity unless the sampling considers the requirements of the TOS. Such methods also increase the likelihood that the answer for one item is "given away" by the stem of some other question because most banks contain multiple items for each concept.

▪ *Leakage of items.* Problems arise when different instructors have different procedures about releasing test bank items to their students after the test has been administered. A professor who reviews each item after its use and recycles the good ones each term will likely not want students to keep copies of the items because such copies are likely to be passed to incoming students. But if other professors in the same department who use the same textbook have their graduate teaching assistants just download 50 items from the publisher-supplied test bank for each exam, they will likely not worry about the dispersion of previously used items in the testing population. In some cases, too, the items have made their way onto the Internet, so technologically savvy students can track them down and review them before the test.

In sum, test banks should be used cautiously. They do not free instructors from their professional and ethical obligation to administer psychometrically sound tests to their students. Assessment guidelines do not include a special rule for professors that says "You should use appropriate measures, except when you can blame inadequate items on the text publisher or item-bank author." If the test bank is not adequate, then it should not be used to create a test.

Essay Tests

Like fall afternoon football games and fraternity parties, the essay test is a classic element of the traditional college experience. Students dread, but expect to take, essay tests at various points during their academic career. Given the constraints of time, topic, and process, such tests may not be the best way to assess students' writing skill, but they are excellent means of measuring higher order thinking skills, course content, and facility in the application of course concepts. Also, the writing that essay tests require, even if constrained, allows "students to focus intensely on writing for a limited period of time and, if the question draws out the creativity of at least some students, can elicit some very good writing indeed" (White, 1995, p. 36).

TYPES OF ESSAY TESTS

Essay tests come in two basic varieties: (a) extended response (ER) and (b) restricted response (RR). These two categories, however, are fuzzy sets rather than discrete classes because they are based on variations in essays along such continua as breadth, restrictedness, writing demands, and higher order cognitive demand. An ER asks students a question that is sufficiently general that they must interpret the meaning of the question, organize their thoughts on the matter, and then present those thoughts in appropriate detail. ERs provide few hints about the direction the essay should take, and they require a command of the language as well as the content. An RR requires a more specific answer; the question gives students more directions about the type of information they should provide or skill they should demonstrate, and so the need to plan, organize, and deftly execute the writing is reduced.

Consider, for example, a professor who uses an essay test to measure students' knowledge of the psychological and physiological mechanisms that govern food intake (e.g., Woods, Schwartz, Baskin, & Seeley, 2000). If she uses an ER type item, she may simply phrase it as, "Discuss the psychological, neurological, and hormonal factors that combine to regulate food intake." Or, if she trusts her students to understand the need to demonstrate their knowledge despite the vagueness of the question asked, she might just ask, "Why do people eat?" She may, however, prefer to use an RR item to restrict the variety of responses, such as in the following example item:

Humans need to take in sufficient quantities of food to offset the energy spent during daily activities.

  a. Describe the process of energy homeostasis as it would occur during a typical 24-hour period.
  b. What role does the liver play in this process?
  c. Critique the glucose monitoring model of hunger and contrast it with an explanation that stresses the importance of environmental stimuli.
  d. Discuss the impact of adipose mass on energy homeostasis, and extend your analysis to outline a weight-regulation program that is consistent with studies of adipose-signaling processes.

Both types of questions in these examples demand higher order thinking, but the ER requires more original and critical thinking than the RR. The RR, however, clarifies the topics that must be covered, decreases the amount of time students will need to generate an answer (and thereby frees up time that can be used for answering additional test questions), and simplifies the grading of the responses. Some professors further clarify their expectations by telling students how many points each component of the RR item is worth in determining the overall grade.

SUGGESTIONS FOR WRITING ESSAY TESTS

As with multiple-choice items, superficial essay questions are easy to write. You could ask students to generate a list, such as, "What are the six types of outcomes specified in Bloom's taxonomy?" or you could ask a very general question, such as, "Summarize and identify the problems that limit group-based student learning activities." Writing *effective* essay items, in contrast, takes time and effort. Essay tests require fewer questions, but each one must be well-crafted.

Use Essays to Measure Higher Order Outcomes

Essays are ideal tools for measuring higher order learning outcomes so, given the amount of time they take to grade, they should be used for that purpose. They should not, therefore, ask students to recall information or define terms but instead to think critically about issues, apply their knowledge of course concepts to specific issues, identify possible solutions to problems, express their ideas in their own words, and explore their own position on controversial issues. Words such as *analyze, apply, appraise, compare and contrast, create, critique, demonstrate, develop, discuss, formulate, gauge, evaluate, estimate, integrate, judge, rate, relate, review,* and *use* signal a better fit between an item's form and its assessment function than such words as *define, describe, identify, list, recall,* or *repeat.*

Align the Questions With Course Objectives

One student, asked to "evaluate the Yale group's theory of persuasion," wrote "I found it unconvincing." Then there was the student, when asked the question, "Why?" on his philosophy test, answered only "Why not?" And the physics student who answered the question "How would you discover the height of a tall apartment building using a barometer?" with "I would find the building superintendent and say, 'I'll give you this swell barometer if you will tell me the exact height of the building.'" Good answers, yes, but ones that did not demonstrate students' achievement of the course objectives.

You can minimize the possibility of receiving such answers by wording items carefully so that students cannot satisfy them with any odd consortium of ideas they muster on the fly. Items should pertain to the course's instructional objectives, or at least students must know that their answers should pertain to those objectives. Assessment experts therefore recommend that if wide-open, unrestricted essay questions are asked, the instructions on the test should remind students that, to receive credit, their answers must demonstrate an understanding of the course material. The phrasing of vague, ill-defined essay questions can also be honed by providing a stimulus for students to react to in their answer.

Clarify Procedures and Standards

Some students perform poorly on essay tests, not from a lack of knowledge of the issues addressed by the question but from a lack of knowledge about essays themselves. Therefore, instead of assuming that everyone has been trained by some previous professor in the elements of writing an essay, review with your students the basic elements of a good essay (Hairston, Ruszkiewicz, & Friend, 1999, p. 160):

- A clear thesis statement in the first paragraph or, better yet, in the very first sentence. Do not worry about crafting a dramatic introduction; there isn't time.
- Logical organization with a single key idea developed in each paragraph and with clear transitions between points.
- Adequate support and evidence for each point, drawn from course readings and lectures.
- Your own views or analysis when the question asks for them. Remember, though, to justify your ideas with evidence and support.
- A conclusion that ties together main points and summarizes their importance, even if you have time for only a sentence or two.
- Clear prose free of major grammatical and mechanical errors.

Students should also be informed about time and page limits and the procedures that you plan to use in grading their essays.

Require Students to Answer the Same Questions

Many instructors give students the option of selecting which items they will answer on the essay test. They may, for example, ask four ER items but let students select which two they will answer during the 50-minute testing period. Another instructor may ask 12 RR items and let students select which 10 they will answer. A choice of questions protects students from the grade-fatal consequences that occur when they cannot answer, even partially, an essay question that comprises 10% to 50% of their grade. A choice among items functions as a kind of mini-portfolio, in which students can control the work that they present for grading. This method may also reduce their pretest anxiety by limiting the chance that a topic overlooked during their preparation will doom them to failure. Providing students a choice of which questions to answer also allows the instructor to ask questions that probe for more specific learning outcomes.

Psychometrically speaking, however, this practice limits the validity of the assessment. The grades are based on different, nonparallel forms, so score-based comparisons can no longer be drawn among students (Wang, Wainer, & Thissen, 1995). The practice also undermines the content validity of the measure. Essay tests themselves tend to be lower in content validity, and providing options lowers that validity further. Students who realize that they have a choice may also be less thorough in their preparation, choosing to omit an entire topic from review because they know they can side-step it on the test. The only exception to the general recommendation against letting students make choices is when the essay test has a large writing-skill component. In such cases, when the students' ability to express themselves eloquently will have a large impact on their grade, then perhaps they should be able to choose a topic that excites their creative muse.

Many professors deal with the problem of gaps in students' preparation causing irreparable harm to their score by giving students a set of possible essay questions in advance of the test day. The actual test will contain some, but not all, of the questions, and students will not be able to use any previously prepared materials during the test. Such methods may encourage more thorough preparation and the formation of collaborative learning cells if students split up the questions and assign them to specific individuals for thorough review.

Take-Home, Online, and Open-Book Essays

When time is limited and the questions asked are numerous and complex, the essay test that is supposed to be a power test becomes a speed test. Converting the exercise into a take-home or online test addresses this problem, but it raises other difficulties. On the one hand, essays completed outside of the constrictions of the classroom may stimulate learning. The process of putting into words answers to complex questions often improves comprehension, and this process will be far more profound when it takes place at a slower pace as students work on the items using text, lecture, and library materials. When Onifade, Nabangi, and Trigg (1998) compared the final exam scores of students who had previously taken a series of take-home quizzes with those of students who had taken the same quizzes in the classroom, they discovered the students who took at-home quizzes outperformed those who took the quizzes in class. Take-home tests may also have more external validity, in that the testing conditions more closely approximate the actual work conditions students will confront in non-educational settings. As Walvoord (1982) pointed out, essays written in class are at best first drafts only. Students also report experiencing less anxiety about their tests when they know that they can decide when to take them (e.g., Weber, McBee, & Krebs, 1983).

Take-home tests have limitations, however. R. Marsh (1984) found that his students did not study as much for take-home tests than they did for in-class exams, and this lack of preparation may undo any gains in learning that the take-home format stimulates. Take-home and online test scores may also be distorted by cheating. Onifade and his colleagues, for example, found that students tend to collaborate with other students on such essays even when the instructions for the test explicitly forbid such group efforts (Onifade, Nabangi, Reynolds, & Allen, 2000).

Allowing students to use the text and other course materials during the exam—the so-called open-book test—also involves benefits and costs. An open-book exam confirms the test's emphasis on higher order learning skills and comprehension by giving unrestricted access to the specific facts of the course. However, when students know they will be able to consult their materials, they may not study as diligently and, even more problematic, they may not use their materials appropriately during the test. As Boniface (1985) discovered, during open-book tests students who made more extensive use of materials generally got lower grades, and these students were the same ones who had lower scores on previous assessments. Some professors let students prepare a "study sheet" to use during the test but restricting them to, for example, an index card or a single page of notes. Research suggests, however, that the use of such study sheets neither increases students' diligence in preparing for the exam, nor provides much help to students during the test itself (Burns, 2014; Dickson & Bauer, 2008).

A Note on Time

Even when professors are committed to giving essay exams, their classes may be so large that they cannot act on their assessment principles. The feasibility of giving an essay exam depends on factors such as the grading skills and experience of the professor, the nature of the questions (ER or RR formats), and the type of grading rubrics used. In classes with 30 or more students, however, the time needed to grade a CR test becomes too great, in particular when papers must be graded in a fixed period of time. In small class of 10 or fewer, time favors the CR test, because the SR test takes longer to prepare. Once a class becomes too large (more than 50), however, professors should explore other ways of assessing students' ability to express themselves (e.g., writing assignments, projects).

SCORING ESSAY TESTS

Grading essay tests is similar to conducting a content analysis in which one assigns numeric identifiers to qualitative data. Just as coding procedures reduce the extent to which subjective impressions of the data determine that identification process, scoring rubrics reduce the impact of rater biases on the grades assigned to the essay. One general type of rubric, *analytic scoring*, specifies the elements that the answer must contain to receive maximum credit. These elements are derived from the points identified in one's response, in the case of an RR item, or from the points made in a model answer written by the grader or culled from the pool of essays generated by the class. An analytic scoring approach for a hypothetical question about energy homeostasis is provided in Table 5.1.

Instead of breaking the answer down into component parts or rating the essay on individual dimensions, a *holistic scoring* rubric assumes that the whole of the essay is greater than the sum of its parts. The scorer uses this procedure to assign the essay to one of a series of graded categories that range from low to high in quality. The number of categories generally corresponds to the university's grading system, such as 4 = A, 3 = B, 2 = C, 1 = D, and 0 = F, or just *pass/fail* in certain situations, and ideally the attributes of the typical essay in each category are described in a scoring key like that shown in Table 5.2.

Holistic scoring takes less time, in most cases, than analytic scoring, in particular when the essay responses are lengthy and the item is an unrestricted one. Such items are difficult to score using analytic methods because students' responses may be so diverse that required elements

TABLE 5.1

Example of an Analytic Scoring Rubric for a Restricted Essay Item Dealing With Hunger and Food Intake

Item	Points	Elements of successful answer
1. Describe the process of energy homeostasis as it would occur during a typical 24-hour period.	3	▪ Defines the concept of homeostasis as it applies to fluctuations in energy levels from high to low in relationship to activity, ambient temperature ▪ Notes that stored food reserves provide energy for processes, with intake of food monitored and regulated by neural, hormonal, and biological mechanisms
2. What role does the liver play in this process?	2	▪ Summarizes briefly Laghans's (1996) work that suggests that when the liver detects too low a level of usable, energy-producing fat, it signals the decline to the brain via the vagus nerves
3. Critique the glucose-monitoring model of hunger and contrast it with an explanation that stresses the importance of environmental stimuli.	4	▪ Describes the concept of glucose monitoring ▪ Notes weakness of the model (e.g., too slow to adjust, humans eat at fixed times independent of blood glucose levels) ▪ Summarizes evidence supporting the concept of cue-dependent food consumption
4. Discuss the impact of adipose mass on energy homeostasis, and extend your analysis to outline a weight-regulation program that is consistent with studies of adipose-signaling processes.	6	▪ Discusses the notion of a set-point and the implications of adiposity levels over time ▪ Describes a diet program that includes changes in activity level, reconditioning of responses to food-related cues, and administration of drugs that control food intake processes

TABLE 5.2

Example of a Holistic Analytic Scoring Rubric for a Restricted Essay Item Dealing With Hunger and Food Intake

Characteristic	Grade
Elaborates extensively in answering all the elements of item. Demonstrates clear and consistent use of the language, offers examples when relevant, or uses citations appropriately to support theoretical points with empirical evidence. The essay is unified and coherent, and conveys information in a precise, lively, or original way. The mechanics, spelling, and grammar are superior.	4
Develops ideas efficiently, answering at least generally all the elements of the item clearly and concisely. The answers indicate that the material is clearly understood, and in several cases additional examples or material are used to support arguments. Errors in understanding are minimal, although in some cases details and implications are not presented. The writing is above average in quality, showing some energy or originality, and mechanics are not problematic.	3
Answers the basic question asked but does so without providing extra detail, depth, or analysis. The basic issues appear to be understood, but the answer rarely takes material beyond the descriptive level and/or relies heavily on the wording used in the text, readings, notes, or item itself. The organization is clear enough to follow without difficulty, although there are a number of errors in mechanics, spelling, and so forth.	2
Offers some material relevant to the item, but the content is sparse and the answer itself is very short. The answers are vague or incomplete, and/or errors suggest that portions of the content are not clearly understood. Some key points are omitted, and much of the analysis deals only with generalities. The response is not well organized, with little flow from one idea to the next. No citations are given to support the points made, and very rarely is evidence used to buttress a theoretical point. The mechanics are poor in places.	1
Fails to indicate that the author understands the issues. Very little information is presented, the answer is too short, and/or errors in interpretation outnumber correct interpretations. The writing is difficult to follow and contains severe composition errors.	0

cannot be specified in advance. Analytic scoring, which narrows the criteria to be used, is likely to be more reliable and valid, in particular because inconsistencies in the application of standards across students can be quickly detected and corrected.

Regardless of type of scoring system is used, to minimize scorer biases and increase validity one should

- prepare a scoring rubric or a model solution,
- read over a sample of the answers before beginning to grade the tests,
- mask the students' identities,
- grade only one item at a time (grade all Item 1s, then all 2s, etc.),

- avoid contaminating evaluations of subsequent questions by masking scores during the grading process (e.g., record scores on a separate sheet of paper),
- grade (if possible) each item at a single sitting,
- re-grade a sample of the papers as needed to prevent rater drift,
- vary the order of the grading by shuffling papers before scoring the next item, and
- resist the temptation to let style and writing quality influence the grading process.

Ideally, too, students should be provided with some kind of feedback—in addition to a grade or the analytic-rubric's points—about the quality of their work.

Test Analysis

Psychologist Jane Loevinger (1998, p. 347) described her years of work devising a test of ego development as a "life sentence" because she created, administered, tested, and revised the instrument over and over in what seemed to be an unending iterative process with no parole in sight. Similarly, professors will spend their entire academic careers constructing, analyzing, and revising their tests. Because each new class offers fresh insights into the course's material, the tests must be adapted to include new items pertaining to that material.

GENERAL REVIEW

In the best of all possible worlds, tests and final exams are written weeks before they are to be given, with ample time for the departmental staff to desktop publish them and duplicate the number of copies needed. In reality, of course, deadlines creep up and tests are generated at the last minute, leaving little time to catch errors, correct formats, or even carry out a thoughtful review of the questions. But professors who are giving a test in a new area, with items they have never used before, should leave time to carefully review the test before it is duplicated and administered. They should also seek out colleagues' comments, if time allows. A fresh set of eyes often can spot errors and limitations that escaped the test developer's review, and seasoned colleagues can use prior experiences in teaching the course to catch problems. Even this process, though, may need to be structured to increase its usefulness. Because colleagues are sometimes reluctant to comment negatively, or the request gets lost in the mountain of other to-be-done tasks, ask them specific questions about the exam, such as the following:

- Given your experience with the class and the unit the test covers, does the test cover the content adequately?
- Is the balance between fact-oriented questions and higher order, conceptual questions about right?
- Would you flag the five most problematic items on the test (ones that seem too picky, poorly worded, trick questions, etc.) and annotate them as needed?
- Is the test too easy or too difficult? Are any specific items too difficult to include? Were you uncertain of the answer to any of the items?
- Will students have enough time to complete the test?
- Does the test match up well with the usual types of assessment methods used in the department?
- Does the test seem to be a fair one?
- Will any phrases or wordings irritate or be more difficult for individuals from various ethnic, gender, and racial groups?
- Would you please mark any typos or errors that I overlooked in my own proofreading?
- Would you please make editorial suggestions or reword as needed?

ANALYSIS OF SELECTED-RESPONSE TESTS

The accurate evaluation of a test's reliability and validity requires data, and so test developers must conduct their work postmortem (as it were). And because even the most skilled question-writers sometimes generate items that fail to perform as they are designed, a test analysis is required whenever new items are used or old items are administered to populations of students unlike those tested in the past. Such an analysis generally begins with a review of descriptive statistics and reliability before the more conceptually intriguing question of validity and item discrimination is addressed. This review is accomplished far more easily if the test is administered online, in particular if your course software provides test-analysis tools.

Descriptive Statistics

Descriptive statistics provide an overall indication of how well students performed on the test and serve as indicators of any unrecognized instructional problems. Consider, as an example, a test covering five basic topics with eight to12 items written per topic and each item worth 2 points (so a score can range from 0 to 100). When administered to 275 students, the mean score on the test was 68.47 and the mode and median were both 68. The standard deviation was 14.84, and scores ranged from 36 to 100. The convergence of the mean, mode, and the median at 68 suggests that the scores are normally distributed, but the kurtosis (deviation from standard normal distribution) of −.82 indicates a slight flattening of the distribution. Inspection of the frequencies (which are presented in Table 6.1 in this volume) also reveals a negative skew (−.12) caused by the relatively larger number of low scores.

Reliability

Most estimates of reliability use internal consistency as an indicator of stability. In the split–half procedure, for example, one divides the test in half (usually combining odd- and even-numbered items instead of the first half of the items and the second half) and then correlates the two halves. This index underestimates reliability because reliability is positively associated with length, so a correction factor (Spearman–Brown) is often applied to correct this estimate. The Kuder–Richardson formula and Cronbach's alpha offer other ways to calculate reliability. The Cronbach's alpha coefficient for the sample test was .83, which is considered adequate, although not that impressive given the large number of items on the test and the range of students' scores.

Item Analysis

The heart of a test evaluation is the analysis of each question's performance as an indicator of student achievement. Test developers craft items to discriminate between students who have achieved an important instructional objective and those who have not, but items do not always reach this standard. Some questions are so easy that incapable students answer them correctly, whereas others are so hard that not even the students who have mastered the objective answer them correctly. And some items are neither too hard nor too easy, yet they do not discriminate between the incapable and the capable. Many of the students who have mastered the material get such items wrong, and many of the students who have not prepared adequately answer them correctly.

Various indexes of item difficulty, or p, exist, but the most frequently used indicator is also the simplest: the proportion of students who answered the question correctly. A p of .50 means that half of the class responded correctly to the item. A p of 1.0 indicates that everyone answered the question correctly, and question with a p of .0 was never answered correctly. Psychometrically speaking, the ideal test question has a difficulty of .50 although, as Sechrest, Kihlstrom, and Bootzin (1999) noted, such a test may be too demoralizing for students. They recommend questioning any item with p above .80 or below .20, and stated that the average of p should be about .70. Such a test would yield an average score of about 70% correct.

Many different indexes of discrimination, or D score, have also been developed, but most are based on the assumed relationship between the individual item and the total score. These procedures assume that the total score, although possibly distorted by the inclusion of invalid items, is a reasonably accurate indicator of overall performance. Therefore, any individual item should predict, at least partially, the overall score: Most high scorers in the class should have answered it correctly, and those who performed poorly should have gotten it wrong. One can, therefore, calculate a D score by subtracting the proportion of high-scoring students who answered correctly from the proportion of low-scoring students who answered correctly. A scores of 1.0 would indicate maximum discrimination, and a value of .0 implies no discrimination, but a D score of −1.0 suggests the item has been coded incorrectly, because every high scorer missed it and every low scorer got it right.

In Table 5.3, I apply this basic logic to three questions from a hypothetical classroom test. First, the students are separated into three groups: (a) the top 25% of the scorers, (b) the middle 50%, and (c) the lower 25% (according to level of overall performance). Inspection of the far right column of the table reveals the key data needed to critique the items. For example, for Item 1, we see the desired decline in correct answering moving from the top-scoring students (71%) to the middle-range students (25%) to the lowest scoring students (13%). The table also provides the data needed to calculate the D score: .58. These numbers all suggest

TABLE 5.3

Item Statistics for Three Items That Vary in Difficulty and Discrimination

Level of overall performance	No. of students at each level who selected this alternative					Proportion who correctly answered the item
	A	B	C	D	E	
Item 1						
High (top quartile)	1	0	10	27	0	.71
Middle (middle two quartiles)	6	5	33	15	0	.25
Low (lowest quartile)	2	1	31	5	11	.13
Totals	9	6	74	47	1	.34
Item 2						
High (top quartile)	37	0	0	1	0	.97
Middle (middle two quartiles)	45	1	4	8	1	.76
Low (lowest quartile)	20	1	2	13	4	.50
Totals	102	2	6	22	5	.74
Item 3						
High (top quartile)	14	0	0	24	0	.63
Middle (middle two quartiles)	23	0	0	34	2	.58
Low (lowest quartile)	15	2	0	17	6	.43
Totals	52	2	0	75	8	.55

that Item 1 is a tough but valid one. Many students missed it (66%), but it discriminates well among students. Its D score is adequate but somewhat disappointing because of the number of high-scoring students who missed it. Note, too, that Option "b" was chosen rarely and that only one student in the class answered "e." This test item could be improved by editing it, but the large proportion of errors among high-performing students suggests that an instructional intervention is needed.

Conversely, the D score for Item 2 in Table 5.3 is lowered by the ease of the item ($p = .74$). Nearly all the high scorers answered the question correctly, and half of the low scorers did so as well. This item could be improved by checking the distractors for flaws in content and design. Distractor "b," for example, was not plausible. However, even a rarely chosen alternative is not necessarily a bad alternative. In some cases, distractors may be checks of very basic instructional objectives, so when students avoid them they are demonstrating mastery of these objectives. If the tester's goal is to maximally discriminate among students, foil "b" should be revised, but if the tester's goal is to measure students' achievement of course learning objectives, and students' aversion to distractor "b" provides evidence they have attained that goal, then it should be retained. The item statistics also confirm the usefulness of distractor "d."

The statistics in Table 5.3, however, offer a less rousing endorsement of Item 3. The item was difficult: Only 55% of the students answered it correctly, but many of those who missed it were the students who answered other questions correctly. The D score for this item is a dreary .20, and more than 90% of the choices were concentrated on only two of the alternatives. A test with too many questions like this one will not yield the information needed to fairly assign grades to students.

Dropping Items

In some cases, item analysis will indicate that an item performed so poorly that it should not be used in the assessment. Items with extremely low p scores—ones that 90% of the class missed, for example—are sometimes, but not always, candidates for deletion. If the instructor feels that the item measures a key, although obviously very challenging, aspect of the course and the question has a decent D score, then retaining it is completely appropriate. However, if inspection of the item's content suggests that the question was badly worded, focused on a trivial aspect of the course, or was a trick question, then a question missed by nearly the entire class should be dropped. A D score near .0—or, even worse, a negative D score (indicating that more of the low-scoring students answered it correctly than did the high-scoring students)—should trigger a careful inspection of the item's design and its possible elimination.

Dropping items, even when done with care, creates a number of procedural problems. If the question listed two alternatives that are arguably correct, then the tests should be rescored to give credit to those students who selected either option. But skipping a question altogether (e.g., basing grades on only 48 of the 50 questions on the test) is often viewed, with some justification, as unfair by the students who answered the faulty items correctly. A less preferable alternative involves simply adding the points the invalid items contributed to total scores to all students' tests, in effect changing the invalid items into bonus items. These procedures should be carried out before the tests are returned to students to reduce confusion.

These procedures can also be avoided (in all but the most extreme cases) by including several extra items on each exam. Just as some standardized tests include a few uncounted items that are examined for possible inclusion on future administrations, a class-based test can include extra items so that faulty items can be deleted without distorting the numerical requirements of the grading system.

Criterion Validity

Students' grades are typically based on several tests, rather than just one, as well as other types of classroom-based assessments: lab work, written assignments, attendance, participation in discussion, term papers, and so on. An examination of the intercorrelations among these various indices of achievement will help one note patterns of high and low correlations, providing evidence of concurrent and discriminant validity. If, for example, a professor administers three major exams in a class, he or she can examine the correlations among those test scores to determine whether they are appropriately related.

Power and Data Limitations

Just as the power of any research study depends on the number of individuals who participated, the usefulness of detailed statistical information about a test depends on the number of students who took it and the number of items on the test. Item analysis procedures are correlational techniques, so they must be interpreted cautiously when the sample size is low (fewer than 50). Most item analyses also assume that the test is a reliable one, and this assumption is not always borne out by the data. The classroom exam, even though it examines multiple topics, is assumed to be unidimensional: a single, unified scale instead of a collection of theoretically and empirically distinct subscales. If the reliability is low, this assumption is not justified, so the total scale score should not be used to create the known groups (high-performing and low-performing students) for the item analysis. Preliminary work may be needed to identify a subset of reliable and valid items, which can then be used to create the aggregates needed for the subsequent item analysis.

ANALYSIS OF CONSTRUCTED-RESPONSE TESTS

A detailed statistical analysis of a CR test is usually not appropriate. As I noted earlier, statistical exploration requires an adequate number of students and an adequate number of items, but essay tests generally contain few items, and they are usually not given in large classes. As a consequence, CR tests require a more qualitative rather than quantitative approach.

Rater Reliability

Essay tests cannot be dropped off at the campus testing center for machine scoring (yet); instead, they must be hand-graded by the professor or a well-trained and knowledgeable assistant, and these graders may not apply scoring standards consistently as they work their way through the essays. Even when they use a scoring rubric, they may drift in their application of this rubric over the course of the grading period. For example, after reading a particularly good essay, a scorer may think that the mediocre essay that follows is particularly weak. As a check for intrarater reliability, the raters should re-grade a sample of the essays and check for agreement in the two sets of scores. If the scores do not match, then the grading system should be revised and the entire set re-graded. If several individuals grade the exam, then interrater reliability should be checked because one grader may have applied a different set of standards than another. These variations will not be detected until scores are compared on a sample of the scores that both raters grade.

Item Analysis

CR items must pass the same standards as SR items. They must not be too difficult or too easy. They should discriminate between students who have reached the class's instructional objectives and those who have not. They should also be related to each other because scores on each item will be added together to yield a total score. Their success in reaching these standards can be checked by inspecting the spread of scores across items and students. The information needed to carry out the analysis is illustrated in Table 5.4, which contains hypothetical data from 10 students who took a 10-question test. Each entry in the matrix reflects the score, on a 4-point scale generated using a holistic rubric, of each student on each item (although the scorer gave one student a bonus point and another partial credit).

The information in Table 5.4 is only suggestive, given the small number of data points. That said, the mean on the exam was 28.8, or 72%, and the standard deviation was 7.2. Scores ranged from 16 (40%)

TABLE 5.4

Example of Score Distribution on a 40-Point Exam

Student	Item 1	2	3	4	5	6	7	8	9	10	Total points	%
Kellie	5	4	4	4	4	4	3	4	4	4	40	100.0
Hope	4	2	3	4	4	4	3	4	4	4	36	90
Felinta	3	4	3	3	4	4	3	4	4	4	36	90
Shauna	4	2	3	3	3	2	3	3	4	4	31	77.5
Aimee	4	3	3	3	4	2	1	2	3	4	29	72.5
Kelly	3	2	2	3	4	2	2	3	2	4	27	67.5
Joshua	3	0	3	3	3.5	3	2	1	2	4	24.5	61.3
James	2	2	3	2	1	2	3	2	3	4	24	60
Jennifer	1	0	4	2	1	2	3	4	3	4	24	60
Ian	1	1	2	1	2	0	2	3	2	2	16	40
Item *M*	3.0	2.0	3.0	2.8	3.1	2.5	2.5	3.0	3.1	3.9	28.8	72
Item *SD*	1.3	1.4	0.7	0.9	1.3	1.3	0.7	1.1	0.9	0.6	7.2	
p score	.70	.30	.80	.70	.70	.40	.60	.70	.70	.90		
D score	.60	.75	.40	.60	.60	.80	.60	.40	.60	.20		

Note. The *p* score is the percentage of students who received scores of 3 or 4. The *D* score for an item (discrimination) is estimated by subtracting the proportion of students who received overall scores of 0 or 1 (*D/F* range) from the proportion of students who received overall scores of 3 or 4 (*A/B* range).

to 40 (100%). If, for the sake of illustration, students are assigned a letter grade based on the percentage of points they earned, and these assignments are based on a simple 10% rule whereby 90%–100% = A, 80%–89% = B, and so on, then the distribution of grades would then be one F, four Ds, two Cs, no Bs, and three As. The difficulty of each item is indicated by the average of students' scores. For example, Item 2 was the most difficult one on the test (*M* = 2.0), whereas Item 10 was the easiest (*M* = 3.9). If a *p* score–like index is required, then the proportion of students who received scores in the 3 and 4 range could be calculated, yielding a *p* of .30 for Item 2 and a .90 for Item 10.

You can also calculate a D score–like discrimination index by subtracting the proportion of students who received overall scores of 0 or 1 (D/F grade range) from the proportion of students who received overall scores of 3 or 4 (A/B range). This index indicates that Item 2, despite its level of difficulty, discriminated well. One high-scoring student missed it, but so did all of the low-scoring students. The very easy Item 10, however, did not discriminate among students, so it should be reviewed and rewritten so that it contributes to the test's validity. The remaining items are adequate, given that no item was consistently missed by high-scoring students yet answered correctly by the students who got lower scores.

Testing Redux: Align Teaching With Testing

Tests, exams, and quizzes are not just academic rituals that are repeated with each class for old times' sake. A brilliant lecture, a deft discussion, a well-designed class project—any act of teaching—must be more than just well conceived and engaging; it must also result in learning. Professors' work is aspirational: designed to transform students in certain desired ways. Testing, however, is confirmational: A good test determines whether the professor's hoped for outcomes have been realized. Regardless of the testing method—grading essays, scoring multiple-choice tests, critiquing student portfolios, evaluating a presentation with a rubric, and so on—evidence is needed to confirm the link between what professors teach and what students learn.

Grading (and Aiding)
Helping Students Reach Their Learning Goals

6

rofessors are categorizers. We slot things into mental bins, automatically and inexorably; even our students cannot escape our relentless cataloguing. As we gather more and more data about each student we classify them on the basis of their performance and potential, distinguishing among those who struggle, those who are getting it, and those who are immune from our attempts to teach them. By the semester's end, our classification is reified in the form of a grade: Exceptional students receive As, good students get Bs, students doing satisfactory work get Cs, weak students receive Ds, and the worst students receive Fs. Of these, only the F label is acronymic: F stands for *Failure* (Schneider & Hutt, 2014).

These grades serve a variety of useful functions. Tests, and the grades they generate, are motivational. Most students, when asked what their primary goal is in taking a class, mention a specific grade or the completion of the course with a passing grade before they mention the material they will learn (Senko, Hulleman, & Harackiewicz, 2011). Students carry out

http://dx.doi.org/10.1037/14777-007
College Teaching: Practical Insights From the Science of Teaching and Learning, by D. R. Forsyth

the required work in a class to raise or maintain their GPA, rather than achieve nebulous learning goals. But most important of all, grades on tests, quizzes, and other assignments also function as feedback and thus help students calibrate their perceptions of their work. Educational systems are cybernetic: To function effectively, they require constant infusions of feedback, and grades provide that feedback.

Grades are also the gold standard for judging performance in the classroom. Verbal judgments, such as "Nice job," "Excellent work," or "Inadequate," are open to interpretation, but a letter grade is readily understood by professors, students, parents, and employers alike. A C represents average, middle-of-the-road work; Bs and Ds identify work that falls above or below this norm, respectively; and As and Fs are reserved for exceptionally good or bad work. Grades also legitimize the educational process itself. Just as laypersons are more impressed when such symptoms as difficulty sleeping, negative affect, self-blame, and low energy are labeled "depression" rather than "feeling blue," so too do stakeholders in the education process consider grades to be objective, meaningful ratings of student achievement. Parents, teachers, and employers question the value of an educational experience that is not graded (Pollio & Beck, 2000).

These benefits come with a cost, however. Grades are massive external rewards, so they shift the locus of students' motivations from the intrinsic side to the extrinsic side. Students who are intrinsically motivated "experience interest and enjoyment, they feel competent and self-determining, they perceive the locus of causality for their behavior to be internal, and in some instances they experience flow" (Deci & Ryan, 1985, p. 34). Students who are extrinsically motivated (sometimes saddled with the epithet *grade-grubbers*) value only the grade and the rewards it brings. When grades, rather than learning, become the goal, students sometimes feel as though they can negotiate for grades in the same way they might haggle for a better deal on a used car.

Grades fail as feedback mechanisms if they do not provide the kind of clarity students need to understand their performance (Hattie, 2009). When students check their posted grade and read "64%, D," all they know is they failed to learn one third of the material covered on the test, but they do not know which items gave them problems or how they can improve their scores in the future. Grades are, in essence, summative: They scale the quality of performance in terms of the success in reaching criteria or in terms of the quality of a student's performance relative to others. But students need formative evaluation: specific, useful, and focused information about strengths and weaknesses that they can use to guide their learning activities.

The value of grades as standards can also be questioned. Although As, Bs, Cs, Ds, and Fs are the Euros of higher education, these classifications are not equivalent across professors, courses, and universities. Because of grade inflation, a B average of the 1960s is not the same as a B average in the 2000s (Rojstaczer & Healy, 2012). Specific professors grade more leniently than others, just as some are more casual, calculating, consistent, or even careless than others. In many cases, grades are based not on how much the student learned but on altogether irrelevant criteria. Although college professors are not likely to use grades the way my sixth-grade teacher did—she would lower our grades in subjects that were most important to us if we challenged her authority in class—they sometimes let personal biases influence the grading process (Tabachnick, Keith-Spiegel, & Pope, 1991). This ambiguity means that the grades, because they are not determined wholly by objective factors, can unfairly classify people and their products. When students are given a grade of D or F, for example, these labels can leave them feeling inferior to other students, undermine their self-efficacy, and erode their motivation. Even professors can be influenced, in a negative way, when they learn that a student is a C− student rather than a B student. For example, a student who asked several penetrating questions in the first few weeks of class but earned a low grade on the first test may be deemed by a professor—fairly or not—as having transformed from a "curious seeker" into a "clueless underachiever."

Are these problems with grades so substantial that the question "Shall we get rid of grades?" should be answered in the affirmative? R. L. Ebel (1974) said no, arguing that professors can address these limitations of grading, in large part, simply by doing a better job grading students. Grading systems, whether intricate or simple, comparative or criterion based, quantitative or qualitative, or old-fashioned or high tech, must reliably connect specific grades to specific levels of achievement. *Educationally effective* grading systems provide students with the information they need to identify the causes of their good and bad performances as well as possible remedies should their performance be inadequate. Instead of just communicating to students that they have failed, an effective grading system should tell them why they failed and what they can do to avoid failure in the future.

Grading Systems

Some students seem to be convinced that their professors toss a dart at a target for each student on the roster, and only if the dart lands in the bull's-eye is an A awarded. Contrary to this myth, however, most professors carefully track student performances and use some sort of grading system to rate these performances. These grading systems, as systems, accept information about student performance, combine that information in ways that are specified by the rules of the system, and then generate grades as output. However, the rules of the system vary from professor to professor. Some use *criterion-referenced systems* (or task-referenced, absolute standards) that compare the student's performance to some benchmark. Others use *norm-referenced systems* (or group-referenced, relative grading, grade curving) that compare students to each other. Still others use systems that combine elements of criterion-referenced grading or norm-referenced grading (Brookhart & Nitko, 2015).

CRITERION-REFERENCED SYSTEMS

Consider a hypothetical example of a professor, Dr. Criter. After completing her instruction of a 3-week unit, she administers a 50-item test to her 275 students. The items are all deemed psychometrically adequate, so she calculates the percentage of questions each student answered correctly and charts the results as shown in Table 6.1. Before she returns the graded tests to the students, though, she must decide what grade to assign to each score. Is a score of 68% a C or D? Is an 88% an A or B? Which score is so low that the student should be given a failing grade?

If she uses a criterion-referenced method, she will base grades on preset standards that define the quality of performance that each grade designation—A, B, C, D, or F or, in some cases, pass/fail—requires. If, for example, she uses the *fixed-percentage method* with 10% cutoffs, her grading scale may allocate an A only to those students who answered at least 90% of the questions correctly. She then applies this standard for each lower grade, so that an score of 80%–89% earns a B, 70%–79% is give a C, and 60%–69% is assigned a D. Students who did not manage to answer 60% of the items correctly are given a grade of F. The distribution of grades, as Table 6.2 indicates, would then be 27% Fs, 23% Ds, 24% Cs, 17% Bs, and 9% As.

Dr. Criter uses criterion-reference grading because it bases students' grades on their personal accomplishments, independent of the performance of others in the class. If all of the students reach all of the course objectives that she measured on her exam, then every one of them can earn a high grade in her class. But should they all fail to reach her standards, then all will receive low grades. The criterion-referenced method also automates that ever-so-difficult decision—who will pass and who will fail—by providing clear standards for each grade. Dr. Criter can tell her students, in class and on the syllabus, precisely what scores they must earn to receive particular grades. Although students who earn grades such as 88%s or 89%s on exams may feel that they are "close enough" to the A criteria to deserve that grade—and they may carefully review their tests, searching for the points they need to reach the

TABLE 6.1

Example of a Score Distribution on a 100-Point Exam

Score	Frequency	%	Cumulative frequency	Cumulative %
36	2	0.73	2	0.73
38	2	0.73	4	1.45
40	3	1.09	7	2.55
42	3	1.09	10	3.64
44	7	2.55	17	6.18
46	7	2.55	24	8.73
48	10	3.64	34	12.36
50	13	4.73	47	17.09
52	8	2.91	55	20.00
54	6	2.18	61	22.18
56	5	1.82	66	24.00
58	8	2.91	74	26.91
60	9	3.27	83	30.18
62	16	5.82	99	36.00
64	11	4.00	110	40.00
66	8	2.91	118	42.91
68	20	7.27	138	50.18
70	12	4.36	150	54.55
72	15	5.45	165	60.00
74	12	4.36	177	64.36
76	12	4.36	189	68.73
78	16	5.82	205	74.55
80	8	2.91	213	77.45
82	8	2.91	221	80.36
84	12	4.36	233	84.73
86	7	2.55	240	87.27
88	12	4.36	252	91.64
90	7	2.55	259	94.18
92	7	2.55	266	96.73
94	4	1.45	270	98.18
96	2	0.73	272	98.91
98	2	0.73	274	99.64
100	1	0.36	275	100.00

criterion—Dr. Criter can stand firm against their entreaties, supported by her standards.

Criterion grading has its drawbacks. The method assumes that the items on the test measure the key learning objectives for the course. A score of, say, 90% is persuasive evidence that the student has mastered 90% of the course's objectives, but only when the test measures those objectives. If the assessment does not comprehensively sample the domain, then percentages are only proxies for a student's grasp of

Impact of Different Grading Methods on the Test Scores Shown in Table 6.1

Example	Criteria for A, B, C, D	Percent of students who earned each grade				
		A	B	C	D	F
10% As	90/80/70/60	9	17	24	23	27
15% Bs	85/70/55/40	15	35	28	21	1
20% Cs	90/80/60/50	9	17	48	14	12
Normed	88/74/60/50	13	27	33	15	12
Bell curved	98/83/53/38	1	19	60	19	1

the domain. Although the specificity of the percentage grades suggests that students' learning has been measured precisely, given the error in measurement, a score of 90% is only an estimate of actual mastery.

Criterion-grading systems also depend, fundamentally, on the boundaries for each grade, and in some cases only convention or habit can explain why a particular set of cutoffs is imposed on students. As indicated in Table 6.2, Dr. Criter's standard of 10% may be defensible given the difficulty of the material, the education level of the students, and the quality of the instruction, but it produces far more failures than the second example in Table 6.2, in which a more lenient 15% rule is used. And why are the intervals for each grade equal? The third example in Table 6.2 illustrates how a grading scale that expands the cutoff for Cs from 70%–79% to 60%–79% will also redefine the criteria for Ds and Fs. If Dr. Criter discovers that too many students fail when the criteria she set on the syllabus is used, she may find herself in the uncomfortable position of having to change her standards, which undermines one of the key strengths of criterion-referenced grading.

NORM-REFERENCED SYSTEMS

Consider a hypothetical second professor, Dr. Norm. He uses a norm-referenced approach that compares students to one another rather than to some preestablished criterion. Dr. Norm, like Dr. Criter, sets cutoffs for each type of grade, but he bases these cutoffs on the number of students who will qualify for each type of grade. Instead of assigning a grade of A to students who "learned most of the material presented in the course," Dr. Norm thinks an A should indicate students who "learned significantly more of the course material than the average student."

Dr. N scores the exam by ordering the students from the lowest scoring to the highest scoring (see Table 6.1) and sets his cutoffs on the basis of a relative standard. If he decides that approximately 15% of the class should receive As, 30% receive Bs, 30% Cs, 15% Ds, and 10% Fs, then he adjusts the cutoffs to create clusters of this size. This method, applied to the example test, yields the cutoffs shown in the fourth example of Table 6.2: 100%–88% is an A, 86%–74% is a B, 72%–60% is a C, 58%–50% is a D, and anything below 50% is an F. Even though the specific cutoffs can be determined only after the test because the distribution of grades depends on the difficulty of the test and the average skill level of the students who take it, the percentage of students in each grade category can (and should) be defined in advance of the testing.

Norm-referenced grading is sometimes described as "grading on a curve" because it is based on the distribution of grades within the population, and such distributions often display the characteristic bell-curve shape. But Dr. Norm's grades need not be normally distributed in order for him to use this method, and he does not have to base cutoffs on the standard deviation (*SD*, an index of dispersion) or the averages (distribution mean). If Dr. Norm did adjust the test according to a bell curve, then he might decide that all students whose grade falls within 1 *SD* of the mean should receive Cs; those whose grades are 1 *SD* above and below the means get Bs and Ds, respectively; and those whose grades fall within 2 *SD* above or below the mean should receive As and Fs, respectively. The cutoffs, as the last example ("bell curved") in Table 6.2 indicates, would therefore be 98, 83, 53, and 38. Dr. Norm may, however, increase the "curve" of this relatively stringent grading scheme because so few students qualify for A grades. He might, for example, set the interval for a C grade around 0.5 or 0.7 *SD* rather than 1 *SD* to decrease the size of the C range and increase the proportion of other grades.

Normative grading's greatest strength is its flexibility. Even when nearly all the students unexpectedly get very high or low scores, the test items have low reliability and validity, and the test is a poor indicator of the unit's learning objectives, norm-referenced methods offer a way of assigning grades by rewarding students who outperform their peers. Normative approaches also mesh well with students' natural tendency to evaluate themselves through comparison with others (Senko et al., 2011). Professors who do not use normative grading methods and insist that students need worry only about their ability to reach the criteria set for the course often find that students demand information about the mean, the score spread, and so on. As social comparison theory suggests, individuals spontaneously evaluate their own abilities and attitudes by comparing themselves to others, and the need for comparison data is particularly strong when people work in achievement-focused groups (Forsyth, 2000).

However, norm-referenced methods can be criticized for not basing grades on students' mastery of the material in the course. Most people, on hearing a student earned an A in a class, would assume that the student learned a prodigious amount in that course, but norm-referenced grading does not guarantee that interpretation. All that is known for certain is that the A student outperformed many others, but the entire class may have learned very little in an absolute sense. The method theoretically also requires that some students be given low grades, even if they learned a substantial proportion of the course material. Students who have the bad luck to end up in classes with a large proportion of high achievers will get lower scores than those who have the good luck to end up in classes with weaker students. Natural variations in the composition of the class may also require changing the cutoff levels for grades from class to class and from test to test. As K. E. Ebel (1988) suggested, when one teaches a course composed of excellent students, fairness dictates using smaller deviations from the mean when setting grade cutoffs. Similarly, the cutoffs for grades will need to be adjusted for each test because they tend to vary in degree in difficulty. A score of 88% may earn a student an A on Test 1, but if Test 2 is easier and more students perform well, an 88% becomes a B. Standards will also shift as the composition of the class changes over the course of the term. If students who are performing poorly drop out of the class after the first or second test, the overall level of ability of the class will increase accordingly, making it harder for students to distance themselves above the ever-increasing mean for the class.

Norm-referenced grading methods may motivate students as they struggle to outperform others in their class, but these methods will likely damp down peer-to-peer learning and collaboration. Kohn (1986), after examining the reward structures of most classrooms, concluded that many beliefs about competition—that it builds character or improves performance—are more myths than certain assurances. Ames (1987) similarly recommended excising all forms of competition from the college classroom by using criterion-based grading schemes (instead of norm-referenced schemes), by not posting grades and not grading on a curve, and by stressing the cooperative nature of learning.

Norm-referenced grading methods, in sum, are interpersonal rather than personal. Whereas criterion-referenced methods evaluate students relative to the course's learning goals, a norm-based approach evaluates them by comparing them to other students. Students who earn Ds or Fs in criterion-referenced classes are told, in essence, that they did not learn very much of the material covered on the test. The grades of D and F students in norm-based classes, in contrast, tell them that they are inferior to many of their peers.

VARIATIONS AND ISSUES IN GRADING

Many professors use hybrid systems to avoid the limitations of criterion- and norm-referenced grading systems. Some opt to reduce the evaluative impact of grades by grading on a pass–fail basis, taking into account students' progress during the term, or rewarding students who exert effort. Some of these variations, and other issues pertaining to grading, are considered in the following sections.

Curving Grades

Even though "grading on the curve" generally refers to the use of a norm-referenced approach, many students think that "curving" means adding points or softening designated cutoffs so that their grades are raised. When they ask, "Will you be curving the grades?" they generally want to hear answers such as, "Yes, I'm changing the curve so that an 85% will be enough for an A" rather than "Yes, the grades are curved such that 68% of the class will receive Cs."

Norm-referenced grades are always curved, but criterion-reference graders sometimes curve their grades when they discover that their test is so hard that very few students will get high grades. Faced with too many low scores, and recognizing that the scores may reflect problems with the test and their teaching instead of low ability on the part of their students, they abandon their commitment to their preset standards and fudge the scores by lowering the cutoffs or adding points to all students' grades. In some cases, a criterion-grader may revert to normative methods by considering the distribution of grades and adding the points needed to shift the distribution of scores upward so that a reasonable number of As and Bs result. They may, for example, feel that the distribution of grades for the test summarized in Table 6.2, in which half of the class received Ds and Fs, is too harsh and add points to limit the number of low grades. The number of points added might also be determined by the highest scorer's grade. If the best score in the class is only a 95%, then all students are given 5 percentage points so that the top score is then a perfect 100%. With this method, the top scorer is said to have "set the curve" for the class. A more subtle approach to curving involves adding points to offset items on the test that were too difficult (e.g., missed by 80% of the class or more) or were psychometrically inadequate.

Gap Grading

Some faculty modify their norm-referenced cutoffs to take advantage of natural breaks in the distribution of students' scores. Although they may have a general idea about how many As, Bs, Cs, Ds, and Fs they will give to students, they modify these percentages to maximize the distance between adjacent grade categories. They may, for example, initially decide that scores of 90 or more will be As because this cutoff gives 20% of the class an A grade. However, further inspection of the distribution of scores may reveal a gap just below this cutoff: Two students got 89%, but then the next highest score was an 86% earned by eight students. In such a case, the professor may drop the curve down so that the students who earned a grade of 89 receive an A as well.

Gap grading (or *gapping*), as this is called, serves one valuable purpose: It reduces the number of students in class who are on the borderline between grades (McMillan, 1997). These students, if they understand the fundamentals of psychological measurement, can reasonably argue that the assessment they have just taken is not so precise that their scores do not contain several points' worth of measurement error. The professor can argue that their score might overestimate their true score and so they deserve an even lower grade, but students almost always assume that the error goes in their favor rather than against them. Gapping, however, is very subjective and likely capitalizes on chance variations in grade distributions (Jacobs & Chase, 1992). Gaps are also rare in larger classes. The scores for the 250+-member class shown in Table 6.1, for example, reveal very few gaps, so this method of sculpting the class curve would not be very effective with these scores.

Grading by Growth

Davis (2009) described the issues that complicate grading methods that consider how much a student improves over the course of a semester. Such methods are norm referenced, but the norm is based on the individual student's average scores rather than a comparison to the class average. Students who show gains by the term's end are rewarded with better grades than students who have shown little improvement, or whose performance has declined. As Davis noted, such practices can result in unfair grades, in particular when students who earn the highest scores in the class on all tests get lower grades than students who start with low scores and end up with mediocre ones. Many professors, however, take growth into account by awarding bonus points to students who show steady improvement over the course of a semester.

Minimal and Developmental Objectives

Gronlund (1998) recommended using criterion-referenced grading methods when deciding who passes and who fails a course but then applying norm-referenced methods when assigning the grades of A, B, C, and D to those who pass. Gronlund based this recommendation on the distinction between minimal objectives and developmental objectives. *Minimal objectives* are ones that the student must complete in order to receive credit for having taken the course. To pass a course in statistics, for example, the student must be able to perform certain basic calculations and conduct a number of specific tests. These minimal requirements do not change relative to the capability of other students in the class because they represent the basic information students must know in order to take more advanced classes. *Developmental objectives*, in contrast, are typically higher order outcomes that some students, but not all, will be able to attain. Students' success in reaching these objectives will be determined by comparisons among students.

Pass–Fail and Mastery

In some cases, the five-category system of A, B, C, D, and F is collapsed into the dichotomy of *pass–fail*. This practice is often used in advanced courses, such as independent study projects or dissertation research, where students are expected to be self-motivated. Students at many universities can also choose to take some of their regular courses on a pass–fail basis. Pass–fail grading reduces the burden on the professor to evaluate critically the student's work, for the only question asked is "Should the student get credit for taking the course?" Pass–fail grading may also undo some of the damage that grades can do to students' intrinsic motivation. When students are not working toward a grade, they feel they are free to explore more controversial topics, carry out more creative and unusual projects, and enjoy learning for learning's sake. On the other hand, however, they may do only the minimal amount of work needed to pass the course, knowing that a pass produced by A-quality work is equal to a pass produced by D-quality work.

Mastery learning is, in some respects, a form of pass–fail grading. This approach to teaching assumes that students should not stop their studies until they have mastered the essential elements of the course. Instead of rewarding them with a C or D for learning only a portion of the required material, students should be given the resources and time they need to reach a basic level of achievement of all material. Students whose work exceeds these basic standards can receive special recognition in the form of a grade of A or B, but those who do not reach the level of competency required for credit receive no grade. Most PhD programs are mastery-oriented systems in which students work for an extended period of time to become subject matter experts. Review committees rarely say, "Time's up! Here is your PhD, but we are giving you a B– on your dissertation."

When tested against more traditional grading approaches, mastery methods have proven themselves to be more effective (e.g., Hattie, 2009). The method, however, is technically complicated to implement, in particular for college-level learners. It requires the continuing and highly precise assessment of learning outcomes; thus, it is best suited to courses that are content focused. The method is also highly individualized, and so it inevitably increases the amount of time needed for instruction. Preparing and grading a midterm and final take far less time than testing students' mastery of each unit during the semester and not permitting them to progress onward until they have reached a designated level of proficiency.

Some of these logistics are at least partially remediated when courses are taught online. Keller's (1968) personalized system of instruction, for example, is regaining popularity because its core elements—self-pacing, repeated assessment, peer review, and mastery—can be more easily implemented in online teaching. The online form of the personalized system of instruction, called *computer-assisted personalized system of instruction* (CAPSI), lets students progress at their own pace through online leaning modules but requires that students complete a module's assessment successfully before they continue to the next (Pear, Schnerch, Silva, Svenningsen, & Lambert, 2011). Svenningsen and Pear (2011) compared a traditional lecture-style class to a blended class that combined both lecture and CASPI instruction and found that both types of teaching were equally effective for promoting students' understanding of course content but that students who completed the CASPI activities scored higher on measures of critical thinking.

Extra Credit

Faculty are far from unified on the issue of extra credit. Opportunities for students to earn extra credit, because they are not based on criteria described in the syllabus or on a comparison of a student's performance to other students' achievements, step outside both criterion- and norm-referenced grading systems. Students view extra credit as a second chance to earn a good grade, but faculty worry that it can "encourage a lax or irresponsible attitude and that it is unfair when offered only to selected students" (Palladino, Hill, & Norcross, 1999, p. 57). Be advised, however, that in one survey of students' judgments about professor's policies, fully 22.6% maintained that the denial of any opportunity for extra credit, even if stated on the syllabus (e.g., "In no event and under no circumstances will any student be allowed to earn extra credit") was considered rarely or never appropriate. Moreover, if you do wilt and offer extra credit to a student crying in your office, know that the other students believe this opportunity should then be extended to all the other members of the class (Moen, Davies, & Dykstra, 2011).

Rewarding Effort

Students, more than faculty, believe in the idea of an "A for effort": that effort should be recognized and factored into the grading process. Zinn and her colleagues (2011) examined this expectation by asking professors and students to consider this situation:

> Edna, a student in a general-education class you teach, performed unsatisfactorily, failing to meet the minimum course requirements. At the same time, she put a great deal of effort into the course. What grade would you recommend the student receive? (paraphrased from p. 10)

Some professors, but not all, were swayed by Edna's plight; 65.5% gave her an F, 25.9% bumped her up to a D, and 8.6% suggested a grade of C would be appropriate. Students, in contrast, felt effort was far more important than did faculty: More than three quarters (76.1%) of the students recommend a grade of C or better, and a few even felt Edna deserved an A for effort. Although students recognized that accurately estimating Edna's effort would prove difficult, they felt that regular class attendance, office hour visits, and doing extra credit were all valid indicators of effort and so should influence grades. These findings suggest that when Edna complains, "But I put a great deal of effort into this class!" she may feel that she has said something that is relevant to the issue under discussion.

COMPUTING FINAL GRADES

Grades must be assigned after each test, homework, exercise, and project, as well as at the completion of the term. This final assignment of grades is the most important step in the grading process, but it is also the most complicated because it requires the creation of a composite score that accurately integrates all the scored assessments completed by the students. Although professors who give only midterm and final exams have a relatively easy time of it, those who use many different types of assessments, of varying complexity and importance, must integrate this information so that the final scores are consistent with their assessment plans. Computers, and the spreadsheet and grade book programs they support, make this task easier, but the process nonetheless requires checking the accuracy of records, aligning metrics if some assignments were given letter grades and others numeric grades, weighting the various activities appropriately, and calculating the composite score.

Giving Students Feedback

Grades are key cogs in the self-regulation/learning system. Few people can decide, using only their own good judgment, whether their achievements, their learning, or their teaching are superlative, complete, or noteworthy. Instead, most must compare their outcomes to official standards that define what is "correct," "successful," or "satisfactory" and then, if necessary, take steps to decrease the discrepancy between those standards and their outcomes. In the case of learning, these official standards are grades, which professors must relay to students so students can assess their performance, reset their goals, and possibly increase their effort. Grades serve as reality checks. Vast numbers of undergraduate students want to become physicians, lawyers, psychiatrists, scientists, and even professors, yet only a small proportion of them have the drive, the intellectual skills, and the self-control needed for success in the arduous training that will qualify them for those careers. Receiving a well-deserved C provides them with the feedback they need to reset their level of effort and/or set more achievable goals (Husman & Lens, 1999).

Giving students feedback is psychologically, interpersonally, and procedurally complicated, however. When the feedback is negative, students may need help coming to terms with their failure. They may, for example, prefer to blame a poor performance on the quality of the instruction they have received rather than on themselves, and such perceptions may prevent them from adjusting their studying to enhance their grades. Some students also need to be reassured that, even though they did not perform well on an exam, they should not abandon their quest to achieve a good grade in the class. Others, in contrast, may need to consider other options, such as withdrawing from the course before they fail it. Students should be informed of their performance as soon as possible, but this feedback process should be a discreet one that respects their privacy. Family Educational Rights and Privacy Act of 1974 regulations, for example, forbid posting of students' grades with their names or leaving their papers (graded or not) in a box outside your office.

PROVIDING SUMMATIVE FEEDBACK

Students seek, and sometimes even appreciate, detailed feedback about their specific strengths and weaknesses, but only after they are informed of their overall score and grade. Some, while dropping off their test, cannot help but ask what the answer was to a particularly bothersome item. Others gather in clusters outside the room, sharing opinions about specific items and the answers they gave. Some professors help their students quench their thirst for immediate feedback by letting them keep copies of the exam questions and providing them with solution sheets or sample answers. Others e-mail scores to students, post them in their learning management system (LMS; e.g., Blackboard, Moodle, Sakai), or just hand back papers in class. Online assessment usually obviates the need for these procedures, but when tests are given in paper-and-pencil format some means is needed to get students their scores.

Some professors prefer to discuss the test's characteristics, and provide students with their scores, during a post-exam review session. During this review, the instructor can present the class with general information about the reliability and validity of the exam, a histogram of the class's grades, and the connection between the items and the course objectives, and can review any problematic items that many students missed as well as items that the class mastered surprisingly well. These sessions must be handled carefully because reviewing a test with a class, en masse, can be an unpleasant experience for both the students and the professor. Tests are very important events in the lives of students, and a low score on one can trigger a complex of affective, cognitive, and behavioral reactions. Students who receive a score that is lower than they expected may question the validity of the score in general or of the items themselves. *Snipers*, the most rebellious cluster of student types identified by R. D. Mann and his colleagues (1970) in their analysis of student types in college classrooms, are particularly likely to express their displeasure during such sessions. Others may become very upset and angry about their grades and will display these emotional reactions openly in class. Schweighart Goss (1999) offered suggestions for dealing with such students, including meeting with them in private, allowing them to express concerns without challenging them, and responding professionally and unemotionally despite their hostile manner. Research on emotional reactions to assessments has suggested that such student reactions are normal ones, in particular when students set high standards for themselves and the grade is very discrepant from their usual level of performance (e.g., Forsyth & McMillan, 1981).

Exam review sessions generally go more smoothly if they focus squarely on summative feedback rather than formative feedback. The professor can ask and answer such questions as "How well did the class perform?" "Were any of the test questions too hard or too easy?" and "Did the test indicate that many of students in the class misunderstood some key concept, study, or finding?" but he or she would do well to avoid such questions from students as "On Question 12, why wasn't Option 'b' considered correct, too?" and "Did we ever cover that stuff that Question 45 asks about in class?" Instead of responding defensively or angrily to such pointed remarks, one should instead note that the available data confirm the validity of the test and that students with specific questions should raise them during office hours. Research also has indicated that the intensity of the emotional reaction will abate rapidly over time as students regain their composure, so a short cooling-off period between the time the feedback is given and any discussion of the feedback will dramatically reduce tension (Forsyth, 1986). Alternatively, when a portion of a class session is spent discussing the test, ban any requests for individualized, follow-up discussions for at least 24 hours. Tell students that they are welcome to discuss their grade during office hours or after class—and even require students with Ds and Fs to contact you—but ask them to wait 24 hours before they approach you.

PROVIDING FORMATIVE FEEDBACK

R. L. Ebel (1974) wrote, "Grades provide a concise summary of . . . a vast amount of specific detail. Often that summary is all that is wanted" (p. 2). However, students need to know more than just their percentage score and grade; they need to know which items they missed; why their essay answers were marked down; and, most important, to identify the learning objectives that their test indicates they have not yet mastered. They also need to understand the meaning of the score in terms of their overall expectations for the class. Posting students' grades is not the last step in the assessment process; providing them with feedback that helps them reach their learning goals is.

Test Review Sessions

Formative feedback must be tailored to the individual student, so these sessions must be conducted in small groups or one-on-one sessions. They generally have three components: (a) an *individual review* period, during which students work alone, reviewing the items they missed and comparing their solutions to the key; (b) a *tutorial review*, during which any questions the student missed and does not understand are discussed; and (c) a *diagnosis review*, which involves identifying any systematic types of errors the student made. Although general tendencies cannot always be identified, in some cases the pattern of students' errors will indicate that they missed mostly items that were covered only in the lecture or only in the textbook, items that required particular cognitive skills (e.g., applying course materials to novel examples), or particular types of items (e.g., analogy items, definition items).

If possible, these sessions should be delegated to teaching assistants, not because they are time consuming (they are), and not because they are unimportant elements of teaching (they are very valuable pedagogical tools), but because the sessions are often more effective when students meet with another student rather than their professor. Students who cannot bring themselves to confess their confusion about a topic that the professor has examined for 30 minutes in class can disclose their concerns more freely with a third party. Students who also want to use the session to merely ingratiate, manipulate, or irritate also take less pleasure and time in these machinations when the target is a teaching assistant rather than their professor.

Written Feedback on Essay Tests

Professors who use constructed-response (CR) tests—essays, short-answer questions, research papers (see Chapter 5, this volume)—can provide students with information about their work by sharing their grading rubric, but they should provide formative feedback as well. Some professors relay their comments to their students orally, during one-to-one or small group sessions, but others use the tried-and-true comments-in-the-margin technique or its more modern variant: commenting and editing with the tools in such programs as Word and Adobe Acrobat. As I noted in Chapter 3, these comments have more value as formative feedback if they are content focused rather than mechanics focused, specific rather than vague, constructive rather than bluntly critical, and heartening rather than discouraging. Professors, too, should be careful to not give too much negative feedback at one time. Students may claim they appreciate receiving detailed feedback, but not if it is too bluntly negative. Students respond more positively to extensive feedback if they have the opportunity to revise and resubmit the work (Ackerman & Gross, 2010).

Professors who use an LMS such as Blackboard or Moodle can use a variety of courseware tools to provide students with feedback. An LMS simplifies the basic task of letting students know their scores; there is no need to post grades on a wall in a classroom when they are posted in students' online gradebooks. Also, when tests are administered online, students can receive immediate feedback about their performance along with detailed explanations of questions they missed. Most LMSs provide excellent rubric tools as well, which can be used to both structure grading and provide students with explicit information about strengths and weaknesses. Some LMSs even allow professors to record comments directly from their laptop cameras or microphones, thereby personalizing the feedback process.

Challenges of the Score

Review sessions will often result in students challenging the validity of a particular item or the fairness of an essay's scoring. These challenges can be handled during a negotiation session with students, but Schweighart Goss (1999) and Whitford (1992) recommended using a more formal procedure to structure these disagreements. Schweighart Goss asked students to complete a form to identify the troublesome item and the basis for their challenge of it. She also informed students that she will reread any essay item that students feel was unfairly graded, but because she provides students with a written commentary on each question few chose this option. Whitford asked students who felt that a question had been unfairly scored to write a paragraph explaining why their choice deserved credit and bring their statement to him during office hours. Whitford noted that, in most cases, the students cannot generate a persuasive paragraph because their answer was, in fact, wrong. These students, by reviewing the material, relearn the concept correctly. A few students had a good argument to support their solution, and in these cases Whitford awarded them credit for their answer.

Grading Fairly

Students often assume that any low grade is an unfair one. Like most people, they do not believe that negative information is accurate, but they wholeheartedly accept the validity of positive feedback. The student who fails a test says, "What an ambiguous, invalid test." The student who received an A replies, "I thought it was an excellent, comprehensive exam" (Snyder, Shenkel, & Lowery, 1977; compare with Johnson, Cain, Falke, Hayman, & Perillo, 1985). College students often have been highly successful in academics in the past, so low grades often take them by surprise. Faced with an unexpected outcome, they tend to blame external factors, such as a substandard textbook or the professor's alleged ineptitude (Forsyth, Story, Kelley, & McMillan, 2009). Redding (1998) related the comment of one of his students who rejected the validity of his low score: "Remember that we are highly successful college students. . . . We do not need to be told how to write or be given low grades!" (p. 1227).

Student' reactions to their grades also depends on their perceptions of their professor's *interactional fairness*: the extent to which the professor's interactions with students are considered impartial, respectful, supportive, sincere, and appropriate. Faculty who extend special privileges to certain students, treat students rudely, show little concern when students experience problems, change key aspects of the course without warning or explanation, and act in sexually provocative ways are not considered to be interactionally fair teachers. Students' judgments also take into account their estimates of the professor's *procedural fairness* and *outcome fairness*. Professors who design valid tests, give appropriate amounts of work, and regularly give students feedback about their progress are considered to be fair in the procedural sense, whereas those faculty who base their grades on well-defined objective standards that are neither too difficult nor too easy are considered to be fair in the outcome sense. Whitley and his colleagues (Whitley, Perkins, Balogh, Keith-Speigel, & Wittig, 2000) offered additional suggestions to faculty who wish to maximize one, two, or all three of these forms of fairness in their teaching.

Helping Students Learn

Some students use highly effective methods in their studies, but others rely on strategies that are not consistent with basic principles of learning and cognition. Many students, for example, read too quickly, without actively processing the information in the text or integrating the new information with their initial conceptions. Some students have a predilection for massed practice: They are binge learners who immerse themselves in their studies only when tests and papers loom. They also rely on some methods, such as just rereading some parts of the materials and highlighting pertinent passages, that are more tried than true (Dunlosky, Rawson, Marsh, Nathan, & Willingham, 2013). Reteaching students the course's content during office hours and in study sessions may help them in the short term, but just as the old adage "Give a man a fish and you feed him for a day, but teach a man to fish and you feed him for a lifetime" suggests, helping students learn to learn may yield more lasting benefits.

DEVELOPING ACADEMIC SKILLS

Pastorino (1999) recommended taking into account students' backgrounds before delving too deeply into the analysis of their academic shortcomings. Struggling graduate students, for example, likely have the basic academic skills needed for success, so their difficulties must spring from some other source. Similarly, the problems of transfer students, nontraditional students, students who speak English as a second language, and students who are working full- and part-time jobs may not be caused by their lack of motivation, poor study habits, or the quality of their academic preparation but by life circumstances that are negatively affecting their academic work. However, many new college students are hindered by a basic lack of academic skills. They thought they knew how to take notes, read a text, write papers, and prepare for an exam, but in reality their skill levels are not sufficient for college-level work. So, in addition to teaching them the course's content, one must also teach them the metacognitive skills they need to monitor their performance, improve their learning, and prepare for tests.

Judgments of Learning

Students' judgments of learning are often poorly calibrated. In many cases, people can, through careful monitoring and self-testing, accurately determine whether they are ready for an upcoming test or presentation. A number of factors, however—including anxiety, overconfidence, and self-serving attributional biases—can cause students who have not yet mastered material to think they have. Like most people, students tend to assume they are above average in their learning. This effect is sometimes referred to as the *Lake Wobegon effect*, after Garrison Keillor's fictitious Lake Wobegon, where "all the women are strong, all the men are good-looking, and all the children are above average." Dunning, Johnson, Ehrlinger, and Kruger (2003) documented this tendency by asking students who had just finished an exam to estimate their score on the test relative to the other students taking the exam. When they separated the students into four different groups based on actual performance, they discovered the high scorers were quite accurate, but low scorers erred in their judgments: They estimated their score to be in the middle range C (73%), when in fact they had failed, answering, on average, only 55% of the items correctly. Because this metacognitive glitch can prompt them to reduce their studying when they need to remain on task, students should avoid this error by self-quizzing as they study. They can also capitalize on the *delayed judgment-of-learning effect*, whereby inserting a delay between the completion of studying and estimating one's learning reliably improves accuracy (Rhodes & Tauber, 2011).

Study Skills

Skilled students encounter few surprises when they take tests. They have such a firm grasp on the material the test covers that they could list, on a blank sheet of paper, all the core outcomes (e.g., major headings, subheadings, key theorists, names, concepts, central points) without prompting. Realizing that their professor will eventually ask them questions about the material they are studying, they generate their own sample test questions as they study. If permitted, they make use of questions asked on their professor's old exams, and they take all the practice quizzes they can. They also adapt their preparations to fit the type of test they will be taking. If the test will use a selected-response format such as multiple choice, they review all of the material thoroughly, being careful to not overlook any important topic. If the test will use a CR format, such as essays, they worry less about comprehensiveness and more about depth of understanding.

Many students, however, do not know how to study. As Gardiner (1998) discovered when he surveyed nearly 800 college students, only 14% reported having received any formal instruction on studying. As a consequence, their idea of studying may amount to little more than skimming the textbook and reviewing their notes the night before the exam. Similarly, students in online courses reported that they appreciated the many study tools available to them—practice quizzes, annotation tools, threaded discussions, and so on—but few of them actually used these support tools to facilitate their learning (Winters, Greene, & Costich, 2008). Students may need to be explicitly told to actively engage the material by using these steps:

- *Setting goals.* When studying a unit of material, students should have clear goals about the major topics that will be covered. They should complete required readings before class and review their understanding of what they have read.
- *Preparing materials.* Students should spend a significant portion of their time preparing the materials and resources they will use in their review sessions. These materials should include personalized outlines of the texts and lectures, copies of any instructional materials, detailed notes from lectures, and so on.
- *Reviewing.* Students frequently complain "I read the book and came to class!" yet could not remember the information later, when taking the exam. They failed to consolidate the material by organizing the information they extracted from the textbook and lecture. They should be encouraged to develop a systematic approach to reviewing lecture and text material and to use their approach consistently.
- *Practicing.* Students should be told about the *spacing effect*—one of the oldest empirically verified recommendations for improving memory (Dempster, 1988). The spacing effect favors multiple review sessions rather than a few and mixing in multiple subjects and topics during these many sessions rather than concentrating on only one subject. If, for example, students use flash cards, they should use large rather than small stacks of cards. Even though students feel they are learning more if they go through a small stack rapidly, larger stacks create more spacing and significantly improve learning (Kornell, 2009).
- *Self-testing.* Study methods that help students practice retrieving information from their memories are more effective than recognition or review methods. Self-testing, for example, has proven to be a reliable aid to learning across students, settings, and a range of outcomes (e.g., recall, recognition, problem solving, argument development, essay writing). Elaborative interrogation and self-explanation, two variants of self-testing, also are effective methods of enhancing memory (Dunlosky et al., 2013).

Avoiding Ineffective Study Methods

Many students study diligently, but their hard work yields little in the way of learning gain because they use ineffective methods. Late-night study sessions, study groups, highlighting, and rereading, and rehearsal are favorite study methods, but the scientific evidence argues against them.

Cramming

Students have apparently always crammed for tests. Back in 1899, William James opined,

> Cramming seeks to stamp things in by intense application immediately before the ordeal. But a thing thus learned can form but few associations. On the other hand, the same thing recurring on different days, in different contexts, read, recited on, referred to again and again, related to other things and reviewed, gets well-wrought into the mental structure. (pp. 102–103)

Students tend to engage in cramming (aka "massed practice") because they do not begin their studies until just before a quiz or test. If they read regularly, they would be less likely to have to cram.

Study Groups

Students often join with others to form study groups, but these assemblages are not always efficient or effective. Some groups enhance members' motivation and help students stay focused on their academic goals (Finn & Rock, 1997). If students are assigned specific topics that they will teach to others, the student doing the teaching will likely benefit (Nestojko, Bui, Kornell, Bjork, 2014). Study groups are, however, groups, and they may therefore suffer from the problems common to many collaboratives. For example, the members may not prepare diligently for the study sessions and may spend too much time on off-task discussions. Although in some cases one of the students may lead the group by setting an agenda, clarifying responsibilities, and regulating the group's meetings, the group may try to complete its work without a leader and so never reach a high level of efficiency (Forsyth, 2014).

Highlighting and Rereading

Many students, when asked how they study, report that they use highlighters, underline text passages, or make notes in margins. Students like seeing their books all colorized, and research suggests that highlighting helps students identify facts and terms. However, highlighting does less to promote the connection of ideas, even when students are trained to highlight with more care (Dunlosky et al., 2013). A small subset of students do benefit from highlighting but, oddly enough, those who have the most confidence in the method's effectiveness tend to benefit the least from it (Yue, Storm, Kornell, & Bjork, 2015).

Rehearsal

Repeating a phrase, definition, or list repeatedly is an effective method of keeping the information accessible in working memory, but it does little to ensure that the information will make its way into long-term memory. Repetition, with spacing, and interleaved with other content, is a far more effective way to remember things (Dunlosky et al., 2013).

Time on Task

Even though those individuals who sit in our classes are usually called *students*, they do not spend much time actually studying. When surveyed, students report spending less than 2 hours in preparation for each hour in class, so their weekly investment in each class they take is about 6 hours—and that's counting class time. Seniors spend no more time preparing for classes than do first-year students, although the quality of their preparation may be superior (National Survey of Student Engagement, 2013).

Unfortunately, time on task is one of the most, if not the most, important predictors of learning. The many suggestions for improving learning by using so-called high-impact teaching procedures to promote deep learning—capstone courses, study abroad experiences, student–faculty collaboration, learning communities, and so on—will be for naught if students do not put in sufficient amounts of time in deliberate, effortful, goal-directed studying. Chickering and Gamson (1987) selected time on task as one of only seven basic principles for effective teaching and learning. As Astin (1993) put it, "students learn what they study" (p. 423).

Reading Skills

Students tend to be inefficient readers. They assume that they can read a textbook chapter much like they read a magazine article or a novel, so they watch television with their textbook open in their lap or fall asleep reading their book in bed. Unfortunately, most textbooks must be studied, not merely read. *Active reading* involves, at minimum, three components: (a) previewing contents, (b) reading, and (c) deliberately committing critical information to long-term memory. Instead of simply reading and rereading chapters, students should first read the chapter summary, study the organization of topics, and generate an outline of the major topics the chapter covers. Only then should they read the text itself, in a situation where they can monitor their understanding of the material, remain alert, and take memory-enhancing notes. They should also be reminded to do the following:

- Read assignments prior to any lectures or discussions that will cover the topics, and be careful to allocate enough time to complete that task.
- Take advantage of the pedagogical features of their texts. If the book or website contains outlines, chapter previews, or summaries, students should study these sections as they develop their

overall conception of the material. They should also learn to make use of the headings and subheadings, which may be based on an implicit outline format that students fail to recognize.

- Generate a verbal interpretation of any information presented in the textbook's charts and graphs.
- Pay particular attention to key points, spend extra time reading complicated or detailed sections of the text, and be mindful of expository elements embedded in the text such as lists, summaries, transitions, and pointer words (e.g., "more important," "unfortunately," and "first of all," "second," etc.).
- Use a general note-taking system, such as SQ3R: This approach to active reading involves *Surveying* the chapter content, formulating a *Question* for each major topic or section, *Reading* the text for information that answers the question, *Reciting* the answer several times (aloud or in writing), and *Reviewing* the material without referring to the text or notes.

Taking Notes

Note-taking is a demanding cognitive task given that it requires listening to and understanding the information presented by the lecturer, separating the key points from background information, and then writing down that material in a form that will facilitate retrieval from long-term memory. Advanced students may already know how to take effective notes, but first-year students and those with weaker academic backgrounds may need help. Most students will gain more from their notes if they use an organized note-taking system, such as the Cornell System (Pauk & Owens, 2014). Students with weaker working memories, however, may have trouble organizing their notes and may therefore benefit from taking more detailed notes (Bui, Myerson, & Hale, 2013).

Effective note-takers prepare for each lecture by taking notes on the readings before class or by watching the lecture online, acquiring any lecture outlines or PowerPoint presentations the professor has made available, and reviewing the notes from the previous topic. If the notes from the readings or PowerPoint slides are posted, students can take fewer notes while concentrating on the presentation.

Recall of information presented in lecture is highly dependent on the completeness of the notes that are taken (Aiken, Thomas, & Shennum, 1975). Notes should be sufficiently detailed so that they can be understood when reviewed weeks later, but they should not be verbatim transcriptions of the lecture. Writing notes by hand, instead of typing them with a laptop computer, may also facilitate learning. Mueller and Oppenheimer (2014), for example, found that students who used laptops, besides multitasking, also tended to just transcribe lectures instead of consolidating them. As a consequence, they did not process the information thoroughly and so performed more poorly on subsequent tests of conceptual learning. In contrast, good note-takers wait to write down phrases and partial sentences after listening to the entire idea that the lecturer is presenting (Bjork, 2001).

If lecturing offline and not using lecture-capture software, professors should consider letting students record the lectures but urge those who do to continue to take notes during class. Taking notes results in some improvement in encoding, but much of the memory-related benefits come from a review of the notes after they have been written: In other words, the notes must be studied outside of class for memory consolidation to occur. Pauk and Owens (2014), for example, stressed the steps that occur after recording the notes, including reducing (questioning), reciting, reflection, recapitulation, and review. One way to review notes is to enter them into a database or document after class.

Students should be encouraged to build networks of note-takers who share notes throughout the term. If the members of the group are similar in their note-taking ability, they can rotate the note-taking responsibility among members of the coterie, leaving the others free to listen attentively to the lecture.

Preparing for Tests

Academically skilled students are not just better at preparing for tests; they are also better at taking tests. They focus their attention on the test itself, and they use all the recommended strategies for testing success. They read questions completely and carefully. They ask questions about confusing items. They don't waste time puzzling over "stumpers" but skip them and come back to them. They double check their work, if time allows. They avoid careless errors. When taking selected-response tests, these test-wise students use a set of heuristics that helps them identify the answers to questions even when they have failed to master the learning objective that the question addresses (Millman, Bishop, & Ebel, 1965). Also, when taking CR tests, they bluff when they do not know the answer (Gronlund, 1998). They carefully restate the question in their answer, add some factually correct but irrelevant information, and include such phrases as "Scholars have been studying this fundamental issue for many years" or "This question lies at the heart of many important and time-honored debates in the field." Graders should not give students points when they use such tactics exclusively, but they often reward students whose essays combine comprehensive content with skillful packaging.

Resources

Professors need not face the task of tutoring students on study skills alone, however. Many excellent books on college-level study skills are available, and students who have poor study habits should be urged to order them and review them (e.g., Foss, 2013; Pauk & Owens, 2014). Most schools also offer academic support for students, from workshops on study skills to entire "Introduction to College" classes that cover the basic ingredients for academic success. Other resources, including the English department's writing clinic, the university's counseling center, and tutorial programs coordinated by your department's undergraduate organizations, can also be used (Pastorino, 1999).

DEVELOPING SELF-REGULATION SKILLS

Some students fail not because they lack the academic skills needed for success but because they cannot bring themselves to exercise those skills on a regular basis. They know how to study, take good notes, and read, but they do not. They have the time they need to complete assignments and make every session of class, but they never get around to doing their homework, and they skip classes. They have plenty of potential, but they do not realize it because they are poor self-regulators (Schunk & Zimmerman, 2013).

One of the profound differences between high school and college is the level of self-regulation college requires. In high school, parents, teachers, and administrators regulate many aspects of learning for students. In college, these external sources of self-control are relaxed, and the students themselves must take responsibility for nearly all the tasks associated with learning. Some students may rise easily to the challenge, but others may need to learn about, and practice, the self-regulatory skills Zimmerman (1998) identified in his studies of successful athletes, writers, musicians, and students. The following recommendations are "practical techniques that the resourceful acquire and hone to a fine degree" (Zimmerman, 1998, p. 79):

- *Goal-setting:* identifying desired outcomes and end-states, including the topics to be covered in a review session, lists of chapters to be read and reviewed, and learning activities to complete before an exam
- *Task strategies:* developing and using personalized strategies for studying, such as compressing all the unit's notes into a single page, developing extensive outlines of text material, or developing examples for concepts reviewed in class
- *Imagery:* creating images that capture the essence of material, as well as enhancing motivation by imagining oneself taking and acing the upcoming exam

- *Self-instruction:* talking to oneself about the material to be learned, as well as reviewing material aloud, urging oneself on (e.g., "Let's do it!"), and prompting or praising oneself
- *Time management:* developing schedules for daily and weekly studying, attending classes, completing homework, and non-school activities
- *Self-monitoring:* keeping track of progress toward one's goals, including keeping a personal grade book; counting all pages, articles, or books read; and updating a graduation worksheet
- *Self-evaluation:* developing and taking self-quizzes covering material to be learned, reviewing papers carefully prior to turning them in
- *Self-consequences:* establishing contingencies of self-reward and self-punishment, such as making social contacts, television, and music-listening, dependent on whether one meets one's study objectives
- *Environmental structure:* controlling the area where one studies to maximize stimulus control over learning and minimize distractions
- *Help seeking:* seeking support from others, such as attending review sessions or optional discussion forums, joining study groups

Zimmerman and Pons (1986) interviewed students in both undergraduate and graduate courses and found that the successful students used these techniques regularly.

Zimmerman's (1998) recommendations, with their emphasis on ratcheting up and maintaining engagement, are particularly relevant for online or blended courses. If students are not yet acclimated to the unique demands and freedoms of online classes, they may not be sufficiently diligent in reading and responding to their correspondence, completing required quizzes, taking part in discussions, reviewing closely all the assigned readings, and so on (Winters et al., 2008). Students in such classes will require more in the way of orienting guidance so that they stay engaged at a consistent level across the entire term.

PROFESSORIAL SOCIAL SUPPORT

Professors can help their students overcome their academic difficulties by giving them instrumentally tinged social support: advice, ideas, and suggestions for improving their study and self-regulatory skills. However, students may also need social support. When students encounter difficulties in their academic work, they will appreciate some how-to advice about studying, but they will also respond positively to sympathy, compassion, and understanding. Researchers who studied college students' coping with social and academic setbacks found that students seek the counsel of those they admire (*idols*), but when they are struggling to cope with the emotional consequences of a failure they turn to *encouragers* and *confidants*. Students need to be "shown the ropes," but they may also need a "shoulder to cry on" (Harlow & Cantor, 1995).

Emotional Support

Some students may need help managing the emotions they experience in the academic setting in general, and in testing and grading situations in particular (Sapp, 2013). Stress levels surge just before and during exams, and then ease off afterward (Jemmott & Magloire, 1988). However, they rise once again when students learn whether they have passed or failed the exam. Studies of students' reactions to success and failure confirm what every professor knows: Students experience a range of emotional reactions after they succeed on or fail exams. Students who fail, relative to successful students, describe themselves as less relaxed, satisfied, content, elated, and pleasantly surprised, and more unhappy, tense, incompetent, inadequate, upset, depressed, guilty, and hostile (Forsyth & McMillan, 1981).

Test Anxiety

If students' emotions are particularly intense, distracting, and negative, they may be experiencing *test anxiety* (Sapp, 2013). In many cases, students experience test anxiety simply because they have not studied for the exam. Such students *should* be worried that they might fail, if they have not prepared properly (Naveh-Benjamin, McKeachie, Lin, & Holinger, 1981). In some cases, however, a student's claim of anxiety is a legitimate one, characterized by high levels of tension, pronounced worrying, intrusive thinking, and physiological interferences. If students agree with the following types of statements about their reactions to tests, they may need help learning ways to control their test-related anxieties (Sarason, 1984, p. 932):

- I feel distressed and uneasy before tests.
- I find myself becoming anxious the day of a test.
- Before taking a test, I worry about failure.
- During tests, I think about past events.
- Irrelevant bits of information pop into my head during a test.
- During tests, I find myself thinking of things unrelated to the material being tested.
- I get a headache during an important test.
- My stomach gets upset before tests.

Test anxiety responds well to treatment, but professors should help anxious students by referring them to counseling rather than by attempting treatment themselves.

MOTIVATIONAL SUPPORT

When students perform poorly on exams, the wind goes out of their motivational sails. They may still value a good grade and mastery of the material, but their score lowers their expectations. As a consequence, their self-confidence may wane and they may consider giving up their goal rather than redoubling their efforts to reach it. They may also engage in self-protective strategies that buoy their sense of self-worth while undermining their chances for success in the future (Covington & Beery, 1976). They may blame their failure on external factors—bad luck, an unfair test, the professor's alleged lack of instruction skills, or the opacity of the text—rather than personal limitations and lack of effort (Forsyth et al., 2009). They may also engage in *self-handicapping*: Instead of working hard to overcome factors that stand in the way of success, they protect their self-esteem by deliberately seeking out impediments: They skip class, take drugs, binge drink, and so on (Schwinger, Wirthwein, Lemmer, & Steinmayr, 2014). Because such defense machinations can have ruinous effects on students' learning, professors must sometimes intervene to steer students away from these motivational pitfalls (Forsyth & McMillan, 1991; McMillan & Forsyth, 1991).

Emphasize Growth and Change

Students' self-confidence can also be threatened when they begin to question their own ability, in general, or their capacity to further improve. As I noted in Chapter 2, Dweck and her colleagues predicted that students' *mindsets*—their implicit personal theories about their intellectual and academic abilities and skills—influence their reaction to challenging experiences (e.g., Dweck, 2012). Those who adopt a fixed, entity-oriented mind-set assume that their basal aptitude in a particular domain sets limits on how much they can learn. Students who adopt an incremental mind-set, in contrast, believe that their qualities are fluid rather than fixed, and so with effort they can reach the highest levels of competency. Dweck and her colleagues found not only that an incremental mind-set is generally associated with more positive reactions in the face of setbacks, but also that these mind-sets can be shifted through direct instruction (e.g., Burnette, Hoyt, Lawson, & Dweck, 2015). For example, T. D. Wilson and Linville (1985) found that first-year students who were told that most college students' grades steadily rise over the course of their college career were less likely to drop out at the end of their second year and achieved greater increases in their GPAs.

Encourage Psychological Controllability

Students who feel that they can control their academic outcomes show no loss of motivation even when they fail repeatedly; those who feel that their outcomes are unrelated to their efforts tend to give up rather than persevere after a failure (Dweck & Leggett, 1988). Professors should therefore emphasize the extent to which educational outcomes are caused by factors that are under students' control—time spent studying, note taking, diligence, preparation—rather than factors beyond their control, such as test difficulty, native ability, and academic background. In one study, researchers succeeded in shifting the failure attributions of a group of low-scoring students away from external, uncontrollable factors (e.g., a "difficult test") to internal, controllable causes (e.g., "effort," "motivation") through a brief counseling intervention. On subsequent tests and on the final exam, students in the experimental condition earned higher grades than the control students who had received no attributional information. By the end of the course, the students in the experimental condition earned Cs, but most of the students in the control group received Ds and Fs (Noel, Forsyth, & Kelley, 1987).

Provide Positive Feedback

Give students a ray of hope to brighten the shadow cast by an F by complimenting something about their work. Even a student with a low score on a test will have answered something correctly, and this success should be mentioned. Be careful, however, to highlight the student's ability to answer these items rather than mentioning the ease of the items. Also, focus on specific strengths, rather than simply bolstering students' overall sense of self-esteem. Theory and prior research suggest that a positive sense of self-worth helps students maintain high levels of motivation in the face of negative feedback, but praise should be deserved. When one team of investigators sought to help college students who had performed poorly on the first class exam by telling them, "Hold your head—and your self-esteem—high," the intervention backfired. Bolstering self-esteem led to poorer performance, especially among the weaker (D and F) students (Forsyth, Lawrence, Burnette, & Baumeister, 2007).

Grading and Aiding Redux: Grade Them but Also Help Them

How do students know when they have reached their learning goals? How, for example, can they determine whether their writing is sufficiently clear and concise, that their knowledge of a particular subject is reasonably comprehensive, that they can solve mathematics and scientific problems correctly, or recognize faulty reasoning in someone's argument? In most cases, their professors provide them with the information they need to calibrate their learning success by grading them, that is, by evaluating their performance by reference to some standard that defines which outcomes are correct, successful, or satisfactory. A grade of A sends a clear message—you have reached a high level of proficiency in your learning—as does a grade of D or F.

Grades, however, should be coupled with feedback that helps students further calibrate not only their level of proficiency but also the adequacy of the methods they are using in their studies. Some students will benefit from feedback that helps them identify their weaknesses. They may, for example, be spending too much time memorizing definitions instead of cultivating a deeper understanding, or they may have misunderstood a key concept that is critically important for mastering a range of interrelated course topics. Other students, however, may benefit from guidance as they strengthen their academic proficiencies. For example, some students may not be sufficiently engaged in their studying and so would be helped by feedback that critiques their study habits and methods. Other students may require more in the way of reassurance to be certain that they recognize that grades are not indelible stamps that define their worth but only signals of the progress they are making in their learning. Grades help students adjust their current level of mastery, but they should be coupled with the resources that students can use to improve their performance.

Managing

Fostering Academic Integrity, Civility, and Tolerance

7

Television and film often juxtapose scenes of raucous high schools with images of serene college classrooms as temples of learning. Teachers in high schools are shown struggling with unruly adolescents who talk constantly to friends and show little respect for the teacher. Professors, in contrast, pontificate to stylishly dressed students seated in elegantly appointed lecture halls listening respectfully to their teachers' every word. College "view books"—those carefully constructed, image-rich informational brochures sent to prospective students and their parents—send a similar message: They are filled with pictures of idyllic landscapes, happy students, and dedicated faculty, who are "are a mixture of Marie Curie, Mr. Chips, and Mr. Rogers, notable for their international scholarly reputations, commitment to teaching and nurturing attentiveness to each special student in the academic neighborhood" (Hartley & Morphew, 2008, p. 677).

But college and university classes do not emerge fully formed and populated by earnest seekers of wisdom who are

http://dx.doi.org/10.1037/14777-008
College Teaching: Practical Insights From the Science of Teaching and Learning,
by D. R. Forsyth

committed to the pursuit of inquiry and understanding. These complex social settings must be managed to establish a learning environment that encourages preparation, reflection, and cooperation but discourages disengagement and disunity. Thus, professors must create communities of learners who feel safe exploring new ideas and dealing with the interpersonal and personal conflicts that inevitably arise when people with varying skills, interests, and motivations join in a shared pursuit. They must also make certain that the golden rule of the academy—do your own work—is heeded without exception. Professors are not just scholars, teachers, and researchers; they also are managers (Evertson & Weinstein, 2011).

Managing the Class

Classes, whether taught in face-to-face classrooms or online, are governed by implicit and explicit social norms that prescribe the appropriate way to respond in a particular situation as well as proscribed actions students should avoid if at all possible. Social norms are what transform a room full of disinterested students into hardworking, engaged students who are committed to their learning. When the norms support learning, students are more likely to ask questions, seek feedback, complete assignments on time, reflect on ideas, and join in discussions (Zimmerman & Pons, 1986). Learning rates are higher in classes whose norms support high levels of student engagement (e.g., Reyes, Brackett, Rivers, White, & Salovey, 2012).

Not all class norms, however, encourage learning. In some classes, preparation, interest, and intellectual mastery are more unusual than expected. Norms of incivility, too, can disrupt the smooth flow of learning in the classroom, as students arrive late and then leave early, do not pay much attention during class, or attempt to multitask with electronic devices. Professors are often reluctant to confront such indiscretions, but research confirms what all elementary school teachers know: These kinds of norms interfere with learning. Hirschy and Braxton (2004), for example, documented two types of incivilities in college classes: (a) disrespectful disruption (students leave class early, make sarcastic comments, groan aloud, use cell phones, interrupt the professor) and (b) insolent inattention (e.g., students sleep, attend class intoxicated). As they predicted, incivility was associated with decreased self-reported intellectual development growth and interest in learning new ideas. Their findings suggest that professors should take steps to develop a culture of learning and inquiry in their classrooms.

CRAFTING THE CLASSROOM CULTURE

Carbone (1998) provided case studies of three professors' approaches to classroom management. One professor establishes the norms on the first day of class and zealously maintains them throughout the term. He explains, "As an instructor I'm not afraid to act as a policeman and squash that type of behavior" (Carbone, 1998, p. 78). A second, more laissez-faire–style professor pays little attention to social goings on and side conversations, asking only that people who talk consistently sit at the back of the room. He concludes, "They're paying for it, they're grown-ups." (Carbone, 1998, p. 78). A third professor permits students to come late and go early but requires that they submit a written request for each occurrence. She also intervenes if students talk excessively in class.

These professors have created three very different classroom cultures: One expects that students will come to class prepared to learn and creates a uniformly attentive classroom by pressuring inattentive students to either act appropriately or to skip class, one is willing to put up with disruptions to learning so that he can maintain rapport with his students, and one maintains control through an elaborate hall-pass system. Each approach is defensible, but their range means that students do not have clear expectations about how to act in class. As a consequence, professors must build the kind of culture they prefer at the start of the term and reinstate the culture's standards whenever students stray too far from the norm.

Setting the Norms

Classes, as groups, rapidly develop a set of norms that will become powerful determinants of members' actions. Norms will develop, quite naturally, in the class over time, but those that grow organically might not be the most conducive for learning. Professors should therefore encourage the formation of the types of norms they prefer by doing one or more of the following:

- Stating the norms clearly in the syllabus and reiterating them as needed (Davis, 2009).
- Linking norms to a more general framework of social and moral principles that provides a rationale for the class's procedures. Students can be reminded, for example, that their highest priority should be learning and that all other concerns must be set aside (Billson, 1986).
- Stressing the need for cooperation and teamwork, in particular in larger classes where the actions of a minority can substantially disrupt the quality of the experience for the majority. Remind

students of the importance of putting their personal, individual needs aside for the good of the collective.

- Sharing responsibility for maintaining norms with the students. Remind students they are collectively responsible for maintaining norms, and so attentive students should feel free to tell talkative students to be quiet.
- Comparing the class to other types of social aggregates, such as audiences, congregations, and mobs. Inform students that the classroom is not like a movie theater, where patrons can step out for popcorn whenever they like. For online classes, tell students that the class is not an anonymous chat room but an online community.
- Using rituals to start and end each session. For example, begin class each day with the same stock opening phrase (e.g., "Good morning, scholars!" or "Silence those phones!") and end class crisply with a ritual closing phrase, such as "And so ends the lesson" or "How time flies."
- Highlighting descriptive norms to make the amount of conformity to the preferred standards salient to students. For example, after a class discussion, explicitly state to the class whether the level of student participation met your standard for good engagement. When teaching online, let students know about base rates for engaging with class material, such as the number of questions and comments posted to a forum. Saying such things as "I've noticed very few people are streaming the online lectures" will reduce rather than encourage that behavior (Schultz, Nolan, Cialdini, Goldstein, & Griskevicius, 2007).
- Nipping undesirable emergent norms in the bud. For example, never tolerate the "There are only 5 minutes left, so I'm going to get ready to leave" habit. If students get noisy and start packing up their materials, stop class, remind them you are aware of the time remaining and state that you will end class on time but that you must have their attention during the class's final minutes so you can complete the day's teaching.

Using Social Influence

Even in classes with well-ensconced pro-learning norms students will sometimes slip up and violate standards you have established. They must modify their behavior from class to class to match the unique normative demands of each professor's class, and if something else requires their attention—such as studying, socializing, or working—then they may engage in actions that are appropriate for another class they are taking but that contradict the norms you have set for your class. In such cases you may need to intervene more directly by using informational, normative, or interpersonal influence (Forsyth, 2014). A professor may

- move from the dais and stand close to students who are talking among themselves;
- use the class and the students in the class frequently as examples of topics under discussion;
- ask students who are not paying attention simple questions: ones that they can easily answer with a personal opinion or by restating a point just made in class;
- reward students on days when they remain attentive to the very end of class by praising them and thanking them effusively;
- monitor the class carefully and focus attention on students and clusters of students who are not acting appropriately; and/or
- convince students who are the informal leaders within the class to act as role models for other students of positive, learning-centered behavior.

Modeling Respect

Boice (2000) pointed out that students are not the only ones who sometimes act uncivilly in the classroom. During his observation of hundreds of classes, Boice recorded many instances of faculty treating students coldly, abruptly, or "with unmistakable rudeness and condescension" (p. 84). He concluded that professors are often partners with students in producing incivility and suggested that faculty can reduce rudeness by remaining positive and approachable.

MANAGING CONFLICT

Nearly all classes experience periods of conflict. As the term wears on, networks of likes and dislikes will enfold the students, and tensions will arise as individual students and in-class cliques vie for the professor's approval. When exams approach and major papers are due, apprehension will mount; a postexam class is often one marked by debate and argument even in courses that had previously been remarkably placid. Many classes, too, move into a period of conflict, or *storming*, at some point, often as a result of students' struggle against what they perceive to be the professor's authority (Tuckman, 1965). Although people react to conflict in many ways, most of these responses vary along two basic dimensions: (a) passive versus active and (b) positive versus negative. Passive methods involve downplaying and minimizing the conflict (Morris-Rothschild & Brassard, 2006). The professor may, for example, apologize to the class for the conditions that created the conflict and offer to resolve the problem by making the changes the students request: Points can be added to grades, assignments that were viewed as too demanding can be dropped, and so on. Alternatively, the professor can simply explain that the issue is obviously a controversial one that is causing strong feelings and invite students to discuss the matter with him or her privately. In many cases students will not take advantage of such an opportunity, so the conflict is effectively avoided. A different professor may quash conflict by using more negative methods, such as invoking his or her privilege as the authority in the class or explaining the nature of classroom power differentials to students (e.g., "If you don't like it, tough"; "If you don't agree with this policy, there's the door"). Such negative methods (i.e., avoidance and fighting) tend to be viewed by students as more disagreeable and unjust, whereas the positive methods (yielding and cooperation) are viewed as more agreeable and fair (De Dreu, 1997). Avoidance, fighting, and yielding are also only temporary solutions; they smooth over conflicts at the surface, without considering the underlying source. Cooperation, in contrast, is an active, positive method that yields immediate and long-term benefits for the class. Most faculty, when they experience a "seditious" class, cope with the conflict by openly discussing issues with students. In many cases, but not all, this conflict management strategy proved to be an effective means of quelling the discord (Forsyth, 2012).

When the cooperative spirit a class needs to function effectively is replaced by tension, hostility, and competitive maneuverings, consider

- meeting with disaffected students in your office, but keep the door open or alert colleagues with nearby offices;
- allowing students to express their concerns and focus on helping them clarify their feelings, thoughts, and position by using basic skills of empathy, reflection, and reframing;
- stating your interpretation of the problem in writing, including your preferred resolution to the problem, and deliver this interpretation to the student in class or through e-mail;
- keeping a file of dated notes pertaining to the incident;
- keeping colleagues informed about the problem and seek their input; if appropriate, ask them to mediate; and
- referring the students to your superior; to the student counseling center; or to an ombudsperson, if available.

In extreme cases, such as when a student (or group of students) disrupts class so thoroughly that instruction cannot continue, check with your college's administrators to determine what options are available to you. Some institutions, recognizing that other students' right to receive instruction is violated by a disruptive student, permit professors to expel miscreants from their classes. But if the disruptive student does not obey such an order, then even more extreme steps must be taken, such as adjourning the class or contacting campus police. In any case, the intervention must be consistent with the standards and procedures adopted by your institution. The intervention must also be lawful. One should not, for example, physically touch a student or subject a student to verbal abuse.

MANAGING DIVERSITY

As I noted in Chapter 2, the notion of the "traditional" college student is disappearing. In the 1950s, when professors walked into their class-rooms, they were usually greeted by students who were similar to each other in terms of sex, race, nationality, and age. As the demographic characteristics of America and its colleges have changed, however, so too have students gradually shifted from homogeneous assemblages into heterogeneous ones.

Classes with students from diverse, multicultural backgrounds offer many advantages over homogeneous ones (R. E. Phelps, 2012). Although higher education has long been considered the protected pre-serve of the wealthy, the White, and the privileged, this narrow view-point can be revised and enlarged when classes include students with different backgrounds, life experiences, and cultural outlooks. Diversity in groups also tends to promote creativity and enhance innovative thinking, so any collaborative, active learning experiences should be particularly dynamic when members bring very different opinions and ideas to the task (Forsyth, 2014). A diverse class can also become a laboratory for learning about diversity itself. For many students, college will be their first contact with people who differ from them in regard to culture, race, ethnicity, and religion. A diverse student body gives them the opportunity to interact with and learn from people who are outside of their usual circle of friends and family (Littleford et al., 2010).

Diversity can, however, lead to complexities: conflict over values, disputes over the fairness of traditional procedures, and communicative misunderstandings (D. A. Harrison & Klein, 2007). Because segregation is still pervasive in U.S. society, students may be uncomfortable with, or unskilled, when interacting with people from different cultural, ethnic, racial, and religious groups. Diverse groups are often less cohesive than homogeneous ones, for differences in values, background, and interests create fault lines, and the group can fission along those lines. In some cases, too, students may be prejudiced, and these attitudes may surface in their comments, actions, and demeanor. When diversity increases, so does the need to monitor relationships among individuals and inter-vene to correct any problems that arise. As Chism (1999) explained, all students, irrespective of their background, personal or social qualities, and abilities should "feel welcome" in the class, "feel that they are being treated as individuals," "feel that they can participate fully," and "feel they are being treated fairly" (p. 221).

Ethnic, Gender, and Cultural Diversity

The result of the increasing diversity of students on college campuses is often a vibrant, unique learning experience that profoundly changes students intellectually and attitudinally (Alwin, Cohen, & Newcomb, 1991; Newcomb, Koenig, Flacks, & Warwick, 1967). Yet college campuses, once oases in a sea of American prejudice, frequently serve as venues for ethnic, racist, and sexist conflicts. Students may express their prejudices against others openly in class, as when a White racist openly denounces African Americans or a sexist student expresses reactionary opinions pertaining to the role of women in contemporary society. In most cases, however, bias is more subtle (Kleinpenning & Hagendoorn, 1993). For example, whenever a nontraditional student offers his or her opinion during a discussion, the younger students glance at each other and roll their eyes. None of the students respond to comments made in the class by an Asian student. The White students in classes keep to themselves by forming exclusive interpersonal networks. When more than 2,500 professors and students were surveyed about classroom biases, approximately one quarter of the instructors, and one half of the students, reported observing instances of bias, including offensive humor, insults, slurs, and noninclusion (Boysen, Vogel, Cope, & Hubbard, 2009). Regrettably, those surveyed suggested professors rarely responded effectively to these biases and, in some cases (12%), were the source of the bias.

Instructors should monitor their classes for evidence of bias and dispel it as needed by following the recommendations of researchers in the field of prejudice reduction (e.g., Paluck & Green, 2009). First, status differences between students should be minimized by insisting that all members of the class treat one another respectfully. Second, when possible, collaborative activities should be used to create informal, personal interaction among students. Third, the professor should respond actively to any instances of intergroup bias because ignoring this problem can be misinterpreted as tacit approval. Social biases are contagious: When students believe that their campus tolerates the unfair treatment of others, they are more likely to express racist opinions themselves, even to the point of condoning the harassment of people in other racial groups (Blanchard, Tilly, & Vaughn, 1991). Fourth, because situations that require cooperative interdependence in the pursuit of common goals tend to reduce prejudice, professors with classes of diverse students should use noncompetitive grading procedures when possible.

Professors, too, should monitor their own behaviors for evidence of unintentional bias. The term *prejudiced professor* is an apparent oxymoron, given that education is the antidote to closed-minded bigotry. But individual biases produced by years of living in a segregated society may nonetheless surface when certain professors interact with their students. Despite reductions in sexism, the college classroom climate remains a chilly one for women. Some male professors make blatantly sexist remarks about women and their role in contemporary society. More frequently, instead of singling women out for ridicule, sexism takes the more subtle form of simply discounting them, or using patterns of language that exclude them (Allan & Madden, 2006; R. M. Hall & Sandler, 1986).

Professors may also treat students differently depending on their ethnicity and race because the professors themselves are not sufficiently experienced with multicultural environments. Some professors may use dated terms to describe members of a group, thereby unintentionally insulting the members of the group. More likely, however, they will use examples, ideas, stories, and illustrations drawn from their own particular social background, so students who share that background feel included but students who do not feel left out. Their examples always refer to "Johnny" or "Jill" instead of "Rafael" or "Lakeisha." When they talk about a romantic couple, they assume that the couple are heterosexual. They offer unwarranted generalizations about activities and interests that are more prevalent in one group rather than another: They denounce certain styles of music, call some neighborhoods "ghettos," and characterize social organizations as "gangs." Some professors make the grave error of calling on a student who is a member of a specific cultural group and asking him or her to provide commentary from that group's perspective. Davis (2009) and M. J. Allen (2000) have suggested ways to increase one's sensitivity to issues of diversity in the class.

Nontraditional Students

Like all "non" categories, nontraditional students are a diverse group themselves, including part-time students returning for a single class each semester, college graduates returning to take more courses, and older students who are restarting their educational careers after a long hiatus. These students are mature adult learners, so their motivations, strengths, and limitations are different from those of the college students who are fresh out of high school. Nontraditional students have already sharpened their self-regulatory skills, so they tend to be responsible, self-directed, goal-oriented learners. They therefore prefer student-centered learning over purely lecture-centered classes and readings of authoritative sources. These individuals' life experiences are often myriad and much more varied than those of the other students in the class, so when discussions turn to such topics as politics, public policies, educational practices, drug use, religion, parenting, management, and values these students are a rich source of insight and examples. They tend, however, to be more practical learners, and so must learn to tie their own experiences into broader theories and perspectives, just as more theoretically oriented instructors must learn to recognize the pedagogical value of sharing students' unique experiences with the class (Wlodkowski, 2008).

Nontraditional students are sometimes rusty when it comes to performing routine academic tasks, so they may initially need to be given more time and support. They may also lack confidence in their abilities and experience the self-consciousness that comes from being different from the average student in the class. In most cases, however, nontraditional students' serious work ethic and problem-solving skills more than compensate for their academic greenness (Taylor, Marienau, & Fiddler, 2000).

Students With Disabilities

Students with disabilities are also headed off to college in ever-increasing numbers. The innovations in helping students with disabilities are based on changes in federal law that prohibit the exclusion of people with physical and psychological impairments from any postsecondary education programs that receive any form of federal funding. Physical impairments include sensory losses, such as total or partial blindness and deafness; physical conditions that limit mobility (e.g., cerebral palsy, multiple sclerosis); and chronic diseases (e.g., diabetes, seizure disorders, AIDS) that can influence students' attentiveness, stamina, behavior, and so on. Mental impairments include learning disabilities (e.g., dyslexia, expressive dysphasia, aural receptive dysphasia), processing impairments caused by injury to the brain (e.g., traumatic brain injury), and some psychological conditions (e.g., depression, schizophrenia, adult attention-deficit disorder).

Institutions that receive federal funds are legally required to facilitate the full participation of students in all aspects of campus life. They cannot, for example, put into place admissions standards that are biased against students with disabilities, or deny housing to students because of their disability. Professors are also legally and ethically required to provide to students with disabilities the resources they need to succeed in their courses. Instructors should willingly arrange their classrooms to take into account the special needs of these students, including providing extra space for any assistive technology the students may require. They should also permit people who are not registered for the class but who are assisting the student, such as note-takers or interpreters, to attend class. Service animals, too, cannot be excluded. They should also adjust the content of curricula and course content, activities, and testing procedures as necessary for qualified students with disabilities. These modifications are termed *adjustments* or *accommodations*, and they can include substitution of one course for another, elimination of certain requirements, adjustment in the length and type of exams, and the substitution of one type of activity or assignment for another.

Most institutions have policies in place that determine how students with disabilities can certify their need and thereby qualify for accommodations, adjustments, and support services. Faculty should ask students with disabilities to contact them at their earliest convenience to discuss accommodations. Some universities, for example, ask that faculty insert an informational paragraph in their syllabi for all courses, such as this:

> Section 504 of the Rehabilitation Act of 1973 and the Americans with Disabilities Act of 1990 require educators provide an "academic adjustment" and/or "reasonable accommodation" to any individual who advises us of a physical or mental disability. If you have a physical or mental limitation that requires an academic adjustment or an accommodation, please arrange a meeting with me at your earliest convenience.

Students with disabilities are not obligated, however, to identify themselves to their instructor by any deadline, so in some cases students seek accommodations late in the term.

HELPING STRESSED STUDENTS

Stress is a part of every student's daily life. Each day brings an avalanche of minor hassles, including broken-down cars, parking tickets, overdue library books, malfunctioning computers, and shortages of cash. Many students are experiencing developmental changes and relational distress, and some are also dealing with traumatic life events (e.g., sexual assault, severe illness). Academic stressors, such as: excessive homework, difficult or ambiguous assignments, and overall time pressures, also play a role in students' lives (Novotney, 2014). Most manage to cope with this stress, but some do not. These students should be heard, supported, comforted, and referred to counseling if their problems appear to warrant it.

When to Refer a Student for Counseling

Most colleges and universities have centers on campus that provide struggling students with extended reviews and tutorials for basic academic skills. Students who have not yet learned some of the basic skills needed for academic success often visit their professors' offices seeking extensions, adjustments, extra credit, and sympathy, but the campus study-skill and learning centers are better suited to give them the help they need to become more successful students.

Other students, however, are seeking not academic advice but help in dealing with a personal or emotional crisis. Some will be content to share, briefly, that personal information, so that you have an understanding of the factors that may be undermining their academic work. Others, however, may display significant disruptions in mood, thought, and action. They may say things or act in ways that are odd or unusual. Their affect may be flat and unchanging, hostile to the point of fury, or depressed and listless. They may reveal their anxiety by crying uncontrollably. Their attention to their clothes and appearance may decline noticeably; some may also show signs of drug abuse. In such circumstances the professor should help the student seek counseling. Eagan et al. (2014) noted that far fewer male faculty (13.9%), compared with female faculty (24.6%), reported having helped students with personal problems at some point.

How Should One Refer a Student?

Students often seek out one of their professors when they become concerned about their mental health, for they often assume that professors function in an *in loco parentis* capacity. But professors' primary mission is teaching, and they risk becoming involved in a dual-role relationship if they also become a student's therapist, friend, or parental figure. Concerned professors should, instead, use their best judgment to determine whether the student's problems are so substantial that he or she would benefit from counseling and then refer him or her to the appropriate campus service agency (Allitt, 2005).

Referral involves more than simply saying, "You should get some help"; instead, the referral should take place in the context of a consultation with the student, during which the professor shows appropriate interest and concern for the student's well-being. During this meeting the professor should try to gauge the severity of the problem and help the student separate distress caused by academic concerns from distress caused by personal difficulties. If the root cause of the student's problems is academic, then the professor should recommend strategies the student can use to deal with those issues. If the source of the student's struggle is personal distress, however, the professor should suggest ways the student can deal with his or her problems. The professor should express concern, but also ask if the student has shared their problems with family or friends. He or she may also want to discuss more formal methods of dealing with the problem, including treatment. These options should be discussed as matter-of-factly as possible. Students can be reassured that most adults turn to counselors whenever they must deal with significant life events, such as divorce, crises in their careers, and so on.

In extreme cases, you may need to take additional steps. You may, with the student still in your office, call the counseling center personally and make an appointment for the student. You can also walk the student to the center. Colleagues can also be contacted, as well as the police, if the student threatens suicide or violence. In most cases, however, all students need is a sympathetic listener who is experienced in working with students and their problems.

Managing Academic Integrity

A college or university, like any complicated social system, is governed by sets of norms that regulate the actions of the individuals in that system. *Descriptive* norms define what is commonplace and conventional—the normal course of action most people display in the situation. Some norms, the *injunctive* ones, include an evaluative component, for they comprise not only actions that will garner praise and adulation but also those that are prohibited or at least frowned on (Forsyth, 1994). For example, some of the prescriptive injunctive norms of a college class are "Listen to the professor," "Sit in the available chairs," and "Take notes," whereas the proscriptive ones are "Do not sleep in class" and "Do not talk on your cell phone in the middle of the lecture."

People who violate injunctive norms are not just acting atypically; they are being "bad" and hence opening themselves up to condemnation by others. This condemnation can include hostility, pressure to change, negative sanctions, and punishment, but the reaction depends on the importance of the norm, the magnitude of the discrepancy, and the characteristics of the person who violates the norm. If the norm reflects current social standards pertaining to minor aspects of conduct, violations are often overlooked, in particular if a prestigious or powerful person is doing the violating. Some norms, however, are considered so essential to the integrity of the class that their violation will be roundly and quickly condemned (Sabini & Silver, 1978). Examples of such norms include "Do not cheat," "Do not plagiarize," "Do not help others cheat," and "Do not abuse library books and other academic materials." Individuals who break moral norms risk severe penalties if their violation is proven, but because the consequences are so severe, in many cases accusers must present evidence that substantiates the charge.

VARIATIONS AND VIOLATIONS

Standards of morality pertaining to lying, stealing, or breaking promises apply to all members of the university community, not just students.

Colleges and universities have an additional set of standards, however, that are designed to guard against students being (a) credited for learning they did not achieve and (b) gaining advantages or privileges that they do not deserve. Every university or college likely has a list of the specific actions that violate these two principles, but most such lists include the following:

- *Cheating:* Using information from books, notes, other people's tests, other people themselves, or some other source, when these materials are not permitted. Cheating "decreases the accuracy of the intended inferences arising from a student's performance on a test or assignment" and "gives one student an unfair advantage over other students on a test or assignment" (Cizek, 2003, p. 4).
- *Plagiarizing:* Presenting another person's words or ideas as one's own by copying verbatim another author's wording, attempting to paraphrase another's work but failing to change the wording sufficiently, or discussing material drawn from another source and failing to cite the origin of the words or ideas.
- *Self-plagiarism:* Presenting papers and materials prepared for previous classes as original work newly prepared for a current class (often called *recycling*).
- *Collusion:* Working with other students on projects that are explicitly defined as individual projects.
- *Falsifications:* Fabricating explanations for missed work or making false claims in an attempt to secure an unfair advantage in a testing situation.

The number of ways that students can cheat is limited only by their ingenuity, and each day they develop and implement entirely new methods. The following are some examples:

- *Signaling and texting:* Cooperating students send answers back and forth during the exam using a signaling system, such as notes on a shared eraser, hand signals, facial cues, smart phones, and so on.
- *Creative cribbing:* Instead of using a bit of paper with critical bits of information jotted on it, creative cribbers write codes on the paper covers of notebooks, on their skin (wrists, hands, ankles), in files they access using their cell phones, on their clothing (e.g., the bills of caps, shirt cuffs), on food wrappers (e.g., on the inside of a gum wrapper), and on food items themselves (e.g., on a stick of gum, which is then eaten to destroy the evidence).
- *The bomb scare:* Unprepared students call in a bomb threat for the building where the final exam is given. In a less dramatic approach, some unprepared students have arrived at the classroom before the professor and write on the board, "Due to illness, class and test canceled for today." By the time the professor

arrives, many students have already departed, and the test must be rescheduled.

- *The "lost" test:* A student, sensing failure, asks several questions of the professor during the exam so that the professor will remember that she was in class that day. She then leaves the class without turning in her test, and contacts the professor when grades are posted complaining that her test was lost. She has studied the test thoroughly since the exam date, willingly takes the test again, and aces it.
- *Ghosting:* A skilled student who is not registered for the class (a *ghost* or *ringer*) comes to class on test day and takes the test for another student, or lets that student copy his answers.
- *Scouting:* When quizzes are administered online, one student (the scout) quickly completes the test, fails, but gets his score and item-by-item feedback. He passes this information on to the students seated around him. For the next quiz or exam, someone else in the clique becomes the scout so others can get 100s. Students also scout for friends in other sections of the same class by using their phones to scan or photograph the test and send it to the students in the later sections.
- *Hacking:* A student breaks into computer databases and alters records of performance.

These sorts of actions violate a number of principles that most professors hold sacrosanct. Academic dishonesty opposes higher education's fundamental mission, which is the creation of knowledge and the dissemination of knowledge to others. Those who cheat or plagiarize not only fail to expand the scholarly stock of knowledge but also undo processes that were designed to help them learn. Such actions also suggest that grades and test scores are all that matter, when in fact it is the learning that matters most. Cheating and plagiarizing are also unfair to the professor and to other students. When students cheat, they increase their individual scores even though they have not achieved the learning that their scores suggest. When grades are based on normative evaluation systems, their cheating unfairly lowers the grades of students who did not cheat. As a consequence, students who do not cheat may be tempted to cheat themselves when they see others cheat successfully. Cheating and plagiarism are also specialized cases of a class of behavior that is widely condemned as immoral: the lie. When students cheat and plagiarize they are lying to their professor by falsely claiming "I wrote this," "I answered this question," or "I learned the material you asked me to."

MAINTAINING ACADEMIC INTEGRITY

Surveys of college students indicate that cheating is no rare avis: Three in four students report having engaged in a relatively serious forms of academic dishonesty, such as using crib notes, copying off of someone else's exam, working with others on projects that were supposed be done by individuals only, and plagiarizing material (e.g., McCabe, Butterfield, & Treviño, 2012). When asked if they had cheated in a particular class or during a given semester, 20% to 30% of students surveyed reported having committed an infraction, and some students reported having cheated repeatedly in the same class throughout the term (Stearns, 2001; Ward & Beck, 1990). Neither is cheating limited to undergraduate students: More than half of the graduate students surveyed in one study admitted plagiarizing (by inadequately paraphrasing the sampled text rather than copying entire sections), and one in four reported working collectively on individual assignments (Wajda-Johnston, Handal, Brawer, & Fabricatore, 2001). Students in online classes cheat as well, although most studies suggest this happens at rates that are similar to those seen in traditional lecture classes (Moten, Fitterer, Brazier, Leonard, & Brown, 2013).

Who is more likely to cheat? Men are slightly more likely to cheat than women, as are students whose time is more limited—say, by a job or participation in extracurricular activities—and students who are younger (Whitley, 1998). Students who are members of sororities and fraternities cheat more frequently than other students, as do student athletes (McCabe et al., 2012). Those who cheat tend to be lower in the Big Five personality constructs of Conscientiousness and Agreeableness (Giluk & Postlethwaite, 2015).

Human beings in general, and college students in particular, have a great capacity for moral goodness, but in many educational settings students fail to fulfill that potential. In the sections that follow, I discuss ways to encourage more positive forms of behavior and discourage antisocial actions (Cizek, 2003; McCabe et al., 2012).

Clarify and Review What Is Acceptable and What Is Unacceptable

The words *cheating* and *plagiarism* are ominous but nebulous in meaning. Students may do things that their professor considers cheating but because they did not think their actions fell in the value-laden category of "cheating," tell themselves, "I didn't cheat." Students may not realize that a take-home test should be completed when they are alone if the test's instructions do not explicitly state "This test must be completed by single individuals, without any discussion, help, or communication from others." They can justifiably claim that the old tests given them by friends are legitimate study aids, for they did not know that the tests were stolen from the classroom by students who skirted the professor's test-security procedures. They may even feel that glancing at another student's test paper is only "checking their own answers" rather than cheating, in particular if they claim that they did not change their own answers after their visual incursion into their neighbor's test. Students should therefore be given guidelines that turn gray ethical areas into sharply delineated black-and-white ones.

Reviews of standards pertaining to plagiarism are particularly useful because professors themselves do not always agree on the proper rules of citation and referencing. Although most students realize that copying an article out of a journal or purchasing a paper online and turning it in instead of writing their own paper is plagiarism, some do not think that taking a few sentences from someone else's work qualifies as plagiarism. Students are also surprised to learn that even when only the ideas, and not the words, are presented, a reference to the source of the ideas is still required. In courses with large amounts of writing, the professor may also want to assign an activity that requires students to identify

- instances of plagiarism,
- paraphrasing that retains so much of the original phrasing that it remains plagiarism,
- allowable paraphrasing, and
- failures to reference the source of ideas.

In one study that confirmed the importance of teaching students about standards, plagiarism rates dropped from 25.8% to 6.5% when students completed an online academic integrity module before starting their papers (Belter & du Pré, 2009).

Prescribed behaviors should also be reviewed, if appropriate. Some universities, for example, require that students must report all honor violations, so students in such institutions should be reminded of their responsibilities. They should also be urged to take steps to reduce the possibility of cheating by others by safeguarding their work from theft.

Establish a Code

What's wrong with taking a few answers from another student? Working together on a project that the professor said was to be individual work only? Borrowing the words of another author and using them to make a point in one's own paper? If students are simply given a list of banned behaviors, with no explanation for why these behaviors are untoward, then their compliance may be minimal. Academic integrity experts therefore recommend making cheating a moral issue by developing an honor code or set of academic integrity principles (e.g., McCabe et al., 2012). Whitley and Keith-Spiegel (2001), for example, suggested that an academic integrity policy should specify clearly

- the reasons for the policy;
- types of behavior that are forbidden;

- responsibilities of all parties, including students, faculty, and administrators;
- procedures that will be followed when a student is suspected of academic dishonesty; and
- penalties for violations.

Faculty themselves should be familiar with their college or university's ethics policy, if one exists. Although many professors prefer to handle cases of cheating themselves—for example, by conducting their own investigations and lowering grades, if warranted—their institutions' ethics policy may not permit this. In many cases such policies explicitly require that all instances of suspected violation be handled formally, using specified procedures, rather than informally by the professor. Faculty, too, are limited in terms of the severity of the sanction they can impose. Whereas individual faculty members can only fail a student in individual classes, more formal procedures can recommend expulsion of the student from the university.

Encourage the Internalization of Academic Integrity Codes

Evidence has indicated that fewer students cheat on campuses that have a well-conceived honor code, but the code's impact depends in large part on the extent to which students have accepted the academic values it represents (McCabe et al., 2012). If students do not personally accept the moral claim of the rules prohibiting cheating or plagiarism, then they will likely look to the situation to define what is right or wrong and will disobey a moral rule if everyone else is doing it, if no one can detect the violation, or if the potential benefits are substantial. Steps such as the ones in the following list should therefore be taken to increase the extent to which students internalize the code:

- Involve students in the discussion and development of an academic integrity policy. Just as managers have discovered that people are more likely to comply with workplace policies if they had a hand in developing those policies, so too will professors find that students are more likely to endorse and comply with ethical standards if they have contributed to the development of the standards.
- Give students the opportunity to endorse, formally, their adherence to the code (e.g., by signing a paper copy of it).
- Encourage the development of mastery goals that focus on learning and development (Jordan, 2001).
- Encourage the development of a full range of attitudes and values pertaining to academic integrity. Individuals who are generally opposed to cheating, but who have yet to formulate a position on specific types of cheating (e.g., cribbing or buying term papers),

are more likely to cheat than those who have action-specific attitudes (Homer & Kahle, 1988).

■ Increase the accessibility of anti-cheating attitudes by mentioning them prior to each exam and when creating assignments. Individuals sometimes act in ways that are inconsistent with their values only because they do so without considering their personal position on the matter.

Structure Longer Writing Assignments

When assigning papers, reports, and other written assignments, consider taking some of the following steps:

■ Consult with students on their topics rather than allowing them to pick freely the subject of their paper (because their choice might be based on papers available to them from nonpersonal sources, such as websites).

■ Require students complete a series of steps as they develop their papers, including describing the topic in a paragraph, listing the references they plan to consult, annotating key references, and drafting one section of the paper. These stages help students begin their work, and they also create a paper trail that confirms that their work is original (McBurney, 1999).

■ Explicitly ban the use of papers written for other classes if you do not permit such recycling.

■ Change the nature and topics of required exercises and papers routinely so that students are not tempted to use papers written by other students who took the class in a previous term.

■ Ask students to save early drafts of their papers and turn in those dated files with their final paper submission.

■ Let students work in three-person groups to reduce the temptation to collaborate secretly. Each student still turns in an individual paper but shares resources with others in the group.

■ Have students maintain an online writing journal in which they document the development of their paper.

Regulate the Classroom Environment

Milgram (1974), in his famous obedience studies, found that everyone wilted when pressured: Every single one of the men and women he tested obeyed initially a command to deliver painful shocks to a helpless victim, and 65% were completely obedient, even when the victims (who were in fact confederates) seemed to clearly be experiencing extreme pain. Similarly, studies of cheating have suggested that students, if subjected to strong, focused situational pressure that demands cheating, will cheat

(Forsyth & Berger, 1982). Given the power of the situation to compel even the best-intentioned student into cheating, testing situations and assignments should be designed so that acting dishonestly is difficult and risky and acting honestly is simple and easy. Consider using one or more of these tactics when giving a test in a traditional classroom setting:

- Ask students to sit with an empty seat between them if possible. If necessary, break up clusters of friends, or have students sit in assigned seats.
- Reserve one row of a class for students who are tardy, who ask frequent questions, or who engage in suspicious behavior and must be moved.
- Create at least two versions of the test by reordering the items. Have the versions printed on different-colored paper and interleave the tests prior to class so that no student is seated beside another student taking the same test version. As students work, visually inspect each row for adjacent students with same-colored tests and move them if necessary.
- In large classes, ask students to display a photo ID when they drop off their test. If very cautious, ask each student to sign an attendance list and their question booklet before leaving the room.
- If the college honor code does not limit proctoring, observe students carefully as they complete the exam, moving to the rear of the room frequently. In large classes, additional proctors will reduce cheating, in particular during the end of the period when attention is diverted to the collection of the tests.
- Guard the exams prior to test day. Lock them away, or keep them with you before the test day.
- Change the content of the exams as frequently as you can, given time limitations and the need to verify the psychometric adequacy of items by first using them in testing settings.
- Periodically exchange tests and test banks with professors who teach at other universities.
- If students provide their own blue books, collect them at the start of class and redistribute them at random.

Regulate the Online Class Environment

Fears that cheating would be rampant in online courses (it even has a special name: *e-cheating*) appear to be unjustified: Evidence suggests that cheating is no more likely to occur in an online class than in a traditional classroom (Moten et al., 2013). Even so, steps can be taken to further prevent cheating in such classes, including the following:

- Administer frequent low-stakes quizzes with time limits set so that students do not have time to review their materials in answering the items. If possible, vary the order of the items in the quiz, and display only a single item at a time on screen.

- Use a well-developed test bank and quiz program that randomly selects items from the bank, so each student is asked a unique set of questions.
- Review the time stamps of submitted work (or Internet protocol addresses, if available), to determine whether students are taking quizzes at time indicated.
- For major exams require students contact you via e-mail or the learning management system's virtual office software at a specific time scheduled in advance for the assessment. Verify their identity, and then provide them with the unique password for the test.
- Rely more on alternative methods of assessment. For example, because online classes provide an excellent environment for discussion, require that students engage frequently with one another on discussion forums, and regularly and rigorously grade their contributions. Require that students collaborate with each other on essay-type exams in their online learning groups.

Be Alert to, and Investigate, Possible Instances of Cheating

Sometimes faculty look the other way when their students cheat (Tabachnick, Keith-Spiegel, & Pope, 1991). When asked why, most traced their leniency to evidentiary concerns: They did not think they had the proof they needed to make a strong case against the student. Other inhibiting factors, identified through factor analysis, include emotional consequences, such as stress and lack of courage; concerns about the amount of time and effort the process would take; fears of retaliation and legal entanglements; and various denials that rationalized not intervening, such as assuming that the student would fail even if he or she were not confronted (Keith-Spiegel, Tabachnick, Whitley, & Washburn, 1998).

Inaction, however, leaves the cheater's unfairly high grade intact, reinforces students' beliefs that they can get away with cheating, and might even instill the implicit norm "cheating is allowable," so professors should be firm in their enforcement of academic integrity principles:

- Enforce the honor code. Social learning theory, developed by Bandura (1977), emphasizes learning through observation. This theory maintains that students will learn to act in socially acceptable way by observing and imitating their peers' actions. However, people do not imitate just any behavior, only those that earn positive outcomes for the person being observed (the *model*). This theory offers one clear recommendation for dealing with academic dishonesty: Make certain anyone guilty of a violation experiences an observable negative consequence.

- Announce that you will be asking people to move during the exam when you see any sign at all of copying. Note that in many cases the people being asked to move are innocent of copying but are being moved away from the individual who is suspected of copying.
- During the exam, if you notice suspicious behavior, announce to the entire class the reminder about cheating while staring directly at the possible cheater.
- Establish a clear policy pertaining to attendance on exam days and deadlines for papers, and require documentation of students' excuses for missing tests or deadlines (Caron, Whitbourne, & Halgin, 1992).
- Use statistical or computer-based detective methods to detect cheating and plagiarism, if possible, and warn students about these procedures. Statisticians have developed procedures for identifying unlikely coincidences in answer patterns of students (e.g., Belov, 2013), and several computer programs and Web sites (e.g., http://www.turnitin.com) allow instructors to search for statistical evidence of cheating and plagiarism.
- Assemble as much evidence as possible pertaining to an incident of academic dishonesty. Describe the incident in writing and send a copy of the report to your department chairperson. If proctors witnessed the infraction, have them write and sign a statement describing the incident. Statements can also be obtained from students in the class.
- Respect the suspected student's rights to due process by following scrupulously your institution's academic integrity guidelines. If those codes prohibit you from handling the infraction personally (e.g., by giving a cheater a zero on a test), then turn the matter over to the office that handles such matters.

Reduce Pressures That Sustain Cheating

Some students may cheat as a last resort, feeling that it is the only way they can pass the class or test. Indeed, one of the best predictors of cheating is level of preparedness, with unprepared students cheating more than prepared ones. One could therefore eliminate all cheating by giving all students As, but less extreme interventions, such as these, may be just as effective:

- Make certain that the demands of the course are appropriate for the types of students you are teaching.
- Use clear grading criteria, and communicate those criteria clearly to students.
- Test frequently so that students' grades are not based on just one or two major assignments.

- Give students sufficient time to complete their work.
- Accept valid excuses for missed work and absences.
- Consider letting students prepare one page or index card of notes for their use when taking tests.
- Do not let norms that encourage cheating (e.g., "Everybody cheats around here," "The only way to pass this class is to cheat") develop. Even students with well-internalized values may cheat if the norms of the situation prevent them from acting on the basis of their values.

Maintain Rapport With Students

McBurney (1999) predicted that a professor who enjoys a sense of rapport and a good relationship with his or her students—for example, by acting positively toward them and treating them respectfully—may be rewarded with fewer problems pertaining to cheating in their classes. Stearns (2001), in support of McBurney's suggestion, found that students who admitted cheating in a particular class were also more likely to report less liking of and respect for their professor. Although the students who cheated may have derogated their professor after the fact so as to rationalize their untoward actions and reduce their sense of guilt, their negative opinion of their professor may have contributed to their cheating. Students who like and respect their professor, but then cheat in his or her class, could resolve this attitude–behavior inconsistency by deriding the professor, claiming they had little choice, or telling themselves that their cheating had yielded no negative consequences, but these modes of dissonance resolution require far more cognitive ratiocination than a single behavioral change: not cheating.

THE PROFESSOR'S CODE OF CONDUCT

Students' civility and academic integrity are determined, in part, by standards set by the faculty. Just as social learning theory warns that students learn by observing their peers, the theory also suggests that professors can influence students by modeling actions and expressing values that are consistent with high standards of academic integrity (Bandura, 1977). A professor who prepares diligently for classes, develops sound methods for testing students' achievements, treats students and teaching assistants fairly, and enthusiastically supports the academy's emphasis on scholarship provides students with an admirable ideal to emulate. But if students are taught by a professor who treats students unfairly, teaches badly, or acts inappropriately, then they will likely learn a different lesson. Professors who want students to obey the rules must obey the rules, too.

Questions of morality must be discussed and debated because different people—and that includes professors, administrators, and students—vary considerably in their moral values and ideologies. However, Braxton, Bayer, and their colleagues, through a series of surveys of nearly 1,000 faculty in a range of disciplines, identified 10 tenets that they suggested should be considered for inclusion in a code of conduct for professors (Braxton & Bayer, 1999, 2004; Braxton, Proper, & Bayer, 2011). These tenets all serve to safeguard the psychological and physical well-being of students in classes, and all were supported by a substantial proportion of the faculty Braxton and his colleagues surveyed. They include (Braxton & Bayer, 2004, pp. 49–51) the following:

1. Undergraduate courses should be carefully planned.
2. Important course details should be conveyed to enrolled students.
3. New and revised lectures and course readings should reflect advancements of knowledge in a field.
4. Grading of examinations and assignments should be based on merit and not on the characteristics of students.
5. Various perspectives on course topics should be presented, examinations should cover the breadth of the course, and scholars' or students' perspectives at variance with the instructor's point of view should be acknowledged.
6. Students should be treated with respect as individuals. Students must not be treated in a condescending and demeaning way.
7. Faculty members must respect the confidentiality of their relationships with students and the students' academic achievements.
8. Faculty members must make themselves available to their students by maintaining office hours and being prepared for student advising, including being prepared to identify special services available for students with problems outside the expertise of the faculty member.
9. Faculty members must not have sexual relationships with students enrolled in their classes.
10. Faculty members must not come to class intoxicated from alcohol or drugs.

These principles are also frequently mentioned in college and university policy documents (Lyken-Segosebe, Min, & Braxton, 2012). A university that asks its students to abide by shared rules pertaining to civility, cheating, and plagiarism likely also asks the faculty to make certain their actions are consistent with the academy's standards for scholarship, teaching, and service. Professors, too, if they are members of a professional association, are likely bound by set of professional ethics, such as the ethical code of the American Association of University

Professors or that of the Society for Teaching and Learning in Higher Education (B. Murray, Gillese, Lennon, Mercer, & Robinson, 1996). Professors may also be bound by the code of ethics for their specific discipline. For example, the American Psychological Association's (2010) "Ethical Principles of Psychologists and Code of Conduct" sets forth a set of basic principles that define the professional responsibilities of psychologists in general. Although the ethics code focuses primarily on the complex issues that face therapists, many of its rules and principles are relevant to professors as well. For example, "Principle B: Fidelity and Responsibility," requires psychologists to "uphold professional standards of conduct" (p. 3). "Principle C: Integrity," stresses the importance of dealing with others fairly and honestly, and enjoins them to "keep their promises and to avoid unwise or unclear commitments" (p. 3). The rules themselves offer relatively clear standards for professional conduct in a variety of areas related to teaching, including testing, relationships with students, and competence.

Faculty must, however, exercise caution and sensitivity in such matters. As employees of their college/university, and as members of the community, professors are expected to act in ways that are consistent with their institution's regulations and their community's standards. Although particular classes of actions, such as out-of-date lecture content or sexual harassment, may not be inconsistent with one code of ethics, they may be condemned by another. A professor who cites one code of ethics to support his or her actions may quickly discover that the college's administrators base their appraisals on an altogether different code. If local norms condemn certain behaviors, considering them tantamount to moral turpitude, then faculty would be well advised to conduct themselves accordingly. At minimum, any professor who is considering engaging in questionable behaviors should discuss the matter with colleagues and supervisors.

Managing Redux: Foster Civility and Integrity

Professors do not just walk into a classroom or open up the course's learning management system and teach the students they find there; they must also create and manage that class. Even though their top priority is promoting students' learning and achievement, they must also enforce basic principles of academic integrity, civility, and tolerance. Teaching is a profoundly interpersonal activity and, like all interpersonal activities, it can be disrupted by conflict, crises, misunderstandings, and antagonisms. Some of these problematic aspects of teaching are inconsequential, but others can significantly disrupt the learning experience unless they are handled swiftly and carefully. When students violate principles pertaining to academic integrity, the professor must intervene with sanctions for the violators and rewards for those who conform. Professors, as teaching professionals, are duty bound to help their students achieve their learning outcomes, all the while making sure to safeguard their welfare and rights.

Upgrading
Using Technology Creatively in Teaching

8

Methods of teaching change over time—but very slowly. For centuries, professors lectured and led discussions, but professors after Johannes Gutenberg added required readings. In the 1800s, cutting-edge instructors began to use the latest innovation in visual aid technology: the blackboard. One student of the time remarked,

> On entering this room, we were struck at the appearance of an ample blackboard suspended on the wall, with lumps of chalk on a ledge below, and cloths hanging at either side. I had never heard of such a thing before. (quoted in Rocklin, 2001, p. 1)

Today, professors continue to use books and boards (black-, white-, and smart-), but they also use information technologies to make the ideas and insights of their discipline more accessible, enhance student engagement, improve the way they assess learning, and forge stronger connections to their students. Just as information technology has changed nearly every aspect of society—how people acquire news and

http://dx.doi.org/10.1037/14777-009
College Teaching: Practical Insights From the Science of Teaching and Learning, by D. R. Forsyth

information, the forms of entertainment they seek, the way they conduct their business, and even the way they manage their social relationships—so too is it changing the way professors teach and students learn.

Upgrading Classrooms

As the Internet became faster and more reliable, professors began experimenting with new methods for interacting with their students. When students started getting e-mail accounts, faculty began to e-mail them reminders, assignments, and updates. When the Internet provided a means of browsing hyperlinked texts, professors started developing web and course pages. When the old newsgroups and computer bulletin boards upgraded to forums, professors started discussing ideas online. Many professors still teach only when their students are gathered with them, collocated in a shared physical space. They take roll each day, lecture from a podium, collect students' printed papers, and work the chalk-and-talk method. Others, however, have updated their methods by doing some or all of their teaching online.

VARIETIES OF ONLINE CLASSES

Using technology in teaching in not an all-or-nothing undertaking. For example, the hypothetical Dr. Lillbit does her teaching in a physical classroom with an assembled class, but she posts the syllabus, readings, and grades to her college's course learning management system (LMS). Dr. Moroline, in contrast, teaches what he calls a *hybrid*, or *blended* class. He meets with his students each week in a physical classroom to discuss course topics and readings, to work on collaborative activities, and take tests. However, he also requires that his students complete many assignments and activities online. For example, Dr. Moroline is a master of the threaded discussion forum. Each week, he posts five provocative questions related to the course readings and requires that students post responses to both the original question and to other students' responses. Dr. Allon's class, in contrast, is a fully online one. His students never join with each other or Dr. Allon in a physical place; they meet only virtually, through online interactions. Dr. Allon, like Drs. Lillbit and Moroline, e-mails his students regularly, leads discussions, and asks students to work in groups, but he interacts more extensively with his students via the Internet. With the assistance of his information technology department, he video-records lectures that cover course materials, and students take low-stakes quizzes after they watch each one. His students keep personal, reflective journals, and Dr. Allon reads and comments on their posts weekly. Students write reaction papers, and he grades them with a rubric but also records an audio clip of his critique, which he posts to each students' grade book. He also carefully monitors his students' online activity and sends personalized, motivational e-mails to students who are too inconsistent in their engagement. Dr. Allon's is not a self-paced class, for it has an established start and end date and deadlines for completion of coursework that are clearly defined in the course syllabus.

As with all forms of teaching, no two professors use technology in their teaching in exactly the same way. Some professors use Internet-based technology to post readings and to e-mail reminders to students, but they do not actually do any teaching online. In a hybrid or blended course, a significant portion of the teaching (e.g., 30% or more) relies on technology, but in an online course all teaching is distance education. Blended and online courses also include both asynchronous and synchronous activities. Students complete *asynchronous* activities at their own pace. They drop off papers, take quizzes, post replies in forum discussion areas when they can—but often within a specified time period. *Synchronous* activities, in contrast, require students interact with each other and/or the professor in real time: watching a live video stream, visiting the professor during virtual office hours, taking part in a tele-conference or webinar, or messaging one another in an Internet relay chat are examples of synchronous learning activities.

Flipped (Inverted) Classes

A *flipped*, or *inverted* class is an example of a hybrid online class. This format asks students to do many of the things they once did in a traditional, face-to-face class online, before the traditional class. They should, for example, read and study the assigned texts. They can also discuss the assigned readings with each other on forum areas in their LMS. What about lectures? Downloadable lectures, usually prepared by the course professor, are one of the defining characteristics of a flipped class. Instead of lecturing in class, professors capture and post their lecture, and students watch the lectures online before coming to class. One might then ask, what is class time used for? It is used for more active forms of learning, such as small group discussion, working problem sets, group activities, demonstrations, simulations, and quizzing (Braseby, 2014).

This method is often paired with other techniques, including Just-in-Time Teaching. With Just-in-Time Teaching, students are given several specific questions to answer before the day's class. The questions are due only an hour or two before class convenes, and students submit them via e-mail, a wiki, or a discussion forum. The professor uses those responses to identify sources of confusion and prepare activities that are targeted to address students' misunderstandings and continuing uncertainty (Witney & Smallbone, 2011).

Massive Open Online Courses

Massive Open Online Courses (MOOCs) are examples—if extreme ones—of all online courses. These courses are offered through various commercial services, such as edX, Udacity, and Coursera, as well as larger universities, including Harvard, Stanford, MIT, and the University of California system. Some courses are self-paced but all are well structured, with clearly defined learning goals established at the beginning; frequent reviews and assessments during the course; and, in some cases, a final assessment that is required for certification of successful completion. These courses take advantage of online lectures to provide content, with the material provided by experts in the field. Some MOOCs stress high levels of interaction among the students, creating a community of learners who work collectively to share resources and information related to the course. Some MOOCs can be taken for course credit at universities, although many offer certification only for students who complete the course and its requirements successfully (Haber, 2014).

COURSEWARE

There is little mystery about the mechanics of teaching and learning in a traditional course. Students and professor gather in some designated place where they communicate with each other in various ways—by talking together, sharing documents, making presentations, and answering questions—and then they disperse. These same interactions occur in online classes, but they are made possible by the Internet and the programs that make communication among networked individuals possible.

Learning Management Systems

At about the time that the digital projectors started pushing overhead projectors out of classrooms, computer scientists were developing the hardware and software needed to enhance the exchange of information through the Internet. Their work developing e-mail protocols, servers, file storage systems, modems, Ethernet, and faster operating systems yielded a collection of new tools for teaching, including forums, blogs, wikis, cloud storage and file sharing systems, social networking, and other ways to use the web to facilitate collaboration. This general shift from a static, one-directional flow of information to dynamic, interactive, user-generated content is sometimes referred to as *Web 2.0*.

These tools are useful when teaching traditional face-to-face courses, and they are particularly valuable when teaching students at remote physical locations. Although students have been taking college courses without actually attending classes on campus for decades, technological advances in courseware and networks now provide the staging, delivery, collaborative, interactive, and assessment tools needed to create dynamic distance learning experiences for both professors and their students (Singh, Mangalaraj, & Taneja, 2010):

- *Staging tools* provide the basic structures needed to manage and deliver course material to students. With them, one can create a password-protected area on the Internet where the records and documents for the course can be securely stored.
- *Delivery tools* provide a way to more easily generate web-based content, such as video, text, or audio information. Originally, anyone wishing to build a page of information for the Internet needed to use specialized programs or code their pages in hypertext markup language (HTML). Web 2.0 made generating content much easier.
- *Collaboration tools* let students and faculty exchange information dynamically, in discussions, commentaries, and more extensive and elaborate text-based documents. Now students can not only access static information on the Internet but also contribute their own content as well.
- *Interactive communication tools* provide students with the means to contact each other and their professor. E-mail was the traditional tool used for this purpose, but texting and applications that support texting have grown more popular among users.
- *Assessment tools* provide the instructor with methods for testing students' performance.

Apps and Applications

LMSs such as Blackboard meet the basic needs of online classes, but their one-size-fits-all approach means that they do not always provide the functionality professors require for specific courses. And, in many cases, these programs—designed to still work with limited bandwidth and older computers—provide a less than pleasing user interface. In many cases, too, they were not designed for mobile devices, which students use with more regularity and enthusiasm. Many online teachers therefore use *apps* (specialized programs that usually perform just one function very well) and *applications* (programs that perform a wider range of interrelated functions) to supplement the functions of their LMS. But not all innovations in online instruction have stood the test of time. Second Life, for example, created a far more vibrant online experience for learners, but many felt it was more trouble than it was worth. And what about the poor Flip Cam—so popular as a means of capturing video until the rise of the smartphone. The following are examples of tools and apps that can be used effectively in teaching, but by the time you read this some of them may already be laughably archaic.

- Audacity is an open source audio editor and recorder that can be used for creating podcasts and recording voice feedback and critiques. Students can use Audacity to record study sessions, interviews, and so on.

- Wordpress, Blogger, and other blogging programs allow users (bloggers) to post their comments, ideas, thoughts, and so on, but they come with a number of gadgets and add-ons that streamline the process. But if you want all of your students to blog, consider using Ning, which combines both blogging and social networking functions for all registered members.

- Mindmapping programs, such as Bubbl.us and MindMeister, facilitate the development of outlines, mapping of associations, and cause–effect relationships.

- Bookmarking programs, such as Delicious and Pocket, and browsers that can be personalized, such as Google and Firefox, solve the problem of lost or just disorganized bookmarks. Once you log into your account, your bookmarks are available, no matter what device you are using.

- Facebook is the leading social network application and is designed to work smoothly across all platforms. Students are heavy users of Facebook, so if you establish a group page for your class, students are more likely to visit that page and learn from its contents.

- If you need to make use of images in your teaching, but hope to keep them organized, then Flickr, Photobucket, or a similar online image file system will help you not only organize them but also share them with others.

- Google continues to develop useful tools, including its Google Docs, spreadsheet, calendar, and e-mail programs. Google Docs are particularly useful because this tool lets students edit together in real time, and automatically saves each revision. And Google Scholar helps students draw information from more reputable sources on the Internet.

- If you are teaching online, you will eventually need to create video and audio recordings. Some of these recordings will walk students through the use of the website, and so should be capable of capturing your screen and audio, and combining this information in downloadable files. In other cases, you will wish deliver short lectures on specific topics, which students can download and review asynchronously. You will need a program like Camtasia, Jing, or Snagit to create those files.

- Wikipedia sets the standard for an informational resource created and edited by a community, but you and your students can build wikis as well, focusing on specific course topics. You could install MediaWiki, the open source software that runs Wikipedia, but Wetpaint, Wikispaces, and PBworks are easier to learn and use.

- Cloud storage has become common, nearly replacing portable drives as storage systems. Your university likely offers students file storage on its servers, but they may be more comfortable using commercial storage systems, such as Onedrive, idrive, and Google Drive.

▪ Reference storage applications facilitate the identification of sources of research and the saving of those sources for eventual citation in documents. Zotero and Refworks are two sophisticated and easy-to-use systems for tracking sources.

Gaming Applications and Simulations

Computer-based learning tools facilitate the development of conceptual skills by creating virtual problems, cases, and laboratories. One specialized type of instructional program, *interactive simulations*, re-creates situations that illustrate course concepts in virtual reality. These programs create hypothetical situations for students and then guide their exploration of these situations. In a psychology course, for example, students can converse with the artificial intelligence program Eliza, who simulates a nondirective, client-centered Rogerian therapist (Suler, 1987). Medical students, in a course in human anatomy, can combine traditional lectures and readings with an online application that simulates a dissectible human cadaver. The simulator bases the three-dimensional model on the National Library of Medicine's Visible Human Project database and permits full rotation of the images (Forsyth, Johnson, Baronian, Newton, & Stewart, 2003). In a business management course, teams of students can gather online in an attempt to scale Mount Everest and along the way encounter challenges that threaten the group's success (Edmondson & Roberto, 2007). Students studying educational leadership can spend a simulated day as a principal in a high school, making one choice after another as unexpected situations arise (D. Mann, Reardon, Becker, Shakeshaft, & Bacon, 2011). As might be expected, students find these educational experiences to be highly engaging (Carnes, 2014).

Modularized Instruction

Many of technology's earliest contributions to education were designed to help students study more effectively, both by providing study tools and by structuring their methods of studying. Many computer-based learning programs, for example, are tutorials that can trace their ancestry back to Skinner's early vision of a teaching machine that shapes students' behavior through reinforcement (L. T. Benjamin, 1988). These tutorials usually segment material into modules, and students must demonstrate proficiency on a quiz before they are given credit for completing the module. Other tutorials are sophisticated nonlinear hypertexts with various tools added for students: self-quizzes, search boxes, indexes, pop-up dictionaries, libraries of additional titles, or animated professors who provide comic relief. These programs are interactive; they allow students to control the pace of their movement through the topics. Most programs also ask students to respond to questions as a check of their comprehension and will direct students to different material depending on their responses. These tools all structure students' learning and at the same time teach them how they should study the material.

Authoring Applications

Writing remains a core literacy in college, for students must know how to express themselves and communicate their ideas clearly to other people. Fortunately, some of the most difficult and time-consuming aspects of writing, composition, and critique are made easier, and are partially streamlined, when classes are online. When students submit their paper to the course LMS, professors use advanced editing and commenting tools to identify specific tracked changes and offer general commentary—they can even record audio files containing their more general comments and suggestions for improvements. When students write using blogging software, such as Wordpress, they can invite other students to review and comment on their writing before they "publish" the paper in its final form. Students can also write collaboratively using such online writing tools as Google docs, blogs, and wikis (Radclyffe-Thomas, 2012). As long as their identities are properly safeguarded, students' work can be shared more widely than in just the class. Students are sometimes more motivated and committed to producing higher quality work when they are writing for a larger audience.

Upgrading Professors

Why are some professors increasing their reliance on information-based technologies in their teaching? Some, I suspect, use them because they just like gadgets and gizmos. They are early adopters of technology, and so they make use of it in their classes; they will use any cool new tool. Others use it because someone made them. They were, for example, asked to teach an online course one semester, or the faculty at their university passed a resolution to stop wasting paper by printing syllabi. Some educators consider and sometimes adopt new technologies to enhance their teaching. They have recognized a problem—or number of problems—and they are turning to technology for solutions to them. They may, for example, realize that they are supposed to be teaching students to be lifelong learners, yet they are not helping students learn to search out and make use of online information resources. They worry that their lectures are not sufficiently engaging, yet their classes are so large that discussion and group activities are not an option. They may feel that they are not connecting personally to their students in the classroom and wonder whether a professor who is available to students on the Internet will be more approachable than one in an office located in some hard-to-find building on campus.

NETWORKING

Bill Gates (1999), in his book *Business @ The Speed of Thought*, offered rules for using technology to improve business practice. Nearly all of his rules stress the tremendous potential of technology for creating connections between people. He insists, for example, that all his employees use e-mail to communicate with one another. He also recommended reviewing digital documents online, so that workers can share their interpretations, and creating virtual teams using networking software. These insights apply equally well to teaching because computer-based technologies increase, rather than decrease, interaction among students and faculty. When professors encourage their students to exchange e-mail and confer online, students can interact with their instructor and other students in the class 24 hours a day, 7 days a week. As a consequence, the "total communication increases and, for many students, the results seems more intimate, protected, and convenient than the more intimidating demands of face-to-face communication with faculty" (Chickering & Ehrmann, 1996, p. 3).

E-mail

Technological advances have added one after another new method for communicating with other people, including Skype, texting, Instagram, Snapchat, Twitter, GroupMe, video conferencing, conference calls, and on and on. But of these many tools, e-mail remains a "killer app": The most frequently used tool for information exchange in the world (Ipsos, 2012). E-mail, although a technologically simple program, is quick, flexible, and reliable, and it works across all platforms and devices. It can be used not only for short announcements and reminders but also to provide additional information about ideas discussed in class, suggestions for further readings, and new questions for students to mull in preparation for the next class. Unlike the course LMS or a static website—which students must visit before they can be influenced by the information they contain—e-mails push information directly to students, increasing the chances that they will read the information (Forsyth & Archer, 1997). The following ideas suggest ways to use e-mail effectively:

- Require all students to use e-mail. Test their e-mail aptitude at the start of the term by sending each one an e-mail and requiring they respond (perhaps with a short description of their reasons for taking the class).

- Send messages to students regularly. These messages should contain not only information about class logistics but also content information that is assessed on the class tests. The e-mails should be written in a personal tone that students will come to identify as your e-mail "voice."
- Keep paragraphs short; students often read them on hand-held devices that will truncate longer messages. Put critical information at the front of each e-mail rather than at the end. If you need to communicate substantial content, state explicitly at the start of the e-mail that it is a long one, and use embedded links in the e-mail to route recipients to the information posted online.
- Use the features of your LMS to streamline the e-mail process. Most LMSs, for example, will not only post messages to a class announcement page but also e-mail a copy of that announcement to all members of the class. Use this system for e-mailing, if at all possible, so that each message to students is automatically archived.
- Use a mailing program, such as Microsoft's Mail Merge, to send personalized bulk template-based messages.
- Most LMSs provide excellent tools (reliable, trackable, and so simple as to be nearly foolproof) for students for submitting their assignments. However, if you permit students to turn in assignments via e-mail, standardize the process (e.g., require that they paste them directly into the body of the e-mail or that they write them using a popular word-processing program and attach them to an e-mail message).
- Install and regularly update a good antivirus program, and regularly check websites that provide information about viruses. Do not delegate this task to anyone else.

Social Network Tools

Some professors use of other forms of information-based communication, such as Twitter, blogs, texting, and Facebook, to increase their online social presence. These forms of communication are ones that students use frequently, and so they increase the reliability of the information exchange. Some students, however, feel that these technologies should be reserved for personal communication. The majority of the students in one study that made use of Facebook for class purposes (posting information, communication, completing online apps) rated the experience positively (64.6%), but a small minority (13.4%) responded negatively to the professor's intrusion into their social network (Forsyth, 2008).

Care should be taken so that these messages do not (a) violate the Family Educational Rights and Privacy Act of 1974 or (b) express personal opinions that others may inappropriate. You can, for example, require students follow your Twitter account and subscribe to your blog. These social networking tools will increase students' engagement with you and the material, but requiring that they respond to your posts is a gray area. Just as you cannot post students' grades on a sheet of paper tacked to your door or leave graded papers in a box outside of your office, so too can you not make public information about your students' grades, their enrollments, and so on. If using social media, be clear with students that they are voluntarily taking part in the exchange and, if they wish to maintain their privacy, ask them to use an alias account. Also, if asking other students to write comments and reviews on other students' posts, caution them to never "grade" the posts (Drake, 2014).

Professors, too, should be mindful of what they write in tweets, blogs, Facebook posts, and the like. Naming a student, for example, is a violation of the Family Rights and Privacy Act, and in the last few years more than a few faculty have expressed themselves unguardedly in social media, with subsequent negative consequences for them.

Maintaining an Online Presence

Most universities provide faculty space on the university web server that they can use to create personal home pages, pages for their research and professional work, and pages for their classes. These sites provide faculty with another means of communicating information to students. Although faculty routinely post most course-related information in the LMS, they can post more general ideas, information, and analyses related to their courses on public web pages (and blogs, of course) so that students who want to know more about the course can review it before they gain access by enrolling and gain access through the LMS.

Online Office Hours

Information technologies also have increased the effectiveness of some of teaching's most conventional practices, such as office hours and guest lectures. Because some students, in particular nontraditional ones, cannot attend office hours held on campus, virtual office hours can be held at night and on weekends in a discussion area or virtual office area of the LMS. You can, before an exam, create a new discussion forum in the class and invite students to post any questions that arise as they study, but set a deadline so that you have a chance to respond before the test. Technology also creates greater connections among scholars and students. When students raise questions that go beyond their professor's interests and expertise, the professor can then involve other experts and scholars in classes by arranging them to visit class through Skype or a video capture lecture.

CURATING WEB RESOURCES

In the 1990s, when the Internet was taking root on computers around the world, people actually called it the "information superhighway," for even then they recognized that this technology would make it possible to access information more easily. The term did not catch on, but the Internet has lived up to the promise of making information that was once hidden away in libraries, journals, books, and other archives readily available to anyone who know how to use a web browser.

Information scarcity is no a longer problem for most students, but information overload is. Students can, with the help of Google, Siri, or similar search tools, find their way to thousands of online resources, including blogs, media sites, journal articles, books, and magazines. When they visit their university library's website they gain access to a variety of archives and databases of images, almanacs, newspapers, journals, theses, dissertations, encyclopedias, and dictionaries. When they register at publishers' and commercial news services' sites, students can use their online resources to explore nearly any topic. Students can even take courses at another university, either by registering at that university or by taking advantage of one of their Massive Open Online Courses (MOOCs).

Given this wealth of available information, professors no longer need to create original content as much as they need to curate the content that is already available (Bowen, 2012). Although students can browse the web themselves and use search tools to locate resources, professors can help by pointing them to particularly informative pages. Many pages also contain large amounts of questionable material, so by posting a curated list of links on their pages professors can be certain their students are referred to reputable sources of information. For example, what if physics students want to know more about Bohr's model of the hydrogen atom? They could start by watching an ion-capa applet that shows electron transitions before visiting the University of Colorado's Physics 2000 site to explore both photon emission and absorption. Chemistry students might appreciate a guiding nudge in the direction of Carnegie Mellon University's courses on chemical equilibrium and acid-based chemistry, or Frostburg State University's omnibus links for chemistry research links. Students in the humanities, such as philosophy and literature, may have missed http://www.bartleby.com, the *Encyclopedia Mythica* (http://www.pantheon.org), or Project Gutenberg (http://www.gutenberg.org) in their travels through the Internet. History students could begin their work at http://www.biography.com or the "Making of America Project" at Cornell University rather than Wikipedia. The Internet provides a rich bounty to the tech-savvy professor and their students.

ONLINE LECTURING

Ten years ago, when the student who skipped a class casually asked, "Did I miss anything?" most professors—after stifling their irritation at the impertinent question itself—answered, "Get the notes from someone." Nowadays the answer might be, "Come by and see me if you have any questions after you review the online recording of the lecture." Recording lectures was formerly so technically complex, and the files so massive in size, that only the highest of the high-tech professors went digital, but the proliferation of webcams, free video archiving services such as YouTube, and easy-to-use capture software (e.g., Tegrity, Panopto) have put lecture capture within even the technophobe's reach.

Recording one's lectures provides a number of benefits. Students can review, repeatedly and at their own pace, each lecture. Those who miss a lecture need not wonder what they missed, and office hour reviews become less frequent. Captured lectures can be broadcast to more than the students in the class itself, providing the opportunity to increase the number of potential learners well beyond those listed on the roster. Bowen (2012), however, argued strongly in favor of podcasts rather than capturing lectures given in classrooms. Lecture captures re-create the classroom experience online, but they are usually filled with inaudible comments, distracting sounds from the students, and "dead air." A podcast, in contrast, is an audio or video recording that can be sent directly to students, who can listen or watch the lecture on their phone, laptop, or web-ready televisions. An alternative form of podcasting, the *screencast*, captures the information displayed on the professor's screen and so can be used not only to display images, graphics, presentations, and videos but also to demonstrate how to do things using a computer, such as using a spreadsheet or searching in a sophisticated way for information on the Internet.

Podcasts and screencasts are more easily edited than recordings of lectures, and their content can be controlled to accentuate points in more detail, include additional examples, or provide visual images that were not used in the classroom. Podcasts and screencasts also need not track the lecture given in the classroom so closely that students feel no need to attend classroom lectures any longer. Although some research suggests that making lecture captures available to students does not reduce classroom attendance, other studies have suggested that some students disappear from the room when they can get their lectures online—and that these may be the very students who will most benefit from the enforced structure of a face-to-face lecture experience (Drouin, 2014).

LEADING DISCUSSIONS

As I noted in Chapter 3, discussions are not just student-centered methods of teaching; they are also very engaging. When used online, however, you will need to actively lead the discussion—at least until the discussion norms become well entrenched in the class. Experienced online instructors regularly identify discussions as the best ways to increase student engagement in the course and have offered the following recommendations for enhancing one's discussion-leadership skills (M. D. Miller, 2014):

- Provide students with a tutorial on how to navigate the discussion forum and post comments so that threads remain intact.
- Include discussions as a regular part of the weekly or biweekly class activity. For example, each Monday post five questions in the class forum area and tell students they must respond to one of the prompts by Wednesday. Also require and set deadlines for students to comment on other students' responses and comments.
- Comment on students' responses and comments during the discussion period (e.g., don't wait until the weekend to read all the comments). Be brief, and positive, but ask for development and clarification as needed.
- Know that students will participate more regularly if they are graded on their postings.

Upgrading Students

Few college students would likely be surprised if they were told, on the first day of class, that some part of their learning experience would make use of information technologies. These students are, after all, digital natives—members of the "net generation" who have been using the Internet since they were in grade school (Prensky, 2001). In one study, more than two thirds of incoming freshmen reported having visited an online instructional resource site just to expand their learning rather than to meet the demands of a course (Eagan, Lozano, Hurtado, & Case, 2013). They are prepared to take advantage of technology to enhance their learning outcomes.

THE ONLINE ENVIRONMENTS

Maria Montessori, best known for the teaching method that bears her name, believed that students absorb knowledge through their own actions:

> Education is not something which the teacher does, but . . .
> a natural process which develops spontaneously in the human being. It is not acquired by listening to words, but in virtue of experiences in which the child acts on his environment. The teacher's task is not to talk, but to prepare and arrange a series of motives for cultural activity in a special environment made for the child. (Montessori, 1949/1995, p. 8)

Advances in information technology have created that "special environment" for learning online. Students learn more easily when they have identified their educational goals, value these goals, and are confident that they can achieve them. Information technologies can increase all these aspects of motivation. In offline, more traditional college classes instructors decide what topics will be covered and in what depth. In contrast, in blended and online classes students gain more control over their learning experiences. Students, with the help of the faculty, can create personalized educational experiences that match their unique interests, needs, and goals. When a particular topic interests them, they can delve more deeply into it. If they feel challenged by a concept or topic, they can re-run programs and move through them slowly, at a pace that suits their need. If they are visual learners, they can study multimedia presentations that combine graphics, images, and text information. If they are text learners, they can spend their time studying information-dense websites and e-books.

Students can also control *when* they will learn in classes that use technology. Provided that students can gain access to the Internet and class resources, they can learn anytime and anywhere: When teaching is asynchronous, then dorm rooms, private residences, or the library at 11:00 p.m. all become classrooms. Students who express positive attitudes about online learning tend to use them more, and these students also earn higher grades in the course. An analysis of students' emotions when they were using technology also suggested that they enjoy this form of learning (Forsyth & Archer, 1997). When researchers examined, meta-analytically, the emotions experienced by students using such learning technologies as intelligent tutors, simulations, and computer-assisted instruction, they discovered that negative emotions such as anger, disgust, sadness, and anxiety were rare, but engagement and flow (as well as a little bit of frustration) were more common (D'Mello, 2013).

INCREASING ENGAGEMENT

In the long run, technologies should save students time and effort (and some money) by making course resources available for their use on their desktops: Students will make fewer trips to the library, spent less time waiting in line at the bookstore, and not have to waste time tracking down their hard-to-locate professors. If Camilia, while studying for tomorrow's test, realizes she is confused about the theory discussed in class 2 weeks ago, she can e-mail other class members and ask for their input. When Kim, Earl, and Demarco start to work on their group project for class, they can stay in touch using Facebook's messaging program, the GroupMe phone app, or the group function in their LMS. Professors and their students now connect with one another not only over coffee, in classes, or at the dining hall, library, and fitness center but also through the Internet.

Online learning does not suit every student, however. Just as some students prefer to learn through attending lectures and others prefer discussion and student-centered learning opportunities, online learning suits some students better than others. Students who feel they have the technical skills needed for success in an online environment, and who express a positive attitude about online learning (e.g., "Learning is the same in class and at home on the Internet"), tend to earn higher grades in their online classes (Bernard, Brauer, Abrami, & Surkes, 2004). However, students who are more interested in the social, interpersonal side of their college experience do less well in online classes, in comparison with those who are self-regulated. Not all students are capable of maintaining the consistently high level of engagement in their studies that an online class requires, so attrition rates tend to be higher for online classes than for offline ones (Hart, 2012). Fortunately, those experienced with teaching online classes offer many suggestions for increasing students' persistence in their learning, including (M. D. Miller, 2014; Sung & Mayer, 2012):

- Balance students' need for autonomy with their need for structure. Particularly during the early weeks of the course, set clear deadlines for assignments, grade those assignments quickly, and give students detailed (but optimistic) feedback if they do not meet your expectations.
- Use rubrics in grading discussions and papers, but also allow students access to the rubrics so that they can understand, more clearly, what are the criteria for a successful performance.
- Interact regularly with students though one-to-one channels of communication; do not just grade their work and post feedback, but also e-mail them (personally) with general comments about their work. Always interact with students in ways that demonstrate your respect for them.

- Most LMSs allow you to track students' access to course materials. During the first 2 weeks of the course, cap review the digital footprints your students are leaving in the course website, and offer support to any student who is not investing sufficient time in the course.
- Be flexible enough to make changes in the schedule and assignments if circumstances interfere with students' progress. Students tend to respond very positively when asked what adjustments should be made to improve the learning process.
- Shrink the psychological size of the class by creating subgroups of students within the larger class. Assign these small groups tasks and discussion areas, which are graded relative to the performance of other groups.

SENSE OF COMMUNITY

Students in large traditional lecture classes sometimes complain of feeling anonymous and unrecognized as individuals: Although they are together, they feel alone. Ironically, students in online classes who have developed a strong sense of community report feeling close, meaningful connections with other students. Even though they are alone, they feel like they are together (Turkle, 2011).

Online classes do not automatically grow into communities; that process must be nurtured through strategic interventions. Communities, for example, have well-defined memberships and clear boundaries. When students are reminded to never share their class login credentials with others, they should also be told that the class is a private, members-only place. They should therefore feel comfortable when in the online environment because they are among friends and fellow students. Communities are also usually differentiated, in some way, from other communities. Frequently referring to the class using its official designation, such as "ABS212 Spring," does little to set the class apart from others. Instead, when students choose the course name, collaborate on its group-level goal, and identify its unique standards and features, they will be more likely to take on the qualities of a true social group rather than remaining just an association of individuals. As a sense of community increases, students are more likely to think that their membership in the class is personally significant. They feel connected to and interdependent with other members, are glad they belong to the group, feel good about the group, and experience strong attachment to the group. Their connection to the group also becomes more affectively toned—a "hot" cognitive reaction rather than a "cold" recognition of membership (Forsyth, 2014). In general, the stronger the sense of community within the students in an online class, the more likely they will be to take part in activities, complete assignments, and perform at higher levels on graded assignments (Boling, Hough, Krinsky, Saleem, & Stevens, 2012).

INFORMATION LITERACY

Students regularly communicate with friends, relatives, and teachers via text messaging and e-mail. When working on papers and projects they frequently acquire information via Facebook, Wikipedia, and online media outlets rather than visiting a bricks-and-mortar library and pulling books off a physical shelf. They are heavy users of entertainment content providers, such as YouTube and Netflix, and are comfortable with streaming audio and video content. However, surveys of their competencies suggest that even so-called digital natives still have much to learn about how to use technology. Many students know about Google, but not Google Scholar. They make use of Wikipedia's content, but they have more difficulty accessing professionally edited and authored resources, such as the *Oxford English Dictionary* site or JSTOR. They read blogs and web postings, but they themselves do not blog or contribute their insights to online discussion forums (Margaryan, Littlejohn, & Vojt, 2011). Although graduates may continue their learning by returning to campus for public lectures or visiting the public library, in all likelihood most will rely on information technologies to search out the information they need. Technology-based classes do not explicitly teach networking, use of e-mail, or word processing, but students must learn these skills in order to accomplish the course's content-based goals (see Table 8.1).

ACADEMIC INTEGRITY

Online classes raise new problems for professors who are concerned with cheating and plagiarism. Online classes strongly endorse collaboration, so students may work together on assignments even when they were instructed not to. Students need not face their instructor in a classroom, and without that threat of detection and public embarrassment they may worry a little less about the consequences of plagiarism. Some surveys suggest that students think they would be more likely to cheat in online classes, but in actuality they don't cheat any more frequently than students in traditional, offline classes (Moten, Fitterer, Brazier, Leonard, & Brown, 2013).

When students work online, however, more can be done to check their work for evidence of cheating. Because students submit their papers as electronic files, these files can be reviewed using plagiarism-detection programs that search for identical strings of words. The site www.turnitin.com, for example, lets professors check the integrity of every document students submit. Once they have registered with the

TABLE 8.1

Learning Goals and the Technologies That Facilitate Their Attainment

Learning goal	Technologies
Knowledge: deep understanding of the field	Streaming online lectures, posted presentations, screencasts, podcasts, e-books, blogs, lab and research pages, wikis, learning modules, online libraries, TED talks, flash cards, shared resource sites
Literacies: proficiency in reading, writing, science, numeracy	Discussion groups, forum participation, peer commentary and review, wikis, web page development, simulations, virtual problem based learning groups, online research
Cognitive capacities: efficient, effective, critical thinking	Interactive simulations, programming, web page design, research simulations, statistical programming, research papers, searches of databases
Application: practical skills	Creating and using spreadsheets, word processing, graphic design, web page development, file management and manipulation
Personal development: study skills, self-regulation, ethics, and interpersonal skills	Computerized tutorials, online guides to academic success, self-quizzing programs, e-mail, document sharing and authoring, conferencing, virtual learning teams

site, students turn in their written papers by submitting them to the turnitin.com portal. The site's software then checks for plagiarism by comparing the student's work against a database of documents submitted by students at all other registered universities. The site also checks the work against text material available on the web and flags cases of identical strings of words. Other methods for dealing with cheating, that are specific to online courses, are discussed in Chapter 7.

Upgrading University Teaching

Creative innovators rarely keep their achievements to themselves. Once they find that their methods are effective, they encourage others to adopt their approach. Early users of the overhead projector and the blackboard, for example, eventually convinced others to use these innovations, and soon these became standard features of the college classroom. Innovative technologies such as online classes and flipped classrooms are still moving from "interesting idea" to widespread acceptance. The innovators are convinced they are onto something, but many others are skeptical.

CHANGE IS SLOW

Each year, surveys of faculty and administrators at colleges and universities find that a few more professors have become more willing to consider teaching a blended or online course, but the rate of change has hardly been dramatic. For example, in 2014 only 28.0% of the academic officers at 4-year colleges and universities agreed with the statement "Faculty at my school accept the value and legitimacy of online education." That percentage has not changed since the poll was first conducted in 2002. These administrators, however, were generally more positive than their faculty; 16.2% considered online classes to be superior to offline ones, 57.9% felt they were equivalent, but only 25.9% felt they were inferior (I. E. Allen & Seaman, 2015).

Faculty, when recently polled about their teaching practices, indicated they were more familiar with technologically enhanced teaching methods than in previous years, yet less than one quarter of them had actually used such basic tools as online discussion and testing in their teaching. When asked if they had considered using more technology in their teaching, many replied that using technology was too challenging and time consuming. They noted that teaching hundreds of students who meet for 3 hours a week in a large auditorium is an extremely time-efficient strategy and that technology only adds more chores to this task. They did report, though, that they had increased their use of one type of technology: videos harvested from YouTube and elsewhere. More than one third (35.6%) reported using videos frequently in their teaching. However, not many—only 16.1%—used online discussion forum boards regularly (Eagan et al., 2014).

TESTING ONLINE LEARNING

Professors' slow acceptance of technology is understandable, given what is known about resistance to change (Oreg, 2003). Online instruction, however, is no longer a risky, untried method: Thousands of studies, of varying methodological rigor, have examined the efficacy of on- and offline learning. These studies have been reviewed in dozens of meta-analyses that have consistently concluded that students learn as much, and often more, in classes that are taught partly or fully online (e.g., Bernard, Borokhovski, Schmid, Tamim, & Abrami, 2014; Cook et al., 2008; Schmid et al., 2014). For example, Hattie (2009), in an examination of the previous multianalytic reviews of computer-assisted instruction, concluded that technology improved learning consistently across studies, students, and contexts. Their impact, he noted, depends on factors that influence any other type of educational intervention. If faculty are not technologically skilled or receive little support in implementing technology, their classes do not improve when they are technologically enhanced. Technology improves learning when it supplements traditional teaching, for in such cases it provides students with an alternative means of learning and, in general, more strategies for learning the better.

Research also has consistently found that technologies that are student centered—ones that give students control over the timing and pace of their learning—are superior to those that create a more system-regulated learning experience. For example, in one project researchers transformed a number of existing courses, and created new ones, so that courseware resources were used more effectively to promote student learning. This program did not reach one of its important goals: to increase the number of students who completed the courses. It did, however, find significant increases in student learning, in particular in courses in which students completed problems online, with individualized pacing, and the use of adaptive instructional and testing algorithms (Means, Peters, & Zheng, 2014).

In sum, research suggests that online teaching is effective—so effective, in fact, that Schmid and his colleagues (2014) lamented that it is "quite incredible . . . that educators are still concerned about, even debating, the benefits of computers and associated computer technologies on teaching and learning in higher/postsecondary education" (p. 271).

Becoming an Online Professor

Psychologist Robert Sternberg (1997a) argued that intelligent people meet the challenges they confront by using all three of their basic types of intellect. They use their skills of *synthesis* to help them identify approaches and methods that more conventional thinkers either overlook or fail to consider. Their *analytic* skills then allow them to select, from the many ideas they discover, the ones that are most worth pursuing. Their *practical-contextual ability* provides them with the drive and good sense they need to put their idea into practice. Professors who want to upgrade their classes but who are not familiar with the relevant technologies will need to use all three forms of their intelligence as they transform themselves from novice (noob [a shortened form of *newbie*]) to expert. They should also heed the recommendations of experts (see, e.g., Dawley, 2007; Ko & Rossen, 2010).

ORIENTATION AND PLANNING

As I noted in Chapter 1, the most skilled, successful innovators begin the problem-solving process not by immediately leaping into action but by first studying and conceptualizing the issue as a whole. Whereas novices often skip this step and immediately start clicking buttons and pulling down menus, experts say they begin by thinking things over, stepping back and taking a second look, or turning the problem over in their mind. Professors who aspire to using more high-tech instruction methods may, for example, first review their teaching thoroughly, identifying goals, satisfactions, and problems. They may then imagine ways to use technology to solve problems, or at least reduce the length of the "Things I Like Least About Teaching" list. They may also review their existing technology skills and identify areas in which they wish to improve through study and practice.

PRACTICE

Ericsson and Lehmann (1996) reported that most experts become experts through sheer practice. Every grand master, maestro, and gourmet chef was once a novice, but through weeks, months, and years of practice they acquired the behavioral and information skills that others now admire. Thus, to become experts at teaching online, professors must use technology extensively in all aspects of their teaching, research, and service. Most already have basic computer skills; they can use e-mail, word process a document, navigate an operating system such as Windows, and use a web browser. They should, however, learn to use fully the features built into these programs and add a few new skills to their repertoire.

NETWORK

Creative innovation is a surprisingly interpersonal process. Although many people intuitively assume that people who generate new ideas and innovations do so through hours spent working alone, in many cases these individuals were part of a network of other creative persons.

Find a Local Expert

Even when faculty are willing to increase their use of appropriate technologies they may not have the technical skills needed to integrate technology in their classrooms, so they must turn to the technology experts at their university in such offices as "IT: Information Technology," or "Media-Support Services," or "Instructional Development Center." The individuals in such offices are a rich resource of technical information, for they actually understand what terms like *bandwidth*, *parity*, *vertical risers*, and *tcp/ip stack* mean. They also know how to get the equipment to work. The skills of a field anthropologist, however, are sometimes needed when learning to decipher their colorful dialect. D. M. Murray (1985) described how many professors still feel about technology staff when he wrote, "They spoke a private language that I could not under-stand, and it was so filled with offensive jargon that I did not want to understand it" (p. 70).

Find a Colleague

Some faculty do not feel confident in their use of computers and higher level technology. Whereas such individuals may be willing to work with colleagues in an informal, information-sharing setting, they would be less likely to work with experts in computing. New information and technology flow best from colleague to colleague rather than from tech experts to professors. Virtually all recommendations for increasing the use of technology in teaching argue in favor of discipline-based programs rather than centralized, technology-based programs.

One of the best places to find a colleague, and an expert, is in a local workshop on teaching technologies. These sessions are often, ironi-cally, examples of poor teaching. These presentations, though, are good places to meet colleagues who also are learning to use the tech-nology and connect with experts who can offer advice about specific problems.

Advance Your Technology Skills in Increments

Innovations are not always the result of radical plans that replace the status quo with something completely unprecedented. In many cases they reflect modifications and improvements of existing systems; they can be incremental changes rather than reconstructive ones. In an incremental approach, you can add to your existing teaching methods gradually as you acquire and implement new skills. Begin, for example, by creating an online version your syllabus (not a pdf) and moving it onto your LMS. Then add more files as they become available. You eventually should learn how to (a) link them together to create learning modules; (b) add sophisticated features, such as graphics and interactive elements; and (c) develop assignments that are based on these materials. Also, rather than agreeing to shift an entire courses to an online, it would be wise to first experiment with blended formats.

Innovating Redux:
Using Technology Appropriately

The nature of college teaching is being reshaped by technology as more campuses are upgrading their older versions of Professor 1.0, jumping to the faster, slicker, but buggier Professor 2.0. It was not so long ago that professors punctuated their lectures with chalk marks on a blackboard, guided students' discussions from the front of the classroom, insisted that the papers they assigned be typed, and assessed learning with paper-and-pencil tests and quizzes. Professors still use these tools in classes today, but they have integrated new technologies—e-mail, e-books, online discussion forums, quiz-giving programs, virtual teams, learning simulations and the like—into their teaching, and the results in terms of student engagement and learning have been positive.

Richardson (1992) wrote that when it comes to the future, there are three kinds of people: "Those who let it happen, those who make it happen, and those who wonder what happened" (p. 2). Although the potential of innovative online teaching is only beginning to be realized, Professor 2.0 offers many advantages over the well-worn Professor 1.0. If you are teaching today the same way you did 10 years ago, you should consider an upgrade.

Evaluating

Assessing and Enhancing Teaching Quality

9

T he professor's world is an evaluated one. Just to join it, we must pass a succession of tests, graded papers, oral exams, and defenses. To land that first job, prospective faculty members are interviewed, quizzed, and critiqued by search commit-tees, deans, department chairs, and other faculty. The papers we write, if published in the best journals, are often written, reviewed, and revised again and again until they are even-tually deemed acceptable. If we seek external funding, our grant proposals are sent to banks of experts who scrutinize our ideas before deciding whether the proposals warrant further review, let alone funding.

This evaluative edge extends to the classes we teach. Most colleges and universities evaluate the quality of instruc-tion by regularly reviewing the adequacy of course offerings; tracking retention and graduation rates; and monitoring the quality of the library (or libraries), technologies, and other resources students will use to reach their learning goals. Most universities also collect data about each teaching professor's

http://dx.doi.org/10.1037/14777-010
College Teaching: Practical Insights From the Science of Teaching and Learning,
by D. R. Forsyth

competence in the classroom. In many cases the term's end turns the assessment tables on professors: They grade their students' learning with final exams, but the students grade their instructors' skills with teaching surveys. Professors typically pass through a relatively detailed review each year when administrators make decisions about wage and salary increases, but the most elaborate evaluations are saved for promotion and tenure decisions.

All this evaluation is needed to sustain personal and professional standards. After all, professors are supposed to be "fully trained, keep up-to-date, and be good at what they do. Otherwise they should stop doing it" (Swenson, 1997, p. 64). *Personal evaluation* double checks individuals' subjective, and potentially biased, assessment of their adequacies. *Formative evaluation* functions as feedback to professors as they refine their skills and extend their expertise; it is through practice paired with constructive criticism that the unskilled become skilled, novices become experts, and rookies become pros. *Summative evaluation* serves the profession's and institution's purposes and can influence employment and career outcomes, including annual merit pay and awards, contract renewal, and promotion (Arreola, 2007).

Few would argue against evaluation, but the specifics of how, when, and why are more often points of critical debate. Lines on a vita can be counted to gauge research productivity, but how can one's teaching effectiveness be measured? Courses vary dramatically in size, level, and content, and professors' approaches to their classes run the gamut from formal lecture to open-ended discussion, structured to unstructured, cautious to risky, slow to fast paced, practical to theoretical, face-to-face to online, and on and on. Most classes, too, are boundaried social interactions. Sometimes, teams of professors teach students and so can observe one another's work. Some classes, such as Massive Open Online Courses, are enormous public forms of teaching. In most cases, however, the only witnesses of professors' teaching are its beneficiaries: their students. As a consequence, most colleges evaluate teaching effectiveness by surveying the students themselves.

Student ratings of instruction, or SRIs, yield a great deal of useful information about teaching, but many faculty question the meaning of the scores themselves. The most vehemently debated issue concerns their validity—can students accurately discern teaching excellence?—but a number of related issues must also be considered: Are general impressions of teaching effectiveness more accurate than ratings of specific aspects of teaching? Does the use of student ratings contribute to grade inflation? Should these ratings be used to make decisions about wages, tenure, and promotion?

Student Ratings of Instruction

Dr. F never saw it coming. He and his students had just shared a splendid semester-long educational experience. He had deftly mixed original readings, engaging class discussions, illuminating lectures, and thoughtful assessments with a community-based project that gave students the opportunity to apply course concepts in a real-world setting.

Or had he? You would think that, after many years of teaching and opening packets of students' ratings at the semester's end (and now, downloading them from the university's evaluation website), there would be no surprises. Besides, Dr. F had taught the course last year and received solid ratings from the students—lots of 4s and even a few 5s on his university's 1-to-5-point scale. Thus, he was not expecting the sting of a rating that was so negative, comprising not 4s and 5s but 2s, 3s, and critical comments about his overall worth expressed with far more eloquence than the students' exam essays suggested was possible: *circuitous, operose, apodictic, importunate,* and *unremittingly opaque.* Dr. F's first thought was "Where did the students acquire this level of proficiency with invectives?" His second thought was "Are these SRI's good indicators of my teaching effectiveness?"

The best way to answer the latter question is to examine the evidence that confirms or questions the validity of SRIs. These surveys are nothing more than psychological instruments designed to assess students' perceptions of their experience in a specific class, and so the field of psychology provides clear criteria for that review. Psychologists are, after all, the people who brought us questionnaires, measures of intelligence, attitude scales, and the first valid measures of personality. Psychologists take their measurement very seriously, to the point that their ethical guidelines prohibit them from using or drawing conclusions from any measure that does not meet psychometric standards. Those standards are clear: If SRIs lack the two essential qualities of a measure—reliability and validity—then they should not be used in faculty evaluations.

RELIABILITY OF STUDENT RATINGS OF INSTRUCTION

Reviews of the vast research literature dealing with SRIs—estimated by Benton and Cashin (2012) on the basis of well over 2,800 studies—generally agree that students' ratings of a given instructor are reliable: They are reasonably stable across different rating forms, times (e.g., midterm vs. end-of-term rating periods and immediately after class vs.

delayed postclass follow-up), and courses taught in the same year. If SRIs were unreliable, they would fluctuate widely each time a class is rated. But even after a considerable gap between two SRIs, ratings often match. Researchers have even explored the idea that teaching evaluations, like fine wines, improve with age, for only when students look back at their courses do they realize how much they learned. But students' ratings 1 year after taking a course are nearly the same ($r = .83$) as their ratings just before the final exam (Overall & Marsh, 1980).

If SRIs were unreliable, then they would be internally inconsistent: Students would give different ratings on conceptually similar items. However, the correlations among the various items are so high that they can usually be summed to yield a total score with little loss of information. The average alpha coefficient of the items for the subscales of a widely used SRI developed by H. W. Marsh (2007), the Students' Evaluations of Education Quality (SEEQ), is .92, indicating very high consistency.

If SRIs were unreliable, then different students would give widely varying ratings, yet ratings are so highly correlated they meet the standards for observers who code data in psychology research. Sixbury and Cashin (1995), for example, found that the median intraclass correlations across all items of an SRI ranged from a low of .69 for a 10-student class to a high of .91 for a 40-student class.

If SRIs were unreliable, then Dr. F's experience—receiving high ratings in some classes but low ratings in others—would be common instead of rare. But when researchers examined professors' ratings across their classes, and across semesters, they found that most professors exhibited a stable ratings profile that varied little from class to class and year to year. When, for example, H. W. Marsh and Bailey (1993) studied 123 instructors over a 13-year period they found evidence of consistency: The average correlation among ratings across all courses was .61, and for professors teaching the same class repeatedly it was .71. Hativa (2014b), in a study of ratings in chemistry and physics over 2 years, did find that some professors' ratings shifted, but they were the ones who had participated in a faculty development project for improved teaching.

CONTENT VALIDITY: THE STRUCTURE OF STUDENT RATINGS OF INSTRUCTION

SRIs do not all use the same items. Some universities use a standard SRI, such as the aforementioned SEEQ, the IDEA (http://ideaedu.org/), items drawn from Purdue University's item bank, or a form supplied by a commercial service. But many use homegrown SRIs that were developed locally, usually by a committee of well-meaning faculty (Keeley, 2012). Most SRIs also include both global and specific items. The global items ask students to rate the general quality of their instructor, the course, and their learning with such questions as "On a scale from 1 to 5, how would you rate this instructor?" The specific items focus on the elements of good teaching, including knowledge of the subject, enthusiasm for the material, respect displayed to students, and so on. The forms may also invite students to express their rating of the course in their own words with open-ended items such as "Why did you rate this instructor as you did?" In many cases, too, professors can select the items they wish to have included on the ratings from a bank of items, or they can devise their own unique queries about their teaching.

Do SRI items capture the meaning of effective teaching? Some investigators, noting the complex, multifaceted nature of the teaching process, have argued in favor of a complex, multidimensional inventory (Berk, 2013; Braskamp & Ory, 1994; Centra, 1993; Feldman, 1989). Marsh and Roche (1997), for example, argued against the use of global items because teaching is too complex to be measured with a single item such as "How effective was your instructor?" They based this conclusion on more than two decades of work by Marsh and his colleagues with the SEEQ (e.g., H. W. Marsh, 1982, 1983, 1984; H. W. Marsh & Hocevar, 1991; H. W. Marsh & Roche, 1997). This measure asks students to rate specific characteristics of the class and the instructor—such as degree of organization, skill in stimulating discussion, rapport with students—and a statistical analysis of these items yields the following key components of effective teaching:

- *Organization of presentations and materials:* use of previews, summaries, clarity of objectives, ease of note taking, preparation of materials
- *Group interaction:* stimulating discussion, sharing ideas, exchanging knowledge, asking questions of individual students, asking questions to the entire class
- *Breadth of coverage:* contrasting implications, conceptual level, and giving alternative points of view
- *Learning/value of the course:* challenge to students, value of material, amount of learning, increases in understanding
- *Rapport, or student–teacher relations:* friendliness toward students, accessibility, interest in students
- *Exams/grading:* value of exam feedback, fairness of evaluation procedures, content validity of tests
- *Instructor enthusiasm:* dynamism, energy, humor, style
- *Workload/difficulty:* perceptions of course difficulty, amount of work required, course pace, number of outside assignments
- *Assignments/readings:* educational value of texts, readings

These specific factors, however, tend to be highly intercorrelated. D'Apollonia and Abrami (1997), after reexamining the results of prior factor analytic studies of SRIs, concluded that a single principal component accounts for 63% of the variance in SRIs. These analyses suggest that this teaching *g factor* can be divided into subcomponents, including presentation, facilitation, and evaluation skills, but these subskills are all included in a general instructional skill factor (Spooren, Mortelmans, & Christiaens, 2015).

Given this high level of convergence of specific items, some investigators feel that the global items on SRIs may be more valid than the more specific ones for three reasons: they (a) make no assumptions about what ingredients are the necessary conditions for effective teaching; (b) do not ask students to render judgments of aspects of teaching that they may not be able to directly observe (e.g., degree of preparation), and (c) are highly correlated with measures of student learning (e.g., P. D. Harrison, Douglas, & Burdsal, 2004; McMillan, Wergin, Forsyth, & Brown, 1987). Berk (2013), however, worried that global items are too low in reliability and content validity to be used as measures of teaching effectiveness but, even worse: they are "inappropriate for personnel decisions according to U.S. professional and legal standards" (p. 64).

CRITERION VALIDITY OF STUDENT RATINGS OF INSTRUCTION

Researchers and educational experts have yet to agree on a single indicator of "teaching quality," so a definitive study of SRIs has yet to be conducted. As I discuss in the next sections, though, researchers have examined the relationship between SRIs and a number of variables that should be related to teaching quality, and the results support the validity of SRIs.

Student Ratings of Instruction and Student Learning

If SRIs are valid measures of teaching effectiveness then, *ceterus paribus*, students in classes from teachers with very positive SRI ratings should learn more than students taking classes from professors whose SRI scores are less admirable. Many investigators have examined this prediction, usually by studying the correlation between SRI scores and students' scores on exams. Some of these investigations cast doubts on the SRI's validity because they find that SRIs are unrelated—or, even worse, negatively related—with student learning (e.g., Carrell & West, 2010; Clayson, 2009; Rodin & Rodin, 1972). Others, however, lend strong support to the strength of the SRI–learning relationship (e.g., Abrami, Cohen, & d'Apollonia, 1988; Beleche, Fairris, & Marks, 2012).

Most reviews of the entire research literature on the topic, including meta-analytic reviews, endorse SRIs as valid indicators of teaching effectiveness (e.g., Cohen, 1981; Feldman, 1989; Hativa, 2014b). For example, Cohen (1981), in his classic review, combined findings from 41 studies that reported correlations between the average SRI a professor received in a course and the average grades of students in those courses on exams. Some of these correlations were negative, but most were positive: The average correlation was .43. This relationship was strongest for students' ratings of the professor's teaching skill, knowledge of the subject, and rapport with students. Students also learned more in courses that they felt were well organized, and ones in which they received feedback about their learning, but ratings were not related to the perceived difficulty of the course.

These findings suggest that some instructors teach better than others and that SRIs are accurate indicators of who these teachers are. However, this strong causal conclusion is not warranted by the correlational nature of the research evidence. Teaching effectiveness, as indicated by SRIs, may improve student learning, but higher grades also could be the causes of the higher SRIs ratings. The *leniency explanation* of the findings assumes that students appreciate receiving higher grades than they deserve and so they reciprocate by rating these kindly professors more favorably. The *reciprocity (retaliation) bias* suggests that students retaliate against tough graders by giving them low ratings (Clayson, Frost, & Sheffet, 2006). The *validity hypothesis* suggests that SRIs and grades are correlated only because they are both caused by a third variable: the professor's superior teaching skills. The students in the class get better grades not because their professor is a lenient grader and the course is not demanding but because the professor teaches so well that students learn more and thus score higher on assessments. The *preexisting differences hypothesis* suggests that students' prior interest in the course determines both their grade and their rating of the professor. Students who are excited about learning course material do well, and their excitement regarding the course raises the professor's rating, but students who are uninterested in the subject do less well and therefore they do not give their professor high marks. Researchers continue to investigate these alternative explanations, but most assessment experts favor the validity hypothesis.

Student Ratings of Instruction and Other Criteria

Students may be the most familiar with the professor's teaching, but they are not the only people who can observe and evaluate teaching. For example, peers observe us when we guest lecture to their classes, alumni can be asked to recall their experiences with us after they graduate, and observers can be sent into our classes and study us as we teach. When these observers' judgments are compared to SRIs, they generally match: Peer observers, alumni, objective observers, and coders trained to look for specific types of instructional behaviors rate professors with higher SRIs more positively than those with lower SRIs (Braskamp & Ory, 1994; Feldman, 1989; Kulik, 2001; H. G. Murray, 1983). SRIs even predict professor's own evaluations of their teaching. When Feldman (1989) combined the results from 19 different studies that measured both SRIs and professors' ratings of instruction he found that each predicted the other; the correlation was .29.

Student Ratings of Instruction and Students' Comments

Just as many faculty think essay tests are better indicators of student learning than multiple-choice tests, so too do some feel that the most useful information they receive about their teaching comes from student responses to the open-ended, constructed-response type items such as, "Do you have any additional comments?" These comments, however, are usually consistent with SRI ratings. Braskamp, Ory, and Pieper (1981), after carefully coding the written comments made in 14 classes, correlated the codes with students' responses to the global items in the SRI: The correlation was .93. Burdsal and Harrison (2008) replicated this finding in a sample of 208 classes. These finding suggest the comments are useful for both formative and summative evaluations.

BIASES: SOURCES OF INVALIDITY

People are active social perceivers; they are constantly forming impressions of others' qualities, characteristics, strengths, and weaknesses. They are not, however, entirely objective perceivers, given that their preferences, moods, attitudes, values, and so on, influence their appraisals of others. I once had a student who gave me a 2 on a 5-point scale on teaching effectiveness, who explained his rating in the comments section: "I would have rated you higher but in class one day you said you did not like the Rolling Stones."

Researchers have identified a number of factors—some situational, some personal, some interpersonal—that can suppress or inflate SRIs. Ratings are slightly higher, for example, for younger faculty than older faculty, but graduate student instructors receive the lowest ratings of all (Braskamp & Ory, 1994). Professors who students consider to be physically attractive get higher ratings (Riniolo, Johnson, Sherman, & Misso, 2006), as do lecturers who use more pictures in their PowerPoint presentations (D. A. Johnson & Christensen, 2011). Women faculty receive ratings equal to those of men, except in certain types of courses and disciplines (Benton & Cashin, 2012). For example, some evidence suggests male faculty are rated more positively by male students in STEM classes (science, technology, engineering, and mathematics; Basow &

Martin, 2012). STEM courses, in general, are rated more negatively than courses in the humanities (Cashin, 1990).

Are your classes large or small, lower level or advanced? SRIs are higher in smaller classes than larger classes (Sixbury & Cashin, 1995) and higher in advanced courses than lower level, introductory courses (Aleamoni, 1981). Is your course a required one? SRIs are higher in elective courses and courses that students rated as more interesting prior to enrolling (H. W. Marsh & Dunkin, 1992). By the way, many believe that class meeting time (e.g., time of day/evening) influences SRIs, but if it does the influence is so small it is undetectable (Aleamoni, 1981).

The way the ratings are collected matters, as well: Ratings are lower if students are anonymous and the professor is not present (H. W. Marsh & Dunkin, 1992). In general, however, there is no difference if ratings are taken at mid-semester or the end of the semester (Feldman, 1978). SRIs tend to be higher if the survey states that responses will influence tenure/promotion and salary decisions (Braskamp & Ory, 1994). Response rates are lower if SRIs are administered online, but so long as 80% of students respond, the ratings are similar to offline ratings (Berk, 2013).

SRIs, then, are influenced by a number of non-instructional variables—factors that have little or nothing to do with the quality of teaching. However, what faculty may not realize is that these factors account for only a small percentage of the variance in ratings. For example, one study indicated that teachers who voluntarily have their courses rated get better ratings, but this statistically significant relationship accounted for less than 1% of the total variance in ratings (Cashin & Perrin, 1983). H. W. Marsh (1980) suggested that extraneous factors taken together probably account for only 12% to 14% of the variance in ratings. As H. W. Marsh and Roche (1997) came to this conclusion:

> Particularly for the more widely studied characteristics, some studies have found little or no relationship or even results opposite to those reported here. The size, or even the direction, of relations may vary considerably, depending on the particular component of students' ratings that is being considered. Few studies have found any of these characteristics to be correlated more than .30 with class-average students' ratings, and most relations are much smaller. (p. 1194)

ARE STUDENT RATINGS OF INSTRUCTION VALID INDICATORS OF TEACHING EFFECTIVENESS?

Is the use of student surveys an accurate and efficient means of evaluating an instructor's effectiveness? Researchers have yet to reach complete consensus on matters of construct, convergent, and discriminant validity. D'Apollonia and Abrami (1997), for example, felt that ratings reflect students' general appraisal of their instructors, but H. W. Marsh and Roche (1997) felt that ratings, and the perceptions they measure, are differentiated and multidimensional. Whereas Greenwald and Gillmore (1997) concluded that ratings are substantially influenced by irrelevant factors, including the grades students expect to receive, d'Apollonia and Abrami (1997), H. W. Marsh and Roche (1997), and McKeachie (1997) all felt that these biasing factors account for so little of the variance in ratings that they can be ignored with little risk. Most investigators are convinced that SRIs provide a relatively accurate picture of a professor's classroom skills, but even they worry that SRIs can be easily misinterpreted.

Using and Improving Student Ratings of Instruction

Few current professors can remember a time when their work was not evaluated using student rating forms. This practice began as a means for faculty to gather useful feedback about their teaching and to give students a way to express their opinions about the quality of the instruction they were receiving. But even though SRIs are an old topic in academia, they are still a hot topic, with debates continuing over their effects and usefulness.

NEGATIVE EFFECTS OF STUDENT RATINGS OF INSTRUCTION

SRIs are meant to measure professors' performance, but they may have some deleterious effects. They provide faculty with useful feedback to improve their teaching and help administrators weed out ineffective instructors and reward those who are most effective at their craft. However, they may also contribute to the use of teaching methods that will win student's favor but not facilitate their learning.

Ratings and Morale

Surveys of faculty at various universities suggest that ratings may undermine faculty morale, in particular among faculty with weak publication rates or a strong involvement in teaching (Armstrong, 1998). Because these faculty's careers are defined more by their teaching than by their research and service, a failure in this sphere will have more profound emotional and motivational consequences (Niedenthal, Setterlund, & Wherry, 1992). These professors may, for example, lose interest in teaching, in particular if the ratings do not reflect the amount of time and energy they put into their teaching. As Armstrong (1998) wrote,

> Faculty members with poor ratings might decide that teaching is not rewarding and spend less time teaching. Teachers might get discouraged by ratings if they see no clear relationship between their attempts to provide a useful learning experience and their ratings. Teachers may get discouraged because time spent on teaching activities has little relationship to ratings or because, as they develop knowledge in the field through their research, there is no increase in their teacher ratings. (p. 1223)

Changes in Teaching Styles

McKeachie (1997) worried that faculty may alter the way they teach to increase their ratings, but because students "prefer teaching that enables them to listen passively" (p. 1219), professors may unwittingly adopt less effective but more student-pleasing methods. When Levy and Peters (2002) asked a sample of college students, "What makes the best college course?" these students most frequently mentioned a comfortable atmosphere, interesting content, and reviews before each test. The U.S. students A. Miller and Pearson (2013) surveyed preferred lectures to discussions and professors who were Americans rather than of other nationalities. Meeting students' preferences may generate higher SRIs, but at a cost to many forms of learning.

Grade Inflation

SRIs may contribute to *grade inflation*: the awarding of higher and higher grades for work of lower and lower quality (V. E. Johnson, 2003). Of the factors that can influence SRIs, only students' expectations about their grades are under the direct control of the instructor. Some educators therefore fear that professors may be tempted to use grades to "buy" better ratings from students. They grade more leniently and lighten the workload for students, who reciprocate by giving them higher ratings. Given the compressed nature of SRIs on most campuses, if a lenient grading policy gains the instructor as little as a half-point on his or her average class rating, he or she may be catapulted from the lower third of teachers in the department to the upper third (Redding, 1998). Whereas Greenwald and Gillmore (1997), drawing on their structural equation modeling of the relationships between expected grade and course rating, recommended that statistical interventions should be taken to adjust SRIs for leniency, McKeachie (1997), H. W. Marsh and Roche (1997), d'Apollonia and Abrami (1997) and other researchers in this area did not feel the findings are sufficiently strong to warrant this step.

Faculty may not deliberately "dumb down" their courses to get higher ratings; instead, once-strict graders may unwittingly relax their standards as a result of pressure from students and administrators. Faced with complaints that their courses are too difficult and grades too low, they alter the way they test, the number of readings they assign, and reduce the students' workload. The course becomes easier, and grades rise, as do SRIs (Greenwald & Gillmore, 1997). On the other hand, professors may grade leniently on purpose to game the system. Tabachnick, Keith-Spiegel, and Pope (1991), in their survey of teaching psychologists, found that only 40% felt that deliberately inflating grades was unethical, and a substantial proportion admitted they sometimes gave students better grades than they deserved just to "ensure popularity with students" (p. 510).

Even though SRIs stand accused of fueling grade inflation, they may not deserve the blame. Professors may believe that easy graders get higher ratings, but the validity studies reviewed earlier have yielded only slight support for that assumption. Extremely challenging professors—tough graders—are often viewed negatively, but so are professors whose classes do not challenge even the least prepared students (Hativa, 2014b). Professors would likely achieve much higher ratings of their teaching if they just examined their teaching practices carefully and identified ways to improve them.

IMPROVING FORMATIVE ASSESSMENTS

Teaching evaluation systems, like professors' systems for grading their students' performance, serve formative and summative functions. As formative reviews, they can provide specific, useful feedback about what does and does not work in the classroom. When the review is positive, the formative review inspires faculty to continue their good work, but when it is negative it guides their personal development efforts. As summative reviews, evaluation systems provide evidence of the overall quality of the institution's effectiveness, and they provide information relevant to administrative decisions on faculty hiring, salary, contract renewal, tenure, and promotion. Formative evaluations may help faculty improve their teaching skills, but summative evaluations provide the extrinsic motivation that translates the feedback into action (McCarthy, 2012).

Formative assessments are more descriptive than evaluative because they are designed to give context-specific information about professors' progress toward their teaching goals. Professors who have not yet mastered all the intricacies of teaching should use these assessments to identify the factors that are blocking their progress. Even highly successful teachers should use formative assessments to check for unexpected problems in their teaching.

Student Rating Scales

Most SRIs are designed to ask students to rate specific aspects of a professor's instruction, including its clarity, the caliber of the assessment methods, the impact assignments, and the professor's willingness to respond to students' questions. Students' ratings, as noted previously, are not in all cases 100% veridical, but when their opinions about strengths and weaknesses converge professors should take heed.

The global items (e.g., "How effective is your instructor?") and the average of the specific items provide only the most general of feedback—did the students consider this course to be well-taught, poorly taught, or something in between. But the more specific items provide the more diagnostic information, for there students are asked to focus on more concrete, and easily discerned aspects of the class. The SEEQ, for example, collects students' judgments on a series of relatively specific items, such as "You found the course intellectually challenging and stimulating," "Instructor's explanations were clear," and "Methods of evaluating student work were fair and appropriate" (H. W. Marsh, 1982, pp. 90–91). Other assessment systems let faculty select the items they wish to have included on their assessment from a bank of items, and the faculty at some universities can develop their own list of items to include on a survey to gather feedback about a particular nuance or innovation.

Constructed-Response Ratings

Many faculty find that the information provided in students responses to open-ended questions, such as "Identify ways this course could be improved," as the No. 1 most useful information provided by SRIs. Completing these open-ended items, however, takes more time than checking boxes, so consider explicitly asking students to add written comments and assuring them that these comments will be read. If students will be completing the surveys offline, during class, administer your SRIs at the beginning of class rather than at the end so students do not hurry through them. The best way to improve responses to open-ended questions, however, is to administer the surveys online. Online and offline ratings tend to be equivalent, except in one way: The comments are more detailed when student do their evaluations online. Not only can they type their comments, but also you can extract them and organize their responses to more easily identify consistent themes.

Rubrics of Assessing Online Instruction

If you teach a hybrid or online class, the SRI most often used at your university may meet only some of your need for feedback about your teaching. Some of the items apply equally well to both on- and offline classes, but the standard form may fail to measure critically important aspects of the online learning experience, including student–student interaction, the structure of the learning modules, the quality of online lectures, instructor support and mentoring, and so on (Drouin, 2012). Online professors may need develop their own items or even better: incorporate one of the many emerging student ratings of online instruction—into their learning management system. Examples include the Student Evaluation of Web-Based Instruction (I. Stewart, Hong, & Strudler, 2004), the Student Evaluation of Online Teaching Effectiveness (Bangert, 2008) and Quality Matters (http://www.qmprogram.org/rubric).

Individual and Group Feedback

Faculty, mindful that the official SRIs will be administered at the end of the semester, sometimes overlook opportunities to assess their teaching *during* the semester. Such assessments, because they can be gathered quickly and analyzed informally, provide useful information about the current class and may suggest changes that can be made immediately.

In the *midterm course check* procedure, for example, students' responses to the following three questions are collected: (a) "What do you like the most about this class?" (b) "What do you like the least about this class?" and (c) "What one thing would you like to see changed?" Alternatively, as Angelo and Cross (1993) recommended, one could ask students to give examples of specific things that facilitate their learning, specific things that make learning more difficult, and practical suggestions for improving their learning. Students should be cautioned to not put their names on their comments and be reminded to try to focus on things that can be changed (e.g., amount of discussion, lecture style) rather than things that cannot be changed (e.g., when the class meets). Their comments can be categorized and discussed in a feedback session in the following class.

This approach can also be carried out as a collaborative group activity by asking a colleague to administer a small-group instructional diagnosis. The colleague should separate the class into groups of five and give the groups about 20 minutes to answer the three questions listed in the previous paragraph. The groups must also select a recorder or spokesperson. Then, in a plenary session, the colleague pools all the ideas on a flip chart and pushes the group toward a consensus. Later, in a private meeting, the colleague relays the feedback to the instructor. This approach promotes collaboration and the development of consensus among class members on issues of classroom management and evaluation (W. E. Bennett, 1987).

Students can also be consulted through informal conversation, focus group–like sessions, and by using more formal review panels. Nuhfer

(1997), for example, recommended gathering information about one's teaching by forming what he called a *student management team* (SMT). He recruits the three or four students for the team during the first few weeks of the semester and asks them to meet with him throughout the semester to provide him suggestions about teaching. He recommended that one student be selected by the professor, on the basis of interest, enthusiasm, and leadership, but the others should be elected by the class or from volunteers (after they have experienced the first few weeks of class). The professor meets with the team every other week, but the group should meet weekly and keep a log of its meetings, which is turned over to the professor at the end of the semester. Nuhfer found that this method provides a variety of benefits, in particularly if a professor learns (before the end of the semester) about an issue that requires resolution. A recent experimental comparison of classes that included SMTs and those that did not revealed another advantage of this technique: Students who are members of the SMTs became more engaged in the course, and this engagement led to improved course performance (Troisi, 2014).

Collaboration With Colleagues and Students

Colleagues can be an excellent source of formative feedback. Informally, they can act as a sounding board for new ideas, a supportive audience to listen to difficulties, and an advisor who can recommend solutions. More formally, they can review the course materials—syllabi, tests, lecture notes, web materials, and so on—and identify strengths, weaknesses, and revisions. Colleagues also can visit the classroom itself and write up the results of their visit in a report or share them with the instructor over a cup of coffee. Faculty observers, however, tend to be lenient reviewers, and one colleague's high appraisal of a learning strategy might not be shared by another colleague down the hallway (Centra, 1975). One may therefore wish to consider providing a checklist for observers to use to structure their comments. H. G. Murray (1983) and Mintzes (1979) have described observational inventories that are less vulnerable to observer bias because they focus on discrete, specific types of behavior. These low-inference ratings ask observers to indicate only the extent to which the professor displayed behaviors that are related to effective and ineffective teaching, such as speaking clearly and expressively, smiling or laughing, using concrete examples, using headings and subheadings, showing interest in the subject, showing concern for students, and so on (H. G. Murray, 1983, pp. 140–141). Chism (2007) described a detailed system of peer review for teaching, including suggestions for procedures, standards, and assessment protocols.

Classroom Assessment Techniques

Some of the most useful information about teaching effectiveness can be gathered by focusing on a particular aspect of the class instead of by seeking general information about overall course quality. A professor may, for example, wonder whether students have too much time or too little time to complete the work assigned. Another may worry that students' notes do not accurately reflect the contents of his lecture. Another may hope that students are learning to apply class material in their everyday lives but be unable to assess their success.

Angelo and Cross (1993) recommended using *classroom assessment techniques* to measure these specific instructional outcomes. They outlined a series of nine steps that faculty should follow in such assessments:

1. Identify a single course that you will review using a classroom assessment technique: one that you teach regularly, that you would like to improve in some way, but that has no glaring problems.

2. Review your goals for the class, and narrow the focus of the review as much as possible. For example, you may want to identify portions of the class that usually do not go as well as you think they should, or a specific problem, such as why students are not interested in the material.

3. Develop an assessment that will yield information about the goal or question, with a focus on what students have learned. Angelo and Cross and Table 9.1 in this chapter describe several of these relatively simple qualitative approaches to assessment.

4. Conduct the session that you wish to examine as you normally would. The assessment intervention, because it focuses on student learning, should fit naturally into the session's teaching and provide students with feedback about goals.

5. Carry out the assessment, being certain that students understand that the intervention is not a test of their learning but an indication of the adequacy of the lesson. Angelo and Cross recommended giving students credit for participating but also keeping responses anonymous.

6. Review the responses, to get a general sense of the results, and then more thoroughly, by taking counts on the number of students who missed specific types of material or voiced similar concerns about the class. Specific cases should also be culled to use as illustrative examples of strengths, weaknesses, and areas for improvement.

7. Review the results. If they are unexpected or inconsistent, spend some time mulling them over, discussing them with

TABLE 9.1

Examples of Classroom Assessment Techniques Discussed by Angelo and Cross (1993)

Assessment technique	Objective checked	Description
Empty outlines	Accuracy and depth of student's notes	At the end of the day's lecture the professor gives students a sheet of paper with only the major headings of the lecture listed and asks students to fill in subheadings and key points.
Memory matrix	Students' ability to compare and contrast concepts	Students complete a table that lists concepts or theories down the rows and their characteristics across the columns (e.g., *classical* and *operant conditioning* are row entries, and terms such as *reinforcement*, *extinction*, and *shaping* are column headings).
Minute paper	Grasp of key points of presentation	Students are given 1 minute to identify the points they feel were the most important ones in the day's presentation and ask questions they want answered.
Muddiest point	Identification of areas of uncertainty	Students are asked to identify the area of the lesson that was the muddiest, or least clear, to them.
One-sentence summary	Students' ability to integrate information	Students must write a grammatically correct single sentence that summarizes a topic; one variation asks students to answer the questions "Who does what to whom, when, where, how, and why?" in one sentence.
Application cards	Students' ability to apply course material to new examples	The professor hands out large index cards to students, who are asked to write down at least one application of the day's presentation to a real-world situation or problem.

students in the class individually, or sharing them with colleagues. Consider such general questions as, "Do your data indicate how well (or poorly) students achieved the teaching/learning goal or task?" and "Can you interpret why you got the results you did?" (p. 55).

8. Give the students feedback about the assessment. If the results suggest changes in method, these possible changes should be discussed carefully with students and, depending on the specificity of the syllabus, initiated the next time the course is taught.

9. Evaluate the assessment. Angelo and Cross recommended reviewing the effectiveness of the assessment procedures, noting any ways that the intervention could be improved to yield clearer, more interpretable information.

Consider, as an example, a professor who teaches a course in learning and cognition. His assessment is triggered by his suspicion that students are not connecting the course content to problems that they face in their own lives. After explaining the reasons for the exercise with the class, he puts this question to the class (Angelo & Cross, 1993):

> Have you tried to apply anything you learned in this unit on human learning to your own life? If "yes," please give as many specific, detailed examples of your applications as possible. If "no," please explain briefly why you have not tried to apply what you learned in this unit. (p. 68)

Students were asked to write a one-page answer, due the next class. Students did not put their names on their papers, but they were given credit if they turned in a response.

One professor who used this method reported that 60% of his students claimed they were using the course's content to improve their studying methods, enhance their memory, reduce their stress, deal with their children's behavior, and so on. At the next class he reviewed the findings with students and, with the class, developed a more detailed listing of possible applications. The professor now stresses applications as a specific goal in this course and conducts the assessment regularly to check his teaching effectiveness.

IMPROVING SUMMATIVE ASSESSMENT

In evaluative contexts, a distinction is often made between a *rating* and an *evaluation*. A rating is a single indicator of some outcome, such as students' learning or a teacher's effectiveness. An evaluation (or assessment), in contrast, is a strategic analysis of learning or teaching that combines information from a variety of sources instead of just one. As Benton and Cashin (2012) explained

> Using the term "rating" rather than "evaluation" helps to distinguish between the people who provide the information (sources of data) and those who interpret it (evaluators) in combination with other sources of information. (p. 1)

SRIs are examples of ratings. They are data, but they are not evaluations. They are useful sources of information for carrying out a faculty evaluation, but they should not be the only source of information. A summative review should take into account not only professors' classroom teaching but also the caliber of the instructional and evaluative materials they develop and use in their classes, the academic quality of the course's contents, the quantity and quality of their nonclassroom teaching activities, and their overall contributions to the discipline's educational mission (Berk, 2013; Hativa, 2014a).

Classroom Teaching

What is the best source of information about professors' competence in the classroom itself: their skill when lecturing, when leading discussions, and when answering questions; their ability to motivate students to learn the material; their work in a teaching laboratory; or their effectiveness as tutors when discussing recent empirical findings with advanced students? As I noted earlier in this chapter, studies of the validity of student ratings of their teachers' effectiveness, although not entirely consistent in their conclusions, suggest that summative evaluators should solicit students' opinions instead of relying on their own. Annual reviews of faculty, tenure and promotion decisions, and considerations for wage increase, if they are at least partially based on the quality of a professor's teaching, should therefore consider what students say about what goes on when their professor is teaching. The following are some specific suggestions:

- SRIs, if used for summative evaluation, should be administered during a specific time during the semester—ideally, just prior to the end of the term (Berk, 2013). Berk (2013) also strongly recommended the use of standardized SRIs instead of ones developed locally.
- SRIs should be used to generate only overall ratings of faculty's teaching—for example, "exceptional," "meets standards," or "unacceptable"—rather finely grained, multicategory discriminations (d'Apollonia & Abrami, 1997). This conservative approach prevents reviewers from reading too much into the numbers and reaching conclusions that are not warranted given the possibility of measurement error. Moreover, as McKeachie (1997) noted, in most cases, "personnel committees do not need to make finer distinctions" than "promote" or "do not promote." (p. 1218)
- Because SRIs are survey data, they should be discounted if their validity is threatened by unusual administrative procedures and inadequate sample sizes. Cashin (1995) recommended that evaluations should be based on at least five sections, taught in different years. SRIs should be interpreted cautiously in classes with fewer than 10 students and in cases when a substantial portion of the class (30%) did not complete the forms.
- SRI information should also include data pertaining to grade expectations, grade distribution, and student motivation; scores can also be statistically adjusted to control for these influences (Greenwald & Gillmore, 1997).
- If merit pay and promotions are based, in part, on teaching effectiveness, then SRIs should be administered in all classes, and the same generic questions should be used on all surveys. The use of standardized items promotes the development of norms pertaining

to teaching, but only if all faculty are required to have students complete ratings: Professors should not be given the option of not evaluating their instruction.

The Quality of Instructional and Evaluative Materials

Outstanding teachers, in addition to stimulating learning through direct instructional activities, also teach by developing effective instructional materials, activities, assignments, and assessment methods. They may not be mesmerizing presenters or skilled discussion leaders, but they can teach effectively online, by giving students detailed feedback about their individual work, by setting clear classroom goals and providing students with the resources they need to achieve them, and so on. The quality of these procedures will likely be indicated by students' ratings of the course itself, rather than their rating of the instructor. Colleagues can also review these instructional materials. As Centra (1975) noted, colleagues are too inaccurate for use as classroom observers. They are, however, excellent judges of instructional material and course management. Just as faculty are skilled in reviewing a scholarly article and determining its publishability, faculty are capable of reviewing a colleague's teaching materials to determine whether they are excellent, adequate, or in need of improvement. As I explain in Chapter 10, professors can facilitate this process by preparing a dossier, or portfolio, that describes their teaching methods and their educational philosophy and includes copies of material used in classes (e.g., syllabi, tests, handouts, classroom exercises, sample lecture notes, graded exams).

The Academic Quality of a Course

There are good courses in college, but there are also great courses. One professor may cover all the course topics carefully and measure students' performance adequately, but another may challenge students to think critically about the field's key issues, coordinate a series of student-generated research studies, provide students with opportunities to express their understanding in their own writing, and have time left over to help students apply course concepts in their everyday lives. Summative evaluations should attempt to gauge the relative academic quality of the course itself by looking beyond *how* the class is taught to focus on *what* is being taught. In most cases, members of the professor's own academic unit can judge whether a course meets the discipline's standards for academic quality by asking such questions as these:

- Is the course material current?
- Is the instructor adequately trained in the subject that he or she is teaching?

- Is the course so easy that students who learn very little nonetheless pass it?
- Does it cover the material that the college catalogue says it is supposed to cover?
- Is the course intellectually challenging?

The Quantity and Quality of Nonclassroom Teaching Activities

When summative evaluators base their ratings of faculty only on classroom teaching, they unwittingly endorse the view of those who criticize faculty for spending too little time teaching. However, much teaching occurs outside of classroom settings, through the following indicators:

- *Advising and mentoring*: the number of advisees; participation as an advisor on undergraduate thesis, graduate thesis, and dissertation committees; any reports (both favorable and unfavorable) from advisees pertaining to advising.
- *Publications dealing with teaching in higher education*, including works on educational topics, manuals developed for classroom use, papers published or presented with student coauthors (both graduate and undergraduate), and textbooks.
- *Specialized teaching*: non–classroom-based teaching, such as (a) public teaching (presentations to the community at large, including speeches, workshops, educational newspaper articles, and interviews); (b) individualized instruction, including mentoring and tutoring; (c) workshops for colleagues and advanced students; (d) distance education; and (e) interdisciplinary teaching.
- *Curriculum development activities*: description of courses that have been developed or substantially changed; innovations in teaching courses or topics should also be noted.
- *Service contributions in teaching*: administrative duties or service that focuses primarily on teaching, such as participation on any departmental, college, or university committees and task forces dealing with teaching.
- *Supervision and mentoring*: guiding students' work on individual research projects, thesis and dissertation research, service learning, and so on.

Overall Contributions to the Discipline's Educational Mission

Ideal professors do all things well. They teach in the classroom, on the sidewalk, in their offices, through technology, and with dramatic effect. Whether they are lecturing, leading discussions, questioning, or mentoring, their students learn. But ideal professors reach beyond fine teaching per se: They make broader contributions to teaching practices in their disciplines and to higher education in general. Such contributions as research into pedagogical practices, curricular reform, university- and national-level service in teaching, public teaching, and mentorship of other teachers dot the vitae of the finest teachers. They are concerned with their own and others' teaching, to the point that they study the process and hone their own skills. They participate in formal and informal analyses of teaching, not because they are experts but because they are always seeking improvement.

Evaluating Redux: Assess Your Success

Both faculty and administrators, seeking feedback about teaching effectiveness in their classes and at their university, often ask their students themselves about the quality of the teaching they are receiving. These SRIs are not perfectly precise measures of students' perceptions, but they are for the most part reliable and valid indexes of teaching. However, faculty evaluations, whether conducted to help faculty improve their teaching or to provide input into personnel decisions, should be conducted with care. Formative reviews can provide professors with suggestions on how to improve their teaching, but not if the questions asked and administrative methods used are problematic. Summative evaluations, too, must be based on more than a simplistic bean count of faculty's gold stars given them by their students. Summative evaluators who factor teaching skill into their reviews of faculty are to be commended for not basing merit awards only on research productivity, but if they base their review on incomplete data their good intentions will be for naught. Faculty should be evaluated, but these reviews must be based on procedures that are consistent with the current state of knowledge in the field of teaching evaluation rather than the personal predilections of faculty or administrators.

Documenting
Developing a Teaching Portfolio

10

P sychologist Gordon W. Allport (1968) summarized his years of research into personality with these questions: "How shall a psychological life history be written? What processes and what structures must a full-bodied account of personality include? How can one detect unifying threads in a life, if they exist?" (p. 377). Allport found these questions to be challenging because each person is a unique configuration of patterns and combinations. He argued that generalities can be identified, for all people are alike in certain ways, but these generalities underestimate the richness of each case. People change over the course of a lifetime as they react to new experiences, make choices based on their goals and values, and grapple with issues of self and satisfactions. As Allport said (1955): "Personality is less a finished product than a transitive process. While it has some stable features, it is at the same time continually undergoing change" (p. 19). Allport, drawing on the work of humanistic psychologists, called this process of change *becoming* or *individuation*.

http://dx.doi.org/10.1037/14777-011
College Teaching: Practical Insights From the Science of Teaching and Learning,
by D. R. Forsyth

Allport's conclusions apply to that part of the professor's life that has been spent teaching. His questions, when put to the professor, ask: How shall the life history of the teaching professor be written? What processes and what structures must a full-bodied account of college and university teaching include? How can one detect the unifying threads that run throughout a career in the classroom? How should you tell the story of your life as a professor?

The Teaching Portfolio

Allport did not favor simple approaches to measuring people. He sometimes gauged traits and temperament with checklists, surveys, and inventories, but he believed that these methods overlook the unique qualities of the individual. He preferred, instead, to examine their personal documents: "any self-revealing record that intentionally or unintentionally yields information regarding the structure, dynamics, and functioning of the author's mental life" (Allport, 1942, p. xii).

A teaching portfolio, or teaching dossier, is just such a personal document because, like the documents that Allport studied so earnestly, it reveals the personality, accomplishments, and plans of its author. The portfolio strategy comes from fields and professions that make things. Marketing firms' portfolios of their prior advertising successes impress new clients. Architects' portfolios of previous designs and structures convey their style and proficiencies. Actors bring with them to each casting call a history of their prior appearances and accomplishments. So too should professors' portfolios include a detailed account of their *products*: the artifacts of their teaching and scholarship, including capsule summaries of the classes they have taught, the lectures they have crafted, the educational materials they have developed, and the curricula they have built. A teaching portfolio, as Seldin (2004) explained, "brings together in one place information about a professor's most significant teaching accomplishments" (p. 3).

Portfolios are personal documents in the Allportian sense because they are created by professors themselves. Each one is unique, given that it documents the activities of a single individual's work in teaching, but portfolios nonetheless include certain common elements. Just as the press of environmental circumstances creates dimensions of variation in people's personalities, so too does the university setting, with its demands for teaching, research, and service, create consistencies in the life history of the professor. These common themes create similarities in professors' portfolios, so that even though each portfolio is a unique description of a unique professor's life, most nonetheless contain the categories of information summarized in Table 10.1: (a) a vitae-like listing of all professional accomplishments related to teaching; (b) a personal statement or narrative that provides the reader with the professor's personal perspective on his or her work in teaching; (c) teaching materials, annotated so that readers can understand their connection to the professor's educational mission; (d) objective and subjective indicators of teaching effectiveness; and (e) ancillaries that the portfolio-builder believes are essential for conveying a sense of their teaching to the reader.

WHY DEVELOP A TEACHING PORTFOLIO?

It takes time to develop a teaching portfolio, and most teaching professors are short on that commodity. So, why take the trouble to document one's teaching in a portfolio? The motivations that prompt professors to create portfolios are as diverse as the motivations that Allport (1942, pp. 69–75) identified in his analysis of why people write diaries, letters, and journals: Some write to explain their actions, others are driven by "a single-minded desire to display one's virtues and vices," and others desire to put their accomplishments in order. Across the gamut of motives, however, portfolio experts most frequently cite these five purposes: (a) documentation, (b) development, (c) enrichment, (d) innovation, and (e) assessment (Cerbin, 2001; J. P. Murray, 1995; Seldin, 2004).

TABLE 10.1

Possible Components of a Teaching Portfolio or Dossier

Component	Characteristics
Vitae	A comprehensive listing of all professional activities related to teaching, including courses taught, service on teaching-related committees, and scholarly activities related to teaching
Personal statement	A narrative describing one's teaching, often containing sections pertaining to personal principles and assumptions about learning, general and specific goals, and autobiographical materials
Teaching materials	An annotated and selective sample of materials used in teaching, including syllabi, lecture notes, reading lists, session plans, self-constructed learning activities and assignments, tests and exams, and unique instructional tools
Assessments	Text, numerical, and graphic summaries of evidence of teaching effectiveness gathered from such sources as student evaluations, peer observations, self-assessments, and exit interviews with students
Supplemental materials	Individualized indicators of teaching style and quality, such as lecture videos, transcribed supervision sessions and discussions, copies of students' graded assignments, scholarly publications pertaining to teaching and learning

Documentation

Teaching portfolios provide a glimpse (ideally, a reassuring glimpse) into the inner world of the teaching professor. Even though teaching is a very public activity, it often occurs in an exclusive, almost secret, setting. The professor typically meets with many students, but in isolation from fellow professors or administrators. Although everyone remembers what is involved in teaching, for they were students themselves at one time, professors' actual activities in and out of the classroom require specification. The portfolio provides that by cataloging the various obligations of a teacher—such activities as meeting the class, lecturing, leading discussions, developing and administering tests, advising, developing curricula, and so on. But the portfolio goes beyond these general, categorical listings by identifying concrete actions and activities that comprise them while also describing any uncommon, unusual, and innovative activities undertaken by the instructor. They also provide a more complete picture of the professor's accomplishments by offering a long-range look at the teacher rather than a time-limited sample of a year or two's work. A portfolio generates longitudinal data that describe the professor's accomplishments across a longer period of time and so provides evidence of changes in patterns and qualities.

Development

The teaching portfolio is a useful tool for stimulating adaptive change across the life history of the teaching professor. Studies of experts in such spheres as sports, chess, problem solving, and science all converge on one conclusion: Experts are particularly good at seeking out feedback about their performances and then using that feedback to improve their overall performance (Ericsson & Lehmann, 1996). The portfolio is an excellent means of gathering such feedback, in particular because it forces the professor to create a context for this information. During the day-to-day demands of teaching, one can easily lose sight of the overall reasons behind one's practices. Teaching becomes a series of discrete actions, such as giving lectures, making up exams, giving out grades, and holding office hours. Preparing a portfolio forces the professor to put these specific actions into a broader context and so see the forest rather than just the individual trees. The very act of developing a portfolio helps professors gain an overarching perspective on their varied accomplishments and activities.

The portfolio-building process also provides the opportunity to discover inconsistencies in one's practices, identify weaknesses, and devise ways to improve. In many cases portfolios include sections that ask the professors to describe ways in which they expect their teaching will change in the future, so that they can identify new goals and plan for their implementation.

Enrichment

Administrators in higher education often confuse job *enrichment* strategies with job *enlargement* strategies. Job enlargement is most useful when individuals, bored with the routine of their work and its minimal demands, are given the opportunity to take on new duties. Job enhancement, in contrast, increases the value of the individual's work, in particular by stressing the intrinsic rewards the work generates.

Teaching portfolios should not be just one more burden placed on an already-overburdened teaching professor; instead, building a teaching portfolio gives professors an opportunity to revisit their motivations for teaching and redefine the intrinsic satisfactions that teaching provides. When professors catalogue all the many and varied activities that are associated with teaching they can better recognize the magnitude of their contribution to others' learning. Portfolios, by providing an opportunity to plan future directions, also increase a sense of efficacy as individual faculty chart out their own goals. Portfolios are also protective and empowering. They protect faculty, to a degree, from the disappointment, disillusionment, and distress that can occur when their students perform poorly despite their best efforts and when their student ratings are more negative than positive. If student grades and ratings are their sole sources of data pertaining to their teaching, then the professor must accept their verdict. But professors who have assembled a cumulative teaching portfolio can consider student grades and ratings in the overall context of their work as teachers. Portfolios also provide professors with the means to influence how their teaching is evaluated by colleagues and administrators because they give professors the opportunity to create and select the materials that will determine how they are evaluated.

Innovation

Portfolios benefit not only individual instructors but also their departments, institutions, and disciplines. Portfolios are often recommended as a tool for refocusing the faculty's attention on teaching, in particular when teaching is afforded little time or energy relative to research. The process of portfolio building can also increase the amount of time faculty spend discussing teaching, as they share ideas for what elements to include in portfolios, gather information from peers to include in their reports, and identify examples of good portfolios to emulate.

Assessment

As I noted in Chapter 9, many colleges and universities use portfolios in their annual review of faculty, when identifying faculty for special awards and honors, and when making tenure and promotion decisions. Portfolios, because they meld many sources of information about teaching, provide a more complete assessment of the quality of the instruction. Portfolios also take some of the sting out of the review process. Faculty reviews can, in some cases, create feelings of competition among the faculty, because when evaluations follow identical formats and use comparative scales, then relative rankings of individuals are unavoidable (e.g., "Relative to the other teachers at this university, how would you rate *this* professor?"). Because they are individualized, portfolios reduce the tendency to rank faculty. Many faculty also feel less threatened by the prospect of portfolio-based reviews. The judgments of students and peers are often summarized in portfolios, but the professor has the opportunity to put this information into perspective for the reader.

TYPES OF TEACHING PORTFOLIOS

Just as the vitae or resumé is deliberately shaped and recast for differing purposes—the vitae one sends when applying for a position as a scientist at a research institute should look very different from the vitae sent with one's application for a tenure-track position at a small, liberal arts college—the teaching portfolios' structure and content change depending on its overall purpose. For example, a *showcase portfolio* that is created when a faculty member is nominated for a teaching award will differ substantially from the *evaluation portfolio* that is requested by the professor's tenure and promotion review committee. A showcase portfolio is deliberately designed to highlight the professor's strengths rather than weaknesses. Just as researchers do not list on their vitae their many failed studies or the papers that never were accepted for publication, the portfolio need not catalogue every teaching catastrophe. It is a "collection of documents that represent the best of one's teaching" (J. P. Murray, 1994, p. 34). An evaluation portfolio, on the other hand, should be a more evenhanded review of the individual's prior work in teaching. Such portfolios, too, should adhere more closely to the standards for such documents as established by the department, college, or school. The evaluation portfolio's goal is to "describe, through documentation over an extended period of time, the full range of your abilities as a college teacher" (Urbach, 1992, p. 71). Other portfolio forms include the *archival portfolio*, the *course portfolio*, the *time-limited portfolio*, and the *developmental portfolio*.

The portfolio will also differ depending on the instructor's stage of development as a teaching professor. A graduate student may begin

TABLE 10.2

Purposes of Portfolios for Particular Professors

Position	Purposes
Graduate student instructors	▪ Gaining a perspective on teaching and its relationship to one's professional identity ▪ Developing the credentials and experiences needed for faculty positions ▪ Increasing one's sense of efficacy in teaching
New faculty	▪ Defining and implementing a balance across demands for research, teaching, and service ▪ Increasing the quality of instruction ▪ Documenting teaching quality for tenure review
Tenured faculty	▪ Developing and diversifying teaching activities ▪ Renewing teaching methods ▪ Maintaining and enhancing motivation for teaching ▪ Documenting teaching quality for honors, awards, promotion, pay
Adjunct faculty	▪ Developing credentials and experiences required by employers ▪ Increasing preparedness for teaching ▪ Developing and sustaining an identity as a teaching professor

building a portfolio to qualify for an academic post, a new professor's motivation may be tenure review, and the full professor's motives may reflect exhibitionism or a quest to find order in the accumulated events of a long and distinguished career. As suggested in Table 10.2, all who teach should develop portfolios, but the final document reflects their varying purposes (Brems, Lampman, & Johnson, 1995).

Building the Portfolio

Languishing in those filing cabinets, archived in your computer's directories, scattered across the Internet, and interweaved randomly into stacks of last semester's correspondence are the raw materials needed to build a teaching portfolio. Teaching evaluations, thank you notes for guest lectures given, old tests and syllabi, handouts and homework assignments, and the lecture notes used on the first day of class that outline the course's larger purposes provide the foundation for what will grow into a more comprehensive life history of the professor.

THE ERUDITIO VITAE

The *curriculum vitae*, or CV, is both the birth certificate and the headstone of the academic. It is literally the "course of the scholar's life," the autobiographical record of all scholarly accomplishments. It should therefore be extraordinarily detailed, with no accomplishment excluded. At the same time, though, the CV is usually a terse document that lists achievements, organizing them into appealing clusters with meaningful headings and subheadings. The traditional CV usually stresses the scholar's own study, training, and research rather than his or her impact on others' learning.

Unlike the CV, the vitae in a teaching portfolio stresses *eruditio*: one's accomplishments as an educator, teacher, and disseminator of knowledge. As suggested in Table 10.3, the *eruditio vitae* (EV) should go beyond information pertaining to degrees received, academic appointments held, membership in professional associations, courses taught, and research published to include sections rarely seen on a CV—sections that provide more detailed information about the course of the scholar's teaching life. Because it is a personal document, designed to convey information about the professor's instructional practices, values, and achievements, its author must consider what impression the EV leaves with the reader. As you build an EV you must ask yourself, "What do I want to tell people about myself and my teaching?" The following sections suggest some answers.

I Am Involved in Teaching

Each publication is usually listed on the CV: every conference paper, chapter, book, and article, gets a line, yet professors who have taught two sections of Introduction to Advanced Studies each semester for 15 years humbly list only Intro to Advanced Studies on their vitae, hoping the reader will imagine the scope of the work summarized by that one line. The EV distrusts imagination and so requires a detailed listing of each semester's classes taught, and it may even include essential details such as size, texts assigned, and so on. The seasoned scholar, looking back at many years of classes, often stops counting each contribution. But if a class is not noted, then a casual reader of the vitae may mistakenly think very little teaching has been done.

My Teaching Takes Many Forms

Professors teach in many places and in many ways. They teach in the classroom, on the sidewalk, in their offices, through technology by lecturing, leading discussions, questioning, and mentoring. The EV should reflect this diversity and so disconfirm the lay belief that teaching involves classroom instruction only. If professors describe their teaching solely in terms of specific classes offered and omit other forms of instruction from the EV, then their message is obvious: These other activities must not qualify as teaching.

The portfolio must document these forms by painstakingly listing supervision of internships, field work, thesis and dissertation research;

TABLE 10.3

Information Often Included in a Curriculum Vitae and in an Expanded Teaching Vitae (Eruditio Vitae)

Category	Examples
	Curriculum vitae
Academic appointments	Professorships, lecturerships, significant work experiences
Awards and honors	Fellowships, memberships in scholarly societies
Education	Universities attended, degrees earned
Grants and contracts	Support garnered from government agencies, private foundations, private industry
Memberships	Disciplinary and professional memberships, state-association membership, and so on
Professional and disciplinary service	Editorships, reviewing for scholarly journals, service to community organizations, and so on
Research and scholarship	Books (monographs, texts, edited volumes, etc.); articles (both refereed or nonrefereed); review articles, semipopular or popular magazine articles; professional reports, journal editorships, proceedings or symposium editorships, conference paper presentations, participation as a panel chair or discussant, invited colloquia, and so on
Service	Involvement with and role taken in departmental, school, and university committees and organizations
Teaching experience	Teaching interests, courses taught, graduate student supervision experience, advising
	Eruditio vitae
Advising	Assisting students in curriculum planning and career exploration
Courses taught	Undergraduate and graduate courses taught, including brief descriptions of topics covered
Curriculum development	Creating new courses, extensively revising existing courses, developing new methods of instruction, developing entirely new educational programs
Faculty development	Activities that enhance other faculty members' skills in teaching (developing and conducting teaching workshops, consulting with faculty regarding their teaching, conducting informal and formal assessments of teaching)
Graduate student mentoring and supervision	Mentoring graduate students in research and practice (e.g., laboratory supervision, thesis and dissertation research)
Grants and contracts	Grants dealing specifically with educational issues, such as projects supported by the Funds for the Improvement of Post-Secondary Education
Memberships	Membership in associations focused on teaching, such as Division 2 (Society of the Teaching of Psychology) of the American Psychological Association, local faculty consortiums
Public teaching	Media interviews, references in the media, opinion/editorials, blogging, TED talks, recognition as a public intellectual or thought leader

(continues)

TABLE 10.3 (*Continued*)

Information Often Included in a Curriculum Vitae and in an Expanded Teaching Vitae (Eruditio Vitae)

Category	Examples
Self-development	Participation in workshops dealing with teaching skills, attendance at conferences on teaching, continuing education enrollments
Service in teaching	Participation in and leadership of committees and task forces dealing with teaching (departmental curriculum committee, university task force on instruction, etc.)
Specialized forms of teaching	Nonroutine types of teaching, including guest lectures, public teaching (speeches to lay audiences, educational newspaper articles, and interviews), Massive Open Online Courses, interdisciplinary teaching, colloquia at one's own university and other universities
Teaching scholarship	Publications, presentations, and talks dealing with teaching and learning (research into teaching effectiveness, publications in teaching journals)
Technology and teaching	Using technology for instructional purposes, including development of multimedia, films, distance education, and Internet-based instruction
Texts and teaching materials	Authored materials used in teaching, including textbooks, instruction manuals, test item banks, and websites
Undergraduate student mentoring and supervision	Individualized forms of instruction (student internships, field work, honors theses, membership on thesis committees)

membership on honors, thesis, and dissertation committees, colloquia; guest lectures; workshops; and so on. Moreover, the concept of teaching itself should be enlarged so that it includes nontraditional forms of instruction, including

- public teaching (presentations to the community at large, including speeches, workshops, educational newspaper articles, and interviews);
- serving as a public intellectual, who is quoted frequently in the media and recognized as an expert in his or her field;
- distance education;
- interdisciplinary teaching;
- colloquia at one's own university and other universities; and
- Internet-based instruction.

The idea here is that outstanding teachers teach—they are literally involved in the act of teaching—in the classroom and in other teaching settings.

I Am a Practicing Teacher

Many professions, including medicine and the law, put great emphasis on improving their work over time. Physicians or lawyers, for example, are called *practitioners*, and their work is called a *practice*. Similarly, the EV should stress teaching professors' development as they practice and hone their technique. The outstanding educator who has never attended a workshop dealing with teaching skills or a conference on teaching or earned continuing education credit while studying his or her teaching is a rarity. If you attend the annual convention of your professional association, find a session dealing with teaching and note your attendance on your EV. If your university offers workshops in teaching skills, take part and record your participation on your EV. Join online e-mail groups devoted to teaching. Even informal meetings during which you and your colleagues discuss teaching can be upgraded into self-development forums by titling the group and formally defining its focus on teaching.

I Contribute to College Teaching

Many of the activities of a professor focus on the way knowledge generated in his or her field can be best conveyed to learners. The EV should, when possible, mention contributions to teaching and to higher education in general. Contributions such as research into pedagogical practices, curricular reform, university- and national-level service in teaching, public teaching, and mentorship of other teachers dot the vitae of the finest teachers. They also provide considerable service to their unit and to their discipline by developing courses, organizing offerings, and providing guidance on curriculum, including

- membership in or leadership of state or national committees or organizations that examine questions of teaching methods and curricula,
- mentorship of other teachers,
- grant activities related to higher education,
- consultations at other universities regarding teaching,
- leadership in faculty development,
- development of educational models adopted elsewhere, and
- conducting workshops for colleagues at professional meetings.

Advanced teaching professors are concerned with their own and others' teaching, to the point that they study the process of teaching itself. The professor's dictum "publish or perish" applies to some degree to the teaching professor given that well-rounded professors communicate their ideas and experiences about teaching to others through articles and papers published or presented on educational topics, manuals developed for classroom use, and textbooks.

I Value Teaching

A traditional CV, with most of its content devoted to research, screams the message "TEACHING DOES NOT MATTER," and although this message is attributed to the individual professor who has crafted the CV it implies that the professor's college or university agrees with this assessment. When students, parents, or legislators read over a traditional CV all they see is evidence of the scholarly credentials and accomplishments. It little wonder that they often complain that teaching is given too low a priority, for they are misled by the CV's myopia. An EV, by giving a voice to accomplishments in teaching, underscores the value of this activity.

PERSONAL STATEMENT OF TEACHING

A teaching portfolio is a personal document that should reflect the unique qualities of the particular teacher, and so no uniform table of contents can be either offered or enforced. But most analyses of portfolios in higher education agree that it should contain a statement by the professor that describes his or her beliefs about learning and education and how these beliefs influence teaching practice. J. P. Murray (1995) wrote, "The only essential component of the teaching portfolio is a statement of what the author believes about teaching and learning" (pp. 24–25).

The actual contents of these narratives vary, but the best teaching philosophies are lucid analyses of the professors' views of their mission as a scholar and as a teacher. They are sometimes written in a personal, revealing style, but they nonetheless contain substantive information about teaching professors' theoretical and conceptual orientation, the goals they seek when teaching their students, and their general assumptions about higher education and learning.

Paradigmatic Assumptions and Outlook

Because college professors integrate the values of the traditional teacher—one who educates and imparts knowledge—and the scholar—a learned person who has a profound knowledge of a particular subject matter—they do not simply serve as relay points for the transmission of information from authorities in the field to the student. Instead, they actively participate in the analysis, construction, and elaboration of their field's basic work. That unique understanding will permeate their teaching just as it permeates their research. The portfolio provides an opportunity to describe your fundamental assumptions about your field and subfield. These brief descriptions of your background and paradigmatic assumptions remind the reader that the author of the portfolio is not simply someone who teaches a particular topic but instead is a subject matter expert who has chosen to advance the discipline by teaching it to others.

Principles

Skilled professors base their teaching interventions on a set of assumptions, or *principles*, about learning and higher education in general. These principles are often only implicit shapers of their classes until the necessity of describing them for the teaching portfolio forces their analysis and description.

These principles can be ones that the teaching professor personally finds to be important, but they can also be drawn from extant analyses of college-level instruction like those discussed briefly in Chapter 1. A professor may, for example, briefly summarize the Boyer Commission's report on reinvigorating undergraduate education (Boyer Commission on Educating Undergraduates in the Research University, 1998), Chickering and Gamson's (1987) "Seven Principles for Good Practice in Undergraduate Education," or the principles of engagement and education as set forth in the National Survey of Student Engagement (2013) before giving examples how the professor applies these principles in his or her classes. Another effective approach is to tie basic principles of a professor's responsibilities directly to the paradigmatic assumptions of one's field. For example, an engineering professor may explain how the class is a complex system of interrelated parts that requires constant review, maintenance, and adjustment. A professor of business may discuss the nature of entrepreneurship and explain how its concepts can be used to create an engaging class experience. A theater professor can examine how theater is both the process of self-discovery and transformation and how both processes are essential to generate transformation in college students. A developmental psychologist could note what theories of cognitive development say about how a college class should be best structured to meet the needs of its students.

Recognized expert teachers in your field, or in higher education in general, are also excellent sources of ideas for the personal narrative (e.g., Epstein, 1981; Perlman, McCann, & McFadden, 1999; Sternberg, 1997b). For example, Weimer (2013) wrote

> Let me distill what I have come to believe are the key ingredients of learner-centered teaching. It is teaching focused on learning—what the students are doing is the central concern of the teacher. Being "focused on learning" is easily understood at a superficial

level, but its delineation reveals more details and intricacies. . . .
It is teaching that engages students in the hard, messy work of
learning. (p. 15)

From Allitt (2005):

"I'm the teacher, you're the student." There are all kinds of
implications. First, as the teacher, I know more about the
subject than the students do, which is why they have to come
to class in the first place. They want to learn things they do not
yet know. . . . Second, some students are more talented than
others and some are more hard-working than others, which
means that their achievements—and their grades—will differ.
Third, despite the steady temptation to make friends with the
students, I have to resist it [lest] I compromise my judgment
and impartiality. (pp. ix–x)

K. E. Ebel (1976) explained:

I will state my philosophic biases at the outset. First, I share one
of the oldest of opinions about learning—that learning is essentially
pleasurable. To me, that opinion puts great weight upon preserving
a sense of play in teaching. I leads me to believe that teaching is
an improviser's art. . . . My broader philosophic bias is that I am
a pluralist: I cannot conceive of any one way of teaching that
will excel all others. (pp. 3–4)

Lefton (1997) described his approach as follows:

I design my class and my textbook according to certain guiding
principles. I try to (a) be selective in what I teach; (b) adapt
to my students' learning styles; (c) teach critical thinking and
learning strategies; (d) work from application to theory; (e) help
students recognize and be sensitive to issues of diversity, including
age, gender, and ethnicity; (f) keep the course current and exciting;
(g) engage students; and (h) teach psychology as a unified,
coherent discipline. (pp. 65–66)

Techniques and Strategies

The generality of the portfolio section that addresses assumptions and
philosophies of learning should be tempered by a section that provides concrete examples of how these principles are applied in specific
courses, to specific topics, and to specific types of students. If your teaching responsibilities include the introductory course, advanced senior
courses, large proseminar courses, and graduate seminars, you need to
describe each of these courses and at least briefly explain your specific
goals, strategies, and procedures. You also may wish to provide far more
details about your methods for one or two of your classes. If, for example, you teach a large section of the introductory course, you may wish
to use this class to illustrate how you put your principles about learning
into practice by stressing critical thinking in your lecturing, breaking

the class down into small groups for collaborative learning, by using computer-based technologies, and so on.

Unique Strengths and Concerns

The teaching narrative part of a portfolio provides professors with the opportunity to explain, and even highlight, features of their teaching that are unique, controversial, or even eccentric. Some professors spend a good deal of time describing some specific, if idiosyncratic, concern that they consider to be of paramount importance; Professor X might discuss the rigor of her course in some detail, noting the close connection among exams, final grades, and the primary objectives of the course. Professor Y might stress the importance of remaining sensitive to how men and women are treated in the classroom because evidence has suggested that in many educational settings women receive less attention relative to men. Professor Z may discuss, at length, the value of service learning and provide details about how students are given the opportunity to earn points in the class by volunteering at local mental health agencies.

Pitfalls of the Personal Narrative

The narrative section of the portfolio is not easily crafted because professors who do not exercise caution often convey the wrong impression to the reader. The reader of the narrative needs answers to many questions about teaching: What are the writer's teaching values? What is her teaching style? Is this instructor liked or disliked by his students? Does the teacher seem experienced and "wise" in her approach to instruction, or naive and uncertain? Does the teacher seem interested in his discipline and in teaching it to others? Does she seem well informed or dogmatic? Does he let his personal values surface unnecessarily, or does he set the correct level of personalization?

These narratives should also be carefully written so they are coherent, articulate, and free of grammatical error. This element of the portfolio gives professors the opportunity to explain the reasons behind their teaching methods, but they can also reveal other, less positive, messages. A narrative that is garbled or unstructured raises, sometimes unfairly, warning signs for the reader. If authors cannot communicate their ideas about the teaching clearly, then how well do they communicate information to their students? A lack of care in developing the narrative can also generate one that sounds pretentious or trite. The professor may explain "I am deeply committed to teaching, for my first obligation is to my students." Another writes, "I love to teach. I've always felt at home in the classroom, surrounded by young minds." A third claims "I strive to instill a love of learning in my students, for I believe that education and the ability to acquire knowledge hold the keys to our world's survival." These statements are the professorial versions of the painful "What my education means to me" essays that students must write on admission applications. These statements should be written not at the last moment but well in advance of the deadline so revisions recommended by colleagues and mentors can be made.

TEACHING MATERIALS

Portfolios should contain actual samples of the professor's work. These samples should be carefully organized so the reader can grasp the connections among the various documents. This section can be prefaced with a brief overview of the scheme that organized the various elements, and annotations should be added as needed to help the reader grasp the importance of each exhibit. Again, these materials should be consistent with, and even elaborate on, the principles and strategies of instruction noted in the personal narrative.

Syllabi

The syllabus, or course outline, is often the very first piece of paper that professors drop into that file folder labeled "Teaching Portfolio Project." Syllabi, as I noted in Chapter 2, are designed to give students a clear idea of the professor's goals, methods, standards, and policies, which is precisely the type of information that should be conveyed in a teaching portfolio. Professors should, however, be mindful of the fit between the principles they espouse in their narrative and the objective data of the syllabus. Professors who claim to use teacher-centered methods and engaging activities that demand critical thinking, but whose syllabi list only the chapter topics and the dates for the multiple-choice exams, signal their hypocrisy rather than competency. A syllabus that omits critical information, such as the course goals, contact information, and course prerequisites, makes a poor impression, as does a syllabus that goes on and on about attendance, make-ups, and classroom etiquette but says little about the course's overall purpose and procedures.

Handouts, Assignments, and Activities

A college course can be the wellspring of a river of documents. During the course of a semester or quarter, professors inundate their students with lecture outlines, learning objectives, exam prep sheets, reading lists, research summaries, homework assignments, exercises, observation guides, study hints, thought questions, and so on, and these documents are telling indicators of teaching practices. Even electronic communications and handouts, such as e-mails to students, screen shots of the course's wiki page, online discussion questions, and forum topics, should be included.

Notes and Planning Materials

College professors rarely develop the elaborate curriculum guides favored by elementary and secondary education teachers, but some use detailed worksheets to describe .topics and objectives, lists of the media to use and readings to cover, key examples to share with students, ideas harvested from such sources as magazines and newspapers, and notes about potential projects. These materials provide background information about the professor's level of preparation, as do the notes they use when giving a lecture or leading a discussion. Lecture and discussion notes, for example, provide the reader with an idea of how each presentation is structured and its relationship to the professor's overall assumptions about teaching. The reading list serves a similar function, even if the list was used only by the professor during his or her preparation for the class and was not shared with the students. Such lists of scholarly books, references, and readings not only impress laypersons but also give colleagues a good indication of the instructor's basic approach and emphases.

Tests, Quizzes, and Exams

The portfolio should include, at a minimum, a description of the procedures used to give students feedback about their progress toward the course's objectives. In many cases, this section will include samples of quizzes, tests, exams, and term paper assignments made in a recently taught class, but professors who use alternative strategies, such as graded participation, term projects, observation of students, and oral exams, should provide some details about how they carry out these evaluations. This section may also contain examples of the types of feedback given to students about their performance, including de-identified (i.e., masked) graded papers.

Given the importance of assessment in teaching, professors should also include additional information about the reliability and validity of the procedures they use. Examples of tables of specification that indicate the relationship between each item and the course's learning objectives, indexes of difficulty and discrimination, item–total correlations, and other psychometric data can give readers of the portfolio reassuring information about the quality of assessment procedures. The professor may also wish to give some indication of the typical distribution of grades, in particular when the portfolio will be reviewed by external audiences who have no way of estimating the difficulty of the exam and the overall course content.

EVALUATIONS OF TEACHING EFFECTIVENESS

The portfolio also should include digests of the results of past and current evaluations of teaching effectiveness based on student evaluations, peer evaluations, and other types of summative evaluation systems. Some of this information may be available on the EV, but this section should provide much more orientation and interpretation so that the reader interprets the data appropriately. A professor might, for example, list on his EV all his PhD students and where they are currently employed but draw attention to these data in this section of the portfolio in a heading named "Mentoring Advanced Students" or "Graduate Student Instruction."

Student Ratings of Instruction

As I noted in Chapter 9, the validity of student rating of instruction is a matter of debate. This information should nonetheless be included in the complete portfolio, for the portfolio's flexibility provides the author with an opportunity to suggest his or her own interpretation of the data. For example, many student ratings of instruction include items with dubious psychometric quality, so the portfolio should focus on the items with the best validity and reliability. The university's feedback report may be online or difficult to interpret, and so the portfolio should provide a verbal interpretation of the numeric data and descriptions of any special conditions that should be taken into account when interpreting the results. Charts, plots, figures, and other graphics also increase the ease of interpretation of the items, in particular when the data are extensive, inconsistent, or confusing. Charts should be annotated, however, to provide an explanation for any trends and to focus the reader on the key points.

Peer-Based Evaluations

Fellow instructors can often provide considerable information about teaching performance: information that goes well beyond that provided by students. In many cases, colleagues have seen each other give colloquia, guest lectures, and presentations at meetings, and these experiences can form the basis for a brief commentary about one's communication and presentation skills. Peers also have considerable information about effectiveness gained by participation in joint teaching situations, such as membership on student committees and team teaching situations. Some universities even have objective "teacher evaluators" visit classrooms and provide analyses of the quality of instruction.

Outcome-Based Evaluations

Most indices of teaching excellence focus on the professor, asking the question "How effective is this instructor?" Yet some universities suggest that the portfolio should also include evidence of the impact of instruction and the question "Did the students learn?" It is difficult to determine instructors' contribution to their students' achievement, but the following types of information provide some evidence of learning outcomes:

- high scores on standardized or locally developed tests of knowledge;
- high-quality essays, projects, and reports written by students;
- publications or presentations with students as coauthors;
- evidence of success after graduation in careers closely connected to a specific course;
- the performance of students in related or subsequent courses; and
- employers' reports after hiring students.

Additional Indicators

In addition to data pertaining to the most critical dependent measure in higher education—Did students learn anything?—one may also wish to include other types of evidence of impact: success in placing students in jobs or graduate schools, comments from parents, testimonials written by students (both those written in response to a direct request and spontaneous submissions), interviews with students or alumni, and special surveys of opinion (often conducted as part of the tenure and promotion process).

SUPPLEMENTAL MATERIALS

The teaching professor's creativity, and not the standards set by others' portfolios, determines what goes into and what is left out of the portfolio. Depending on the individual teacher, the portfolio may include such novelties as the following items:

- a recording of a lecture from a class or a presentation at a national conference;
- interactive programs that teach a range of course topics;
- a map of the United States, with a star marking the location of each PhD student mentored;
- the verbatim, unedited comments made by students on the open-ended portion of the student evaluations, or a word cloud of these ratings;

- copies of the forms, descriptions, and memoranda created when a new course was guided through the various school curricula committees and into the course catalogue;
- dozens of eloquent recommendation letters written for undergraduate and graduate students;
- a letter from the department chairperson describing the professor's teaching skills; and
- photographs of chalk-filled blackboards generated by an old-school, but passionate, lecturer.

All these varied forms of evidence testify to the professor's skills as an educator are possibilities for inclusion in the portfolio. Just as evaluators of teaching quality must cast their net widely if they are to catch all the indicators of teaching discussed in Chapter 9, so too must professors do all they can to provide readers with the information they need to understand what it means to be a professor.

Indicators of sometimes-overlooked aspects of teaching are particularly important to include. *Teaching-related service*, for example, can absorb an enormous amount of time, and yet this contribution to teaching is often overlooked by review committees whose attention is riveted on classroom instruction. However, each new course developed or modified, service on committees devoted to issues related to teaching and curriculum, and administrative duties that are primarily focused on teaching all underscore the professor's commitment to teaching. Evidence of effective mentoring and advising should also be highlighted because all teaching does not happen in a classroom lecture or discussion; the portfolio should not overlook indicators of the professor's accomplishments in one-on-one and small group teaching settings. Evidence of teaching scholarship—such as papers on teaching, manuals developed for classroom use, research into the learning and teaching process, textbooks, and books—that examines critical processes and issues in teaching (like this one!), too, are appropriate additions to the teaching portfolio.

Documenting Redux: Developing a Teaching Persona

Professors' professional responsibilities are staggering, yet their work in and out of the classroom can be ignored and forgotten if it is never documented. A teaching portfolio is insurance against this tragedy because it gathers together the artifacts of one's teaching in a portfolio or dossier that describes the professor's involvement in, and success at, teaching. Portfolios are unique, individualistic summaries of one's work in the teaching arena, but most will include a teaching vitae, a personal statement about teaching, a selective sample of teaching materials, and documents that provide objective evidence of teaching effectiveness.

Given the value of teaching portfolios, professors who are serious about their work as educators are urged to develop one, but this suggestion is only one on a list of suggestions that can be harvested from the chapters of this book. The chapters' analyses of teaching and learning, by drawing on theory and research in psychology and related fields, assumed that knowing more about the cognitive, motivational, personal, and impersonal processes that intermingle to create a college class will likely yield useful suggestions for those who teach. It reminds professors to monitor, measure, and even manipulate those processes and to favor the methods that have withstood the test of empirical procedures rather than the test of time:

1. *Orient: Identify your purposes and priorities.* Before we order the textbooks, prepare syllabi, write lectures, and craft discussion questions, we must first consider the essential purposes we seek. Teaching is a goal-focused, purposive activity and so is far more likely to end successfully when its purposes are well understood by all concerned. Excellent teaching is teaching that serves its intended purpose.

2. *Prepare: Align your purposes with practices.* Our courses are a mix of many different activities, events, and experiences, but each one should be aligned with the course's overall purposes. Excellent teaching requires not only identifying your goals—the changes you will seek in the limited time you have available to help your students learn—but also selecting the means to achieve those ends.

3. *Guide: Use student-centered teaching strategies.* Discussion, activities, writing assignments, independent studies, internships, and other student-centered teaching methods shift the focus of the class away from the instructor to the student. These methods may not be the most efficient means for you to transmit information to your students, but they are more likely to increase students' engagement in their learning. All excellent teaching promotes active learning, but student-centered methods require more observable engagement from students in the teaching–learning process.

4. *Lecture: Communicate engagingly.* Your specialty might be leading a discussion, teaching online, or helping students develop their writing, but nearly all professors must occasionally engage in that tried-and-true form of teaching: the lecture. Not all professors have mastered the art of the lecture, but those who

combine intellectual excitement and interpersonal rapport in their presentations can transform a classroom of passive listeners into one filled with engaged, active learners.

5. *Test: Align teaching with testing.* From time to time, the link between effective teaching and lasting learning must be verified. Even when you have identified specific learning outcomes and have carefully chosen learning activities that should help students reach those goals, you still require objective confirmation that your carefully wrought procedures are working. The ultimate test of teaching excellence is student success. Few would be impressed by professors who claim to be excellent teachers but whose students seem to learn so little.

6. *Grade and aid: Grade them but also help them.* Students need feedback about their level of achievement, and grades provide them with that feedback; they are the definers of success in an academic course. Giving a grade, however, is only the first step in a learning cycle that includes preparation, performance, evaluation, feedback, and remediation. If students are graded, they should also be provided with the resources they need to improve those grades.

7. *Manage: Foster civility and integrity.* Learning requires taking risks: exploring areas of uncertainty, seeking guidance from others, and testing one's limits. Classes must be places of psychological and interpersonal safety, and so you must not only teach students but also work with them to create a civil and ethical learning environment. Excellent teaching promotes excellence in conduct and character.

8. *Upgrade: Use technology creatively and appropriately.* If you have been postponing learning to use technology when you teach, then your procrastination has paid off: The glitches and bugs have now been worked out, and the research evidence confirms that learning online is as intellectually and academically satisfying as offline learning. So, who is now the excellent teacher? The answer to that question is, "Someone who uses technology effectively in their classes—whether they meet in face-to-face classes or online."

9. *Evaluate: Assess your success.* Excellence in teaching manifests itself in any number of ways—from the length of waiting lists to get into your classes and invitations to speak to student groups to glowing ratings on RateMyProfessor and publications with student authors. But many—perhaps too many—still use student ratings of instruction as their primary metric for assessing teaching excellence, so excellent teachers know that students' perceptions are not to be ignored.

10. *Document: Develop a teaching persona.* Professors tend to have the long-range view of things. Each day brings new demands and new experiences: new courses to teach when the developments of your field make the ideas and information offered in older formulations obsolete; new studies and projects to conduct as new questions arise that can only be answered through scholarly research; new students to help understand the discipline core concepts through teaching and training; and new lectures to give, discussions to lead, activities to design and implement, tests to write, grades to assign, classes to manage, technologies to learn, and courses to evaluate. But each activity, each course, each term, and each year contributes to the process of becoming an excellent teacher and so should be catalogued and documented. Building the case for your excellence as a professor is too important a task to delegate to others.

References

Abrami, P. C., Cohen, P. A., & d'Apollonia, S. (1988). Implementation problems in meta-analysis. *Review of Educational Research*, *58*, 151–179. http://dx.doi.org/10.3102/00346543058002151

Acee, T. W., Cho, Y., Kim, J. I., & Weinstein, C. E. (2012). Relationships among properties of college students' self-set academic goals and academic achievement. *Educational Psychology*, *32*, 681–698. http://dx.doi.org/10.1080/01443410.2012.712795

Ackerman, D. S., & Gross, B. L. (2010). Instructor feedback: How much do students really want? *Journal of Marketing Education*, *32*, 172–181. http://dx.doi.org/10.1177/0273475309360159

ACT. (2013). *2013 condition of college and career readiness*. Iowa City, IA: Author. Retrieved from http://www.act.org/readiness/2013

Aiken, E. G., Thomas, G. S., & Shennum, W. A. (1975). Memory for a lecture: Effects of notes, lecture rate, and informational density. *Journal of Educational Psychology*, *67*, 439–444. http://dx.doi.org/10.1037/h0076613

Aleamoni, L. M. (1981). Student ratings of instruction. In J. Millman (Ed.), *Handbook of teacher evaluation* (pp. 110–145). Thousand Oaks, CA: Sage.

Allan, E. J., & Madden, M. (2006). Chilly classrooms for female undergraduate students: A question of method? *The Journal of Higher Education, 77*, 684–711. http://dx.doi.org/10.1353/jhe.2006.0028

Allen, I. E., & Seaman, J. (2015). *Grade level: Tracking online education in the United States.* Oakland, CA: Babson Survey Research Group and Quahog Research Group. Retrieved from http://www.onlinelearningsurvey.com/highered.html

Allen, M. J. (2000, September). Teaching non-traditional students. *APS Observer, 13*(7), 16–17, 21, 23. Retrieved from http://www.psychologicalscience.org/teaching/tips/tips_0900.html

Allitt, P. (2005). *I'm the teacher, you're the student: A semester in the university classroom.* Philadelphia: University of Pennsylvania Press.

Allport, G. W. (1942). *The use of personal documents in psychological science.* New York, NY: Social Science Research Council.

Allport, G. W. (1955). *Becoming: Basic considerations for a psychology of personality.* New Haven, CT: Yale University Press.

Allport, G. W. (1968). *The person in psychology: Selected essays by Gordon W. Allport.* Boston, MA: Beacon Press.

Alwin, D. F., Cohen, R. L., & Newcomb, T. M. (1991). *Personality and social change: Attitude persistence and changes over the lifespan.* Madison: University of Wisconsin Press.

Amador, J. A., Miles, L., & Peters, C. B. (2006). *The practice of problem-based learning: A guide to implementing PBL in the college classroom.* San Francisco, CA: Anker.

Ambrose, S. A., Bridges, M. W., DiPietro, M., Lovett, M. C., & Norman, M. K. (2010). *How learning works.* San Francisco, CA: Jossey-Bass.

American Psychological Association. (2010). *Ethical principles of psychologists and code of conduct (2002, Amended June 1, 2010).* Retrieved from http://www.apa.org/ethics/code/principles.pdf

Ames, C. (1987). The enhancement of student motivation. In M. Maehr & D. Kleiber (Eds.), *Advances in motivation and achievement: Vol. 5. Enhancing motivation* (pp. 123–148). Greenwich, CT: JAI Press.

Anderson, L. W., Krathwohl, D. R., Airasian, P. W., Cruikshank, K. A., Mayer, R. E., Pintrich, P. R., . . . Wittrock, M. C. (2001). *A taxonomy for learning, teaching, and assessing: A revision of Bloom's taxonomy of educational objectives.* White Plains, NY: Longman.

Angelo, T. A., & Cross, K. P. (1993). *Classroom assessment techniques: A handbook for college teachers* (2nd ed.). San Francisco, CA: Jossey-Bass.

Appleby, D. C. (1999). How to improve your teaching with the course syllabus. In B. Perlman, L. I. McCann, & S. H. McFadden (Eds.), *Lessons learned: Practical advice for the teaching of psychology* (pp. 19–24). Washington, DC: American Psychological Society.

Arch, S. (1998). How to teach science. *Science, 279*, 1869. http://dx.doi.org/10.1126/science.279.5358.1869

Armstrong, J. S. (1998). Are student ratings of instruction useful? *American Psychologist, 53,* 1223–1224. http://dx.doi.org/10.1037/0003-066X.53.11.1223

Aronson, E., Blaney, N., Stephan, C., Sikes, J., & Snapp, M. (1978). *The jigsaw classroom.* Thousand Oaks, CA: Sage.

Arreola, R. A. (2007). *Developing a comprehensive faculty evaluation system* (3rd ed.). Bolton, MA: Anker.

Arum, R., & Roksa, J. (2011). *Academically adrift: Limited learning on college campuses.* Chicago, IL: University of Chicago Press.

Arum, R., & Roksa, J. (2014). *Aspiring adults adrift: Tentative transitions of college graduates.* Chicago, IL: University of Chicago Press.

Asch, S. E. (1946). Forming impressions of personality. *The Journal of Abnormal and Social Psychology, 41,* 258–290. http://dx.doi.org/10.1037/h0055756

Association of American Colleges and Universities. (2002). *Greater expectations: A new vision for learning as a nation goes to college.* Washington, DC: Author.

Astin, A. W. (1993). *What matters in college? Four critical years revisited.* San Francisco, CA: Jossey-Bass.

Austin, J. T., & Vancouver, J. B. (1996). Goal constructs in psychology: Structure, process, and content. *Psychological Bulletin, 120,* 338–375. http://dx.doi.org/10.1037/0033-2909.120.3.338

Ausubel, D. P. (1963). *The psychology of meaningful verbal learning.* Oxford, England: Grune & Stratton.

Axtell, J. (1998). *The pleasures of academe: A celebration and defense of higher education.* Lincoln: University of Nebraska Press.

Babad, E., Darley, J. M., & Kaplowitz, H. (1999). Developmental aspects in students' course selection. *Journal of Educational Psychology, 91,* 157–168. http://dx.doi.org/10.1037/0022-0663.91.1.157

Baer, J. D., Cook, A. L., & Baldi, S. (2006). *The literacy of American's college students.* Washington, DC: American Institutes for Research. http://dx.doi.org/10.1037/e539672012-001

Bain, K. (2004). *What the best college teachers do.* Cambridge, MA: Harvard University Press.

Bandura, A. (1977). *Social learning theory.* Englewood Cliffs, NJ: Prentice Hall.

Bangert, A. W. (2008). The development and validation of the Student Evaluation of Online Teaching Effectiveness. *Computers in the Schools, 25,* 25–47. http://dx.doi.org/10.1080/07380560802157717

Banyard, P., & Grayson, A. (1999). Teaching with original sources. In B. Perlman, L. I. McCann, & S. H. McFadden (Eds.), *Lessons learned: Practical advice for the teaching of psychology* (pp. 29–35). Washington, DC: American Psychological Society.

Barkley, E. F. (2009). *Student engagement techniques: A handbook for college faculty.* San Francisco, CA: Jossey-Bass.

Barkley, E. F., Cross, P. K., & Major, C. H. (2005). *Collaborative learning techniques: A handbook for college faculty.* San Francisco, CA: Jossey-Bass.

Barrick, M. R., Mount, M. K., & Li, N. (2013). The theory of purposeful work behavior: The role of personality, higher-order goals, and job characteristics. *Academy of Management Review, 38,* 132–153. http://dx.doi.org/10.5465/amr.2010.0479

Basow, S. A., & Martin, J. L. (2012). Bias in student evaluations. In M. E. Kite (Ed.), *Effective evaluation of teaching: A guide for faculty and administrators* (pp. 40–49). Retrieved from http://teachpsych.org/Resources/Documents/ebooks/evals2012.pdf

Bean, J. C. (2011). *Engaging ideas: The professor's guide to integrating writing, critical thinking, and active learning in the classroom* (2nd ed.). San Francisco, CA: Jossey-Bass.

Becker, A. H., & Calhoon, S. K. (1999). What introductory psychology students attend to on a course syllabus. *Teaching of Psychology, 26,* 6–11. http://dx.doi.org/10.1207/s15328023top2601_1

Beleche, T., Fairris, D., & Marks, M. (2012). Do course evaluations truly reflect student learning? Evidence from an objectively graded post-test. *Economics of Education Review, 31,* 709–719. http://dx.doi.org/10.1016/j.econedurev.2012.05.001

Bell, A. H., & Smith, D. M. (2011). *Learning team skills.* Boston, MA: Prentice Hall.

Belland, B. R., Kim, C., & Hannafin, M. J. (2013). A framework for designing scaffolds that improve motivation and cognition. *Educational Psychologist, 48,* 243–270. http://dx.doi.org/10.1080/00461520.2013.838920

Beloit College. (2014). *Mindset list: 2014.* Retrieved from https://www.beloit.edu/mindset/previouslists/2014/

Belov, D. I. (2013). Detection of test collusion via Kullback–Leibler divergence. *Journal of Educational Measurement, 50,* 141–163. http://dx.doi.org/10.1111/jedm.12008

Belter, R. W., & du Pré, A. (2009). A strategy to reduce plagiarism in an undergraduate course. *Teaching of Psychology, 36,* 257–261. http://dx.doi.org/10.1080/00986280903173165

Benassi, V. A., & Buskist, W. (2012). Preparing the new professoriate to teach. In W. Buskist & V. A. Benassi (Eds.), *Effective college and university teaching: Strategies and tactics for the new professoriate* (pp. 1–8). Los Angeles, CA: Sage. http://dx.doi.org/10.4135/9781452244006.n1

Benjamin, L. T., Jr. (1988). A history of teaching machines. *American Psychologist, 43,* 703–712. http://dx.doi.org/10.1037/0003-066X.43.9.703

Benjamin, R. G. (2012). Reconstructing readability: Recent developments and recommendations in the analysis of text difficulty. *Educational Psychology Review, 24,* 63–88. http://dx.doi.org/10.1007/s10648-011-9181-8

Bennett, R., Rock, D., & Wang, M. (1991). Equivalence of free-response and multiple-choice items. *Journal of Educational Measurement, 28,* 77–92. http://dx.doi.org/10.1111/j.1745-3984.1991.tb00345.x

Bennett, W. E. (1987). Small group instructional diagnosis: A dialogic approach to instructional improvement for tenured faculty. *Journal of Staff, Program, & Organizational Development, 5,* 100–104.

Benton, S. L., & Cashin, W. E. (2012). *Student ratings of teaching: A summary of research and literature* (IDEA Paper No. 50). Manhattan: Center for Faculty Evaluation and Development, Kansas State University.

Benz, J. J., & Miller, R. L. (1996). Panel discussions as a means of enhancing student-directed learning. *Journal of Instructional Psychology, 23,* 131–136.

Berk, R. A. (2013). *Top 10 flashpoints in student ratings and the evaluation of teaching.* Sterling, VA: Stylus.

Bernard, R. M., Borokhovski, E., Schmid, R. F., Tamim, R. M., & Abrami, P. C. (2014). A meta-analysis of blended learning and technology use in higher education: From the general to the applied. *Journal of Computing in Higher Education, 26,* 87–122. http://dx.doi.org/10.1007/s12528-013-9077-3

Bernard, R. M., Brauer, A., Abrami, P. C., & Surkes, M. (2004). The development of a questionnaire for predicting online learning achievement. *Distance Education, 25,* 31–47. http://dx.doi.org/10.1080/0158791042000212440

Berra, Y. (2002). *When you come to a fork in the road, take it! Inspiration and wisdom from one of baseball's greatest heroes.* New York, NY: Hyperion.

Berry, T., Cook, L., Hill, N., & Stevens, K. (2010). An exploratory analysis of textbook usage and study habits: Misperceptions and barriers to success. *College Teaching, 59*(1), 31–39. http://dx.doi.org/10.1080/87567555.2010.509376

Biggs, J., & Tang, C. (2007). *Teaching for quality learning at university.* Maidenhead, Berkshire, England: Open University Press.

Billson, J. M. (1986). The college classroom as a small group: Some implications for teaching and learning. *Teaching Sociology, 14,* 143–151. http://dx.doi.org/10.2307/1318467

Bjork, R. A. (2001, March). How to succeed in college: Learn how to learn. *APS Observer, 14*(3), 3, 9–10. Retrieved from http://www.psychologicalscience.org/observer/0301/prescol.html

Blanchard, F. A., Tilly, T., & Vaughn, L. A. (1991). Reducing the expression of racial prejudice. *Psychological Science, 2,* 101–105. http://dx.doi.org/10.1111/j.1467-9280.1991.tb00108.x

Bligh, D. A. (1998). *What's the use of lectures?* (5th ed.). [Electronic version]. Exeter, England: Intellect.

Bligh, D. A. (2000). *What's the point in discussion?* [Electronic version]. Exeter, England: Intellect.

Bloom, B. S., Englehart, M. D., Furst, E. J., Hill, W. H., & Krathwohl, D. R. (1956). *Taxonomy of educational objectives: The classification of educational goals. Handbook I: Cognitive domain.* White Plains, NY: Longman.

Boice, R. (1982). Teaching of writing in psychology. *Teaching of Psychology, 9,* 143–147. http://dx.doi.org/10.1207/s15328023top0903_4

Boice, R. (1992). *The new faculty member: Supporting and fostering professional development.* San Francisco, CA: Jossey-Bass.

Boice, R. (1994). *How writers journey to comfort and fluency.* Westport, CT: Praeger.

Boice, R. (2000). *Advice for new faculty members*: Nihil nimus. Boston, MA: Ally.

Bok, D. (2006). *Underachieving colleges: A candid look at how much students learn and why they should be learning more.* Princeton, NJ: Princeton University Press.

Boling, E. C., Hough, M., Krinsky, H., Saleem, H., & Stevens, M. (2012). Cutting the distance in distance education: Perspectives on what promotes positive, online learning experiences. *The Internet and Higher Education, 15,* 118–126. http://dx.doi.org/10.1016/j.iheduc.2011.11.006

Boniface, D. (1985). Candidates' use of notes and textbooks during an open-book examination. *Educational Research, 27,* 201–209. http://dx.doi.org/10.1080/0013188850270307

Bowdon, M. A., Billig, S. H., & Holland, B. A. (Eds.). (2008). *Scholarship for sustaining service learning and civic engagement.* Charlotte, NC: Information Age.

Bowen, J. A. (2012). *Teaching naked: How moving technology out of your college classroom will improve student learning.* San Francisco, CA: Jossey-Bass.

Boyer Commission on Educating Undergraduates in the Research University. (1998). *Reinventing undergraduate education: A blueprint for America's research universities.* Stony Brook, NY: Boyer Commission on Educating Undergraduates in the Research University. Retrieved from http://files.eric.ed.gov/fulltext/ED424840.pdf

Boysen, G. A., Vogel, D. L., Cope, M. A., & Hubbard, A. (2009). Incidents of bias in college classrooms: Instructor and student perceptions. *Journal of Diversity in Higher Education, 2,* 219–231. http://dx.doi.org/10.1037/a0017538

Braseby, A. M. (2014). *The flipped classroom* (IDEA Paper No. 57). Manhattan: Center for Faculty Evaluation and Development, Kansas State University.

Braskamp, L. A., & Ory, J. C. (1994). *Assessing faculty work: Enhancing individual and institutional performance.* San Francisco, CA: Jossey-Bass.

Braskamp, L. A., Ory, J. C., & Pieper, D. M. (1981). Student written comments: Dimensions of instructional quality. *Journal of Educational Psychology, 73,* 65–70. http://dx.doi.org/10.1037/0022-0663.73.1.65

Braxton, J. M., & Bayer, A. E. (1999). *Faculty misconduct in collegiate teaching.* Baltimore, MD: Johns Hopkins University Press.

Braxton, J. M., & Bayer, A. E. (2004). Toward a code of conduct for undergraduate teaching. *New Directions for Teaching and Learning, 99,* 47–55. http://dx.doi.org/10.1002/tl.158

Braxton, J. M., Proper, E., & Bayer, A. E. (2011). *Professors behaving badly: Faculty misconduct in graduate education.* Baltimore, MD: Johns Hopkins University Press.

Brems, C., Lampman, C., & Johnson, M. E. (1995). Preparation of applications for academic positions in psychology. *American Psychologist, 50,* 533–537. http://dx.doi.org/10.1037/0003-066X.50.7.533

Brickhouse, T. C., & Smith, N. D. (2009). Socratic teaching and Socratic method. In H. Siegel (Ed.), *The Oxford handbook of the philosophy of education* (pp. 177–194). Oxford, England: Oxford University Press.

Bromage, B. K., & Mayer, R. E. (1986). Quantitative and qualitative effects of repetition on learning from technical text. *Journal of Educational Psychology, 78,* 271–278. http://dx.doi.org/10.1037/0022-0663.78.4.271

Brookfield, S. D., & Preskill, S. (1999). *Discussion as a way of teaching: Tools and techniques for democratic classrooms.* San Francisco, CA: Jossey-Bass.

Brookhart, S. M., & Nitko, A. J. (2015). *Educational assessment of students* (7th ed.). New York, NY: Pearson.

Brophy, J. (2004). *Motivating students to learn* (2nd ed.). Mahwah, NJ: Erlbaum.

Brown, G. A., Bakhtar, M., & Youngman, M. B. (1984). Toward a typology of lecturing styles. *British Journal of Educational Psychology, 54,* 93–100. http://dx.doi.org/10.1111/j.2044-8279.1984.tb00848.x

Brown, P. C., Roediger, H. L., II, & McDaniel, M. A. (2014). *Make it stick: The science of successful learning.* Cambridge, MA: Belknap Press.

Brunell, A. B., Staats, S., Barden, J., & Hupp, J. M. (2011). Narcissism and academic dishonesty: The exhibitionism dimension and the lack of guilt. *Personality and Individual Differences, 50,* 323–328. http://dx.doi.org/10.1016/j.paid.2010.10.006

Bruner, J. (1996). Frames for thinking: Ways of making meaning. In D. R. Olson & N. Torrance (Eds.), *Modes of thought: Explorations in culture and cognition* (pp. 93–105). New York, NY: Cambridge University Press.

Bruning, R., & Horn, C. (2000). Developing motivation to write. *Educational Psychologist, 35,* 25–37. http://dx.doi.org/10.1207/S15326985EP3501_4

Bui, D. C., Myerson, J., & Hale, S. (2013). Note-taking with computers: Exploring alternative strategies for improved recall. *Journal of Educational Psychology, 105,* 299–309. http://dx.doi.org/10.1037/a0030367

Burdsal, C. A., & Harrison, P. D. (2008). Further evidence supporting the validity of both a multidimensional profile and an overall evaluation of teaching effectiveness. *Assessment & Evaluation in Higher Education, 33,* 567–576. http://dx.doi.org/10.1080/02602930701699049

Burnette, J., Hoyt, C. L., Lawson, B., & Dweck, C. C. (2015, February). *Growth theories buffer females against identity threat in computer science.* Paper presented at the Annual Meeting of the Society for Personality and Social Psychology, Long Beach, CA.

Burns, K. C. (2014). Security blanket or crutch? Crib card usage depends on students' abilities. *Teaching of Psychology, 41,* 66–68. http://dx.doi.org/10.1177/0098628313514181

Buskist, W., & Saville, B. K. (2001, March). Rapport-building: Creating positive emotional contexts for enhancing teaching and learning. *APS Observer, 14*(3), 12–13, 19. Retrieved from http://www.psychologicalscience.org/teaching/tips/tips_0301.html

Buttigieg, P. L. (2010). Perspectives on presentation and pedagogy in aid of bioinformatics education. *Briefings in Bioinformatics, 11,* 587–597. http://dx.doi.org/10.1093/bib/bbq062

Cacioppo, J. T., & Petty, R. E. (1979). Effects of message repetition and position on cognitive response, recall, and persuasion. *Journal of Personality and Social Psychology, 37,* 97–109. http://dx.doi.org/10.1037/0022-3514.37.1.97

Campbell, D. E. (2014). The influence of teacher immediacy behaviors on student performance in an online course (and the problem of method variance). *Teaching of Psychology, 41,* 163–166. http://dx.doi.org/10.1177/0098628314530351

Carbone, E. (1998). *Teaching large classes: Tools and strategies.* Thousand Oaks, CA: Sage. http://dx.doi.org/10.4135/9781483328270

Carnegie, D. (1937). *How to win friends and influence people.* New York, NY: Simon & Schuster.

Carnes, M. C. (2014). *Minds on fire: How role-immersion games transform college.* Cambridge, MA: Harvard University Press. http://dx.doi.org/10.4159/harvard.9780674735606

Caron, M. D., Whitbourne, S. K., & Halgin, R. P. (1992). Fraudulent excuse making among college students. *Teaching of Psychology, 19,* 90–93. http://dx.doi.org/10.1207/s15328023top1902_6

Carpenter, S. K., Cepeda, N. J., Rohrer, D., Kang, S. H. K., & Pashler, H. (2012). Using spacing to enhance diverse forms of learning: Review of recent research and implications for instruction. *Educational Psychology Review, 24,* 369–378. http://dx.doi.org/10.1007/s10648-012-9205-z

Carrell, S., & West, J. (2010). Does professor quality matter? Evidence from random assignment of students to professors. *Journal of Political Economy, 118,* 409–432. http://dx.doi.org/10.1086/653808

Carroll, D. W. (2001). Using ignorance questions to promote thinking skills. *Teaching of Psychology, 28,* 98–100. http://dx.doi.org/10.1207/S15328023TOP2802_05

Cashin, W. E. (1990). *Student ratings of teaching: Recommendations for use* (IDEA Paper No. 22). Manhattan: Center for Faculty Evaluation and Development, Kansas State University.

Cashin, W. E. (1995). *Student ratings of teaching: The research revisited* (IDEA Paper No. 32). Manhattan: Center for Faculty Evaluation and Development, Kansas State University.

Cashin, W. E. (2010). *Effective lecturing* (IDEA Paper No. 46). Manhattan: Center for Faculty Evaluation and Development, Kansas State University.

Cashin, W. E., & Perrin, B. M. (1983). Do college teachers who voluntarily have courses evaluated receive higher student ratings? *Journal of Educational Psychology, 75*, 595–602. http://dx.doi.org/10.1037/0022-0663.75.4.595

Centra, J. A. (1975). Colleagues as raters of classroom instruction. *The Journal of Higher Education, 46*, 327–337. http://dx.doi.org/10.2307/1980806

Centra, J. A. (1993). *Reflective faculty evaluation: Enhancing teaching and determining faculty effectiveness.* San Francisco, CA: Jossey-Bass.

Cerbin, W. (2001, April). The course portfolio. *APS Observer, 14*(4), 16–17, 30–31. Retrieved from http://www.psychologicalscience.org/observer/0401/tips.html

Chen, J., & Lin, T. F. (2008). Does downloading PowerPoint slides before the lecture lead to better student achievement? *International Review of Economics Education, 7*(2), 9–18.

Chickering, A. W. (1969). *Education and identity.* San Francisco, CA: Jossey-Bass.

Chickering, A. W. (1981). *The modern American college: Responding to the new realities of diverse students and a changing society.* San Francisco, CA: Jossey-Bass.

Chickering, A. W., & Ehrmann, S. C. (1996). Implementing the seven principles: Technology as a lever. *AAHE Bulletin, 49*(2), 3–6.

Chickering, A. W., & Gamson, Z. F. (1987). Seven principles for good practice in undergraduate education. *AAHE Bulletin, 39*(7), 3–7.

Chism, N. V. N. (1999). Taking student social diversity into account. In W. J. McKeachie (Ed.), *McKeachie's teaching tips: Strategies, research, and theory for college and university teachers* (pp. 218–234). New York, NY: Houghton Mifflin.

Chism, N. V. N. (2007). *Peer review of teaching: Sourcebook* (2nd ed.). Bolton, MA: Anker.

Cizek, G. J. (2003). *Detecting and preventing classroom cheating: Promoting integrity in assessment.* Thousand Oaks, CA: Corwin Press.

Claxton, C. S., & Murrell, P. H. (1987). *ASHE–ERIC higher education report: Vol. 4. Learning styles: Implications for improving educational practices.* Washington, DC: Association for the Study of Higher Education.

Clayson, D. E. (2009). Student evaluations of teaching: Are they related to what students learn? A meta-analysis and review of the literature. *Journal of Marketing Education, 31*, 16–30. http://dx.doi.org/10.1177/0273475308324086

Clayson, D. E., Frost, T. F., & Sheffet, M. J. (2006). Grades and the student evaluation of instruction: A test of the reciprocity effect. *Learning & Education, 5,* 52–65. http://dx.doi.org/10.5465/AMLE.2006.20388384

Cohen, P. A. (1981). Student ratings of instruction and student achievement: A meta-analysis of multisection validity studies. *Review of Educational Research, 51,* 281–309. http://dx.doi.org/10.3102/00346543051003281

Cook, D. A., Levinson, A. J., Garside, S., Dupras, D. M., Erwin, P. J., & Montori, V. M. (2008). Internet-based learning in the health professions: A meta-analysis. *JAMA, 300,* 1181–1196. http://dx.doi.org/10.1001/jama.300.10.1181

Corrigan, J. D., Dell, D. M., Lewis, K. N., & Schmidt, L. D. (1980). Counseling as a social influence process: A review. *Journal of Counseling Psychology, 27,* 395–441. http://dx.doi.org/10.1037/0022-0167.27.4.395

Covington, M. V., & Beery, R. (1976). *Self-worth and school learning.* New York, NY: Holt, Rinehart & Winston.

Cowan, J. (2014). Noteworthy matters for attention in reflective journal writing. *Active Learning in Higher Education, 15,* 53–64.

Cronbach, L. J., & Meehl, P. E. (1955). Construct validity in psychological tests. *Psychological Bulletin, 52,* 281–302. http://dx.doi.org/10.1037/h0040957

Dahlgren, L. O. (1984). Outcomes of learning. In F. Marton, D. Hounsell, & N. Entwistle (Eds.), *The experience of learning* (pp. 19–35). Edinburgh, Scotland: Scottish Academic Press.

d'Apollonia, S., & Abrami, P. C. (1997). Navigating student ratings of instruction. *American Psychologist, 52,* 1198–1208. http://dx.doi.org/10.1037/0003-066X.52.11.1198

Davis, B. G. (2009). *Tools for teaching* (2nd ed.). San Francisco, CA: Jossey-Bass.

Dawley, L. (2007). The tools for successful online teaching. Hershey, PA: IGI Global. http://dx.doi.org/10.4018/978-1-59140-956-4

Deci, E. L., & Ryan, R. M. (1985). *Intrinsic motivation and self determination in human behavior.* New York, NY: Plenum Press. http://dx.doi.org/10.1007/978-1-4899-2271-7

De Dreu, C. K. W. (1997). Productive conflict: The importance of conflict management and conflict issue. In C. K. W. De Dreu & E. Van de Vliert (Eds.), *Using conflict in organizations* (pp. 9–22). Thousand Oaks, CA: Sage. http://dx.doi.org/10.4135/9781446217016.n2

Delbanco, A. (2012). *College: What it was, is and should be.* Princeton, NJ: Princeton University Press.

Dempster, F. N. (1988). The spacing effect: A case study in the failure to apply the results of psychological research. *American Psychologist, 43,* 627–634. http://dx.doi.org/10.1037/0003-066X.43.8.627

Dewey, J. (1910). *How we think.* New York, NY: D. C. Heath. http://dx.doi.org/10.1037/10903-000

Dickson, K. L., & Bauer, J. J. (2008). Do students learn course material during crib sheet construction? *Teaching of Psychology, 35,* 117–120. http://dx.doi.org/10.1080/00986280801978343

Dillon, J. T. (1979). Paper chase and the Socratic method of teaching law. *Journal of Legal Education, 30,* 529–535.

Dillon, J. T. (1988). The remedial status of student questioning. *Journal of Curriculum Studies, 20,* 197–210. http://dx.doi.org/10.1080/0022027880200301

Dillon, J. T. (1994). *Using discussion in classrooms.* Buckingham, England: Open University Press.

D'Mello, S. (2013). A selective meta-analysis on the relative incidence of discrete affective states during learning with technology. *Journal of Educational Psychology, 105,* 1082–1099. http://dx.doi.org/10.1037/a0032674

Döring, N. (2002). Personal home pages on the web: A review of research. *Journal of Computer-Mediated Communication, 7.* http://dx.doi.org/10.1111/j.1083-6101.2002.tb00152.x

Drake, P. D. (2014). Is your use of social media FERPA compliant? *EDUCAUSE review, 24.* Retrieved from http://www.educause.edu/ero/article/your-use-social-media-ferpa-compliant

Drouin, M. (2012). What's the story on evaluations of online teaching? In M. E. Kite (Ed.), *Effective evaluation of teaching: A guide for faculty and administrators.* Retrieved from http://teachpsych.org/ebooks/evals2012/index.php

Drouin, M. A. (2014). If you record it, some won't come: Using lecture capture in introductory psychology. *Teaching of Psychology, 41,* 11–19. http://dx.doi.org/10.1177/0098628313514172

Duffy, D. K., & Jones, J. W. (1995). *Teaching within the rhythms of the semester.* San Francisco, CA: Jossey-Bass.

Dunlap, J. C. (2005). Problem-based learning and self-efficacy: How a capstone course prepares students for a profession. *Educational Technology Research and Development, 53,* 65–83. http://dx.doi.org/10.1007/BF02504858

Dunlap, J. C. (2011). Down-and-dirty guidelines for effective discussions in online courses. In P. R. Lowenthal, D. Thomas, A. Thai, & B. Yuhnke (Eds.), *The CU online handbook.* Retrieved from http://www.ucdenver.edu/academics/CUOnline/FacultySupport/Handbook/Documents/GuidelinesEffectiveDiscussions.pdf

Dunlosky, J., Rawson, K. A., Marsh, E. J., Nathan, M. J., & Willingham, D. T. (2013). Improving students' learning with effective learning techniques promising directions from cognitive and educational psychology. *Psychological Science in the Public Interest, 14,* 4–58. http://dx.doi.org/10.1177/1529100612453266

Dunn, D. S. (2000). Letter exchanges on statistics and research methods: Writing, responding, and learning. *Teaching of Psychology, 27,* 128–130.

Dunning, D., Johnson, K., Ehrlinger, J., & Kruger, J. (2003). Why people fail to recognize their own incompetence. *Current Directions in Psychological Science, 12*, 83–87. http://dx.doi.org/10.1111/1467-8721.01235

Dweck, C. S. (2012). Implicit theories. In P. A. M. Van Lange, A. W. Kruglanski, & E. T. Higgins (Eds.), *Handbook of theories of social psychology* (Vol. 2, pp. 43–61). Thousand Oaks, CA: Sage. http://dx.doi.org/10.4135/9781446249222.n28

Dweck, C. S., & Leggett, E. L. (1988). A social-cognitive approach to motivation and personality. *Psychological Review, 95*, 256–273. http://dx.doi.org/10.1037/0033-295X.95.2.256

Eagan, K., Lozano, J. B., Hurtado, S., & Case, M. H. (2013). *The American freshman: National norms fall 2013*. Los Angeles: Higher Education Research Institute, University of California, Los Angeles. Retrieved from http://www.heri.ucla.edu/monographs/TheAmericanFreshman2013.pdf

Eagan, K., Stolzenberg, E. B., Lozano, J. B., Aragon, M. C., Suchard, M. R., & Hurtado, S. (2014). *Undergraduate teaching faculty: The 2013–2014 HERI faculty survey*. Los Angeles: Higher Education Research Institute, University of California, Los Angeles. Retrieved from http://heri.ucla.edu/monographs/HERI-FAC2014-monograph.pdf

Ebel, K. E. (1976). *The craft of teaching*. San Francisco, CA: Jossey-Bass.

Ebel, K. E. (1988). *The craft of teaching* (2nd ed.). San Francisco, CA: Jossey Bass.

Ebel, R. L. (1974). Shall we get rid of grades? *Measurement in Education, 5*(4), 1–5.

Edmondson, A., & Roberto, M. A. (2007). *Leadership and team simulation: Everest*. Cambridge, MA: Harvard Business School.

Egeth, H. E., & Yantis, S. (1997). Visual attention: Control, representation, and time course. *Annual Review of Psychology, 48*, 269–297. http://dx.doi.org/10.1146/annurev.psych.48.1.269

Elliot, A. J., & Church, M. A. (1997). A hierarchical model of approach and avoidance achievement motivation. *Journal of Personality and Social Psychology, 72*, 218–232. http://dx.doi.org/10.1037/0022-3514.72.1.218

Emmer, E. T., & Stough, L. M. (2001). Classroom management: A critical part of educational psychology, with implications for teacher education. *Educational Psychologist, 36*, 103–112. http://dx.doi.org/10.1207/S15326985EP3602_5

English, S. L. (1985). Kinetics in academic lectures. *The ESP Journal, 4*, 161–170. http://dx.doi.org/10.1016/0272-2380(85)90018-6

Epstein, J. (1981). *Masters: Portraits of great teachers*. New York, NY: Basic Books.

Ercikan, K., Schwarz, R. D., Julian, M. W., Burket, G. R., Weber, M. M., & Link, V. (1998). Calibration and scoring of tests with multiple-choice and constructed-response item types. *Journal of Educational Measurement, 35*, 137–154. http://dx.doi.org/10.1111/j.1745-3984.1998.tb00531.x

Ericsson, K. A., & Lehmann, A. C. (1996). Expert and exceptional performance: Evidence of maximal adaptation to task constraints. *Annual Review of Psychology, 47*, 273–305. http://dx.doi.org/10.1146/annurev. psych.47.1.273

Evertson, C. M., & Weinstein, C. S. (Eds.). (2011). *Handbook of classroom management: Research, practice, and contemporary issues.* New York, NY: Routledge.

Ewell, W. H., & Rodgers, R. R. (2014). Enhancing student preparedness for class through course preparation assignments: Preliminary evidence from the classroom. *Journal of Political Science Education, 10*, 204–221. http://dx.doi.org/10.1080/15512169.2014.893760

Ewens, W. (1985). Teaching using discussion. *Footnotes, 13*(10), 8.

Exline, R. V., & Messick, D. (1967). The effects of dependency and social reinforcement upon visual behaviour during an interview. *The British Journal of Social and Clinical Psychology, 6*, 256–266. http://dx.doi.org/10.1111/j.2044-8260.1967.tb00528.x

Family Educational Rights and Privacy Act of 1974, 20 U.S.C. § 1232g

Fay, N., Garrod, S., & Carletta, J. (2000). Group discussion as interactive dialogue or as serial monologue: The influence of group size. *Psychological Science, 11*, 481–486. http://dx.doi.org/10.1111/1467-9280. 00292

Feldman, K. A. (1978). Course characteristics and college students' ratings of their teachers: What we know and what we don't. *Research in Higher Education, 9*, 199–242. http://dx.doi.org/10.1007/BF00976997

Feldman, K. A. (1989). Instructional effectiveness of college teachers as judged by teachers themselves, current and former students, colleagues, administrators and external (neutral) observers. *Research in Higher Education, 30*, 137–194. http://dx.doi.org/10.1007/BF00992716

Fink, L. D. (2013). *Creating significant learning experiences: An integrated approach to designing college courses* (updated ed.). San Francisco, CA: Jossey-Bass.

Finn, J. D., & Rock, D. A. (1997). Academic success among students at risk for school failure. *Journal of Applied Psychology, 82*, 221–234. http://dx.doi.org/10.1037/0021-9010.82.2.221

Forsyth, D. R. (1986). An attributional analysis of students' reactions to success and failure. In R. Feldman (Ed.), *The social psychology of education* (pp. 17–38). New York, NY: Cambridge University Press.

Forsyth, D. R. (1994). Norms. In T. Manstead & M. Hewstone (Eds.), *Blackwell encyclopedia of social psychology* (pp. 412–417). Oxford, England: Blackwell.

Forsyth, D. R. (2000). Social comparison and influence in groups. In J. Suls & L. Wheeler (Eds.), *Handbook of social comparison: Theory and research* (pp. 81–103). New York, NY: Plenum Press. http://dx.doi. org/10.1007/978-1-4615-4237-7_5

Forsyth, D. R. (2006). *Classroom performance systems: A primer* (2nd ed.). Boston, MA: McGraw-Hill.

Forsyth, D. R. (2008, August). *New frontiers in teaching with technology: Using Facebook to strengthen social networks in college classes.* Paper presented at the 116th Annual Convention of the American Psychological Association, Boston, MA.

Forsyth, D. R. (2012). The seditious class. *Personality and Social Psychology Connections.* Retrieved from https://facultystaff.richmond.edu/~dforsyth/seditious.pdf

Forsyth, D. R. (2014). *Group dynamics* (6th ed.). Belmont, CA: Cengage.

Forsyth, D. R., & Archer, C. R. (1997). Technologically assisted instruction and student mastery, motivation, and matriculation. *Teaching of Psychology, 24,* 207–212. http://dx.doi.org/10.1207/s15328023top2403_17

Forsyth, D. R., & Berger, R. E. (1982). The effects of ethical ideology on moral behavior. *The Journal of Social Psychology, 117,* 53–56. http://dx.doi.org/10.1080/00224545.1982.9713406

Forsyth, D. R., & Diederich, L. T. (2014). Group dynamics and development. In J. DeLucia-Waack, C. Kalodner, & M. Riva (Eds.), *The handbook of group counseling and psychotherapy* (2nd ed., pp. 34–45). Thousand Oaks, CA: Sage.

Forsyth, D. R., Johnson, J. H., Baronian, N., Newton, C. R., & Stewart, J. E. (2003, April). *Web-based instructional materials derived from surface models of visible human data.* Paper presented at the Emerging Technologies Conference, Richmond, VA.

Forsyth, D. R., Lawrence, N. K., Burnette, J. L., & Baumeister, R. F. (2007). Attempting to improve the academic performance of struggling college students by bolstering their self-esteem: An intervention that backfired. *Journal of Social and Clinical Psychology, 26,* 447–459. http://dx.doi.org/10.1521/jscp.2007.26.4.447

Forsyth, D. R., & McMillan, J. (1981). Attributions, affect, and expectations: A test of Weiner's three-dimensional model. *Journal of Educational Psychology, 73,* 393–403. http://dx.doi.org/10.1037/0022-0663.73.3.393

Forsyth, D. R., & McMillan, J. H. (1991). Practical proposals for motivating students. In R. J. Menges & M. Svinicki (Eds.), *Approaching instructional problems through theoretical perspectives: New directions for teaching and learning* (Vol. 44, pp. 53–66). San Francisco, CA: Jossey-Bass.

Forsyth, D. R., Story, P. A., Kelley, K. N., & McMillan, J. H. (2009). What causes failure and success? Students' perceptions of their academic outcomes. *Social Psychology of Education, 12,* 157–174. http://dx.doi.org/10.1007/s11218-008-9078-7

Foss, D. J. (2013). *Your complete guide to college success: How to study smart, achieve your goals, and enjoy campus life.* Washington, DC: American Psychological Association. http://dx.doi.org/10.1037/14181-000

Fried, C. B. (2008). In-class laptop use and its effects on student learning. *Computers & Education, 50,* 906–914. http://dx.doi.org/10.1016/j.compedu.2006.09.006

Froese, A. D., Gantz, B. S., & Henry, A. L. (1998). Teaching students to write literature reviews: A meta-analytic model. *Teaching of Psychology, 25,* 102–105. http://dx.doi.org/10.1207/s15328023top2502_4

FTI Consulting. (2015). *U.S. postsecondary faculty in 2015: Diversity in people, goals and methods, but focused on students.* Retrieved from http://postsecondary.gatesfoundation.org/wp-content/uploads/2015/02/US-Postsecondary-Faculty-in-2015.pdf

Gage, N. L. (2009). *A conception of teaching.* New York, NY: Springer. http://dx.doi.org/10.1007/978-0-387-09446-5

Galliano, G. (1999). Enhancing student learning through exemplary examples. In B. Perlman, L. I. McCann, & S. H. McFadden (Eds.), *Lessons learned: Practical advice for the teaching of psychology* (pp. 93–97). Washington, DC: American Psychological Society.

Gallup–Lumina Foundation. (2014). *What America needs to know about higher education redesign.* Retrieved from http://www.gallup.com/services/176759/america-needs-know-higher-education-redesign.aspx

Gamson, Z. F. (1991). A brief history of the seven principles for good practice in undergraduate education. *New Directions for Teaching and Learning, 47,* 5–12. http://dx.doi.org/10.1002/tl.37219914703

Gardiner, L. F. (1998). Why we must change: The research evidence. *Thought & Action, 16,* 71–88. Retrieved from http://www.nea.org/assets/img/PubThoughtAndAction/TAA_00Fal_13.pdf

Gates, W. H. (1999). *Business @ the speed of thought: Succeeding in the digital economy.* New York, NY: Warner Books.

Giluk, T. L., & Postlethwaite, B. E. (2015). Big Five personality and academic dishonesty: A meta-analytic review. *Personality and Individual Differences, 72,* 59–67. http://dx.doi.org/10.1016/j.paid.2014.08.027

Gleason, M. (1986). Better communication in large courses. *College Teaching, 34*(1), 20–24. http://dx.doi.org/10.1080/87567555.1986.10532325

Goffman, E. (1971). *Relations in public: Microstudies of the public order.* New York, NY: Basic Books.

Golding, J. M. (2011). The role of attendance in lecture classes: You can lead a horse to water . . . *Teaching of Psychology, 38,* 40–42. http://dx.doi.org/10.1177/0098628310390915

Gopen, G. D. (2004). *The sense of structure: Writing from the reader's perspective.* New York, NY: Pearson.

Grabe, M. (1994). Motivational deficiencies when multiple examinations are allowed. *Contemporary Educational Psychology, 19,* 45–52. http://dx.doi.org/10.1006/ceps.1994.1005

Graham, S., & Perin, D. (2007). A meta-analysis of writing instruction for adolescent students. *Journal of Educational Psychology, 99,* 445–476. http://dx.doi.org/10.1037/0022-0663.99.3.445

Gray, P. (1997). Teaching is a scholarly activity: The idea-centered approach to introducing psychology. In R. J. Sternberg (Ed.), *Teaching introductory psychology: Survival tips from the experts* (pp. 49–64).

Washington, DC: American Psychological Association. http://dx.doi.org/10.1037/10228-003

Greenwald, A. G., & Gillmore, G. M. (1997). Grading leniency is a removable contaminant of student ratings. *American Psychologist, 52*, 1209–1217. http://dx.doi.org/10.1037/0003-066X.52.11.1209

Griffith, C. R. (1921). A comment upon the psychology of the audience. *Psychological Monographs, 30*, 36–47. http://dx.doi.org/10.1037/h0093148

Gronlund, N. E. (1998). *Assessment of student achievement* (6th ed.). Boston, MA: Allyn & Bacon.

Grubb, W. N. (with Gabriner, R.) (2013). *Basic skills education in community colleges: Inside and outside of classrooms*. New York, NY: Routledge.

Haber, G. M. (1980). Territorial invasion in the classroom: Invadee response. *Environment and Behavior, 12*, 17–31. http://dx.doi.org/10.1177/0013916580121002

Haber, J. (2014). *MOOCs*. Boston, MA: MIT Press.

Hackathorn, J., Garczynski, A. M., Blankmeyer, K., Tennial, R. D., & Solomon, E. D. (2012). All kidding aside: Humor increases learning at knowledge and comprehension levels. *Journal of the Scholarship of Teaching and Learning, 11*, 116–123.

Hairston, M., Ruszkiewicz, J., & Friend, C. (1999). *The Scott, Foresman handbook for writers* (5th ed.). New York, NY: Longman.

Haladyna, T. M. (1994). *Developing and validating multiple choice test items*. Mahwah, NJ: Erlbaum.

Haladyna, T. M. (1997). *Writing test items to evaluate higher order thinking*. Boston, MA: Allyn & Bacon.

Haladyna, T. M., & Downing, S. M. (1989a). A taxonomy of multiple-choice item-writing rules. *Applied Measurement in Education, 2*, 37–50. http://dx.doi.org/10.1207/s15324818ame0201_3

Haladyna, T. M., & Downing, S. M. (1989b). Validity of a taxonomy of multiple-choice item-writing rules. *Applied Measurement in Education, 2*, 51–78. http://dx.doi.org/10.1207/s15324818ame0201_4

Haladyna, T. M., & Rodriguez, M. C. (2014). *Developing and validating test items*. New York, NY: Routledge.

Hall, G. S. (1911). *Educational problems* (Vol. 2). New York, NY: Appleton.

Hall, R. M., & Sandler, B. R. (1986). *The classroom climate: A chilly one for women? Project on the status and education of women*. Washington, DC: Association of American Colleges.

Handelsman, M. M., & Krest, M. (1996, March). Improving your students' writing: Arts and drafts. *APS Observer, 9*(3), 22, 23, 31. Retrieved from http://www.psychologicalscience.org/index.php/publications/observer/1996/march-96/improving-your-students-writing-arts-and-drafts.html

Harackiewicz, J. M., Barron, K. E., & Elliot, A. J. (1998). Rethinking achievement goals: When are they adaptive for college students and why? *Educational Psychologist, 33,* 1–21. http://dx.doi.org/10.1207/s15326985ep3301_1

Harlow, R. E., & Cantor, N. (1995). To whom do people turn when things go poorly? Task orientation and functional social contacts. *Journal of Personality and Social Psychology, 69,* 329–340. http://dx.doi.org/10.1037/0022-3514.69.2.329

Harris, M. J. (2006). Three steps to teaching abstract and critique writing. *International Journal of Teaching & Learning in Higher Education, 17,* 136–146.

Harrison, D. A., & Klein, K. J. (2007). What's the difference? Diversity constructs as separation, variety, or disparity in organizations. *Academy of Management Review, 32,* 1199–1228. http://dx.doi.org/10.5465/AMR.2007.26586096

Harrison, P. D., Douglas, D. K., & Burdsal, C. A. (2004). The relative merits of different types of overall evaluations of teaching effectiveness. *Research in Higher Education, 45,* 311–323. http://dx.doi.org/10.1023/B:RIHE.0000019592.78752.da

Hart, C. (2012). Factors associated with student persistence in an online program of study: A review of the literature. *Journal of Interactive Online Learning, 11,* 19–42.

Hart, P. D. (2004). *Summary of existing research on attitudes toward liberal education outcomes for the Association of American Colleges and Universities.* Washington, DC: Peter D. Hart Research Associates.

Hartley, M., & Morphew, C. C. (2008). What's being sold and to what end?: A content analysis of college viewbooks. *The Journal of Higher Education, 79,* 671–691. http://dx.doi.org/10.1353/jhe.0.0025

Hativa, N. (2014a). *Student ratings of instruction: A practical approach to designing, operating, and reporting* (2nd ed.). Oron Publications, Createspace Independent Publishing Platform.

Hativa, N. (2014b). *Student ratings of instruction: Recognizing effective teaching* (2nd ed.). Oron Publications, Createspace Independent Publishing Platform.

Hatteberg, S. J., & Steffy, K. (2013). Increasing reading compliance of undergraduates: An evaluation of compliance methods. *Teaching Sociology, 41,* 346–352. http://dx.doi.org/10.1177/0092055X13490752

Hattie, J. (2009). *Visible learning: A synthesis of over 800 meta-analyses relating to achievement.* New York, NY: Routledge.

Hattie, J., & Yates, G. (2014). *Visible learning and the science of how we learn.* New York, NY: Routledge.

Häussler, P., & Hoffmann, L. (2000). A curricular frame for physics education: Development, comparison with students' interests, and impact on students' achievement and self-concept. *Science Education, 84,*

689–705. http://dx.doi.org/10.1002/1098-237X(200011)84:6<689:: AID-SCE1>3.0.CO;2-L

Havard, B., Ellis, H., & Kingry, M. A. (2013, March). The Team Member Evaluation Tool: Assigning individual grades on group projects. In R. McBride & M. Searson (Eds.), *Society for Information Technology & Teacher Education International Conference Proceedings* (pp. 510–515). Chesapeake, VA: Association for the Advancement of Computing in Education.

Hembrooke, H., & Gay, G. (2003). The laptop and the lecture: The effects of multitasking in learning environments. *Journal of Computing in Higher Education, 15,* 46–64. http://dx.doi.org/10.1007/BF02940852

Hendrix, K. G. (1998). Student perceptions of the influence of race on professor credibility. *Journal of Black Studies, 28,* 738–763. http://dx.doi.org/10.1177/002193479802800604

Hersey, P., Blanchard, K. H., & Johnson, D. E. (2013). *Management of organizational behavior* (10th ed.). Englewood Cliffs, NJ: Prentice Hall.

Hickson, S., Reed, W. R., & Sander, N. (2012). Estimating the effect on grades of using multiple-choice versus constructive-response questions: Data from the classroom. *Educational Assessment, 17,* 200–213. http://dx.doi.org/10.1080/10627197.2012.735915

Hilton, J. L. (1999). Teaching large classes. In B. Perlman, L. I. McCann, & S. H. McFadden (Eds.), *Lessons learned: Practical advice for the teaching of psychology* (pp. 115–120). Washington, DC: American Psychological Society.

Hinkle, S., & Hinkle, A. (1990). An experimental comparison of the effects of focused freewriting and other study strategies on lecture comprehension. *Teaching of Psychology, 17,* 31–35. http://dx.doi.org/10.1207/s15328023top1701_7

Hirsch, E. D., Jr., Kett, J. F., & Trefil, J. S. (1987). *Cultural literacy: What every American needs to know.* New York, NY: Houghton Mifflin.

Hirschy, A. S., & Braxton, J. M. (2004). Effects of student classroom incivilities on students. *New Directions for Teaching and Learning, 99,* 67–76. http://dx.doi.org/10.1002/tl.160

Homer, P. M., & Kahle, L. R. (1988). A structural equation test of the value–attitude–behavior hierarchy. *Journal of Personality and Social Psychology, 54,* 638–646. http://dx.doi.org/10.1037/0022-3514.54.4.638

Horner, D. T., Stetter, K. R., & McCann, L. I. (1998). Adding structure to unstructured research courses. *Teaching of Psychology, 25,* 126–128. http://dx.doi.org/10.1207/s15328023top2502_12

Hovland, C. I., Janis, I. L., & Kelley, H. H. (1953). *Communication and persuasion.* New Haven, CT: Yale University Press.

Howard, D. J. (1990). Rhetorical question effects on message processing and persuasion: The role of information availability and the elicitation of judgment. *Journal of Experimental Social Psychology, 26,* 217–239. http://dx.doi.org/10.1016/0022-1031(90)90036-L

Howard, R., Kline, B., & O'Quin, K. (2014). The Revised Appreciation of the Liberal Arts Scale (ALAS–R): Development, reliability and validity. *International Journal of Research Studies in Education, 3,* 63–78.

Husman, J., & Lens, W. (1999). The role of the future in student motivation. *Educational Psychologist, 34,* 113–125. http://dx.doi.org/10.1207/s15326985ep3402_4

Innes, R. B. (2003). *Reconstructing undergraduate education: Using learning science to design effective courses.* Mahwah, NJ: Erlbaum.

Ipsos. (2012). *Interconnected world: Communication & social networking.* Toronto, Ontario, Canada: Author. Retrieved from http://www.ipsos-na.com/news-polls/pressrelease.aspx?id=5564

Jacobs, L. C., & Chase, C. I. (1992). *Developing and using tests effectively: A guide for faculty.* San Francisco, CA: Jossey-Bass.

James, W. (1892). *Psychology.* New York, NY: Henry Holt. http://dx.doi.org/10.1037/11060-000

James, W. (1899). *Talks to teachers on psychology and to students on some of life's ideals.* New York, NY: Holt. http://dx.doi.org/10.1037/10814-000

Jarvenpaa, S. L., Shaw, T. R., & Staples, D. S. (2004). Toward contextualized theories of trust: The role of trust in global virtual teams. *Information Systems Research, 15,* 250–267. http://dx.doi.org/10.1287/isre.1040.0028

Jemmott, J. B., III, & Magloire, K. (1988). Academic stress, social support, and secretory immunoglobulin A. *Journal of Personality and Social Psychology, 55,* 803–810. http://dx.doi.org/10.1037/0022-3514.55.5.803

Johnson, D. A., & Christensen, J. (2011). A comparison of simplified visually rich and traditional presentation styles. *Teaching of Psychology, 38,* 293–297. http://dx.doi.org/10.1177/0098628311421333

Johnson, J. T., Cain, L. M., Falke, T. L., Hayman, J., & Perillo, E. (1985). The "Barnum effect" revisited: Cognitive and motivational factors in the acceptance of personality descriptions. *Journal of Personality and Social Psychology, 49,* 1378–1391.

Johnson, V. E. (2003). *Grade inflation: A crisis in college education.* New York, NY: Springer.

Jordan, A. E. (2001). College student cheating: The role of motivation, perceived norms, attitudes, and knowledge of institutional policy. *Ethics & Behavior, 11,* 233–248. http://dx.doi.org/10.1207/S15327019EB1103_3

Kahn, W. A. (2009). *The student's guide to successful project teams.* New York, NY: Psychology Press.

Kahneman, D., & Tversky, A. (1973). On the psychology of prediction. *Psychological Review, 80,* 237–251. http://dx.doi.org/10.1037/h0034747

Kay, R. H. (2014). Developing a framework for creating effective instructional video podcasts. *iJET, 9*(1), 22–30.

Keeley, J. W. (2012). Choosing an instrument for student evaluation of instruction. In M. E. Kite (Ed.), *Effective evaluation of teaching: A guide for faculty and administrators.* Retrieved from http://teachpsych.org/Resources/Documents/ebooks/evals2012.pdf

Keith-Spiegel, P., Tabachnick, B. G., Whitley, B. E., Jr., & Washburn, J. (1998). Why professors ignore cheating: Opinions of a national sample of psychology instructors. *Ethics & Behavior, 8,* 215–227. http://dx.doi.org/10.1207/s15327019eb0803_3

Keller, F. S. (1968). "Good-bye, teacher . . . ". *Journal of Applied Behavior Analysis, 1,* 79–89. http://dx.doi.org/10.1901/jaba.1968.1-79

Kessler, C. S., Dharmapuri, S., & Marcolini, E. G. (2011). Qualitative analysis of effective lecture strategies in emergency medicine. *Annals of Emergency Medicine, 58,* 482–489.e7. http://dx.doi.org/10.1016/j.annemergmed.2011.06.011

Kilgo, C. A., Sheets, J. K. E., & Pascarella, E. T. (2014). The link between high-impact practices and student learning: Some longitudinal evidence. *Higher Education, 69,* 1–17.

King, P. M. (1978). William Perry's theory of intellectual and ethical development. *New Directions for Student Services, 1978*(4), 35–51.

Kleinpenning, G., & Hagendoorn, L. (1993). Forms of racism and the cumulative dimension of ethnic attitudes. *Social Psychology Quarterly, 56,* 21–36. http://dx.doi.org/10.2307/2786643

Knight, L. J., & McKelvie, S. J. (1986). Effects of attendance, note-taking, and review on memory for a lecture: Encoding vs. external storage functions of notes. *Canadian Journal of Behavioural Science, 18,* 52–61. http://dx.doi.org/10.1037/h0079957

Knowles, E. S. (1982). A comment on the study of classroom ecology: A lament for the good old days. *Personality and Social Psychology Bulletin, 8,* 357–361. http://dx.doi.org/10.1177/0146167282082026

Ko, S., & Rossen, S. (2010). *Teaching online: A practical guide* (3rd ed.). New York, NY: Routledge.

Kochenour, E. O., Jolley, D. S., Kaup, J. G., Patrick, D. L., Roach, K. D., & Wenzler, L. A. (1997). Supplemental instruction: An effective component of student affairs programming. *Journal of College Student Development, 38,* 577–586.

Kohn, A. (1986). *No contest: The case against competition.* Boston, MA: Houghton Mifflin.

Kolb, D. A. (1984). *Experiential learning: Experience as the source of learning and development.* Englewood Cliffs, NJ: Prentice Hall.

Kornell, N. (2009). Optimising learning using flashcards: Spacing is more effective than cramming. *Applied Cognitive Psychology, 23,* 1297–1317. http://dx.doi.org/10.1002/acp.1537

Kozhevnikov, M., Evans, C., & Kosslyn, S. M. (2014). Cognitive style as environmentally sensitive individual differences in cognition: A modern synthesis and applications in education, business, and management. *Psychological Science in the Public Interest, 15,* 3–33. http://dx.doi.org/10.1177/1529100614525555

Kramer, T. J., & Korn, J. H. (1999). Class discussions: Promoting participation and preventing problems. In B. Perlman, L. I. McCann, & S. H. McFadden (Eds.), *Lessons learned: Practical advice for the teaching of psychology* (pp. 99–104). Washington, DC: American Psychological Society.

Krauss, R. M., Morrel-Samuels, P., & Colasante, C. (1991). Do conversational hand gestures communicate? *Journal of Personality and Social Psychology, 61*, 743–754. http://dx.doi.org/10.1037/0022-3514.61.5.743

Kulik, J. A. (2001). Student ratings: Validity, utility, and controversy. *New Directions for Institutional Research, 109*, 9–25. http://dx.doi.org/10.1002/ir.1

Kuo, Y. C., Walker, A. E., Schroder, K. E., & Belland, B. R. (2014). Interaction, Internet self-efficacy, and self-regulated learning as predictors of student satisfaction in online education courses. *The Internet and Higher Education, 20*, 35–50. http://dx.doi.org/10.1016/j.iheduc.2013.10.001

Laghans, W. (1996). Metabolic and glucostatic control of feeding. *Proceedings of the Nutrition Society, 55*, 497–515.

Lake, D. A. (2001). Student performance and perceptions of a lecture-based course compared with the same course utilizing group discussion. *Physical Therapy, 81*, 896–902.

Lattuca, L. R., & Stark, J. S. (2009). *Shaping the college curriculum: Academic plans in context* (2nd ed.). San Francisco, CA: Jossey-Bass.

Lau, K. V., Fallar, R., & Friedman, E. (2015). Characterizing the effective modern medical school lecture. *Medical Science Educator.* Advance online publication. http://dx.doi.org/10.1007/s40670-015-0102-1

Lawrence, N. K. (2013). Cumulative exams in the introductory psychology course. *Teaching of Psychology, 40*, 15–19. http://dx.doi.org/10.1177/0098628312465858

Leary, M. R., Rogers, P. A., Canfield, R. W., & Coe, C. (1986). Boredom in interpersonal encounters: Antecedents and social implications. *Journal of Personality and Social Psychology, 51*, 968–975. http://dx.doi.org/10.1037/0022-3514.51.5.968

Lefton, L. A. (1997). Why I teach the way I do: Repackaging psychology. In R. J. Sternberg (Ed.), *Teaching introductory psychology: Survival tips from the experts* (pp. 65–71). Washington, DC: American Psychological Association. http://dx.doi.org/10.1037/10228-004

Levine, D. W., McDonald, P. J., O'Neal, E. C., & Garwood, S. G. (1982). Classroom seating effects: Environment or self-selection—neither, either, or both. *Personality and Social Psychology Bulletin, 8*, 365–369. http://dx.doi.org/10.1177/0146167282082028

Levy, G. D., & Peters, W. W. (2002). Undergraduates' views of the best college courses. *Teaching of Psychology, 29*, 46–48.

Light, R. J. (2003). Writing and students' engagement. *Peer Review, 6*(1), 28–31.

Lilienfeld, S. O., Lynn, S. J., Ruscio, J., & Beyerstein, B. L. (2009). *50 great myths of popular psychology: Shattering widespread misconceptions about human behavior.* New York, NY: Wiley.

Lindgren, H. C. (1969). *The psychology of college success: A dynamic approach.* New York, NY: Wiley.

Littleford, L. N., Buskist, W., Frantz, S. M., Galvan, D. B., Hendersen, R. W., McCarthy, M. A., . . . Puente, A. E. (2010). Psychology students: Today and tomorrow. In D. F. Halpern (Ed.), *Undergraduate education in psychology: A blueprint for the future of the discipline* (pp. 63–79). Washington, DC: American Psychological Association. http://dx.doi.org/10.1037/12063-004

Loevinger, J. (1998). *Technical foundations for measuring ego development.* Mahwah, NJ: Erlbaum.

Lowman, J. (1995). *Mastering the techniques of teaching* (2nd ed.). San Francisco, CA: Jossey-Bass.

Ludewig, L. M. (1994). 10 worst student behaviors. *The Teaching Professor, 8*(5), 3.

Lyken-Segosebe, D., Min, Y., & Braxton, J. M. (2012). The existence of codes of conduct for undergraduate teaching in teaching-oriented four-year colleges and universities. *New Directions for Higher Education, 160,* 61–72. http://dx.doi.org/10.1002/he.20037

MacArthur, B. L., & Villagran, M. M. (2015). Instructor misbehaviors as digital expectancy violations: What students despise and what they let slide. *Journalism & Mass Communication Educator, 70,* 26–43. http://dx.doi.org/10.1177/1077695814566046

Mager, R. F. (1962). *Preparing instructional objectives.* Belmont, CA: Fearon.

Mann, D., Reardon, R. M., Becker, J. D., Shakeshaft, C., & Bacon, N. (2011). Immersive, interactive, Web-enabled computer simulation as a trigger for learning: The next generation of problem-based learning in educational leadership. *Journal of Research on Leadership Education, 6,* 272–287.

Mann, R. D., Arnold, S. M., Binder, J. L., Cytrynbaum, S., Newman, B. M., Ringwald, B. E., . . . Rosenwein, R. (1970). *The college classroom: Conflict, change, and learning.* New York, NY: Wiley.

Mann, S., & Robinson, A. (2009). Boredom in the lecture theatre: An investigation into the contributors, moderators and outcomes of boredom amongst university students. *British Educational Research Journal, 35,* 243–258. http://dx.doi.org/10.1080/01411920802042911

Margaryan, A., Littlejohn, A., & Vojt, G. (2011). Are digital natives a myth or reality? University students' use of digital technologies. *Computers & Education, 56,* 429–440. http://dx.doi.org/10.1016/j.compedu.2010.09.004

Marsh, H. W. (1980). The influence of student, course, and instructor characteristics on evaluations of university teaching. *American Educational Research Journal, 17,* 219–237. http://dx.doi.org/10.3102/00028312017002219

Marsh, H. W. (1982). SEEQ: A reliable, valid, and useful instrument for collecting students' evaluations of university teaching. *British Jour-*

nal of Educational Psychology, 52, 77–95. http://dx.doi.org/10.1111/j.2044-8279.1982.tb02505.x

Marsh, H. W. (1983). Multidimensional ratings of teaching effectiveness by students from different academic settings and their relation to student/course/instructor characteristics. *Journal of Educational Psychology, 75,* 150–166. http://dx.doi.org/10.1037/0022-0663.75.1.150

Marsh, H. W. (1984). Students' evaluations of university teaching: Dimensionality, reliability, validity, potential biases, and utility. *Journal of Educational Psychology, 76,* 707–754. http://dx.doi.org/10.1037/0022-0663.76.5.707

Marsh, H. W. (2007). Students' evaluations of university teaching: Dimensionality, reliability, validity, potential biases and usefulness. In R. P. Perry & J. C. Smart (Eds.), *The scholarship of teaching and learning in higher education: An evidence-based perspective* (pp. 319–383). Dordrecht, the Netherlands: Springer. http://dx.doi.org/10.1007/1-4020-5742-3_9

Marsh, H. W., & Bailey, M. (1993). Multidimensional students' evaluations of teaching effectiveness: A profile analysis. *The Journal of Higher Education, 64,* 1–18. http://dx.doi.org/10.2307/2959975

Marsh, H. W., & Dunkin, M. (1992). Students' evaluations of university teaching: A multidimensional perspective. In J. C. Smart (Ed.), *Higher education: Handbook of theory and research* (Vol. 8, pp. 143–233). New York, NY: Agathon.

Marsh, H. W., & Hocevar, D. (1991). Students' evaluations of teaching effectiveness: The stability of mean ratings of the same teachers over a 13-year period. *Teaching and Teacher Education, 7,* 303–314. http://dx.doi.org/10.1016/0742-051X(91)90001-6

Marsh, H. W., & Roche, L. A. (1997). Making students' evaluations of teaching effectiveness effective: The critical issues of validity, bias, and utility. *American Psychologist, 52,* 1187–1197. http://dx.doi.org/10.1037/0003-066X.52.11.1187

Marsh, H. W., & Ware, J. E. (1982). Effects of expressiveness, content coverage, and incentive on multidimensional student rating scales: New interpretations of the Dr. Fox effect. *Journal of Educational Psychology, 74,* 126–134. http://dx.doi.org/10.1037/0022-0663.74.1.126

Marsh, R. (1984). A comparison of take-home versus in-class exams. *The Journal of Educational Research, 78,* 111–113. http://dx.doi.org/10.1080/00220671.1984.10885583

Martinez, M. E. (1999). Cognition and the question of test item format. *Educational Psychologist, 34,* 207–218. http://dx.doi.org/10.1207/s15326985ep3404_2

Mastascusa, E. J., Snyder, W. J., & Hoyt, B. S. (2011). *Effective instruction for STEM disciplines: From learning theory to college teaching.* San Francisco, CA: Jossey-Bass.

Mathie, V. A., Beins, B., Benjamin, L. T., Jr., Ewing, M. M., Iljima Hall, C. C., Henderson, B., . . . Smith, R. A. (1993). Promoting active learning in psychology courses. In T. V. McGovern (Ed.), *Handbook for enhancing undergraduate education in psychology* (pp. 183–214). Washington, DC: American Psychological Association. http://dx.doi.org/10.1037/10126-007

Mayer, F. (1960). Creative teaching. *Improving College and University Teaching, 8*(2), 40–42. http://dx.doi.org/10.1080/00193089.1960.10534088

Mayer, R. E. (1997). Multimedia learning: Are we asking the right questions? *Educational Psychologist, 32,* 1–19. http://dx.doi.org/10.1207/s15326985ep3201_1

Mayer, R. E. (2002). Rote versus meaningful learning. *Theory Into Practice, 41,* 226–232. http://dx.doi.org/10.1207/s15430421tip4104_4

Mayer, R. E. (2004). Should there be a three-strikes rule against pure discovery learning? The case for guided methods of instruction. *American Psychologist, 59,* 14–19. http://dx.doi.org/10.1037/0003-066X.59.1.14

Mayer, R. E., & Anderson, R. B. (1991). Animations need narrations: An experimental test of a dual-coding hypothesis. *Journal of Educational Psychology, 83,* 484–490. http://dx.doi.org/10.1037/0022-0663.83.4.484

Mayer, R. E., & Gallini, J. K. (1990). When is an illustration worth ten thousand words? *Journal of Educational Psychology, 82,* 715–726. http://dx.doi.org/10.1037/0022-0663.82.4.715

Mayer, R. E., Stull, A., DeLeeuw, K., Almeroth, K., Bimber, B., Chun, D., . . . Zhang, H. (2009). Clickers in college classrooms: Fostering learning with questioning methods in large lecture classes. *Contemporary Educational Psychology, 34,* 51–57. http://dx.doi.org/10.1016/j.cedpsych.2008.04.002

Maynard, M. T., Mathieu, J. E., Rapp, T. L., & Gilson, L. L. (2012). Something(s) old and something(s) new: Modeling drivers of global virtual team effectiveness. *Journal of Organizational Behavior, 33,* 342–365. http://dx.doi.org/10.1002/job.1772

McBurney, D. H. (1999). Cheating: Preventing and dealing with academic dishonesty. In B. Perlman, L. I. McCann, & S. H. McFadden (Eds.), *Lessons learned: Practical advice for the teaching of psychology* (pp. 213–217). Washington, DC: American Psychological Society.

McBurney, D. H. (2000). The problem method of teaching research methods. In M. E. Ware & D. E. Johnson (Eds.), *Handbook of demonstrations and activities in the teaching of psychology: Vol. 1. Introductory, statistics, research methods, and history* (2nd ed., pp. 134–136). Mahwah, NJ: Erlbaum.

McCabe, D. L., Butterfield, K. D., & Treviño, L. K. (2012). *Cheating in college: Why students do it and what educators can do about it.* Baltimore, MD: Johns Hopkins University Press.

McCarthy, M. A. (2012). Using student feedback as *one* measure of faculty teaching effectiveness. In M. E. Kite (Ed.), *Effective evaluation of teaching: A guide for faculty and administrators* (pp. 30–39). Retrieved from http://teachpsych.org/Resources/Documents/ebooks/evals2012.pdf

McCroskey, J. C. (2012). Oral communication apprehension: A reconceptualization. In M. Burgoon (Ed.), *Communication yearbook 6 Issue 6,* (pp. 136–170). New York, NY: Routledge.

McGovern, T. V., Corey, L., Cranney, J., Dixon, W. E., Holmes, J. D., Kuebli, J. E., . . . Walker, S. J. (2010). Psychologically literate citizens. In D. Halpern (Ed.), *Undergraduate education in psychology: A blueprint for the future of the discipline* (pp. 9–27). Washington, DC: American Psychological Association. http://dx.doi.org/10.1037/12063-001

McGrath, J. E. (1984). *Groups: Interaction and performance.* Englewood Cliffs, NJ: Prentice Hall.

McKeachie, W. J. (1980). Implications of cognitive psychology for college teaching. *New Directions for Teaching and Learning, 2,* 85–93. http://dx.doi.org/10.1002/tl.37219800208

McKeachie, W. J. (1997). Student ratings: The validity of use. *American Psychologist, 52,* 1218–1225. http://dx.doi.org/10.1037/0003-066X.52.11.1218

McKeachie, W. J. (1999). *McKeachie's teaching tips: Strategies, research, and theory for college and university teachers.* New York, NY: Houghton Mifflin.

McMillan, J. H. (1997). *Classroom assessment: Principles and practice for effective instruction.* Boston, MA: Allyn & Bacon.

McMillan, J. H., & Forsyth, D. R. (1991). Why do learners learn? Answers offered by current theories of motivation. In R. J. Menges & M. Svinicki (Eds.), *Approaching instructional problems through theoretical perspectives: New directions for teaching and learning* (Vol. 44, pp. 39–52). San Francisco, CA: Jossey-Bass.

McMillan, J. H., Wergin, J. F., Forsyth, D. R., & Brown, J. C. (1987). Student ratings of instruction: A summary of the literature. *Instructional Evaluation, 8,* 2–13.

Means, B., Peters, V., & Zheng, Y. (2014). *Lessons from five years of funding digital courseware: Postsecondary success portfolio review, executive summary.* Menlo Park, CA: SRI Education.

Messick, S. (1995). Validity of psychological assessment: Validation of inferences from persons' responses and performances as scientific inquiry into score meaning. *American Psychologist, 50,* 741–749. http://dx.doi.org/10.1037/0003-066X.50.9.741

Milgram, S. (1974). *Obedience to authority.* New York, NY: Harper & Row.

Miller, A., & Pearson, J. (2013). Can I talk to you? The effects of instructor position, nationality, and teaching style on students' perceived willingness to communicate and on teacher evaluations. *Communication Quarterly, 61,* 18–34. http://dx.doi.org/10.1080/01463373.2012.719059

Miller, C. J., McNear, J., & Metz, M. J. (2013). A comparison of traditional and engaging lecture methods in a large, professional-level course. *Advances in Physiology Education, 37,* 347–355. http://dx.doi.org/10.1152/advan.00050.2013

Miller, G. A., Galanter, E., & Pribram, K. H. (1960). *Plans and the structure of behavior*. New York, NY: Holt. http://dx.doi.org/10.1037/10039-000

Miller, H. L., Jr., & Flores, D. (2012). Teaching controversial issues, liberally. In W. Buskist & V. A. Benassi (Eds.), *Effective college and university teaching: Strategies and tactics for the new professoriate* (pp. 155–162). Los Angeles, CA: Sage. http://dx.doi.org/10.4135/9781452244006.n17

Miller, M. D. (2014). *Minds online: Teaching effectively with technology*. Cambridge, MA: Harvard University Press. http://dx.doi.org/10.4159/harvard.9780674735996

Millman, J., Bishop, C. H., & Ebel, R. (1965). An analysis of test-wiseness. *Educational and Psychological Measurement, 25,* 707–726. http://dx.doi.org/10.1177/001316446502500304

Mintzes, J. J. (1979). Overt teaching behaviors and student ratings of instructors. *Journal of Experimental Education, 48,* 145–153. http://dx.doi.org/10.1080/00220973.1979.11011728

Moen, D., Davies, T., & Dykstra, D. V. (2011). Student perceptions of instructor classroom management practices. *College Teaching Methods & Styles Journal, 6,* 21–32.

Montessori, M. (1995). *The absorbent mind* (C. A. Claremont, Trans.). New York: Henry Holt. (Original work published 1949)

Morreale, S., Backlund, P., & Sparks, L. (2014). Communication education and instructional communication: Genesis and evolution as fields of inquiry. *Communication Education, 63,* 344–354. http://dx.doi.org/10.1080/03634523.2014.944926

Morris-Rothschild, B. K., & Brassard, M. R. (2006). Teachers' conflict management styles: The role of attachment styles and classroom management efficacy. *Journal of School Psychology, 44,* 105–121. http://dx.doi.org/10.1016/j.jsp.2006.01.004

Moten, J., Fitterer, A., Brazier, E., Leonard, J., & Brown, A. (2013). Examining online college cyber-cheating methods and prevention measures. *The Electronic Journal of e-Learning, 11,* 139–146.

Mueller, P. A., & Oppenheimer, D. M. (2014). The pen is mightier than the keyboard: Advantages of longhand over laptop note taking. *Psychological Science, 25,* 1159–1168. http://dx.doi.org/10.1177/0956797614524581

Murray, B., Gillese, E., Lennon, M., Mercer, P., & Robinson, M. (1996). *Ethical principles for college and university teaching*. Retrieved from http://www.aahea.org/articles/Ethical+Principles.htm. http://dx.doi.org/10.1002/tl.37219966611

Murray, D. M. (1985). *A writer teaching writing* (2nd ed.). Boston, MA: Houghton Mifflin.

Murray, H. G. (1983). Low-inference classroom teaching behaviors and student ratings of college teaching effectiveness. *Journal of Educational Psychology, 75,* 138–149. http://dx.doi.org/10.1037/0022-0663.75.1.138

Murray, H. G., & Lawrence, C. (1980). Speech and drama training for lecturers as a means of improving university teaching. *Research in Higher Education, 13,* 73–90. http://dx.doi.org/10.1007/BF00975777

Murray, J. P. (1994). Why teaching portfolios? *Community College Review, 22,* 33–43. http://dx.doi.org/10.1177/009155219402200105

Murray, J. P. (1995). *ASHE–ERIC higher education report: Vol. 8. Successful faculty development and evaluation: The complete teaching portfolio.* Washington, DC: Graduate School of Education and Human Development, George Washington University.

National Assessment Governing Board. (2010). *Writing framework for the 2011 National Assessment of Educational Progress.* Washington, DC: Author. Retrieved from http://www.nagb.org/content/nagb/assets/documents/publications/frameworks/writing/2011-writing-framework.pdf

National Council of Teachers of Mathematics. (1991). *Principles and standards for school mathematics.* Reston, VA: Author. Retrieved from http://www.nctm.org/standards/

National Science Foundation. (2000). *A description and analysis of best practice finding of programs promoting participation of underrepresented undergraduate students in science, mathematics, engineering, and technology.* Arlington, VA: Author.

National Survey of Student Engagement. (2013). *A fresh look at student engagement—Annual results 2013.* Bloomington: Indiana University Center for Postsecondary Research.

Naveh-Benjamin, M., McKeachie, W. J., Lin, Y., & Holinger, D. P. (1981). Test anxiety: Deficits in information processing. *Journal of Educational Psychology, 73,* 816–824. http://dx.doi.org/10.1037/0022-0663.73.6.816

Neisser, U. (1967). *Cognitive psychology.* New York, NY: Appleton-Century-Crofts.

Nestojko, J. F., Bui, D. C., Kornell, N., & Bjork, E. L. (2014). Expecting to teach enhances learning and organization of knowledge in free recall of text passages. *Memory & Cognition, 42,* 1038–1048. http://dx.doi.org/10.3758/s13421-014-0416-z

Newcomb, T. M., Koenig, K. E., Flacks, R., & Warwick, D. P. (1967). *Persistence and change: Bennington College and its students after twenty-five years.* New York, NY: Wiley.

Newman, J. H. (1891). *The idea of a university.* New York, NY: Doubleday.

Niedenthal, P. M., Setterlund, M. B., & Wherry, M. B. (1992). Possible self-complexity and affective reactions to goal-relevant evaluation. *Journal of Personality and Social Psychology, 63,* 5–16. http://dx.doi.org/10.1037/0022-3514.63.1.5

Nilson, L. B. (2010). *Teaching at its best: A research-based resource for college instructors.* San Francisco, CA: Jossey-Bass.

Nodine, B. F. (1999). Why not make writing assignments? In B. Perlman, L. I. McCann, & S. H. McFadden (Eds.), *Lessons learned: Practical advice for the teaching of psychology* (pp. 167–172). Washington, DC: American Psychological Society.

Noel, J., Forsyth, D. R., & Kelley, K. (1987). Improving the performance of failing students by overcoming their self-serving attributional biases. *Basic and Applied Social Psychology, 8*, 151–162. http://dx.doi.org/10.1080/01973533.1987.9645882

Novotney, A. (2014). Students under pressure. *Monitor on Psychology, 45*(8), 36–38.

Nuhfer, E. (1997). Student management teams—The heretic's path to teaching success. In W. E. Campbell & K. A. Smith (Eds.), *New paradigms for college teaching* (pp. 102–126). Edina, MN: Interaction Book Co.

O'Connell, T. S., & Dyment, J. E. (2011). The case of reflective journals: Is the jury still out? *Reflective Practice, 12*, 47–59. http://dx.doi.org/10.1080/14623943.2011.541093

Oluoch-Suleh, E. (2014). Teacher level of interaction with learners based on classroom seating position. *Journal of Education and Practice, 5*, 114–121.

Onifade, E. O., Nabangi, F. K., Reynolds, R., & Allen, C. (2000). *The relationship between grade point average and cheating behavior, and the effect of both on the usefulness of take-home tests.* Paper presented at the annual meeting of the Academy of Business Education. Retrieved from http://citeseerx.ist.psu.edu/viewdoc/download?doi=10.1.1.196.9407&rep=rep1&type=pdf

Onifade, E., Nabangi, F. K., & Trigg, R. R. (1998). Comparative effects of take-home tests, quizzes, and home-works on accounting students' performance. *Journal of Accounting and Finance Research, 5*(2), 6–14.

Oreg, S. (2003). Resistance to change: Developing an individual differences measure. *Journal of Applied Psychology, 88*, 680–693. http://dx.doi.org/10.1037/0021-9010.88.4.680

Organisation for Economic Co-operation and Development. (2013). *OECD skills outlook 2013.* Retrieved from http://www.oecd.org/site/piaac/

Overall, J. U., & Marsh, H. W. (1980). Students' evaluations of instruction: A longitudinal study of their stability. *Journal of Educational Psychology, 72*, 321–325. http://dx.doi.org/10.1037/0022-0663.72.3.321

Palladino, J. J., Hill, G. W., IV, & Norcross, J. C. (1999). Using extra credit. In B. Perlman, L. I. McCann, & S. H. McFadden (Eds.), *Lessons learned: Practical advice for the teaching of psychology* (pp. 57–60). Washington, DC: American Psychological Society.

Paluck, E. L., & Green, D. P. (2009). Prejudice reduction: What works? A review and assessment of research and practice. *Annual Review of Psychology, 60*, 339–367. http://dx.doi.org/10.1146/annurev.psych.60.110707.163607

Pashler, H., McDaniel, M., Rohrer, D., & Bjork, R. (2008). Learning styles concepts and evidence. *Psychological Science in the Public Interest, 9*, 105–119.

Pastorino, E. E. (1999). Students with academic difficulty: Prevention and assistance. In B. Perlman, L. I. McCann, & S. H. McFadden (Eds.), *Lessons learned: Practical advice for the teaching of psychology* (pp. 193–199). Washington, DC: American Psychological Society.

Patterson, M. L. (2011). *More than words: The power of nonverbal communication.* Madrid, Spain: Aresta.

Pauk, W., & Owens, R. J. Q. (2014). *How to study in college* (11th ed.). Boston, MA: Wadsworth/Cengage.

Pear, J. J., Schnerch, G. J., Silva, K. M., Svenningsen, L., & Lambert, J. (2011). Web-based computer-aided personalized system of instruction. *New Directions for Teaching and Learning,* (128), 85–94. http://dx. doi.org/10.1002/tl.471

Pearson, P. D., & Cervetti, G. (2013). The psychology and pedagogy of reading processes. In I. B. Weiner (Ed. in Chief), W. M. Reynolds, & G. E. Miller (Eds.), *Handbook of psychology: Vol. 7. Educational psychology* (pp. 257–281). New York, NY: Wiley.

Penner, J. G. (1984). *Why many college teachers cannot lecture: How to avoid communication breakdown in the classroom.* Springfield, IL: Charles C Thomas.

Perkins, D. V., & Saris, R. N. (2001). A "jigsaw classroom" technique for undergraduate statistics courses. *Teaching of Psychology, 28,* 111–113. http://dx.doi.org/10.1207/S15328023TOP2802_09

Perlman, B., McCann, L. I., & McFadden, S. H. (Eds.). (1999). *Lessons learned: Practical advice for the teaching of psychology.* Washington, DC: American Psychological Society.

Perry, W. G., Jr. (1970). *Forms of intellectual and ethical development in the college years: A scheme.* New York, NY: Holt, Rinehart & Winston.

Phelps, R. E. (2012). Diversity and diversity issues in teaching. In W. Buskist & V. A. Benassi (Eds.), *Effective college and university teaching: Strategies and tactics for the new professoriate* (pp. 145–154). Los Angeles, CA: Sage. http://dx.doi.org/10.4135/9781452244006.n16

Phelps, R. P. (Ed.). (2009). *Correcting fallacies about educational and psychological testing.* Washington, DC: American Psychological Association. http://dx.doi.org/10.1037/11861-000

Phelps, R. P. (2012). The effect of testing on student achievement, 1910–2010. *International Journal of Testing, 12,* 21–43. http://dx.doi. org/10.1080/15305058.2011.602920

Piaget, J. (1950). *Psychology of intelligence.* London, England: Kegan Paul.

Pieschl, S., Stahl, E., & Bromme, R. (2008). Epistemological beliefs and self-regulated learning with hypertext. *Metacognition and Learning, 3,* 17–37. http://dx.doi.org/10.1007/s11409-007-9008-7

Pizzolato, J. E. (2006). Achieving college student possible selves: Navigating the space between commitment and achievement of long-term identity goals. *Cultural Diversity & Ethnic Minority Psychology, 12,* 57–69. http://dx.doi.org/10.1037/1099-9809.12.1.57

Pollio, H. R., & Beck, H. P. (2000). When the tail wags the dog: Perceptions of learning and grade orientation in, and by, contemporary college students and faculty. *The Journal of Higher Education, 71*, 84–102. http://dx.doi.org/10.2307/2649283

Prensky, M. (2001). Digital natives, digital immigrants. *On the Horizon, 9*(5), 1–6. http://dx.doi.org/10.1108/10748120110424816

Pressley, N., Van Etten, S., Yokoi, L., Freebern, G., & Van Meter, P. (1998). The metacognition of college studentship: A grounded theory approach. In J. D. Hacker, J. Dunlosky, & A. Graesser (Eds.), *Metacognition in educational theory and practice* (pp. 347–363). Mahwah, NJ: Erlbaum.

Prince, M. (2004). Does active learning work? A review of the research. *Journal of Engineering Education, 93*, 223–231. http://dx.doi.org/10.1002/j.2168-9830.2004.tb00809.x

Pryor, J. H., Eagan, K., Palucki Blake, L., Hurtado, S., Berdan, J., & Case, M. H. (2012). *The American freshman: National norms fall 2012.* Los Angeles: Higher Education Research Institute, University of California, Los Angeles. Retrieved from http://www.heri.ucla.edu/monographs/TheAmericanFreshman2012.pdf

Radclyffe-Thomas, N. (2012). Blogging is addictive! A qualitative case study on the integration of blogs across a range of college level courses. In C. Wankel & P. Blessinger (Eds.), *Cutting-edge technologies in higher education* (pp. 75–107). Bingley, England: Emerald.

Radmacher, S. A., & Latosi-Sawin, E. (1995). Summary writing: A tool to improve student comprehension and writing in psychology. *Teaching of Psychology, 22*, 113–115. http://dx.doi.org/10.1207/s15328023top2202_4

Redding, R. E. (1998). Students' evaluations of teaching fuel grade inflation. *American Psychologist, 53*, 1227–1228. http://dx.doi.org/10.1037/0003-066X.53.11.1227

Reimann, P., & Schult, T. J. (1996). Turning examples into cases: Acquiring knowledge structures for analogical problem solving. *Educational Psychologist, 31*, 123–132. http://dx.doi.org/10.1207/s15326985ep3102_4

Reker, G. T., & Wong, P. T. P. (1988). Aging as an individual process: Toward a theory of personal meaning. In J. E. Birren & V. L. Bengtson (Eds.), *Emergent theories of aging* (pp. 214–246). New York, NY: Springer.

Renner, C. H., & Renner, M. J. (1999). How to create a good exam. In B. Perlman, L. I. McCann, & S. H. McFadden (Eds.), *Lessons learned: Practical advice for the teaching of psychology* (pp. 43–47). Washington, DC: American Psychological Society.

Reyes, M. R., Brackett, M. A., Rivers, S. E., White, M., & Salovey, P. (2012). Classroom emotional climate, student engagement, and academic achievement. *Journal of Educational Psychology, 104*, 700–712. http://dx.doi.org/10.1037/a0027268

Reynolds, W. M., Miller, G. E. (Eds.), & Weiner, I. B. (Ed. in Chief). (2013). *Handbook of psychology: Educational psychology* (Vol. 7). Hoboken, NJ: Wiley.

Rheingold, H. L. (1994). *The psychologist's guide to an academic career.* Washington, DC: American Psychological Association. http://dx.doi.org/10.1037/10146-000

Rhodes, M. G., & Tauber, S. K. (2011). The influence of delaying judgments of learning on metacognitive accuracy: A meta-analytic review. *Psychological Bulletin, 137,* 131–148. http://dx.doi.org/10.1037/a0021705

Richardson, J. M., Jr. (1992). *Making it happen: A positive guide to the future.* Washington, D.C.: U.S. Association for the Club of Rome.

Richland, L. E., Stigler, J. W., & Holyoak, K. J. (2012). Teaching the conceptual structure of mathematics. *Educational Psychologist, 47,* 189–203. http://dx.doi.org/10.1080/00461520.2012.667065

Rietz, H. L., & Manning, M. (1994). *The one-stop guide to workshops.* New York, NY: Irwin.

Riniolo, T. C., Johnson, K. C., Sherman, T. R., & Misso, J. A. (2006). Hot or not: Do professors perceived as physically attractive receive higher student evaluations? *The Journal of General Psychology, 133,* 19–35. http://dx.doi.org/10.3200/GENP.133.1.19-35

Rocklin, T. (2001). Do I dare? Is it prudent? *The National Teaching & Learning Forum, 10*(3), 1–3. Retrieved from http://cgi.stanford.edu/~dept-ctl/tomprof/posting.php?ID=309

Rodin, M., & Rodin, B. (1972). Student evaluations of teachers. *Science, 177,* 1164–1166. http://dx.doi.org/10.1126/science.177.4055.1164

Rodriguez, M. C. (2003). Construct equivalence of multiple-choice and constructed-response items: A random effects synthesis of correlations. *Journal of Educational Measurement, 40,* 163–184. http://dx.doi.org/10.1111/j.1745-3984.2003.tb01102.x

Rodriguez, M. C. (2005). Three options are optimal for multiple-choice items: A meta-analysis of 80 years of research. *Educational Measurement: Issues and Practice, 24*(2), 3–13. http://dx.doi.org/10.1111/j.1745-3992.2005.00006.x

Roediger, H. L., III, Agarwal, P. K., McDaniel, M. A., & McDermott, K. B. (2011). Test-enhanced learning in the classroom: Long-term improvements from quizzing. *Journal of Experimental Psychology: Applied, 17,* 382–395. http://dx.doi.org/10.1037/a0026252

Roediger, H. L., III, & Butler, A. C. (2011). The critical role of retrieval practice in long-term retention. *Trends in Cognitive Sciences, 15,* 20–27. http://dx.doi.org/10.1016/j.tics.2010.09.003

Rojstaczer, S., & Healy, C. (2012). Where A is ordinary: The evolution of American college and university grading, 1940–2009. *Teachers College Record, 114,* 1–23.

Rosenfeld, P., & Anderson, D. D. (1985). The effects of humorous multiple-choice alternatives on test performance. *Journal of Instructional Psychology, 12,* 3–5.

Ross, L., Amabile, T. M., & Steinmetz, J. L. (1977). Social roles, social control, and biases in social perception processes. *Journal of Personality and Social Psychology, 35,* 485–494. http://dx.doi.org/10.1037/0022-3514.35.7.485

Ruef, M., & Nag, M. (2015). The classification of organizational form: Theory and application to the field of higher education. In M. W. Kirst & M. L. Stevens (Eds.), *Remaking college: The changing ecology of higher education* (pp. 84–111). Stanford, CA: Stanford University Press.

Ruhl, K. L., Hughes, C. A., & Schloss, P. J. (1987). Using the pause procedure to enhance lecture recall. *Teacher Education and Special Education, 10*, 14–18. http://dx.doi.org/10.1177/088840648701000103

Sabini, J. P., & Silver, M. (1978). Moral reproach and moral action. *Journal for the Theory of Social Behaviour, 8*, 103–123. http://dx.doi.org/10.1111/j.1468-5914.1978.tb00393.x

Salas, E., & Rosen, M. A. (2013). Building high reliability teams: Progress and some reflections on teamwork training. *BMJ Quality & Safety, 22*, 369–373. http://dx.doi.org/10.1136/bmjqs-2013-002015

Salomon, G., & Perkins, D. N. (1989). Rocky roads to transfer: Rethinking mechanisms of a neglected phenomenon. *Educational Psychologist, 24*, 113–142. http://dx.doi.org/10.1207/s15326985ep2402_1

Sapp, M. (2013). *Test anxiety.* Lanham, MD: University Press of America.

Sarason, I. G. (1984). Stress, anxiety, and cognitive interference: Reactions to tests. *Journal of Personality and Social Psychology, 46*, 929–938. http://dx.doi.org/10.1037/0022-3514.46.4.929

Schank, R. (2011). *Teaching minds: How cognitive science can save our schools.* New York, NY: Teachers College Press.

Schmid, R. F., Bernard, R. M., Borokhovski, E., Tamim, R. M., Abrami, P. C., Surkes, M. A., . . . Woods, J. (2014). The effects of technology use in postsecondary education: A meta-analysis of classroom applications. *Computers & Education, 72*, 271–291. http://dx.doi.org/10.1016/j.compedu.2013.11.002

Schneider, J. (2013). Remembrance of things past: A history of the Socratic method in the United States. *Curriculum Inquiry, 43*, 613–640. http://dx.doi.org/10.1111/curi.12030

Schneider, J., & Hutt, E. (2014). Making the grade: A history of the A–F marking scheme. *Journal of Curriculum Studies, 46*, 201–224. http://dx.doi.org/10.1080/00220272.2013.790480

Schneps, M. (Producer), & Sadler, P. (Producer). (1987). *A private universe* [DVD]. Burlington, VT: Annenberg Media.

Schommer, M. (1998). The influence of age and education on epistemological beliefs. *British Journal of Educational Psychology, 68*, 551–562. http://dx.doi.org/10.1111/j.2044-8279.1998.tb01311.x

Schultz, P. W., Nolan, J. M., Cialdini, R. B., Goldstein, N. J., & Griskevicius, V. (2007). The constructive, destructive, and reconstructive power of social norms. *Psychological Science, 18*, 429–434. http://dx.doi.org/10.1111/j.1467-9280.2007.01917.x

Schunk, D. H., & Zimmerman, B. J. (2013). Self-regulation and learning. In W. M. Reynolds, G. E. Miller, & I. B. Weiner (Eds.), *Handbook of psychology: Vol. 7. Educational psychology* (pp. 45–68). Hoboken, NJ: Wiley.

Schweighart Goss, S. (1999). Dealing with problem students in the classroom. In B. Perlman, L. I. McCann, & S. H. McFadden (Eds.), *Lessons learned: Practical advice for the teaching of psychology* (pp. 209–212). Washington, DC: American Psychological Society.

Schwinger, M., Wirthwein, L., Lemmer, G., & Steinmayr, R. (2014). Academic self-handicapping and achievement: A meta-analysis. *Journal of Educational Psychology, 106*, 744–761. http://dx.doi.org/10.1037/a0035832

Scialfa, C., Legare, C., Wenger, L., & Dingley, L. (2001). Difficulty and discriminability of introductory psychology test items. *Teaching of Psychology, 28*, 11–15. http://dx.doi.org/10.1207/S15328023TOP2801_03

Sechrest, L., Kihlstrom, J. F., & Bootzin, R. R. (1999). How to develop multiple-choice tests. In B. Perlman, L. I. McCann, & S. H. McFadden (Eds.), *Lessons learned: Practical advice for the teaching of psychology* (pp. 49–56). Washington, DC: American Psychological Society.

Seldin, P. (2004). *The teaching portfolio: A practical guide to improved performance and promotion/tenure decisions* (3rd ed.). Boston, MA: Anker.

Selingo, J. (2003, May 2). What Americans think about higher education. *Chronicle of Higher Education.* Retrieved from http://chronicle.com/article/What-Americans-Think-About/21061/

Senko, C., Hulleman, C. S., & Harackiewicz, J. M. (2011). Achievement goal theory at the crossroads: Old controversies, current challenges, and new directions. *Educational Psychologist, 46*, 26–47. http://dx.doi.org/10.1080/00461520.2011.538646

Shanahan, T., & Shanahan, C. (2008). Teaching disciplinary literacy to adolescents: Rethinking content-area literacy. *Harvard Educational Review, 78*, 40–59.

Shepard, L. A. (1993). Evaluating test validity. *Review of Research in Education, 19*, 405–450.

Showalter, E. (2003). *Teaching literature.* Malden, MA: Blackwell.

Simmel, G. (1902). The number of members as determining the sociological form of the group. *American Journal of Sociology, 8*, 1–46, 158–196. http://dx.doi.org/10.1086/211115

Simonds, C. J. (1997). Classroom understanding: An expanded notion of teacher clarity. *Communication Research Reports, 14*, 279–290. http://dx.doi.org/10.1080/08824099709388671

Singh, A., Mangalaraj, G., & Taneja, A. (2010). Bolstering teaching through online tools. *Journal of Information Systems Education, 21*, 299–311.

Sixbury, G. R., & Cashin, W. E. (1995). *Description of database for the IDEA Diagnostic Form* (IDEA Paper No. 10). Manhattan: Center for Faculty Evaluation and Development, Kansas State University.

Skinner, B. F. (1953). *Science and human behavior.* New York, NY: Free Press. Sleigh, M. J., & Ritzer, D. R. (2001). Encouraging student attendance. *APS Observer, 14*(9), 19–20. Retrieved from http://www.psychologicalscience.org/observer/1101/tips.html

Smart, J. C. (1982). Faculty teaching goals: A test of Holland's theory. *Journal of Educational Psychology, 74,* 180–188. http://dx.doi.org/10.1037/0022-0663.74.2.180

Smith, L. R., & Cotten, M. L. (1980). Effect of lesson vagueness and discontinuity on student achievement and attitudes. *Journal of Educational Psychology, 72,* 670–675. http://dx.doi.org/10.1037/0022-0663.72.5.670

Snyder, C. R., Shenkel, R. J., & Lowery, C. R. (1977). Acceptance of personality interpretations: The "Barnum effect" and beyond. *Journal of Consulting and Clinical Psychology, 45,* 104–114. http://dx.doi.org/10.1037/0022-006X.45.1.104

Sommer, R. (1969). *Personal space: The behavioral basis of design.* Englewood Cliffs, NJ: Prentice Hall.

Soysa, C. K., Dunn, D. S., Dottolo, A. L., Burns-Glover, A., & Gurung, R. (2013). Orchestrating authorship: Teaching writing across the psychology curriculum. *Teaching of Psychology, 40,* 88–97. http://dx.doi.org/10.1177/0098628312475027

Spooren, P., Mortelmans, D., & Christiaens, W. (2015). Assessing the validity and reliability of a quick scan for student's evaluation of teaching: Results from confirmatory factor analysis and G theory. *Studies in Educational Evaluation.* Advance online publication. http://dx.doi.org/10.1016/j.stueduc.2014.03.001

Stage, F. K., & Kinzie, J. (2009). Reform in undergraduate science, technology, engineering, and mathematics: The classroom context. *Journal of General Education, 58,* 85–105. http://dx.doi.org/10.1353/jge.0.0038

Stark, J. S., Lowther, M. A., Ryan, M. P., & Genthon, M. (1988). Faculty reflect on course planning. *Research in Higher Education, 29,* 219–240. http://dx.doi.org/10.1007/BF00992924

Statman, S. (1988). Ask a clear question and get a clear answer: An enquiry into the question/answer and the sentence completion formats of multiple-choice items. *System, 16,* 357–376.

Stearns, S. A. (2001). The student–instructor relationship's effect upon academic integrity. *Ethics & Behavior, 11,* 275–285. http://dx.doi.org/10.1207/S15327019EB1103_6

Sternberg, R. J. (1997a). *Successful intelligence.* New York, NY: Plume.

Sternberg, R. J. (Ed.). (1997b). *Teaching introductory psychology: Survival tips from the experts.* Washington, DC: American Psychological Association.

Sternberg, R. J. (1997c). Teaching students to think as psychologists. In R. J. Sternberg (Ed.), *Teaching introductory psychology: Survival tips from the experts* (pp. 137–149). Washington, DC: American Psychological Association. http://dx.doi.org/10.1037/10228-009

Stewart, I., Hong, E., & Strudler, N. (2004). Development and validation of an instrument for student evaluation of the quality of Web-based instruction. *American Journal of Distance Education, 18,* 131–150. http://dx.doi.org/10.1207/s15389286ajde1803_2

Stewart, K. (2009). Lessons from teaching millennials. *College Teaching*, *57*, 111–118. http://dx.doi.org/10.3200/CTCH.57.2.111-118

Stewart, K., & Kilmartin, C. (2014). Connecting the dots: The decline in meaningful learning. *Journal of Faculty Development*, *28*, 53–61.

Strunk, W., Jr., & White, E. B. (2014). *The elements of style* (international ed.). New York, NY: Pearson.

Stulberg, L. M., & Weinberg, S. L. (2011). *Diversity in American higher education: Toward a more comprehensive approach*. New York, NY: Routledge.

Suler, J. R. (1987). Computer-simulated psychotherapy as an aid in teaching clinical psychology. *Teaching of Psychology*, *14*, 37–39. http://dx.doi.org/10.1207/s15328023top1401_10

Sung, E., & Mayer, R. E. (2012). Five facets of social presence in online distance education. *Computers in Human Behavior*, *28*, 1738–1747. http://dx.doi.org/10.1016/j.chb.2012.04.014

Svenningsen, L., & Pear, J. J. (2011). Effects of a computer-aided personalized system of instruction in developing knowledge and critical thinking in blended learning courses. *The Behavior Analyst Today*, *12*, 34–40. http://dx.doi.org/10.1037/h0100709

Sweet, M., & Michaelsen, L. K. (2012). Critical thinking and engagement: Creating cognitive apprenticeships with team-based learning. In M. Sweet & L. K. Michaelsen (Eds.), *Team-based learning in the social sciences and humanities* (pp. 5–32). Sterling, VA: Sylus.

Swenson, L. C. (1997). *Psychology and law for the helping profession*. Pacific Grove, CA: Brooks/Cole.

Sykes, C. J. (1988). *ProfScam: Professors and the demise of higher education*. Washington, DC: Regnery Gateway.

Tabachnick, B. G., Keith-Spiegel, P., & Pope, K. S. (1991). Ethics of teaching: Beliefs and behaviors of psychologists as educators. *American Psychologist*, *46*, 506–515. http://dx.doi.org/10.1037/0003-066X.46.5.506

Taylor, K., Marienau, C., & Fiddler, M. (2000). *Developing adult learners: Strategies for teachers and trainers*. San Francisco, CA: Jossey-Bass.

Thorndike, E. L. (1910). The contribution of psychology to education. *Journal of Educational Psychology*, *1*, 5–12. http://dx.doi.org/10.1037/h0070113

Thorndike, E. L. (1913). *The psychology of learning* (Vol. 2). New York, NY: Teachers College Press.

Thorndike, E. L. (1918). The nature, purposes, and general methods of measurement of educational products. In G. M. Whipple (Ed.), *Seventeenth yearbook of the National Society for the Study of Education* (Vol. 2, pp. 16–24). Bloomington, IL: Public School.

Tindell, D. R., & Bohlander, R. W. (2012). The use and abuse of cell phones and text messaging in the classroom: A survey of college students. *College Teaching*, *60*(1), 1–9. http://dx.doi.org/10.1080/8756755.2011.604802

Tinto, V. (1997). Classrooms as communities: Exploring the educational character of student persistence. *The Journal of Higher Education, 68,* 599–623. http://dx.doi.org/10.2307/2959965

Tomlinson, S. (2002). A management lesson. In C. A. Stanley & M. E. Porter (Eds.), *Engaging large classes: strategies and techniques for college faculty* (pp. 162–169). Bolton, MA: Anker.

Traub, R. (1993). On the equivalence of the traits assessed by multiple-choice and constructed-response tests. In R. Bennett & W. Ward (Eds.), *Construction versus choice in cognitive measurement* (pp. 29–44). Mahwah, NJ: Erlbaum.

Troisi, J. D. (2014). Making the grade and staying engaged: The influence of student management teams on student classroom outcomes. *Teaching of Psychology, 41,* 99–103. http://dx.doi.org/10.1177/0098628314530337

Tuckman, B. W. (1965). Developmental sequences in small groups. *Psychological Bulletin, 63,* 384–399. http://dx.doi.org/10.1037/h0022100

Tufte, E. (2003, September). Learning to love PowerPoint. *WIRED Magazine.* Retrieved from http://www.wired.com/wired/archive/11.09/ppt1.html

Turkle, S. (2011). *Alone together: Why we expect more from technology and less from each other.* New York, NY: Basic Books.

Twenge, J. M. (2006). *Generation Me: Why today's young Americans are more confident, assertive, entitled—And more miserable than ever before.* New York, NY: Free Press.

Twenge, J. M., & Campbell, W. K. (2010). *The narcissism epidemic: Living in the age of entitlement.* New York, NY: Free Press.

Urbach, F. (1992). Developing a teaching portfolio. *College Teaching, 40,* 71–74. http://dx.doi.org/10.1080/87567555.1992.10532272

U.S. Department of Education. (2006). *A test of leadership: Charting the future of U.S. higher education.* Retrieved from https://www2.ed.gov/about/bdscomm/list/hiedfuture/reports/pre-pub-report.pdf

U.S. News & World Report. (2013, September 10). *U.S. News & World Report Announces the 2014 best colleges.* Washington, DC: Author. Retrieved from http://www.usnews.com/info/blogs/press-room/2013/09/10/us-news-announces-the-2014-best-colleges

Vallacher, R. R., & Wegner, D. M. (1987). What do people think they're doing? Action identification and human behavior. *Psychological Review, 94,* 3–15. http://dx.doi.org/10.1037/0033-295X.94.1.3

Wajda-Johnston, V. A., Handal, P. J., Brawer, P. A., & Fabricatore, A. N. (2001). Academic dishonesty at the graduate level. *Ethics & Behavior, 11,* 287–305. http://dx.doi.org/10.1207/S15327019EB1103_7

Walsh, W. B. (2003). Person–environment psychology and well-being. In W. B. Walsh (Ed.), *Counseling psychology and optimal human functioning* (pp. 93–121). Mahwah, NJ: Erlbaum.

Walvoord, B. E. F. (1982). *Helping students write well.* New York, NY: The Modern Language Association of America.

Walvoord, B. E. (2014). *Assessing and improving student writing in college: A guide for institutions, general education, departments, and classrooms.* San Francisco, CA: Jossey-Bass.

Wang, X., Wainer, H., & Thissen, D. (1995). On the viability of some untestable assumptions in equating exams that allow examinee choice. *Applied Measurement in Education, 8,* 211–225. http://dx.doi.org/10.1207/s15324818ame0803_2

Ward, D. A., & Beck, W. L. (1990). Gender and dishonesty. *The Journal of Social Psychology, 130,* 333–339. http://dx.doi.org/10.1080/00224545.1990.9924589

Ware, J. E., & Williams, R. G. (1977). Discriminant analysis of student ratings as a means for identifying lecturers who differ in enthusiasm or information-giving. *Educational and Psychological Measurement, 37,* 627–639. http://dx.doi.org/10.1177/001316447703700306

Weber, L. J., McBee, J. K., & Krebs, J. E. (1983). Take home tests: An experimental study. *Research in Higher Education, 18,* 473–483. http://dx.doi.org/10.1007/BF00974810

Wei, F. Y. F., Wang, Y. K., & Klausner, M. (2012). Rethinking college students' self-regulation and sustained attention: Does text messaging during class influence cognitive learning? *Communication Education, 61,* 185–204. http://dx.doi.org/10.1080/03634523.2012.672755

Weimer, M. (2013). *Learner-centered teaching: Five key changes to practice* (2nd ed.). San Francisco, CA: Jossey-Bass.

White, E. M. (1995). An apologia for the timed impromptu essay test. *College Composition and Communication, 46,* 30–45. http://dx.doi.org/10.2307/358868

Whitford, F. W. (1992). *Teaching psychology.* Englewood Cliffs, NJ: Prentice Hall.

Whitley, B. E. (1998). Factors associated with cheating among college students: A review. *Research in Higher Education, 39,* 235–274.

Whitley, B. E., Jr., & Keith-Spiegel, P. (2001). Academic integrity as an institutional issue. *Ethics & Behavior, 11,* 325–342. http://dx.doi.org/10.1207/S15327019EB1103_9

Whitley, B. E., Jr., Perkins, D. V., Balogh, D. W., Keith-Spiegel, P., & Wittig, A. F. (2000, July/August). Fairness in the classroom. *APS Observer, 13.* Retrieved from http://www.psychologicalscience.org/teaching/tips/tips_0700.html

Widick, P., Parker, C. A., & Knefelkamp, L. (1978). Arthur Chickering's vectors of development. *New Directions for Student Services, 4,* 19–34.

Williams, R. G., & Ware, J. E. (1976). Validity of student ratings of instruction under different incentive conditions: A further study of the Dr. Fox effect. *Journal of Educational Psychology, 68,* 48–56. http://dx.doi.org/10.1037/0022-0663.68.1.48

Williams, R. G., & Ware, J. E. (1977). An extended visit with Dr. Fox: Validity of student satisfaction with instruction ratings after repeated exposures to a lecturer. *American Educational Research Journal, 14,* 449–457. http://dx.doi.org/10.3102/00028312014004449

Willingham, D. B. (1990). Effective feedback on written assignments. *Teaching of Psychology, 17,* 10–13. http://dx.doi.org/10.1207/s15328023top1701_2

Willingham, D. T. (2009). *Why don't students like school: A cognitive scientist answers questions about how the mind works and what it means for the classroom.* San Francisco, CA: Jossey-Bass.

Wilson, J. H., Beyer, D., & Monteiro, H. (2014). Professor age affects student ratings: Halo effect for younger teachers. *College Teaching, 62*(1), 20–24. http://dx.doi.org/10.1080/87567555.2013.825574

Wilson, J. H., & Taylor, K. W. (2001). Professor immediacy as behaviors associated with liking students. *Teaching of Psychology, 28,* 136–138.

Wilson, K., & Korn, J. H. (2007). Attention during lectures: Beyond ten minutes. *Teaching of Psychology, 34,* 85–89. http://dx.doi.org/10.1080/00986280701291291

Wilson, T. D., & Linville, P. W. (1985). Improving the performance of college freshmen with attributional techniques. *Journal of Personality and Social Psychology, 49,* 287–293. http://dx.doi.org/10.1037/0022-3514.49.1.287

Winters, F. I., Greene, J. A., & Costich, C. M. (2008). Self-regulation of learning within computer-based learning environments: A critical analysis. *Educational Psychology Review, 20,* 429–444. http://dx.doi.org/10.1007/s10648-008-9080-9

Witney, D., & Smallbone, T. (2011). Wiki work: Can using wikis enhance student collaboration for group assignment tasks? *Innovations in Education and Teaching International, 48,* 101–110. http://dx.doi.org/10.1080/14703297.2010.543765

Witt, P. L., Wheeless, L. R., & Allen, M. (2004). A meta-analytical review of the relationship between teacher immediacy and student learning. *Communication Monographs, 71,* 184–207. http://dx.doi.org/10.1080/036452042000228054

Wlodkowski, R. J. (2008). *Enhancing adult motivation to learn: A comprehensive guide for teaching all adults* (3rd ed.). San Francisco, CA: Jossey-Bass.

Woods, S. C., Schwartz, M. W., Baskin, D. G., & Seeley, R. J. (2000). Food intake and the regulation of body weight. *Annual Review of Psychology, 51,* 255–277. http://dx.doi.org/10.1146/annurev.psych.51.1.255

Wurdinger, S. D., & Carlson, J. A. (2010). *Teaching for experiential learning: Five approaches that work.* Lanham, MD: Rowman & Littlefield Education.

Yue, C. L., Storm, B. C., Kornell, N., & Bjork, E. L. (2015). Highlighting and its relation to distributed study and students' metacognitive beliefs. *Educational Psychology Review, 27,* 69–78.

Zakrajsek, T. (1999). Developing effective lectures. In B. Perlman, L. I. McCann, & S. H. McFadden (Eds.), *Lessons learned: Practical advice for the teaching of psychology* (pp. 81–86). Washington, DC: American Psychological Society.

Zaman, M. Q. U. (2004). *Review of the academic evidence on the relationship between teaching and research in higher education* (Research Report RR506). Nottingham, England: Department for Education and Skills. Retrieved from http://www.education.gov.uk/publications/eOrderingDownload/RR506.pdf

Zanna, M. P., & Darley, J. M. (1987). On managing the faculty–graduate student research relationship. In M. P. Zanna & J. M. Darley (Eds.), *The compleat academic: A practical guide for the beginning social scientist* (pp. 139–149). New York, NY: Random House.

Zimbardo, P. G. (1997). A passion for psychology: Teaching it charismatically, integrating teaching and research synergistically, and writing about it engaging. In R. J. Sternberg (Ed.), *Teaching introductory psychology: Survival tips from the experts* (pp. 7–34). Washington, DC: American Psychological Association. http://dx.doi.org/10.1037/10228-001

Zimmerman, B. J. (1998). Academic studying and the development of personal skill: A self-regulatory perspective. *Educational Psychologist, 33*, 73–86. http://dx.doi.org/10.1080/00461520.1998.9653292

Zimmerman, B. J., & Pons, M. M. (1986). Development of a structured interview for assessing student use of self-regulated learning strategies. *American Educational Research Journal, 23*, 614–628. http://dx.doi.org/10.3102/00028312023004614

Zinn, T. E., Magnotti, J. F., Marchuk, K., Schultz, B. S., Luther, A., & Varfolomeeva, V. (2011). Does effort still count? More on what makes the grade. *Teaching of Psychology, 38*(1), 10–15. http://dx.doi.org/10.1177/0098628310390907

Index

About the Author

Donelson R. Forsyth, PhD, completed his undergraduate work at Florida State University in 1974, in sociology and psychology with a minor in education. He completed his doctorate at the University of Florida in 1978. He has taught at Virginia Commonwealth University, the University of Kansas, and the University of Richmond. Dr. Forsyth holds the Colonel Leo K. and Gaylee Thorsness Chair in Ethical Leadership in the Jepson School of Leadership Studies at the University of Richmond.

A social and personality psychologist, Dr. Forsyth studies groups, leadership, ethical thought, and educational outcomes. In addition to his general interest in group processes and personality, he explores empirically the psychological and interpersonal consequences of success and failure at the group and individual level, individual differences in ethical ideology, and perceptions of leaders. He has authored more than 140 chapters and articles on ethics, groups, and related topics, and his books include *Group Dynamics* (1983, 1990, 1999, 2006, 2010, 2014); *Social Psychology* (1987); *Psychotherapy and Behavior Change: Social, Cultural, and Methodological Perspectives* (1988, with H. Nick Higgenbotham and Stephen G. West); *Our Social World* (1995); and *The Professor's Guide to Teaching* (2003). Dr. Forsyth also has edited, with C. R. Snyder, the *Handbook of Social and Clinical Psychology: The Health*

Perspective (1991); *The Social Psychology of Leadership* (with Crystal Hoyt and George Goethals, 2008); and *For the Greater Good of All: Perspectives on Individualism, Society, and Leadership* (with Crystal Hoyt, 2011).

Dr. Forsyth has taught thousands of graduate and undergraduate students during his 38 years as a professor in such courses as introductory psychology, educational psychology, environmental psychology, social psychology, group dynamics, research methods, internships, theories and models of leadership, and ethics. He was recognized as the Outstanding Group Psychologist by the Society of Group Psychology and Group Psychotherapy in 1996. He received the State of Virginia Outstanding Faculty Award in 2002 and the Distinguished Educator Award from the University of Richmond in 2010. He is a fellow of the American Psychological Association.